PROPERTY MANAGEMENT IN CALIFORNIA

5TH EDITION
1994

JOSEPH W. DECARLO, CPM, GRI
Professor of Real Estate
at Coastline Community College

J.D. Publications & Seminars
P.O. Box 1230
Costa Mesa, CA 92626
(714) 751-2787

LIBRARY OF CONGRESS CATALOG
   CARD NUMBER: 86-61730

ISBN 0-9-37841-27-7

Printed in USA

Acknowledgments

I want to express my appreciation to all the people who encouraged and helped me write this book. Advice was solicited and received from real estate professionals (CPMs), property management instructors at other colleges, attorneys, the California Apartment Association, California Association of Realtors, California Department of Real Estate, Institute of Real Estate Management, Building Owners and Managers Association International, and International Council of Shopping Centers. The list of reviewers for individual chapters includes Ph.D's, CPMs, CSMs, RPAs, attorneys, and MBAs. My Spring 1986 Rancho Santiago College property management class was also of great help in reviewing the individual chapters. Special thanks for the assistance of illustrator Bill Hankla, typists Mary Usher and Michele Burgess, and publication coordinator Julie Shafii.

And last, but certainly not least, my sincere gratitude to Carla McLelland, CPM, without whose help in writing, research, editing, and reviewing, this book would not have been completed.

i

Acknowledgments of Chapter Reviewers

Lowell Anderson
Real Estate Coordinator
Cerritos College
Norwalk, CA

James Ashcraft, Jr., B.S.
Ashcraft Electric Co.
Long Beach, CA

Russell W. Berry
Executive Vice President
Woodmont Companies
Belmont, CA

Bernie Blume, CPA
Valley View Mortgage
Santa Fe Springs, CA

Terry Calder, Attorney
Calder & Associates
Santa Ana, CA

Gary Conkley, B.A.
United Insurance Agencies
Pasadena, CA

Mike Cook
Windward Investments
Huntington Beach, CA

Evelyn Daniel, Attorney
Real Estate Coordinator
Rancho Santiago College
Santa Ana, CA

Mike Dunn, Attorney
Dunn & Associates
Costa Mesa, CA

Steve Durringer, Attorney
Newport Beach, CA

Michael Easton
Maintenance Manager
J.D. Maintenance & Construction
Costa Mesa, CA

Stanley Feldsott, Attorney
Feldsott and Lee
Newport Beach, CA

Susan Fassnacht, CPM
Eugene Berger Management
Santa Ana, CA

Frank Fowler
Real Estate Coordinator
El Camino College
Torrance, CA

Thomas Gille, CPM, RPA
Catellus Development
San Francisco, CA

Gene Harrison
Victor Valley College
Apple Valley, CA

Cecilia Hopkins, Ph.D
College of San Mateo
San Mateo, CA

Audrey King, RECI
Real Estate Broker
Tustin, CA

Peter Kroosz, CPM, MBA
Peter Kroosz Realty Management
Newport Beach, CA

Mike Lango, RPA
City of San Luis Obispo
San Luis Obispo, CA

Carla McLelland, CPM
J.D. Property Management, Inc.
Costa Mesa, CA

Stevi Meredith
Maintenance Coordinator
J.D. Property Management, Inc.
Costa Mesa, CA

Mike Packard, CPM
The Loomis Company
Carlsbad, CA

John Phelps, CPM, CSM
Tishman West Management Corp.
Orange, CA

Chet Platt, Ph.D
Associate Dean
Coastline Community College
Fountain Valley, CA

Judy Ricker, CPM
Invest West Management
Santa Barbara, CA

Trudy Rideout
Coastline Community College
Fountain Valley, CA

Donald Smith, CPM, CSM
D.W.A. Smith & Co.
Newport Beach, CA

Jim Spivey, GRI
Spivey & Associates
Tustin, CA

Lainy Steinberg
J. Ray Construction
Irvine, CA

Robert Taylor, CPM, MBA
Real Estate Marketing/Management
Santa Ana, CA

Gene Trowbridge, CCIM
Trowbridge Equity Group
Costa Mesa, CA

Acknowledgments

Chuck Alexander, CCIM, Real Estate Coordinator, Solano Community College

Eric Alexander, CPM, Mira Costa College

David Arant, Real Estate Coordinator, Los Angeles Harbor College

Dr. Eugene C. Azamber, Real Estate Instructor, Fresno City College

David D. Bays, Instructor, Mission College

Leslie G. Bellamy, Instructor, Los Angeles Southwest College

Leon Benizio, CPM, Instructor, Glendale College

Jack Bliss, CCIM, El Camino College

Benton Caldwell, Dean, Mount San Jacinto College

Dr. Edward Chapin, Jr., Crafton Hills College

Faz Elahi, Instructor, West Los Angeles College

Warren B. Enos, Director of Division of Business, Ohlone College

Earl Erickson, Instructor, San Francisco Community College

Abraham H. Farkas, Real Estate Program Coordinator, West Los Angeles College

Edward Flores, Instructor, Evergreen Valley College

Gene Geary, Instructor, Cypress College

Betty Gwiazdon, Real Estate Coordinator, American River College

Lou Hansotte, Instructor, Cuyamaca College

Gary Hubbard, Director of Community Development, West Valley College

Ellen Ito, Community Service Specialist, Sacramento City College

Thomas A. Ketelaar, Instructor, Grossmount College

Dr. Peter Kirianoff, Business Division, Fullerton College

Dr. Alan Klofkorn, Instructor, Irvine Valley College

Lowell Knapp, Instructor, Cuyamaca College

Don Long, Real Estate Coordinator, Foothill College

Dr. Charles Mayfield, Real Estate Coordinator, Los Angeles Southwest College

Dr. Ken McDonnell, College of the Desert, Copper Mountain Campus

Otto E. Mielenz, Chairman of Business Division, Chabot College

Gary M. Page, RPA, Instructor, Southwestern College

David Roberts, Business Division Chairman, San Joaquin Delta College

Carey Roth, CPM, Real Estate Instructor, UCLA

Steven Schaefer, Division of Business, Contra Costa College

Kenneth L. Siegel, Instructor, Moorpark College

Dr. Al Silvera, Real Estate Coordinator, Santa Barbara City College

Ken Vise, Instructor, Saddleback College

John B. Weidler, Professor of Real Estate, Los Angeles Mission College

Robert R. Wynne, Instructor, Barstow College

Nick Zoumbos, Professor of Accounting and Real Estate, San Bernardino College

Preface

Property Management in California is written for students and practitioners of property management. It is specifically for California, unlike most property management books which are sold nationally and do not cover individual state practices. This book addresses the laws and regulations governing landlord/tenant relations in California. Addenda covering the Landlord/Tenant Laws in specific states are available as a supplement to this book. For example, addenda on New York, Arizona, Texas, and other states have been written. Over 85 illustrations and forms are used, along with examples, to provide the reader with both theory and a practical understanding of property management. This book is intended to be a basic text, not a comprehensive reference book. It does, however, contain an extensive list of further reference sources, books, and publications.

The book is divided into chapters covering areas such as leases, residential management, shopping centers, office buildings, maintenance, and landlord/tenant law. At the end of each chapter are ten multiple-choice review questions to help the reader better understand the chapter. Answers to these questions are contained in **Appendix E**.

This book also contains a case study beginning with Chapter 5 and continuing on throughout the book. The reader is given background information and facts about a 20-unit apartment building that has serious problems. At the end of selected chapters, questions are asked relating to the material in the chapter to help solve some of these problems. Suggested answers will be found in **Appendix D**. Also included is an extensive list of frequently used property management terms (**Appendix A**).

Contents

Chapter 1

PROPERTY MANAGEMENT AS A PROFESSION

Key Terms

ARM
CPM
CSM
IREM
FIABCI-USA
AMO
ICSC
Property manager
Regional manager
RPA
Mixed-use complexes
Resident manager
BOMI
Asset manager

Food for Thought

"A journey of 1,000 miles begins with a single step."

Property Management as a Profession

Introduction

During the twentieth century the United States moved into an era of urbanization and rapid development. The real estate profession has responded to this revolutionary trend with increased specialization and a higher and more sophisticated level of service to its clients.

Many professional designations originated to coincide with increased levels of professional service and specialization. The appraisal area developed specialists called the "MAI" Appraisers. Commercial real estate brokers designate their specialists as "CCIM."

One of the fastest growing areas of specialization to originate as long-term real estate investments increased was that of Property Manager. The highest designation bestowed on this new professional field was that of CPM® (CERTIFIED PROPERTY MANAGER®). This special recognition is bestowed only after intensive study, including completion of classes, seminars, testing, demonstration reports, and several years of experience in the field while abiding by a strict code of ethics.

Evolution of Property Management

The profession of property management is both an evolving and a rapidly expanding field. The role of being just a rent-collector is disappearing. Instead, property management has emerged as a highly technical and specialized managerial science. The property manager of today must possess communication skills and be a dynamic and effective decision-maker. He or she must act as a market analyst, an advertising executive, a diplomat, and a maintenance engineer as he or she associates with property owners, prospective tenants and investors, tenants, employees, attorneys, accountants, and others involved in the real estate field.

History

During colonial times, the development of American cities occurred at seaports and along major waterways. These early cities — New York, Boston, and Philadelphia — served as living, trading, and shopping areas. During the 1800s the population of America profoundly increased in the downtown centers of cities, and office and commercial buildings soon developed.

In the early 1900s, significant changes were starting to take place. Three important technological advances occurred:

1. The structural advantages of steel-framed buildings.

2. The perfection of high-speed elevators.

3. The continued use of the automobile.

The first two technological advances brought about taller buildings, thereby increasing the density of office, commercial, and apartment buildings. The advent of the automobile permitted both business owners and residents to move away from the congested downtown areas into a newly developing phenomenon, *"SUBURBIA."*

After World War II, assisted by VA and FHA loans, returning soldiers were able to purchase their own homes. Many of these new homes were located away from downtown in "suburbia." Following this migration, developers built office and shopping centers convenient to the growing suburban population.

Initially, these suburban shopping centers tended to be small and convenience-oriented, made up mostly of grocers and small retailers. From the 1960s through the 1980s, as the population migration continued, commercial developers became increasingly interested in serving the shopping needs of suburbia. Larger centers were soon built, offering one-stop shopping, free parking, and climate-controlled malls to meet the needs of the burgeoning "Baby Boomers." Today, over 600 major regional malls exist throughout the United States.

Projections for the Future

Present trends indicate a reversal of this migration pattern. Many areas of the country are now saturated with large shopping centers. As a result, those under construction are frequently smaller in size. The population, growing at a slower rate, is moving back to cities and to small rural towns. America is changing from a nation that produces a product to one that supplies information and services. The property manager, therefore, must keep abreast of changing demographics regarding location, family size, age, and consumer buying habits.

Classification of Properties

The real estate industry is large and diversified, with many types of properties that need to be managed. Properties are defined according to their uses:

Retail —	properties where things are sold; i.e., regional shopping centers to strip centers.
Office —	properties where services are rendered; i.e., skyscrapers to garden offices.
Industrial —	properties where things are made; i.e., large manufacturing plants to small industrial parks.
Agricultural —	properties where food is grown; i.e., large farms to strawberry fields in urban areas.
Residential —	properties where people live; i.e., apartments, condos, single-family homes.
Special-Purpose —	properties where the use dictates the design; i.e., motels, mobile home parks, mini-storage.

Within these general classifications are many subdivisions.

Property Management Designations

The term "Professional Property Manager" has been misunderstood, misused, and abused in the past. Presently, there is no college degree or major in property management, even though property management courses are becoming more common in community colleges throughout the state. There are, however, several professional designations. The three major ones are: Certified Property Manager (CPM), Real Property Administrator (RPA), and Certified Shopping Center Manager (CSM).

The CPM designation is conferred by the Institute of Real Estate Management (IREM), a branch of the National Association of Realtors (NAR). The organization was formed in 1933 by a group of property managers concerned with establishing ethical standards and professionalism in the property management field. To qualify for this designation, already earned by 10,000 property managers in the United States, the property manager must meet stringent qualifying standards in areas of education, experience,

REALTOR®

and ethical conduct. In addition to passing three exams in these areas, a candidate must satisfactorily complete a management plan (mini-thesis). The candidate must also currently manage a set minimum management portfolio, for example, over 300 apartment units or 120,000 square feet of retail space, and have five years experience as a property manager. If directly supervised by a CPM, the time element may be reduced to three years. Additional information concerning this professional designation can be obtained by writing to:

 **Institute of Real Estate Management**
of the NATIONAL ASSOCIATION OF REALTORS®
National Headquarters: 430 North Michigan Avenue, Chicago, IL 60611-4090
(312) 661-1930   Telex (312) 025-3742

The RPA designation is bestowed by the Building Owners and Managers Institute International (BOMI). BOMI has had experience (three years) and portfolio (40,000 square feet) requirements since January 1, 1990. They also have a code of ethics. Each candidate must successfully complete a seven-course educational program. Additional information can be obtained by writing to:

 Building Owners and Managers Institute International
1201 New York Ave., N.W., Suite 300
Washington, D.C. 20005
(202) 408-2662

The CSM designation is conferred by the International Council of Shopping Centers. At the present time no management courses are required, but courses are available to help the candidate pass the required examination. Additional information can be obtained by writing to:

665 Fifth Ave., New York, N.Y. 10022
(212) 421-8181

The AMO® designation (ACCREDITED MANAGEMENT ORGANIZATION®) is also awarded by IREM to firms engaged in property management which have met the high standards IREM has established in areas of education, experience, integrity, and financial stability.

The ARM® (Accredited Resident Manager) designation is awarded by IREM to residential onsite managers who have met experience and educational standards after passing a test at the end of a one-week course.

The terms CPM, ARM, and AMO are registered trademarks of the Institute of Real Estate Management.

The Urban Land Institute (ULI) is an independent, non-profit education and research organization whose stated purpose is to improve the quality standards for land-use planning and development. ULI was founded in 1936 and has published hundreds of publications and held numerous seminars and on-site study projects. These items range from office handbooks, rental housing, and dollars and cents of shopping centers to shared-parking computer programs. A complete list can be obtained by writing to:

THE URBAN LAND INSTITUTE
625 Indiana Ave., N.W., Ste. 400
Washington, D.C. 20004
(202) 624-7000

Other organizations which are very useful sources of information are the National Apartment Association (NAA) and the California Apartment Association (CAA). Legal briefs and updates are sent to the organization members along with red alerts concerning unfavorable legislation, whether it be taxes, rent control, etc. The CAA has also developed an extensive list of forms such as rental applications and security deposit return forms. Many of these forms are included in this book. There are also Apartment Association Chapters in many areas of California that hold monthly meetings, print monthly newsletters, and offer tenant credit checking services to their members. The names and addresses of local chapters near you can be obtained by writing to the CAA. One such chapter, the Apartment Association of Orange County, publishes a 100-page monthly magazine and has over 3,000 members. They also have a designation called the Certified Apartment

Manager (CAM), which is issued after completion of two courses, preparation of an apartment community analysis report, an additional 40 hours of optional credits, two years of management experience, and successfully passing a national examination.

California Apartment Association

CALIFORNIA APARTMENT ASSOCIATION
1414 K Street, Ste. 610
Sacramento, CA 95814

NATIONAL APARTMENT ASSOCIATION
1111 14th N.W., 9th Floor
Washington, D.C. 20005

International Management Organizations

The International Real Estate Institute has a designation "Registered Property Manager" (RPM) which has a code of ethics although no courses or tests are required to earn the designation. They also publish the "International Real Estate Journal."

International Real Estate Institute

8383 E. Evans Rd.
Scottsdale, AZ 85281 USA
(602) 998-8267

The most widely recognized international real estate organization is FIABCI, which was founded in 1949. It is also a National Association of Realtors affiliate. It has over 6,000 international real estate specialists and operates in more than 44 countries. The name is derived from its French origins and means Federation Internationale des Administrateurs de Biens Conseils Immobiliers. FIABCI publishes a world directory, a professional newsletter and holds educational seminars. It has a professional designation called "Certified International Property Specialist" (CIPS). Candidates must fulfill criteria in three main categories: education, participation in FIABCI and work experience.

FIABCI-USA
777 14th Street N.W.
Washington, D.C. 20005
(202) 383-1000

Trends in Property Management

Multi-Family Housing (Apartments)

At the present time there are approximately 30 million rental units in the United States, 9 million of which are single-family houses. The rental ownership is well diversified, with the top 50 largest owners controlling just a little over 4% of the total. This percentage will increase in the future as large investors and syndicators move into the industry with even larger complexes in many locations throughout the country. Approximately 34% of all housing units are rentals with the remaining 66% owner occupied.

Government Participation

Participation by the federal government in rental housing is slowing as funding for rent subsidies and low-cost government housing has been reduced. The use of tax-free bond financing, which in the past helped the development of new projects by lowering debt financing costs, has been curtailed. Under the Tax Reform Act of 1986, the depreciation schedule has been increased to 27½ years for residential (apartments) and 31½ years for commercial buildings. This change reduces the tax shelter benefits — a form of government participation — that real estate enjoyed in the past.

Increase in Condominiums and Smaller Single-Family Homes

As the number of people per household declines (presently 2.5), there is less need for the larger four- and five-bedroom homes preferred by the large families of the past. Houses are getting smaller as high land costs spur the development of condominiums and PUDs (Planned Unit Developments).

Mixed-Use Complexes

These complexes usually include offices, retail shopping, and apartments or condos. By using shared parking, land costs are lowered while providing convenience and aesthetics to the development. Examples are Tricorp Towers in New York and The City complex in Orange, California.

Complexity of Management

The increasing costs, risks, and sophistication of real estate development — leasing, financing, and government regulations — have created a need for professional property management. Landlord/tenant laws and court cases have thrust a considerable amount of the liability upon the shoulders of managers and owners.

Career Opportunities

Steps in achieving the position of property manager have traditionally followed the career path of assistant resident manager, then resident manager, and finally leading to property manager. This is no longer the case, however, as a person who excels at running one building (onsite resident manager) may not have the temperament, skills, or ability to manage several properties (property manager). The old adage of "The best salesperson does not always make the best sales manager" may apply here.

Resident Manager

The terms "onsite manager" and "resident manager" are interchangeable. The main duties of a resident manager are:

1. *Renting units*
2. *Collecting rents*
3. *Responsibility for tenant relations*
4. *Maintenance*
5. *Supervision*
6. *Keeping records*
7. *Completing proper paperwork*

Personality traits usually found in good resident managers or assistant resident managers include:

1. *Conscientiousness*
2. *Congenial personality*
3. *Accuracy*
4. *Salesmanship*
5. *Tact*
6. *Honesty*

**Figure 1-1
Resident Manager**

Property Manager

The terms "property manager" and "property supervisor" are also interchangeable. These persons differ from the onsite manager in that they deal with several properties and supervise the onsite manager. They usually interface directly with the owner. In addition to being problem-solvers, they must also be planners, directors, delegators, and have the ability to organize and implement comprehensive control of the properties they manage.

The main duties of a property manager or property supervisor would include:

1. *Budgeting, reports, and monthly statements*

2. *Onsite inspections*

3. *Supervision*

4. *Controlling expenditures*

5. *Establishing rental rates*

6. *Establishing standard operating procedures*

7. *Maximizing income stream and value*

Personality traits usually found in a property manager include, in addition to those of a resident manager, all of the following:

1. *Analytical and detail-oriented*

2. *Personable*

3. *Self-starting, motivated, enthusiastic*

4. *Assertive and ambitious*

5. *A logical decision-maker*

6 *Able to be firm and say "NO"*

7. *Able to represent both owner and tenant*

Regional Manager

This job description relates to larger property management companies where a manager supervises several property managers or property supervisors. The regional manager must have especially good communication skills, and be able to delegate, motivate, and accomplish objectives through the efforts of subordinates.

Figure 1-2. Employment Opportunities

**EMPLOYMENT OPPORTUNITIES
IN
PROPERTY MANAGEMENT**

- Executive Manager
- Asset Manager
- Property Supervisor — Residential
- Property Supervisor — Commercial
- Property Supervisor — Condominiums
- Onsite Manager — Residential
- Onsite Manager — Commercial
- Leasing Agent — Offsite
- Leasing Agent — Onsite
- Accounts Supervisor — Bookkeeping
- Controller
- Administrative Assistant
- Maintenance Supervisor
- Building Engineer
- General Maintenance

Asset Manager

The most ill-defined job title in property management is that of asset manager. An asset manager may be responsible for a multi-million-dollar portfolio at one company or simply work onsite at another. The correctly defined asset manager is normally an employee of a large investment holding company with little or no responsibility for the day-to-day activity of the portfolio properties. The asset manager is usually responsible for the investment and financial planning aspects of the entire portfolio.

Executive Manager

The executive manager is responsible for the overall property management performance of the company or business. This responsibility includes supervision of property supervisors, accounting divisions, and maintenance departments. The executive manager is usually a Certified Property Manager (CPM), and in smaller companies typically is the owner-operator.

Specialization Within Property Management

Just as there are different types of properties, different management companies specialize in specific types of properties. As an example, some management companies specialize in residential units and would therefore be a poor choice to manage a medical building which has unique individual problems and specific needs. Another example would be a management company which manages large complexes (over 100 units). The supervisor might be qualified to manage this size complex, but probably would not be able to manage smaller complexes (say, 15 units). The systems and procedures geared toward larger properties require more experienced onsite managers. Conversely, a management company that handles single-family houses probably does not have the computerized system necessary to manage larger operations. A full-service company which is fully computerized, however, may have divisions capable of handling the entire management spectrum.

Types of Property Management Operations

Large Insurance and Pension Corporations

These firms usually have salaried staff property managers to handle the corporate property portfolio in-house.

"Ma and Pa" Owners

This type of owner is usually someone who owns single-family houses or a few multi-unit complexes. He or she usually self-manages, which requires minimal training and experience. The professional qualifications usually come from "The School of Hard Knocks."

Local Real Estate Office

Sometimes a real estate agent sells a four-plex, for example, to an investor and tells him about all the benefits of ownership (appreciation and tax benefits). The agent forgets, however, to mention evictions, stopped-up toilets, and tenant phone calls at all hours of the night. The investor then tells the real estate agent that if he wants the listing when the property is to be sold, he must manage the property until the sale. This is called "management by default."

Professional Fee Management Company

Investors (owners) who need a manager in order to bring their operation diversified talents, experience, and controls, including computer operation, all in one package, will hire a professional property management company. The compensation for this service is usually based on a percentage of the collected income. These companies usually have one or more Certified Property Managers (CPMs) on the staff.

Figure 1-3. Local Real Estate Office

Growth of Women in the Field

In the past several years, the number of women entering the field has increased significantly. The reasons for this are many, but include the following considerations.

1. *It is a comparatively new area (non-traditional).*

2. *A formal education is not required for entry.*

3. *Promotions are based on merit.*

4. *Temperament and patience are traits of the successful manager.*

Figure 1-4. Women In Property Management

Future Trends

1. *More specialization* as the property management field becomes more complex, technical and sophisticated.

2. *More formal education* (a college degree) may be required along with accounting and financial courses.

3. *More reliance on the computer*, including systems and procedures.

4. *Standardization of the industry* relative to terms, methods, and procedures.

5. *More government regulations*, including regulation of requirements for property managers beyond the present real estate licensing requirements.

6. *More team play* in which the property manager will be involved from conception in consulting on projects with attorneys, architects, builders, etc.

7. *Greater need* for professional management as tax benefits are reduced and investors are increasingly pressured to manage real estate as a full-time business. Investors will want to hire the best manager to maximize investment income and property appreciation.

8. *Increased salary* compensation along with the increased importance of property management.

Summary

With the advent of urbanization during the twentieth century, the real estate industry became more specialized and sophisticated. The specialized designation of Certified Property Manager (CPM) was instituted in 1933. This designation necessitated taking educational courses (three), having years of experience (five) and, most recently, college education. The evolution of property manager was from a rent collector to that of a sophisticated professional manager who must possess communication skills, technical knowledge, and be a rational decision-maker. The advent of important technological advances (steel framing, high-speed elevators, etc.) in the early 1900s enabled taller buildings and thus increased density. The increased use of the automobile helped create a migration from the city to suburbia. The major classifications of properties that emerged were: retail, office, industrial, agricultural, residential, and special-purpose. The property manager must keep abreast of changing trends in demographics, consumer buying habits, and the economic consequences of a society shifting from manufacturing to service industries.

Professional organizations that have emerged in the property management fields of specialization include: IREM (CPM), BOMI (RPA), ICSC (CSM), NAN (CAM), and FIABCI-USA (CIPS).

Employment opportunities in property management are many and varied and include: asset manager, property manager, leasing agent, controller, maintenance supervisor, building engineer, etc.

The resident or onsite manager is the person who usually resides on the property and is responsible for day-to-day activities such as rentals, rent collection, tenant relations, maintenance, supervision, keeping records, and related paperwork. This person should be conscientious, congenial, accurate, tactful, honest, and possess sales ability.

The property manager is the person who usually supervises the resident managers of several properties. Duties would include budgeting, inspection, supervision, controlling expenditures, establishing rental rates and operating procedures, and maximizing the cash flow and appreciation for the property. The property manager needs to be analytical, personable, self-starting, assertive, and logical.

Types of management operations range from small Ma and Pa owners to large insurance and pension corporations, local real estate offices, and professional fee management companies. Future trends in property management include growth and opportunities for women, more specialization and standardization, more government regulations, and higher salary levels.

We conclude from our analysis that the property management profession is an art and not a science. It has neither an empirical nor exact body of knowledge, nor a standard code of ethics to which all must adhere, nor specific educational requirements. Property management is a mixture of the theories of the management process (getting things done with and through people), empirical theory (the use of past experience), and decision theory (the rational approach to decisions).

Chapter 1 Review Questions

1. *The designation for a property manager is:*

   a. MAI.
   b. REEA.
   c. CPM.
   d. none of the above.

2. *Property management developed as a profession around:*

   a. the early 1980s.
   b. the Middle Ages.
   c. the early 1900s.
   d. the early 1850s.

3. *High-speed elevators, structural steel, and reinforced concrete made possible:*

   a. high-rise buildings.
   b. strip shopping centers.
   c. single-story industrial buildings.
   d. both a and c.
   e. none of the above.

4. *Regional (large) shopping centers developed:*

   a. in the early 1900s.
   b. before World War II.
   c. after World War II.
   d. none of the above.

5. *Major factors affecting real estate management include:*

   a. high-rise buildings.
   b. cities becoming more concentrated.
   c. neither a nor b.
   d. both a and b.

6. *The "CSM" designation means:*

   a. Commercial Skyscraper Manager.
   b. Certified Shopping Center Manager.
   c. Commercial Slum Manager.
   d. Commercial Shopping Center Manager.

7. *The onsite manager designation for apartments is:*

   a. ARM.
   b. CAP.
   c. CSM.
   d. CPM.
   e. none of the above.

8. *BOMI is an organization primarily for:*

   a. shopping center managers.
   b. office managers and owners.
   c. appraisers.
   d. apartment managers and owners.
   e. none of the above.

9. *Which position is usually higher on an organizational chart?*

   a. Onsite Manager.
   b. Maintenance Manager.
   c. Property Supervisor.
   d. Personnel Manager.
   e. Apartment Manager.

10. *The Institute of Real Estate Management bestows which designation?*

    a. CPM.
    b. REEA.
    c. RPA.
    d. CSM.
    e. none of the above.

Chapter 1
Selected Additional References and Reading

Apartment News Magazine
  Apartment Association of Orange County
  12900 Garden Grove Boulevard, Suite 101
  Garden Grove, CA 92643

Cushman, Robert, and Neal Rodin, *Property Management Handbook*, John Wiley & Sons, Somerset, NJ, 1985.

Downs, Anthony, *Rental Housing in the 1980s*, The Brookings Institution, Washington, D.C., 1983.

Downs, James Jr., CPM, *Principles of Real Estate Management*, Institute of Real Estate Management, 12th Edition, Chicago, IL, 1980.

Institute of Real Estate Management, *The Certified Manager Profile*, Chicago, IL, 1984.

International Real Estate Journal (Three Times Per Year)
  8715 Via de Commercio
  Scottsdale, AZ 95258

Journal of Property Management (Bimonthly)
  Institute of Real Estate Management
  430 N. Michigan Avenue
  Chicago, IL 60611

National Network of Commercial Real Estate Women
  1776 Massachusetts Avenue, N.W.
  Washington, D.C. 20036

Walter, William Jr., CPM, *The Practice of Real Estate Management*, Institute of Real Estate Management, Chicago, IL, 1983.

NOTES

Chapter 2

REAL ESTATE ECONOMICS

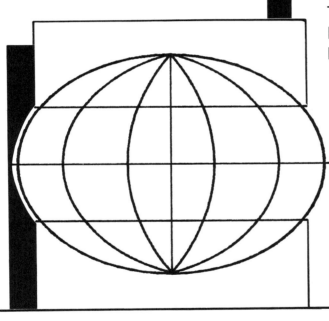

Key Terms

Supply and demand
Technical oversupply
Economics oversupply
Nuisance increase
    Family formations
    Physical
      obsolescence
    Economic
      obsolescence
    Functional
      obsolescence
    Net operating
      income (NOI)
    Population growth
    Reproduction
      approach
    Market approach
    Income approach
    Capitalization
    Cash flow
    Gross multiplier
    Real depreciation
    Tax depreciation

Food for Thought

"There is always time for the things you put first."

Real Estate Economics

Size of the Market

In order to maximize real estate income and appreciation, the property manager must understand the real estate market. This market, due to its large size, has a significant influence on the total economy. The real estate rental industry is the third largest industry in California with over $15 billion per year in total revenues. There are over 4.2 million residential rental units and over 9.5 million rental occupants in the state. The average rent statewide is almost $600 per month, and over $700 per month in affluent areas such as Orange County.

Nationwide, there are over 30 million residential units, with a half million new units being built each year. The national average rent is projected at $450 per month. It can readily be seen that this large market needs capable, trained, professional property managers to shepherd these vast assets.

Business Cycles

With the coming of the Industrial Revolution and the development of sophisticated banking and financial markets, an interdependence of the various sectors of the American economy was created which has led to cyclical economic fluctuations. These cycles are constantly changing. There are differences, however, in the makeup, severity, and duration from cycle to cycle. Cycles can last from one to fifteen years and are usually characterized in three phases:

Phase I   — Expansion — recovery
Phase II — Prosperity — peak
Phase III — Recession (possible depression) — decline

Business cycles are measured by an artificial index made up of individual indicators; i.e., unemployment, industrial production, and gross domestic product. The causes of these cycles are not known, but there are four theories:

1. *Monetary theories* — changes in money supply; i.e., interest rates and credit.

2. *Savings and investments theories* — savings that are used for expanded production will eventually lead to overproduction and recession. In other words, increasing levels of investment cannot be maintained indefinitely and lead to decline as a "normal" business activity.

3. *Business economy theories* — which were championed by John Maynard Keynes, say that business cycles are a self-generating phenomenon, inherent in industrial society.

4. *Social cycles* — society determines the cyclical pattern. In his best seller, *The Great Depression of 1990*, Dr. Ravi Batra states that society is composed of four types of people, each endowed with a different frame of mind:

(1) *Warrior mentality* — soldiers, policemen, athletes, etc.

(2) *Intellectual mentality* — writers, lawyers, physicians, white-collar workers, etc.

(3) *Acquisitors mentality* — merchants, bankers, landlords, etc.

(4) *Physical labor mentality* — unskilled workers.

Dr. Batra's theory states that cycles of prosperity and depression are a result of broad economic and social forces rather than unique events caused by individuals.

Government Efforts to Control Cycles

The United States government, since the Great Depression, has sought to stimulate orderly economic growth while cushioning the adverse effects of cyclical fluctuations. Some of these control mechanisms and devices would include:

1. Margin requirements on stocks to reduce speculation.

2. Federal Reserve Board can increase the money supply (print more money) or reduce the rate it charges member banks to borrow funds.

3. Government programs such as unemployment insurance, welfare, price supports for farmers, social security, food stamps, public works projects, and road building.

In summary, forecasts of real estate market and business cycles are based on monitoring and analysis of four major classes of data:

Demand factors — population, effective buying income of families

Supply factors — existing inventory and new construction starts, etc.

Catalytic factors — mortgage interest rates, unemployment rates, etc.

Psychological factors — perception by consumers of economic changes such as inflation

Causes of Real Estate Fluctuations

Money

As a general rule, real estate values increase during inflationary times and decrease during times of recession or depression. Inflationary conditions are frequently due to behavior rather than to economic causes. For example, if Americans believe the value of the dollar will decrease due to the government printing more money (monetizing) to pay its debts, they will purchase real estate, gold, and items which increase in inflationary times. This action may have little relationship to supply and demand, but rather to a perceived future demand.

Supply and Demand

If demand (tenants) is greater than supply (units), rents will generally increase. This will, in theory, cause developers to build more units to meet the increased demand caused by the low vacancy rate (Figure 2-1).

1. *Vacancy rates* are often incorrectly calculated. Local apartment associations are a good source for vacancy data. Also, the IREM Experience Exchange Apartments for major cities is a good reference.

2. *Excess demand* can lead to overcrowding and doubling up of tenants in existing units. It may also result in rent control.

3. *Technical oversupply* occurs in areas where there are more units than tenants. It frequently occurs in boomtowns or where major sources of employment have moved out (i.e., energy boomtowns like Farmington, New Mexico, or Houston, Texas).

4. *Economic oversupply* occurs when tenants cannot afford the existing rent levels for housing. This happens often in depressed areas where two or more families or non-related parties share an apartment, thereby reducing their housing costs. It frequently leads to accelerated wear and tear on the housing unit and excessive demands for water, gas, and electricity. In addition, these types of arrangements often lead to unsanitary living conditions.

Figure 2-1. Supply and Demand

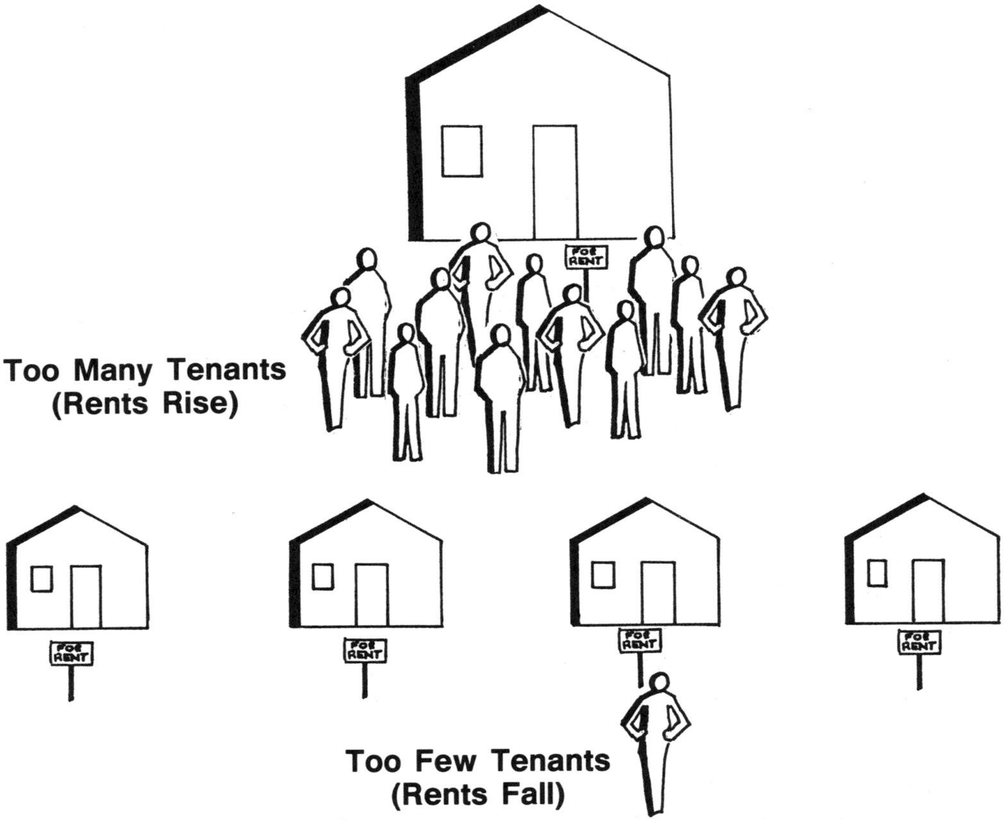

**Too Many Tenants
(Rents Rise)**

**Too Few Tenants
(Rents Fall)**

Figure 2-2. Economic Indicators

Economic Indicators

Dow Jones Average
Balance of Trade
T-Bill Rate
Employment Figures
Bond Prices and Yield
Corporate Earnings
Consumer Price Index
Gold Prices
U.S. Government Borrowing
Federal Reserve Discount Rate
Gross Domestic Product
Housing Starts
Retail Sales
Industrial Production
Wholesale Price Index

Employment Levels

During periods of high unemployment, tenants may not have money to pay rent, resulting in delinquencies and evictions.

Government Policies

These include public assistance in the form of:

1. *Welfare*

2. *Unemployment compensation*

3. *Social security*

4. *Tax or mortgage (loan) benefits* to developers for additional housing

5. *HUD Section 8 payments to subsidize rents of low income tenants*

Rental Rates

The real estate industry produces a fixed product (building) that lasts for 50 years or longer. The manager has no power to reduce the supply by manufacturing fewer products.

Market conditions affect rates. If rents are at market level or higher, you might consider advertising in areas with even higher rents in an attempt to draw those people accustomed to paying higher rents to your building.

Rent increases are generally divided into two parts:

1. *Nuisance.* Usually $10 or less, tenants will pay a nuisance increase rather than incur the cost and hassle of moving.

2. *Economic.* Usually based on what the traffic will bear and usually needed to keep pace with rising costs of operation such as insurance, utilities, etc.

3. *New Tenants.* New tenant rents should be increased as the unit changes tenancy. This accomplishes two goals. First, existing tenants feel they are getting a better deal (a bargain) because of their longevity. Second, it helps establish a new, higher market level for future increases.

4. *Rent Control.* If your units are under some form of rent control, your ability to increase rents to existing and new tenants may be restricted. Local ordinances must be consulted prior to any rent increases.

Home Prices and Affordability

The cost of an existing single-family home increased dramatically from 1977 to 1993 on a national basis by 145%. The median price nationally in 1993 was approximately $108,000. The cost of existing houses is even higher in California, led by the San Francisco area with a median cost of approximately $254,100. The Los Angeles area follows with a cost of $196,300. In the past few years, California home prices have declined.

Population Trends

1. *Increasing supply of renters* due to fewer people being able to afford their own home.

2. *Mobility* as people move to other parts of the country.

3. *Sun Belt* states have the *highest growth rate*, but are more service-oriented.

4. *Frost Belt* areas in the Northeast are showing renewed growth.

5. *Rust Belt* areas of large industries such as steel are being hurt by foreign imports.

6. *Grain Belt* farming areas have little or no *projected growth*.

Family Formations

The average size of households (2.62 persons) is decreasing and will continue to decrease in the future. The traditional family has a male head of household. Single parents — mostly women — now head 26% of all families with children, according to a recent Census Bureau study. This study also found that more than 60% of black families have only one parent. Nearly one American youngster in four lives with just one parent, compared to only 9% in 1960. Unmarried people of the same and opposite sex are forming their own households in increasing numbers. These trends mean the property manager must re-examine screening and selection methods for rental of housing units.

Shifts in Ethnic Groups

The California population will continue to grow to almost 32 million residents in 1995. This is a growth rate of more than 17% compared to the U.S. average of 6.9% between 1987 and 1995. Last year, however, more people left California than migrated here for the first time in history. The projected ethnic population for 1995, according to a study by the Center for Continuing Study of the California Economy as reported by the *Los Angeles Times*, is that 70% of the growth will be by Hispanic, Black, and Asian people. By 1995, Los Angeles will be on the verge of becoming the first region in the country where minorities will make up more than 50% of the population.

Personal Buying Power

In 1977, the typical buyer was 32.5 years old, but this age increased in 1987 to over 37 years of age. Over 50% of the home buyers were two-wage-earner households. The average monthly mortgage payment, including taxes and insurance, rose to $882 in 1987 compared to $400 in 1977. The median income of the home-buyer more than doubled from $22,700 in 1977 to $46,000 in 1987. Less than 30% of the new homeowners spent more than 25% of their income on housing.

Based on these economic data, upward pressure will be exerted upon rental increases in the future. Renters will stay renters for a longer period of time as they save money for down payments to be able to afford the increase in mortgage payments. A Census Bureau study found that only 9% of the renters nationwide can afford to buy a home.

Business Environment

The United States is changing from a producer of goods to a provider of services. Manufacturing jobs are decreasing and service-oriented jobs will, by the year 2000, comprise almost 75% of the work force. The property manager must be aware of how these changes will affect properties now and in the future. For example, the property manager should not submit a plan to upgrade an apartment building next to a steel mill that might be closing as the tenants would be unable to afford the upgraded amenities.

Appraisal

When conducting studies on rehabilitation, refinancing, or possible sale of a property, the property manager must be aware of how to estimate value. Three approaches to value will be examined here, with emphasis on the income approach. The goal is to estimate the property's value at its highest and best use.

Reproduction (Cost) Approach

To determine the reproduction cost, it is necessary to calculate the cost of constructing a similar building at today's construction costs. The steps are shown in Figure 2-3.

Cost statistics can be obtained from Marshall & Swift Valuation Service and are usually based on square footage. The disadvantage of this method is that it ignores cash flow and comparable prices. This method is used mostly for special-purpose buildings (churches, post offices) or where there have been few recent market sales.

Figure 2-3. Cost Approach

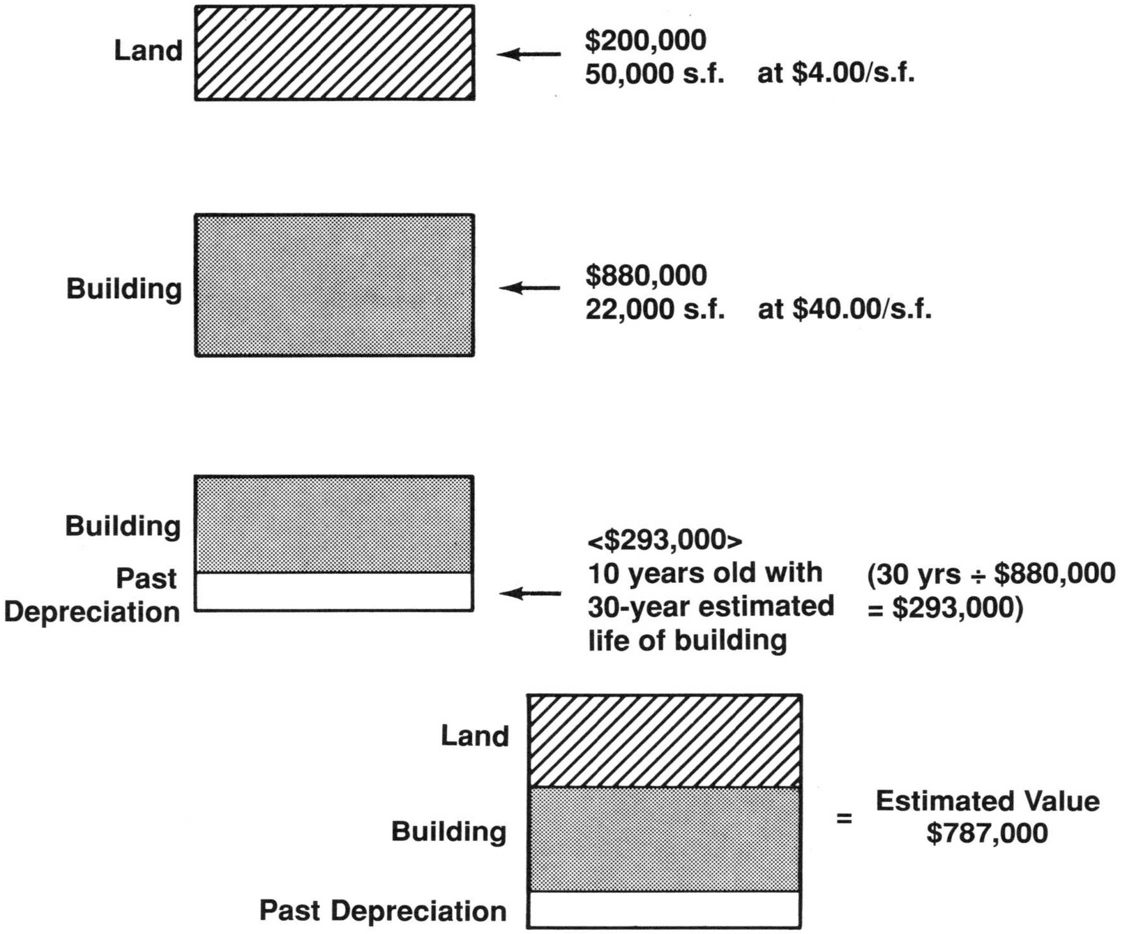

Land ← $200,000
50,000 s.f. at $4.00/s.f.

Building ← $880,000
22,000 s.f. at $40.00/s.f.

Building

Past Depreciation ← <$293,000>
10 years old with
30-year estimated
life of building

(30 yrs ÷ $880,000
= $293,000)

Land

Building = Estimated Value
$787,000

Past Depreciation

Market Approach

This method is valid only if there have been numerous recent similar sales in the property market area. Basically, one compares current selling prices of similar properties and adjusts those prices for differences in amenities such as pool, size of units, etc., and the method of financing. This method works best with single-family homes. A variation is used in apartment sales by comparing the price per unit or square footage. For example, a 20-unit building with 22,000 square feet sold for $787,000. Thus:

Price per unit	$39,350.00
Price per square foot	$ 35.77

A similar 10-unit building with 10,000 square feet sold for $392,000. Thus:

Price per unit	$39,200.00
Price per square foot	$ 39.20

One must be careful to remember not to compare one-bedroom units with two- or three-bedroom units when using the once-per-unit method.

Income Approach

This method basically derives the value based on income generated by the property. Within the income approach, there are several methods used to arrive at value. The most commonly used methods are examined here.

1. *Capitalization (IRV)*. The net income at the time of sale is divided by the purchase price paid, which results in a yield called the capitalization (CAP) rate. This approach works best where there have been some recent sales and reliable data on rents and expenses can be obtained. "Cap rates" from different properties can be compared and allowances made for varying conditions and location of the property. Less desirable locations and conditions, such as "fixer-uppers" in poor neighborhoods, result in higher "cap rates" as investors want higher yields for greater risks.

The historical method of determining the "cap rate" an investor wants to receive is composed of several factors based on subjective assumptions such as:

Bank rate	6.0%
Risk rate	2.0%
Non-liquidity	1.0%
Cap rate	9.0%

A more sophisticated method of determining the investor's "cap rate" would be the <u>Band of Investment</u>. It is sometimes referred to as "debt/equity band of investment." It relies, however, only on interest rates and doesn't take into account the risk or location factors.

25% down payment
75% 1st Trust Deed 10% — 30-year loan constant

Loan constant .1053
(.1053 × 75%) = 7.89
25% equity (owner wants 12% return)
12% × 25% = 3.0
Cap Rate = 10.89 or 10.9%

Figure 2-4. Capitalization (IRV)

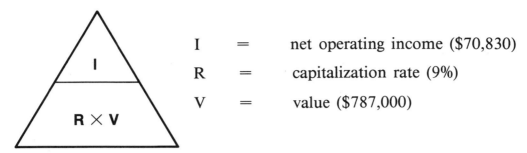

I   =   net operating income ($70,830)

R   =   capitalization rate (9%)

V   =   value ($787,000)

With two of the three factors, the third can be easily found by covering up the desired factor (R or V or I).

To find *net operating income* (NOI), just multiply rate times value.

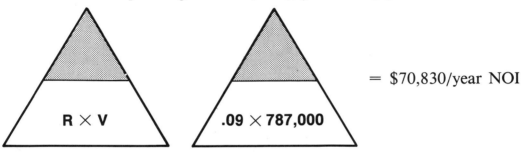

= $70,830/year NOI

To find value, just divide NOI by the cap rate.

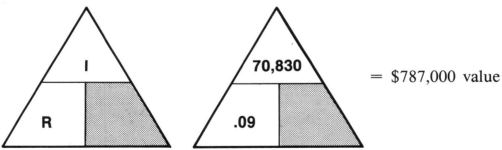

= $787,000 value

To find rate, divide NOI by the value.

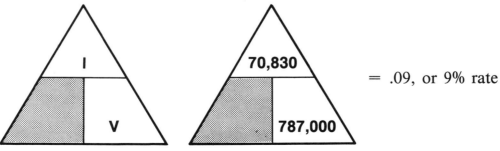

= .09, or 9% rate

2. *Cash Flow.* Net Operating Income (NOI) can be calculated simply by using the following format:

Scheduled gross income	$120,000
Less vacancy (5%)	(6,000)
Plus misc. income (washer, dryer)	2,000
Effective gross income	$116,000
Less operating expenses (taxes, insurance, utilities, maintenance, management fees, etc.)	(45,170)
Net operating income (NOI)	$ 70,830
Less debt service	(79,850)
Cash Flow	($ 9,020)

It can be seen from the above example that the disadvantage of the capitalization rate analysis is that it does not consider debt service (the high loan payment) which may be the result of over-leveraging. Therefore, the 20-unit apartment building in our case study has a negative cash flow. Investors are becoming interested in cash flow as well as NOI when analyzing a real estate investment.

Figure 2-5. Cash Flow

3. *Gross Rent Multiplier.* The "gross rent multiplier" is a rule-of-thumb method of determining value. The gross rent multiplier method recognizes the ratio between the gross rent roll and the sale price. The sale price is divided by the gross rent roll at the time of the sale. The resulting number is then multiplied by the rent roll of the subject property to establish estimated value. For example:

$$\text{Gross rents} \times \text{gross multiplier} = \text{value}$$
$$\$120,000 \times 6.56 = \$787,000$$

To find the gross multiplier:

Sales price ÷ gross rents (gross scheduled income) =
gross multiplier

$787,000 value ÷ $120,000 gross scheduled income =
6.56 gross multiplier

The disadvantage of this method is that it does not take into consideration financing costs or whether a building has separate or master-metered utilities. For example, if a building has master-metered gas representing 7% of gross annual income ($8,400), subtracting this figure which inflates the rent would result in:

$120,000 − $8,400 = $111,600
$787,000 ÷ $111,600 = 7.05 gross multiplier

We have examined the three main methods of income approach (capitalization rate, cash flow, and gross multiplier) and concluded that cash flow is the most critical to the owner. Other methods of valuation are available, but an understanding of the above three will enable the property manager to discuss the proposed rehabilitation, refinancing, or sale and its effects with the owner and other interested parties.

Depreciation

Depreciation is of two basic types: tax and real (physical). Depreciation is defined as a reduction in value of the property as it wears out through age or other causes.

Real Depreciation

1. *Physical.* Physical depreciation is the loss of value by wear and tear from use and decay. Proper repair and maintenance can defer such physical depreciation which is thus, in most cases, curable.

2. *Economic and Social Obsolescence.* Economic and social obsolescence is the adverse influence on the property by changes in zoning, noise, nuisance, population, and industry shifts. For example, if the neighborhood in which your apartment building is located has turned into a "ghetto," the value of your property may decrease.

3. *Functional Obsolescence.* Functional obsolescence is the loss of value due to outdated or poor architectural design or layout and lack of necessary amenities. This type of depreciation, as in economic, is difficult to cure. An example would be an office building with few windows, lots of columns, and inadequate elevator capacity for peak periods.

Figure 2-6. Depreciation

Physical

Economic

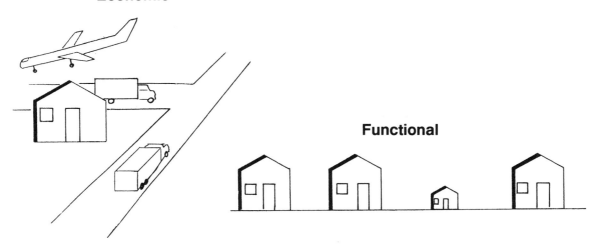

Functional

Tax Depreciation

This form of depreciation calculates a loss in book value, not real value, based on a scheduled number of years. Tax depreciation is sometimes referred to as "phantom depreciation" as the building can, in fact, be appreciating in real value while the government allows you to lower its value by providing a deduction of this pro-rated depreciation from your taxes each year. Under the Tax Reform Act of 1986, and the Omnibus Budget Reconciliation Act of 1993 the minimum recovery period that can be used is:

Residential rental property	27½ years
Non-residential rental property	39 years

Straight-line depreciation, however, is for 40 years for the alternative minimum tax. Using the above schedule results in a tax preference item for the difference between 27½ years and 40 years, which is one of the items used to calculate the alternative minimum tax (AMT) that a taxpayer may owe. The taxpayer will owe the regular tax or the alternative minimum tax, whichever is higher.

One can depreciate only improvements, not the land. Breakdown as to land value can be obtained from sources such as property tax bills or appraisals.

Value of property when purchased	$787,000
Less land value	-196,750
Value of improvements (apt. building)	$590,250

$$\frac{\text{Improvements}}{\text{Depreciated life}} = \frac{\$590,250}{27\frac{1}{2} \text{ years}} = \$21,464 \text{ depreciation per year}$$

Tax Changes

In contrast to the Tax Reform Act of 1986, which affected nearly every taxpayer, the Omnibus Budget Reconciliation Act of 1993 (OBRA) directs new tax increases toward wealthier taxpayers. According to the *Wall Street Journal* (August 15, 1993), people earning more than $200,000 annually will pay an average 17.4% more in taxes. These tax law changes affect the purchase and operation of real estate rental properties and need to be understood in order to better meet the client's investment goals.

Figure 2-7. Tax Brackets

Joint Returns: 1994		Single Returns: 1994	
Taxable Income	Marginal Tax Rate	Taxable Income	Marginal Tax Rate
$0-36,900	15%	$0-22,100	15%
Over $36,900	28%	Over $22,100	28%
Over $89,150	31%	Over $53,500	31%
Over $140,000	36%	Over $115,000	36%
Over $250,000	39.6%	Over $250,000	39.6%

Treatment of Income

The Tax Reform Act of 1986 divided income into three basic categories:

1. *Active* — income actually earned, including wages, tips, salaries, bonuses, etc.

2. *Portfolio* — includes interest, annuities, dividends, and royalty income.

3. *Passive* — The Omnibus Budget Reconciliation Act of 1993 (OBRA) eased the passive activity loss (PAL) rules for those in the real property business for tax years beginning January 1, 1994. All rental activities are now always classified as passive, even if it's the investor's sole business activity. These passive losses from real estate rentals can be offset only if passive income or passive losses are suspended and carried forward until disposition of the properly. Under (OBRA) new rules, a taxpayer can deduct losses from rental activities against non-passive as well as passive income if the taxpayer is in one or more real property businesses and the taxpayer materially participates. The term "real property business" includes most real property "trades or businesses" such as construction, rental, management, leasing, brokerage, acquisition, conversion, etc. The requirements for material participation include:

a. *Regular Participation* — spending more than 500 hours, or at least 100 hours and taxpayer participation is not less than the participation of any other person.

b. *The 50% Rule* — taxpayer must spend more than half of his or her personal-services time in the real property business or businesses in which there is material participation.

c. More than 750 hours spent in the business — taxpayer must spend more than 750 hours in total for the year in real property businesses in which there is material participation. If the taxpayer is married, either spouse can qualify. For example, if the wife is a doctor and the husband is a property manager, the taxpayer would qualify.

Other Tax Changes (1993)

1. *Capital Gains* — on assets held more than one year, the tax rate remains unchanged at 28%. With the top individual rate at 39.5%, a capital gains rate of 28% can now represent considerable tax savings.

2. *Debt Restructuring* — the Omnibus Budget Reconciliation Act of 1993 gives borrowers the option of reducing the depreciable basis of real property by the amount of discharged debt to avoid taxable income in year of discharge. This provides incentive for workouts on delinquent mortgages and depressed properties.

3. *Alternative Minimum Tax* — the rate increased January 1, 1994, to 26% on the first $175,000 and 28% on the balance of alternative minimum taxable income.

4. *Club Dues* — dues for country clubs and business clubs will no longer be a tax-deductible expense.

5. *Business Meals and Entertainment* — now only 50% tax-deductible.

6. *Business Travel* — spouse travel costs are deductive only if the spouse is also an employee and there is a valid business purpose.

7. *Corporate Tax Rate* — increased from 34% to 35% on income over $10 million.

8. *Compensation Limits* — the maximum compensation taken into account for qualified plan contributions is reduced to $150,000.

9. *California State Corporations and Limited Partnership Tax* — has been increased to $800 minimum even if the entity shows a loss.

10. *1031 Tax-Deferred Exchange Rules* — were left in their existing format. This will result in more sellers considering exchanges rather than selling in the future.

11. *Small Business Expensing Allowance* — increased the deduction for otherwise depreciable property to $17,500.

How Does the Tax Reform Act Affect the Property Manager?

Owners in the future will not be granted as favorable tax benefits and will tend to view the property as a business which should generate a monthly profit (positive cash flow). They will need professional help to achieve this goal. The demand for Certified Property Managers (CPMs) will increase, as will their compensation levels.

Owners who do not qualify for the new passive loss rules for real estate professionals may still qualify for the old provision under the 1986 Tax Reform Act. The owner must have an "active role" in the management of the property in order to qualify for a passive loss deduction of up to $25,000 per year. This does not mean the owner cannot retain the services of a property manager. The Senate Finance Committee set forth the following guidelines for "active role":

1. Must own at least 10% of the investment.

2. Must participate in management decisions:

    a. Guidelines for approval of tenants; i.e., income criteria.

    b. Guidelines on rental terms; i.e., pet policy.

    c. Approval of capital and repair budgets; i.e., repaving driveway, reroofing, etc.

In order to satisfy this active role requirement, a written plan of action should be obtained from the owner (Mini Management Plan, Figure 4-7).

When the property manager is involved with depreciation and tax issues, the owner should be advised to seek counsel from a Certified Public Accountant as the laws and regulations are constantly changing. The property manager may not be licensed to practice law or accounting. Some of the forms can be found in Figures 2-8 through 2-11.

Figure 2-8. Form 8582 Passive Activity Loss Limitations

Form 8582

Passive Activity Loss Limitations

► See separate instructions.

► Attach to Forms 1040, 1041, or 1120 (Personal service corporation and closely held C corporations).

Department of the Treasury
Internal Revenue Service

OMB No. 1545 1008

Attachment Sequence No 88

Name(s) as shown on return: Paul and Paige Jones

Social security or employer identification number: 123-00-4567

Part I — Computation of 1987 Passive Activity Loss

Caution: See the worksheets on page 4 of the instructions before completing Part I.

Rental Real Estate Activities With Active Participation (See the definition of active participation under Rental Activities on page 2 of the instructions.)

Activities acquired before 10-23-86:
- 1a Activities with net income — 1a
- 1b Activities with net loss — 1b (3,000)
- 1c Combine lines 1a and 1b — 1c (3,000)

Activities acquired after 10-22-86:
- 1d Activities with net income — 1d 100
- 1e Activities with net loss — 1e (3,100)
- 1f Combine lines 1d and 1e — 1f (3,000)
- 1g Net income or (loss). Combine lines 1c and 1f. — 1g (6,000)

All Other Passive Activities (See Lines 2a through 2g on page 4 of the instructions.)

Activities acquired before 10-23-86:
- 2a Activities with net income — 2a
- 2b Activities with net loss — 2b (3,231)
- 2c Combine lines 2a and 2b — 2c (3,231)

Activities acquired after 10-22-86:
- 2d Activities with net income — 2d
- 2e Activities with net loss — 2e
- 2f Combine lines 2d and 2e — 2f
- 2g Net income or (loss). Combine lines 2c and 2f. — 2g (3,231)

3 Combine lines 1g and 2g. If the result is net income, see the instructions for line 3. If this line and line 1g are both losses, go to line 4. Otherwise, enter -0- on line 9 and go to line 10. — 3 (9,231)

Part II — Computation of the Special Allowance for Rental Real Estate With Active Participation

Note: Before completing Parts II and III, see page 4 of the instructions for how to treat numbers as if they were all positive.

4 Enter the smaller of the loss on line 1g or the loss on line 3 — 4 6,000

5 Enter $150,000 ($75,000 if married filing separately and you lived apart for the entire year) — 5 150,000

6 Enter modified adjusted gross income, but not less than -0- (see instructions). If line 6 is equal to or greater than line 5, skip lines 7 and 8, enter -0- on line 9, and then go to line 10. Otherwise, go to line 7. — 6 147,000

7 Subtract line 6 from line 5 — 7 3,000

8 Multiply line 7 by 50% (.5). Do not enter more than $25,000 ($12,500 if married filing separately and you lived apart for the entire year) — 8 1,500

9 Enter the smaller of line 4 or line 8 — 9 1,500

Part III — Computation of Passive Activity Loss Allowed

10 Combine lines 1c and 2c and enter the result. If the result is -0- or net income, skip to line 16. (See instructions.) — 10 6,231

11a If line 9 is -0-, enter -0- on line 11 and go to line 12.

11b If line 1c shows income, has no entry, or shows -0-, enter -0- on line 11. Otherwise, enter the smaller of line 1c or line 8. — 11 1,500

12 Subtract line 11 from line 10. If line 11 is equal to or greater than line 10, enter -0-. — 12 4,731

13 Subtract line 9 from line 3 — 13 7,731

14 Enter the smaller of line 12 or line 13 — 14 4,731

15 Multiply line 14 by 65% (.65) and enter the result — 15 3,075

16 Enter the amount from line 9 — 16 1,500

17 Passive Activity Loss Allowed for 1987. Add lines 15 and 16 — 17 4,575

18 Add the income, if any, on lines 1a, 1d, 2a, and 2d and enter the result — 18 100

19 Total losses allowed from all passive activities for 1987. Add lines 17 and 18. See page 5 of the instructions to see how to report the losses on your tax return — 19 4,675

For Paperwork Reduction Act Notice, see separate instructions.

Form 8582 (1987)

Figure 2-9. Form 4562 Depreciation and Amortization

Form **4562** Department of the Treasury Internal Revenue Service	**Depreciation and Amortization** ▶ **See separate instructions.** ▶ **Attach this form to your return.**	OMB No. 1545-0172 Attachment Sequence No. **67**
Name(s) as shown on return		Identifying number

Business or activity to which this form relates

Part I **Depreciation** (Do not use this part for automobiles, certain other vehicles, computers, and property used for entertainment, recreation, or amusement. Instead, use Part III.)

Section A.—Election To Expense Depreciable Assets Placed in Service During This Tax Year (Section 179)

(a) Description of property	(b) Date placed in service	(c) Cost	(d) Expense deduction
1			

2 Listed property—Enter total from Part III, Section A, column (h) . . . .

3 Total (add lines 1 and 2, but do not enter more than $10,000) . . . .

4 Enter the amount, if any, by which the cost of all section 179 property placed in service during this tax year is more than $200,000 . . . .

5 Subtract line 4 from line 3. If result is less than zero, enter zero. (See instructions for other limitations) . .

Section B.—Depreciation

(a) Class of property	(b) Date placed in service	(c) Basis for depreciation (Business use only—see instructions)	(d) Recovery period	(e) Method of figuring depreciation	(f) Deduction
6 Accelerated Cost Recovery System (ACRS) (see instructions): *For assets placed in service* **ONLY** *during tax year beginning in 1987*					
a 3-year property					
b 5-year property					
c 7-year property					
d 10-year property					
e 15-year property					
f 20-year property					
g Residential rental property					
h Nonresidential real property					

7 Listed property—Enter total from Part III, Section A, column (g) . . . .

8 ACRS deduction for assets placed in service prior to 1987 (see instructions) . . . .

Section C.—Other Depreciation

9 Property subject to section 168(f)(1) election (see instructions) . . . .

10 Other depreciation (see instructions) . . . .

Section D.—Summary

11 Total (add deductions on lines 5 through 10). Enter here and on the Depreciation line of your return (Partnerships and S corporations—Do NOT include any amounts entered on line 5.) . . . .

12 For assets above placed in service during the current year, enter the portion of the basis attributable to additional section 263A costs. (See instructions for who must use.) . .

Part II **Amortization**

(a) Description of property	(b) Date acquired	(c) Cost or other basis	(d) Code section	(e) Amortization period or percentage	(f) Amortization for this year
1 Amortization for property placed in service only during tax year beginning in 1987					
2 Amortization for property placed in service prior to 1987					
3 Total. Enter here and on Other Deductions or Other Expenses line of your return					

See Paperwork Reduction Act Notice on page 1 of the separate instructions.   Form **4562** (1987)

Figure 2-10. Schedule E, Form 1040

SCHEDULE E
(Form 1040)

Department of the Treasury
Internal Revenue Service   (O)

Supplemental Income Schedule

(From rents, royalties, partnerships, estates, trusts, REMICs, etc.)
▶ Attach to Form 1040, Form 1041, or Form 1041S.
▶ See Instructions for Schedule E (Form 1040).

OMB No. 1545-0074

Attachment
Sequence No. 13

Name(s) as shown on Form 1040: *Paul and Paige Jones*

Your social security number: 123 : 00 : 4567

Part I — Rental and Royalty Income or (Loss)   Caution: Your rental loss may be limited. See Instructions.

1 In the space provided below, show the kind and location of each rental property.

2 For each property listed, did you or a member of your family use for personal purposes any of the properties for more than the greater of 14 days or 10% of the total days rented at fair rental value during the tax year? Yes | No

3 For each rental real estate property listed, did you actively participate in the operation of the activity during the tax year? (See Instructions.) Yes | No

Property		2 Yes	2 No	3 Yes	3 No
Property A	House, Somewhere, U.S.A. ▶ Post		×	▶	×
Property B	Duplex, Somewhere, U.S.A. ▶ Pre		×	▶	×
Property C	Boat Dock, Somewhere, U.S.A. ▶ Post		×	▶	×

Rental and Royalty Income

		A	B	C		Totals (Add columns A, B, and C)
4	Rents received	7,200	6,000	2,400	4	14,400
5	Royalties received				5	

Rental and Royalty Expenses

			A	B	C		Totals
6	Advertising	6					
7	Auto and travel	7					
8	Cleaning and maintenance	8					
9	Commissions	9					
10	Insurance	10	400	300	100		
11	Legal and other professional fees	11					
12	Mortgage interest paid to financial institutions (see Instructions)	12	5,500	6,000	1,200	12	12,700
13	Other interest	13					
14	Repairs	14	150		300		
15	Supplies	15					
16	Taxes (Do not include windfall profit tax here. See Part V, line 40.)	16	1,200	700	200		
17	Utilities	17					
18	Wages and salaries	18					
19	Other (list) ▶						
20	Total expenses other than depreciation and depletion. Add lines 6 through 19.	20	7,250	7,000	1,800	20	12,850
21	Depreciation expense (see Instructions), or depletion (see Publication 535)	21	3,050	2,000	500	21	5,550
22	Total. Add lines 20 and 21	22	10,300	9,000	2,300		
23	Income or (loss) from rental or royalty properties. Subtract line 22 from line 4 (rents) or 5 (royalties)	23	(3,100)	(3,000)	100		
24	Deductible rental loss. **Caution:** Your rental loss on line 23 may be limited. See Instructions to determine if you must file **Form 8582**, Passive Activity Loss Limitations	24	(1,725)	(1,666)	—		

25	**Profits.** Add rental and royalty profits from line 23, and enter the total profits here	25	100
26	**Losses.** Add royalty losses from line 23 and rental losses from line 24, and enter the total (losses) here	26 (	3,880)
27	Combine amounts on lines 25 and 26, and enter the net profit or (loss) here	27 (	3,780)
28	Net farm rental profit or (loss) from Form 4835. (Also complete Part VI, line 43.)	28	
29	Total rental or royalty income or (loss). Combine amounts on lines 27 and 28, and enter the total here. If Parts II, III, IV, and V on page 2 do not apply to you, enter the amount from line 29 on Form 1040, line 17. Otherwise, include the amount from line 29 in line 42 on page 2 of Schedule E	29 (	3,780)

For Paperwork Reduction Act Notice, see Form 1040 Instructions.

Schedule E (Form 1040) 1987

Figure 2-11. Passive Loss and Credit Limitation Determination Chart

Passive Loss and Credit Limitation Determination Chart

Is the taxpayer reporting the activity an individual, estate, trust, closely held corporation or personal service corporation? ——No——— Stop; Limit N/A

—Yes

Is the activity a "trade or business?" —Or— Is the activity a "rental activity?" —No— Stop; Limit N/A

Yes   Yes

Stop; Limit N/A —Yes— Is the activity a working interest (that does not limit liability) in oil and gas?   Is the activity a "rental real estate activity?" —No— Losses and credits are limited.

No   Yes

——Yes— Is the interest a limited partnership interest?   Is the activity a "qualified low-income housing project?" —Yes— Losses and credits are allowed during a special relief period. See "Transition rule." • • •

No   No

Stop; Limit N/A —Yes— Did the taxpayer "materially participate" in the activity?   Is the taxpayer an individual? —No— Losses and credits are limited.

No   Yes

——Yes—— Did the taxpayer own the interest in the activity prior to October 23, 1986?   Did the taxpayer "actively participate" in the rental real estate activity? —No— Losses and credits are limited.

Losses and credits are subject to "phase-in rule." • • •

No   Yes

Losses and credits are limited.   Does the taxpayer's "adjusted gross income" exceed $100,000

————Yes————   No

The special $25,000** allowance for losses and credits ("deduction equivalent") that otherwise would be limited is subject to a "phase-out rule." • • • •   Losses and credits (actually the "deduction equivalent" for credits) that otherwise would be limited are allowed up to $25,000.**

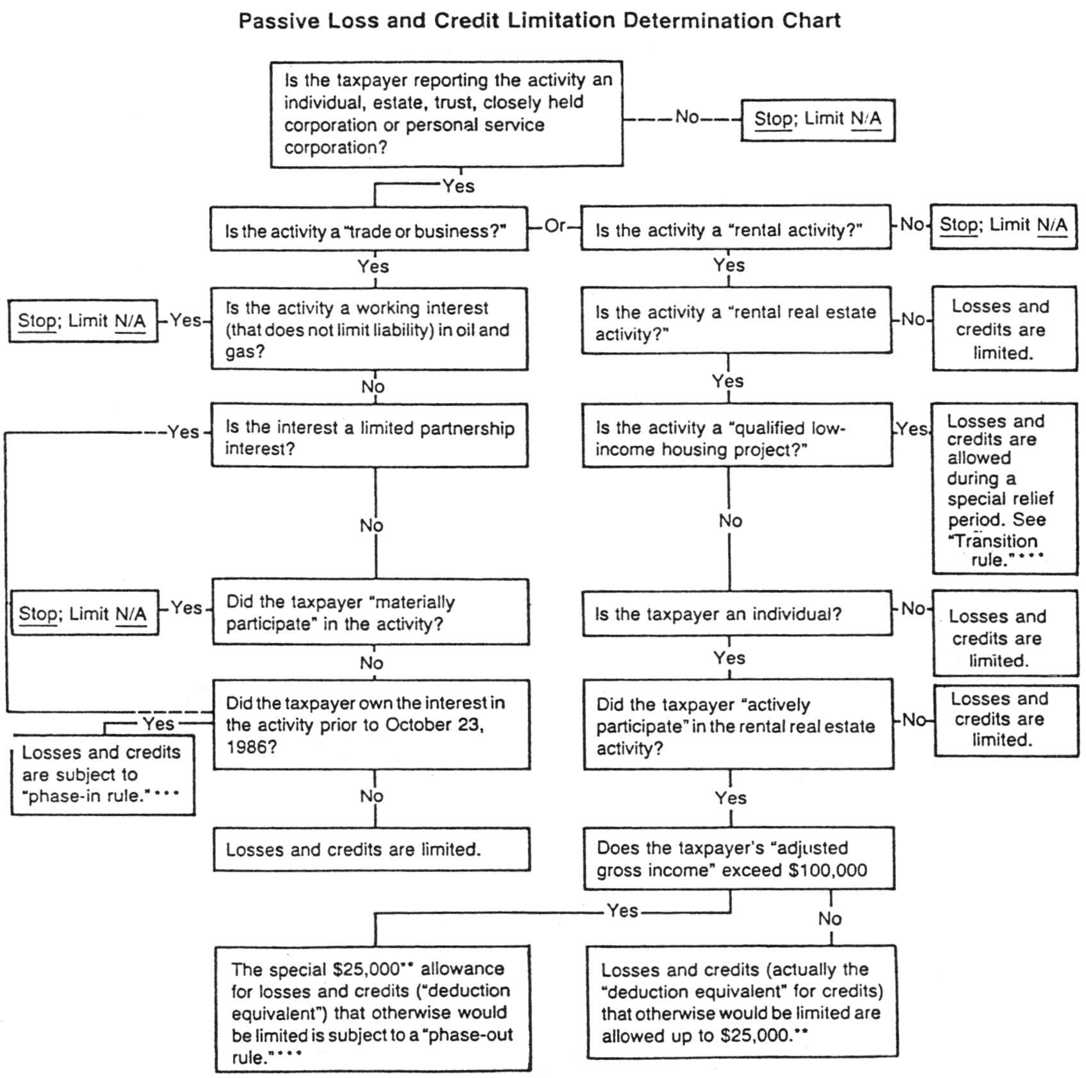

• $50,000 for married taxpayers, filing separate, and living apart at all times during the tax year.

•• $12,500 for married taxpayers, filing separate, and living apart at all times during the tax year.

• • • Discussed in Publication 925-Passive Activity and At-Risk Rules.

Note 1: The phrase "trade or business" is intended to include a research and experimentation activity and, to the extent provided in regulations, any activity in connection with a trade or business and any activity engaged in for the production of income.

Note 2: For credits from low-income housing and rehabilitation activities, the phase-out of the $25,000 offset is required when an individual's adjusted gross income exceeds $200,000 ($100,000 for a married individual filing a separate return and living apart at all times during the year). In addition, the taxpayer need not actively participate in a low-income housing or a rehabilitation rental real estate activity to use the $25,000 offset.

Note 3: The limitation for losses and credits of a closely held corporation is different from the limit for other taxpayers. For other taxpayers, losses (and credits) are allowed only to the extent of "passive income" (or the tax on passive income). For closely held corporations, however, losses (and credits) are allowed to offset "net active income" (non-passive income) as well as passive income, but not "portfolio income."

Summary

In order to understand real estate economics, we examined the size of a market which contains over 30 million residential rental units nationwide and over 4.2 million rental units in California. The real estate cycles analysis showed that we still cannot predict the occurrence or length of the cycles. Two of the causes were money, and supply and demand. The best source for information on vacancies by zip code is the Federal Home Loan Bank. We differentiated between "technical oversupply" and "economic oversupply." Boomtowns such as Houston have a temporary oversupply called "technical oversupply." "Economic oversupply" occurs when tenants cannot afford the rental rates.

Four types of rental rates were discussed: "nuisance increases" ($10.00 or less), economic (market rent), new tenants (top of market), and rent control (restricted). Government policies such as welfare, unemployment compensation, social security, and Section 8 housing were identified as having an effect on real estate economics. The size of the average household is decreasing and is projected to continue to decrease in the future, with one out of four families having only one adult. Different population trends such as mobility were reviewed; the Sun Belt, Frost Belt, Rust Belt, and Grain Belt were analyzed, with the Sun Belt having the highest projected growth rate.

In order to value the real estate investment, an appraisal must always be prepared. Whether it be for refinance, rehabilitation, or sale, the estimated value needs to be known. The three approaches to value were discussed. These are the "cost approach," used mostly for special-purpose buildings; the "market approach," comparing recent sales; and the "income approach," using the cap rate and gross multiplier. The two types of depreciation, real and tax, were discussed. Under real depreciation, we have physical and economic, social obsolescence, and functional obsolescence. Under tax depreciation, the Tax Reform Act of 1986 specified a minimum residential depreciation rate at 27.5 years and 39 years for commercial. We have three methods of treating income: active (wages), portfolio (interest and dividends), and passive (rental income property). The property manager must be knowledgeable of the client's tax bracket and its effects on the property managed.

Conclusion

The purpose of this chapter was to familiarize the property manager with the real estate environment. The basic purpose of property management is to increase the income stream by increasing revenues while minimizing expenses. This subsequently leads to an increase in real estate values.

Chapter 2 Review Questions

1. *How many residential rental units are there in the U.S.?*

   a. Approximately 1 million.
   b. Approximately 10 million.
   c. Approximately 30 million.
   d. Approximately 90 million.

2. *During a recession, real estate values usually:*

   a. increase.
   b. remain the same.
   c. go down.
   d. none of the above.

3. *If the money supply is abundant, interest rates usually:*

   a. go down.
   b. remain the same.
   c. increase.
   d. none of the above.

4. *If the number of renters increases faster than the supply of new apartments, rents will usually:*

   a. increase.
   b. remain the same.
   c. decrease.
   d. none of the above.

5. *The rental population is affected by:*

   a. the baby boom.
   b. earning power.
   c. mobility.
   d. all of the above.
   e. none of the above.

6. *Which of the following is an appraisal method?*

   a. cost approach.
   b. market survey.
   c. income approach.
   d. all of the above.
   e. none of the above.

7. *Net operating income (NOI) does <u>not</u> include:*

   a. debt service.
   b. property taxes.
   c. management fees.
   d. maintenance.

8. *Depreciation of a property for income tax purposes:*

   a. reduces value.
   b. increases value.
   c. has no effect on physical assets.
   d. none of the above.

9. *"Sun Belt" refers to:*

   a. warmer-climate areas.
   b. only the orange-growing areas.
   c. apartment buildings that face east.
   d. properties laid out in a circular manner.

10. *Cash flow is calculated by:*

   a. subtracting NOI from the effective rents.
   b. subtracting operating expenses from effective rents.
   c. subtracting loan payments from NOI.
   d. adding loan payments to NOI.
   e. none of the above.

Chapter 2
Selected Additional References and Reading

Batra, Dr. Ravi, *The Great Depression of 1990*, Simon and Shuster, New York, NY, 1987.

California Department of Water Resources, *California Water; Looking to the Future*, Sacramento, CA, 1987.

Callaghan's Federal Tax Guide
Callaghan & Company
155 Pfingsten Road
Deerfield, IL 60015

Case, Fred, *Real Estate Economics: A Systematic Introduction*, California Association of Realtors, Los Angeles, CA, 1978.

Commerce Clearing House, Inc., *Explanation of the Tax Reform Act of 1986*, Chicago, IL, 1986.

Commerce Clearing House, Inc., *1988 U.S. Master Tax Guide*, Chicago, IL, 1988.

The Journal of Real Estate Taxation (Quarterly)
Warren, Gorham, and Lamont, Inc.
210 South Street
Boston, MA 02111

National Association of Independent Fee Appraisers, *Income Property Appraising*, St. Louis, MO.

Real Estate Finance Journal (Quarterly)
Warren, Gorham, & Lamont, Inc.
210 South Street
Boston, MA 02111

Real Estate Financing Update (Monthly)
Warren, Gorham, & Lamont, Inc.
210 South Street
Boston, MA 02111

Roulac's Strategic Real Estate (Monthly)
Roulac and Company
P.O. Box 3274
San Francisco, CA 94119

U.S. Real Estate Week (Weekly)
Warren, Gorham, & Lamont, Inc.
210 South Street
Boston, MA 02111

NOTES

Chapter 3

LEASES

Key Terms

Estate for Years
Periodic tenancy
Gross lease
Net lease
Assignment
Sublet
Radius clause
CAM
Late charges
Residential lease
Commercial lease
Month-to-month

Food for Thought

"Frustration is not having anyone to blame but yourself."

Leases

Introduction

One of the major functions of a property manager is to rent and lease the property for the owner. One must then be familiar with the duties, rights, and terminology involved in leasing. Successful leasing creates the income that the property manager — "increasing the net operating income while enhancing the appreciation and value" — strives to protect. The property manager may be involved either directly, as the leasing agent, or supervisorially when independent leasing agents are used. In either case, a firm knowledge of leases and their effects on the property is mandatory.

Historically, leases have been drawn by attorneys and usually favor the owner. Many managers use the same "boiler plate" leases and rental agreements over and over again. These documents should be reviewed periodically by legal counsel for updates and changes in the law and business practice. The property manager, if given authority through the management agreement, can usually sign lease and rental agreements as an agent on behalf of the owner. In so doing, the property manager is responsible for the contents of the agreements.

Types of Leasehold Estates

Estate for Years

An "Estate for Years" is an agreement between a lessor (owner) and lessee (tenant) for a fixed period of time. The "Estate for Years" has a specific beginning and ending date. If the term is for more than one year, the lease agreement must be in writing. As the length of time on a commercial lease may be for several years, a very detailed lease agreement is frequently used.

Estate at Sufferance

"Estate at Sufferance" occurs when a tenant holds over (stays) on the premises after the lease has expired or after the tenant has given notice to vacate. If the owner or manager accepts rental payments, the lease will revert to a "Periodic Tenancy." The period of such tenancy will usually be month to month, or in some cases for the period of time between rental payments that is specified in the original lease.

Estate from Period to Period

"Periodic Tenancy" (Estate from Period to Period) is most commonly referred to as a month-to-month rental agreement and is used primarily for residential properties or for small commercial spaces (see Figure 7-11 in Chapter 7). The periodic tenancy has no specific ending date and can be terminated by either party giving notice usually equal to the period of time between rental payments. A written rental agreement is not required by the Statute of Frauds if the period of tenancy is under one year, but is highly advisable. In order to collect attorney's fees, as under any lease, a specific clause must be written indicating that the "prevailing party will be entitled to attorney's fees" in the event of a dispute.

Estate at Will

An "Estate at Will" can be terminated by either tenant or owner at will as it has no fixed time period. California Civil Code requires a termination notice equal to at least the time period between rental payments.

Basic Types of Leases

Gross Lease

In a "gross" lease the tenant pays the owner a fixed monthly rental sum which may include the landlord's taxes, maintenance, insurance, and utilities in the gross fee. This is the common form of residential lease as maintenance and repairs are part of habitability which cannot be delegated to the tenant by the owner. It is also frequently used for small commercial sites where the lease term is for short periods of time and the lessor and lessee desire a simpler form of rental payments. A definite advantage accrues to the tenant in that predetermined rent can be budgeted without worrying about increases in building maintenance costs.

Net Lease

In a "net" lease the tenant pays a minimum rental rate and then pays a prorated share of taxes, insurance, and maintenance. A single net lease refers to the tenant paying one of the above-mentioned items; a double net, two; and a triple net, three. Frequently the lease will specify that the tenant pay for professional management or at least a percentage for supervision in addition to the common area charges. This supervision fee can accrue to the property management firm as part of its management fee. Sometimes this additional fee is referred to as a "quadruple" net lease. Because of the residential habitability issue, net leases refer to commercial leases and are not used in residential management.

Percentage Lease

In a "percentage" lease the tenant pays the higher of either a minimum base rent or a percentage of total sales each month. Used in shopping centers, especially larger ones, it is primarily a retail lease. Nowhere else is the "partnership" relationship between owner and tenant more evident than in a percentage lease. The more successful the tenant, the more successful the center and vice versa.

While the percentage lease is used primarily with large national tenants, it is helpful in charting the success of smaller tenants. The required percentage sales reports help the manager chart the success of the tenant. Are sales going up? Or down? What effect does a particular tenant have on the others? What sort of rental increase can be effected? Should the lease be renewed?

Another major consideration when writing a percentage lease should be the assignable use. The expected rent from a major supermarket could be adversely affected if assignment is made to a cafeteria chain or other use that produces lower monthly sales.

Acceleration (Set-Ups) Lease

In an acceleration lease, the rental rate is accelerated to predetermined amounts at fixed dates during the term of the lease. It protects the landlord against inflation and keeps the base rent closer to market so the rental increase at time of renewal isn't as large. Its use is also very appropriate for a tenant just starting out, but with good potential. The rate may start at lower than market, but end, when the tenant is more financially strong, at a rate higher than expected. The acceleration lease also exemplifies the partnership of landlord/tenant. The landlord defers a return until the tenant succeeds, thereby increasing the expected return at a later date. Example:

Standard Lease	*Accelerated Lease*
1,000 s.f. at $1.00/s.f.	$.75 1st year, $9,000
5-year term	$1.00 2nd year, $12,000
$12,000 per year	$1.25 thereafter, $45,000
$60,000 per term	$66,000 per term

Requirements of a Valid Lease

Lease and rental agreements vary in size and content. No one agreement is perfect. A good suggestion is to use one that has been drawn by a competent attorney who specializes in real estate law. Although the lease must be updated periodically to conform with changing laws and business practices, resist change for change's sake alone or using different agreements from tenant to tenant. The lease will become familiar and comfortable with a "Standard Agreement" such as that issued by the California Association of Realtors (CAR) (see Figure 7-11). Standardization of lease clauses makes implementation easier than when each tenant operates under separate rules.

The requirements for a valid lease are similar to those for a valid contract. Both parties must have legal capacity to enter into a mutual agreement that is legal in nature. The items listed below outline the specifics with which the property manager should be familiar.

1. *Description of Property:* Use address, plot plan, and layout diagram as necessary to adequately describe the space.

2. *Names of Parties:* Both lessor and lessee must be named. If a corporation is a party to the lease, a corporate resolution may be necessary to validate the lease. As lessor, it may be prudent to require a "personal guarantee" from a corporate officer when dealing with small or individually owned corporations.

3. *Signature:* The signature of all parties should be obtained. Payment of rent and taking possession is sometimes considered sufficient acceptance. Common sense dictates, however, that all parties sign and be knowledgeable of the lease contents.

4. *Written:* Required for terms of over one year, but a property manager would be prudent to have *all* rental and lease agreements in writing.

5. *Term of Lease:* The term of lease should specify the duration. Automatic renewal options, if any, must be in BOLD TYPE.

6. *Rental Rate:* The rental rate and accelerations thereof should be specified along with payment dates and the location where the rent should be paid.

7. *Legal Purpose:* The use of the lease must be legal in nature (no bookie operations).

8. *Competence of Parties:* Contracting parties must be over 18 years of age and competent to negotiate.

Commercial Lease Clauses

Rent Increases

Periodic rent accelerations may be based on an increase in the local or national Consumer Price Index (CPI) (published monthly by the U.S. Department of Labor), or for a stated percentage or specified amount at specified intervals. All long-term leases should have an acceleration clause.

SAMPLE CLAUSE

Annual CPI Adjustments — The amount of monthly Minimum Rent due hereunder shall be adjusted annually commencing with the expiration of the first full twelve (12) calendar months following the Commencement Date and every twelve (12) months thereafter on the same day of the year (the "adjustment date"). The adjustment, if any, shall be calculated on the basis of the Consumer Price Index for Urban Wage Earners and Clerical Workers (Revised Series), Subgroup "all items," Los Angeles-Long Beach-Anaheim Average (1982-84 = 100), published by the U.S. Department of Labor, Bureau of Labor Statistics (the "Index"). ---

Renewal Options

Renewal options usually favor the tenant. They specify notice time, future rental rate, and length of option. For example, "upon ninety (90) days prior written notice, Lease shall be extended at tenant's option, provided tenant is not in default under this Lease, for an additional five (5) years. Rent shall be negotiated at the then current market rate with all other terms and conditions remaining the same." Landlord should always get as long a notice period as possible for the renewal option to be able to find a new tenant in the event the option is not exercised.

SAMPLE CLAUSE

Lessee shall, at its option, have the right to _____ successive extensions of this Lease to be exercised separately, each such extension to be for a period of _____ years and to be on the same covenants, terms, and conditions as those of this Lease.

Unless Lessee shall have given Lessor not less than _____ days notice by certified or registered mail, return receipt requested, of his [its] intention to renew or extend this Lease at its expiration or at the expiration of any extended term or period with the exception of the last extension period, Lessee shall be deemed as having elected not to exercise option to extend or renew from term to term. ---

Figure 3-1. CPI Index

UNITED STATES DEPARTMENT OF LABOR, BUREAU OF LABOR STATISTICS
CONSUMER PRICE INDEX, ALL ITEMS, 1982–1984

LOS ANGELES   ANAHEIM   RIVERSIDE

Data prior to January 1978 is used with both the CPI For All Urban Consumers (CPI U)
and the CPI For Urban Wage Earners and Clerical Workers (CPI W)

YEAR	JAN	FEB	MARCH	APRIL	MAY	JUNE	JULY	AUG	SEPT	OCT	NOV	DEC	ANNUAL AVERAGE
1961	89.5	89.6	89.3	89.4	89.4	89.6	89.6	89.4	89.5	89.7	90.0	90.0	89.6
1962	89.9	89.9	90.2	90.4	90.9	91.0	90.8	90.6	91.2	91.2	91.1	91.2	90.6
1963	91.2	91.7	91.6	91.8	91.5	91.3	91.8	92.2	92.3	92.8	92.9	92.4	92.0
1964	93.2	92.7	93.3	93.5	93.5	93.5	93.5	93.7	93.5	94.4	94.6	94.7	93.7
1965	94.9	95.2	95.4	95.7	95.7	96.0	95.8	94.8	95.9	95.8	95.9	96.3	95.7
1966	95.9	96.4	96.7	97.2	97.1	97.4	97.8	97.4	98.4	98.6	98.9	98.9	97.5
1967	98.5	98.4	98.1	98.9	99.4	99.7	99.9	100.6	101.3	101.1	102.0	102.0	100.0
1968	102.5	102.6	103.0	103.0	102.8	103.7	104.0	104.4	104.4	105.3	105.6	105.6	103.9
1969	106.0	106.5	107.7	107.9	107.9	108.8	109.4	109.6	110.2	110.6	110.5	111.5	108.8
1970	111.6	111.9	112.4	113.5	113.8	113.9	114.9	114.2	115.8	116.2	116.2	116.8	114.3

CONSUMER PRICE INDEX FOR ALL URBAN CONSUMERS (CPI U)

YEAR	JAN	FEB	MARCH	APRIL	MAY	JUNE	JULY	AUG	SEPT	OCT	NOV	DEC	ANNUAL AVERAGE
1971	116.7	116.2	116.9	116.7	118.1	118.7	119.1	119.4	119.9	120.2	119.9	120.0	118.5
1972	120.0	120.3	121.1	121.2	121.3	121.6	122.7	122.8	123.8	123.9	124.3	124.4	122.3
1973	124.8	125.5	126.4	126.9	127.4	128.5	129.1	130.9	131.2	132.3	133.6	134.1	129.2
1974	135.2	136.2	137.6	139.0	140.3	141.4	142.9	144.9	147.0	147.1	148.7	150.0	142.5
1975	150.8	152.2	154.2	155.6	156.9	156.7	158.1	158.8	160.4	161.5	162.5	163.7	157.6
1976	164.7	163.8	163.9	164.1	166.3	167.0	168.8	169.7	170.7	171.5	172.1	172.8	168.0
1977	174.8	176.3	176.7	177.9	178.5	179.5	180.4	180.6	181.6	181.6	182.9	184.4	179.6
1978	185.5	186.5	187.4	189.6	191.5	193.4	194.3	194.9	197.3	197.8	198.1	197.1	192.8
1979	199.6	201.9	203.8	207.8	211.0	212.9	214.7	217.5	220.7	221.8	224.2	228.0	213.7
1980	232.6	237.6	241.3	244.6	249.1	250.1	248.7	247.3	249.6	252.6	255.5	258.7	247.3
1981	259.4	261.6	263.3	265.5	267.3	267.9	272.2	274.8	279.3	281.3	281.6	282.1	271.4
1982	285.6	285.4	286.4	286.6	287.1	290.1	289.3	289.1	288.2	289.5	288.5	285.3	287.6
1983	285.6	286.8	287.1	289.5	292.0	293.6	294.5	295.2	296.4	297.0	296.5	297.7	292.7
1984	299.1	300.2	300.7	302.8	305.4	305.6	305.9	308.6	310.2	311.7	311.7	311.1	306.1
1985	313.0	314.1	314.7	315.9	319.1	319.3	321.3	323.9	323.8	326.1	325.0	326.1	320.2
1986	326.8	326.6	328.2	326.8	329.4	331.3	330.9	330.9	334.6	336.2	333.8	332.9	330.7
1987	335.1	338.8	341.4	342.8	345.1	344.2	344.1	346.7	348.6	350.4	349.3	350.2	344.7
1988	351.2	353.7	356.3	357.7	360.4	360.5	360.9	362.3	364.4	366.4	366.5	367.1	360.6
1989	368.2	370.7	372.8	375.8	378.9	380.1	381.2	380.9	384.3	384.2	384.1	385.8	378.9
1990	390.3	394.8	397.3	396.4	397.7	399.0	400.7	402.6	406.7	409.7	410.3	411.4	401.4
1991	413.6	413.2	412.8	415.7	416.1	415.8	418.2	418.7					

CONSUMER PRICE INDEX FOR URBAN WAGE EARNERS AND CLERICAL WORKERS (CPI W)

YEAR	JAN	FEB	MARCH	APRIL	MAY	JUNE	JULY	AUG	SEPT	OCT	NOV	DEC	ANNUAL AVERAGE
1971	116.7	116.2	116.9	116.7	118.1	118.7	119.1	119.4	119.9	120.2	119.9	120.0	118.5
1972	120.0	120.3	121.1	121.2	121.3	121.6	122.7	122.8	123.8	123.9	124.3	124.4	122.3
1973	124.8	125.5	126.4	126.9	127.4	128.5	129.1	130.9	131.2	132.3	133.6	134.1	129.2
1974	135.2	136.2	137.6	139.0	140.3	141.4	142.9	144.9	147.0	147.1	148.7	150.0	142.5
1975	150.8	152.2	154.2	155.6	156.9	156.7	158.1	158.8	160.4	161.5	162.5	163.7	157.6
1976	164.7	163.8	163.9	164.1	166.3	167.0	168.8	169.7	170.7	171.5	172.1	172.8	168.0
1977	174.8	176.3	176.7	177.9	178.5	179.5	180.4	180.6	181.6	181.6	182.9	184.4	179.6
1978	185.6	186.8	187.1	188.9	191.2	193.0	194.1	194.7	196.9	197.2	197.5	197.0	192.5
1979	199.7	202.3	204.4	208.8	212.4	214.5	216.8	219.6	223.0	224.0	225.8	229.9	215.1
1980	235.0	240.0	243.9	247.8	252.6	253.4	251.5	250.1	252.0	254.9	258.4	262.2	250.2
1981	262.7	265.0	266.5	269.1	270.7	271.7	276.3	278.6	282.9	284.9	285.3	285.9	275.0
1982	289.6	289.2	290.2	290.3	290.6	293.9	293.0	292.8	291.7	292.8	291.6	288.0	291.1
1983	288.0	290.1	289.6	290.2	292.1	292.1	293.2	293.7	296.7	299.0	297.8	299.9	293.5
1984	297.9	299.0	297.9	298.9	303.1	303.4	300.3	305.1	304.2	302.5	304.2	306.5	301.9
1985	308.1	309.1	309.8	311.2	314.1	314.1	315.8	318.0	317.7	320.0	319.1	320.1	314.8
1986	320.9	320.4	321.6	320.2	322.7	324.5	323.8	323.5	326.8	328.3	326.3	325.3	323.7
1987	327.4	331.2	333.4	334.8	337.1	336.3	336.2	338.8	340.4	342.1	341.1	342.0	336.7
1988	342.7	344.7	347.1	348.6	351.4	351.2	351.7	353.2	355.5	357.6	357.4	357.9	351.6
1989	358.9	361.4	363.2	366.4	369.5	370.4	371.4	371.0	373.8	373.8	373.5	375.3	369.1
1990	379.7	383.6	385.6	384.9	386.2	387.4	389.1	390.9	394.6	397.6	398.4	399.4	389.8
1991	401.2	400.4	399.8	402.9	403.4	403.2	405.7	406.1					

Assignment and Sublet

1. No assignment for residential as leases are of short duration.

2. In commercial, courts have usually held that "consent cannot be unreasonably withheld." Legal interpretation of what is reasonably withheld consent is usually based on the financial implications of the assigned use. Is the assignee as creditworthy as the original tenant? Will the intended use conflict with other tenants' use, or be detrimental to the landlord's percentage rent potential?

3. The basic difference between an assignment and a sublet is as follows: An assignment is between the owner and tenant(s) and may relieve the original tenant of all rights and responsibilities to the lease by transferring it to the new tenant (see Figure 3-2). A sublet is between the original tenant and a new tenant or concessionaire and keeps the original tenant financially responsible. A sublet can be for less than the entire term, or for only a portion of the space covered under the "master" lease.

SAMPLE CLAUSE

Landlord's Consent Rule — *Tenant shall not, either voluntarily or by operation of law, assign, sell, mortgage, encumber, pledge, or otherwise transfer all or any part of tenant's leasehold estate hereunder, or permit the Premises to be occupied by anyone other than Tenant or Tenant's employees, or sublet the Premises or any portion thereof (refer to CC 1995.230). ———*

Figure 3-2. Assignment of Lease

ASSIGNMENT OF LEASE

For value received, the undersigned,_____

_____ present Lessees in that certain lease dated _____

_____, which was executed by and between _____

_____, as Lessee, and _____ as Lessor, with

respect to premises located at_____

do hereby assign all of their right, title and interest in and to said lease

together with the options and lease security as set forth therein, to_____

_____

Dated this _____ day of _____, 19___.

_____

_____

ASSUMPTION OF LEASE

For value received, and in consideration of the above assignment by the Lessee,

and in consideration of the written consent of the Lessor thereto, the under-

signed hereby assume and agree to make all payments, and to perform all of the

terms, convenants and conditions of the foregoing lease, and which the said

lessee therein had agreed to make and perform.

Dated this _____ day of _____, 19___.

_____

_____

CONSENT TO ASSIGNMENT

For value received, and in consideration of the assumption of the lease re-

ferred to heretofore by the above prior named assignee thereof, the undersigned

lessor hereby consents to the above assignment, but does not thereby waive

any of his rights under said lease or any extensions thereof, as to the lessee,

or as to any assignee. An administrative fee of $100.00 will be charged by the

management company.

Dated this _____ day of _____, 19___.

_____

_____

Figure 3-3. Lease Table of Contents

TABLE OF CONTENTS

Sign Restriction

Sign restriction controls signage by the tenants. Not only may the size and design of signage be addressed, but the content of window dressing (i.e., "no more than 50% of the window space may be utilized for 'special' advertising at one time with content to be approved by property manager").

Permitted Use Clause

Use clauses should clearly specify the type of business activity permitted by tenants under the lease; i.e., a Mexican restaurant with an onsite beer and wine license.

SAMPLE CLAUSE

Permitted Use — *Tenant shall use the Premises for those uses and under that trade name specified in the Fundamental Lease Provisions and shall not use or permit the Premises to be used for any other purpose or under any other trade name.* —

Insurance

The tenant is usually required to carry fire and liability insurance on the contents and leased premises. The owner usually carries the coverages on the buildings and common areas on behalf of the tenant (one of the net charges). This usually results in a lower obligation to the tenant as the owner is able to generally secure a lower insurance cost on the property as a whole. It also ensures that the property is properly insured. The clause may go on to specify that if the tenant's business or practices increase the cost of the landlord's insurance, the tenant will be responsible to pay that increased cost. Usually the manager will want to specify minimum amounts the tenant must carry and require the tenant to name the owner and its management agent as "Additionally Insured" under the policy (see Chapter 13). The landlord should also be given notification upon cancellation.

SAMPLE CLAUSE

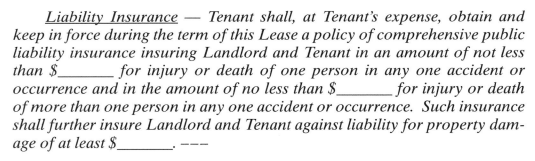

Liability Insurance — *Tenant shall, at Tenant's expense, obtain and keep in force during the term of this Lease a policy of comprehensive public liability insurance insuring Landlord and Tenant in an amount of not less than $_____ for injury or death of one person in any one accident or occurrence and in the amount of no less than $_____ for injury or death of more than one person in any one accident or occurrence. Such insurance shall further insure Landlord and Tenant against liability for property damage of at least $_____.* ---

Property Insurance — *Tenant shall, at Tenant's expense, obtain and keep in force during the term of this Lease a policy of all-risk insurance, including, but not limited to, coverage against direct physical loss such as fire, theft, burglary, structural collapse, sprinkler leakage, vandalism, and malicious mischief, in an amount sufficient to cover at least ninety percent (90%) of the replacement cost.* ---

Insurance Policies — *All insurance to be obtained by Tenant pursuant to this Article 13 shall be provided by Companies rated A-15 or better in "Best's Insurance Guide" or in the event "Best's Insurance Guide" is no longer published, any comparable rating in a similar guide selected by Landlord.* –––

Radius Clause

A radius clause disallows a retailer from opening a new location within a certain radius of the existing store, usually three miles. The purpose of the radius clause is to prohibit the tenant, especially those with percentage rent obligations, from drawing business away from the shopping center and lowering the tenant's percentage rent potential. If the tenant does open a location within the radius, this clause may provide as a penalty that percentage rent be paid on the combined sales of both the old and new operations.

SAMPLE CLAUSE

So long as this Lease shall remain in effect, Lessee shall not, within a radius of _____ (_____) mile(s) straight true measurement from the shopping center, either directly or indirectly, own, operate, or be financially interested in, either by itself or with others, a business like, or similar to, or bearing the name of or selling the same goods and wares as, the business permitted to be conducted under this Lease. –––

Exclusive Use Clause

An exclusive use clause specifies that only one merchant will be allowed to perform a particular "primary use" in a shopping center; i.e., operate a donut shop. This prevents another donut shop from opening, but still allows a coffee shop to offer donuts as part of their menu. This, while in common usage, may be considered "restraint on free trade" by the courts in the event the clause is challenged.

SAMPLE CLAUSE

Landlord covenants that it will not lease, rent, or permit to be occupied as a retail food store, any premises owned, leased, or occupied by it, its legal representatives, successors, or assigns, not presently occupied as such a store within the center, without Tenant's written consent. Without limitation of the meaning of "retail food store," such prohibition shall in particular apply to a supermarket, meat market, grocery store, fruit and vegetable store, and frozen or otherwise processed food store, but shall not apply to a delicatessen, bakery, drugstore, take-out food store, or any restaurant or lunchroom. –––

Continuous Operation Clause

This clause requires that the tenant continuously occupy and operate the business during prescribed business hours and "customary" days over the entire term of the lease. This clause assists the owner in preventing "dark" (closed) stores (i.e., a tax service that is open only for the tax season and closed the balance of the year, or a retail business that opens only three days a week), thus adversely affecting curb appeal and foot traffic in the center.

SAMPLE CLAUSE

Hours of Business — *Tenant shall continuously and uninterruptedly during the entire term hereof conduct and carry on Tenant's business in the Premises and keep the Premises open for business during all business hours customary for businesses of like character in the County in which the Premises are located; provided, however, that this provision shall not apply if the Premises should be closed and the business of Tenant temporarily discontinued therein for not more than three (3) days out of respect to the memory of any deceased officer or employee of Tenant, or the relative of any such officer or employee. Tenant shall, at all times, (a) keep the Premises adequately stocked with merchandise, (b) maintain sufficient sales personnel to care for the patronage to the Premises, and (c) conduct its business in the Premises in accordance with sound business practices. ---*

Condemnation Clause

A condemnation clause sets forth the consequences to the parties in the event the property, or a portion of the property, is taken by condemnation. This clause normally relieves the owner of any responsibility.

SAMPLE CLAUSE

Termination of Lease — *If more than twenty-five percent (25%) of the Floor Area of the Premises shall be taken or appropriated by any public or quasi-public authority under the power of eminent domain, either party hereto shall have the right to terminate this Lease effective upon the date possession is required to be surrendered to such authority. Such right must be exercised, if at all, by written notice to the other party hereunder within thirty (30) days after such effective date. ---*

Recapture Clause
(Triple Net Reimbursement)

Recapture clauses usually fall into four separate areas: common area mainte-nance (CAM), real estate taxes, insurance, and building operating expenses. CAM allows an owner to charge tenants for expenses of the common areas; i.e., landscap-ing, common utilities, parking lot and sidewalk upkeep, etc. Separate clauses may specify payment of property taxes, insurance, and building operating expenses (usu-ally found in office building leases) or increases thereof. In California, specific attention should be given to the payment of property taxes after the sale of the property and the ensuing reassessment. Tenants will desire that increases due to sale be excluded from their tax cost, owners the opposite. The tax clause should also require the tenant to pay for any reassessment caused by his action; i.e., exten-sive remodeling. The charges may be based on a prorated share of actual cost or, on a modified basis, on an increase over a fixed base (usually the costs of a specific "base" year).

SAMPLE CLAUSE

Operating Expenses — *Tenant agrees to pay Landlord, as additional rent for the Premises, the following costs and expenses incurred by Land-lord from and after the commencement date:*

1. Real Property Taxes — . . .

2. Insurance — . . .

3. Building Expense — . . .

Merchants Association Clause

The Merchants Association clause provides that the tenant belong to and participate in the activities of a Merchants Association. This clause should also spell out mandatory dues and special assessments and may include the hours and days of operation in the center.

SAMPLE CLAUSE

Tenant will promptly become a member of the Merchants Association and agrees fully to participate in and to remain a member in good standing of said Association. Tenant agrees to pay the Merchants Association dues, in equal monthly installments, as Tenant's contribution towards the adver-tising, promotion, public relations, and administrative expenses paid or incurred by the Association. . . .

Commercial Lease Summary

We have seen by examining the various lease clauses that negotiations can be very complicated. The long time period the lease is in effect dictates that the relationship between owner and tenant be spelled out in detail to avoid adverse effects on the operation and value of the property. The reader should also be aware that the owner's lease will favor the owner and should have this document reviewed by an experienced commercial real estate agent and an attorney who specializes in real estate law.

In order to understand the lease, Figure 3-2 is Assignment of Lease Form, Figure 3-3 is Table of Contents, Figures 3-4 and 3-5 are first and last pages of a commercial lease. The sample lease clauses are only abstracts in most cases and are not necessarily the full wording of each clause.

The Residential Agreement

Lease vs. Month-to-Month Rental Agreement

The question of whether it is better to put a residential property on a month-to-month rental agreement or lease is frequently asked. As in most areas of property management, there is no absolute answer. It depends on the property. An expensive single-family beachfront rental house may be on a lease since the rental value depends on the season. A suburban apartment building with a low to moderate vacancy rate would probably be best with a month-to-month agreement.

With a month-to-month agreement, rent can increase with only 30 days notice (unless regulated by rent control) (Figure 3-6). Additionally, only a 30-day notice need be given when asking a tenant to vacate (except in areas of rent control or when the reason is based on either retaliation or discrimination by the landlord). This gives the property manager flexibility to maximize the income and offers better saleability if the owner decides to sell the property. In high-occupancy areas the renters benefit more from a residential lease than do the landlords. In areas with high vacancy rates — where the unit might remain unoccupied for a long period of time — a lease might help prevent that vacancy.

Waiver of Tenant Rights

The residential renter cannot waive any rights in areas such as habitability, security deposits, right to sue, notice, entry, or retaliation by the owner. If the owner inserts such clauses, they are void even though the tenant may sign the agreement (see Chapter 14-21).

Figure 3-4. First Page of Commercial Lease

LEASE — SHOPPING CENTER FORM

THIS LEASE, made and entered into this_____day of _____, 19 ____
by and between

and

, hereinafter
respectively referred to as Landlord and Tenant, without regard to number or gender,

WITNESSETH:

1. USE. The Landlord hereby leases to Tenant and Tenant hereby hires from Landlord, for
the purpose of conducting therein

, those certain
premises with appurtenances described as hereinafter set forth,

2. PREMISES: The premises leased to Tenant, together with appurtenances, are hereinafter
referred to as the "demised premises" and are situated in the City of ,
County of , State of California, and are the premises out-
lined in red on the plat of the shopping center commonly known and designated as
; said plat
being marked Exhibit "A" and attached hereto and made a part hereof. The demised premises shall
have a frontage of_____feet (said measurement being from center of partition to center of partition), and a depth of _____feet (outside dimensions).

3. TERM. The Term of this Lease shall be for a period of_____(_____)
years. The term of this Lease, and Tenant's obligation to pay rent, shall commence on the earlier
of the following dates (a) the date which is thirty (30) days after the Landlord, or Landlord's supervising architect, notifies the Tenant in writing that the premises are ready for occupancy, or (b) the
date on which Tenant shall open the leased premises for business to the public, whichever shall
first occur. In the event that the expiration of the said thirty (30) day period does not occur on the
first day of the month, or the Tenant shall have opened the leased premises for business to the public on a day other than the first day of the month, then the term hereunder shall commence on the
first day of the month next succeeding the expiration of said thirty (30) day period, or next succeeding the opening of the leased premises for business, whichever shall first occur. In that event,
however, the Tenant shall pay rent for the fractional month on a per diem basis (calculated on the
basis of a thirty-day month) until the first day of the month when the term hereunder commences
(but the percentage rent shall be paid in accordance with Article 4B hereof); and thereafter the
minimum rent shall be paid in equal monthly installments on the first day of each and every month
in advance.

Landlord and Tenant hereby agree that in the event the demised premises are not completed
and possession delivered to Tenant on or before_____, then and in
that event this Lease shall be deemed null and void, have no further force or effect, and any security deposit made herewith shall be promptly returned to the Tenant.

4. RENTAL.

A. *Guaranteed Minimum Monthly Rental.* Tenant shall pay to Landlord as minimum monthly
rental for the demised premises the sum of_____($_____) Dollars
per month, which sum shall be paid in advance on the first day of each calendar month throughout
the term of this Lease. Said rental shall commence upon the commencement of the term of this
Lease as set forth in Article Three hereof with proration of rentals for any partial calendar month
of the term hereof. All rental to be paid by Tenant to Landlord shall be in lawful money of the
United States of America and shall be paid without deduction or offset, prior notice or demand, and
at such place or places as may be designated from time to time by Landlord.

1

Figure 3-5. Last Page of Commercial Lease

37. TIME. Time is of the essence of this Lease.

38. SUBORDINATION, ATTORNMENT. Upon request of the Landlord, Tenant will in writing subordinate its rights hereunder to the lien of any first mortgage, or first deed of trust, to any bank, insurance company or other lending institution, now or hereafter in force against the land and building of which the demised premises are a part, and upon any buildings hereafter placed upon the land of which demised premises are a part, and to all advances made or hereafter to be made upon the security thereof.

In the event any proceedings are brought for foreclosure, or in the event of the exercise of the power of sale under any mortgage or deed of trust made by the Landlord covering the demised premises, the Tenant shall attorn to the purchaser upon any such foreclosure or sale and recognize such purchaser as the Landlord under this Lease.

The provisions of this Article to the contrary notwithstanding, and so long Tenant is not in default hereunder, this Lease shall remain in full force and effect for the full term hereof.

Within ten (10) days after request therefor by Landlord, or in the event that upon any sale, assignment or hypothecation of the demised premises or the land thereunder by the Landlord, an offset statement shall be required from Tenant, Tenant agrees to deliver in recordable form a certificate addressed to any such proposed mortgagee or purchaser or to the Landlord certifying that this Lease is in full force and effect (if such be the case) and that there are no differences or offsets thereto or stating those claimed by Tenant.

IN WITNESS WHEREOF, the parties have duly executed this Lease together with the herein referred to Exhibits which are attached hereto, the day and year first above written.

_____   _____

_____   _____

_____   _____

_____   _____
              LANDLORD   TENANT'

Sublet

Most residential agreements prohibit sublet or assignment. On a month-to-month agreement, sublet prohibition is a moot point as the owner may terminate the tenancy if the tenant sublets (see Chapter 3-7).

Overcrowding

A good residential agreement should list names, ages, and number of tenants occupying a unit. Families in low-income neighborhoods will often double up, with two or more families living in one apartment. This not only causes additional wear

Figure 3-6. Rent Increase Letter

J. D. PROPERTY MANAGEMENT
3520 Cadillac Ave., Suite B, Costa Mesa, CA 92626
(714) 751-2787

Date_____

Dear Mr./Mrs./Ms. _____,

It is with genuine reluctance that we must inform you of an
increase in the rent you are paying.

Although we regret the necessity of taking this step, we feel
you will recognize that the value of this rental property has
increased since the last rent adjustment.

Please consider this official notice that effective on _____
your rent, which is presently _____ per month, will
increase to _____.

We appreciate your good tenancy and hope you will remain in
residence indefinitely. However, may we remind you of each
resident's responsibility to give thirty days notice when they
plan to move.

Sincerely,
J.D. PROPERTY MANAGEMENT CO.

Joseph W. DeCarlo, CPM

JWD:lr

and tear, but might be illegal in cities which have adopted the Uniform Housing Code. For example, according to Section 503(b), the limit for most one-bedroom units is three people based on bedroom size. Calculation under Section 503(b) is 70 square feet of bedroom space for the first two persons and 50 square feet for each additional person. In the event the tenant increases occupancy after the rental agreement is signed, the owner may waive the right to terminate the rental agreement in the future by accepting rent while knowing of the additional occupants (see Chapter 14-7).

Roommates

When renting to roommates the agreement should read that they are severally responsible. This means that if one roommate does not pay, the other(s) must pay the balance or face eviction. The roommates are thus treated as one entity.

Late Charges

Referred to as late fees, service charges, or administrative fees, some landlords charge a penalty to prompt the tenants to pay rent in a timely manner. The California Civil Code does not specify late charges as a possible remedy, nor amounts chargeable for late fees in landlord/tenant cases. Different California courts have different interpretations as to whether late fees may be charged. You must have a provision in your rental agreement, however, in order to ever be able to collect any late charges.

When preparing a "Notice to Pay Rent or Quit," when a tenant is delinquent in the rental payment, *do not* include the late charge. The notice must state the exact amount of rent (and only rent) due, or the notice may be ruled invalid at time of trial. This would necessitate starting the process over. Again, this increases the possibility of rent loss. In many cases, the hassle of the late charge is not worth the effort. Another more effective method may be to send a month-to-month tenant who is frequently late on the rent a 30-day change-of-terms notice, raising the rent 6% for each month thereafter, telling the tenant the rent increase was caused by continued late payments. The tenant will either move or pay on time thereafter. Another method is to offer "promptness discounts" for rent paid by the first of the month. For example, if the rent is $530 and the tenant pays on time, they would pay only $500, thereby receiving a "promptness discount" of $30. In areas of low vacancy, this could reduce the income to the owner by $30 per month times the number of units (20 units × $30 = $600 per month). The apartments, when advertised for rent, would have to be advertised at $530. Why pay someone for what they are legally obligated to do anyway?

How much should the landlord charge? The typical late charge on a residential home loan is 6% of a monthly payment. If the monthly rent is $500, using this rationale, you would charge a $30 late fee. Some landlords charge a flat $20 or $25, regardless of the rental amount.

House Rules

A clause is usually contained in most rental agreements that the tenant agrees to comply with all reasonable rules and regulations.

Figure 3-7.

The *Uniform Residential Landlord/Tenant Act* is a model law drafted in 1972 by the National Conference of Commissions on Uniform State Laws. This document suggests standardized landlord/tenant laws between states. Not all states adopted the suggested laws, however, and California laws still remain different from those in New York, Texas, and other states. The rental agreement used in California may *not* be legal in another state. See Chapter 7, Figure 7-11, for a sample rental agreement.

Residential Credit Application

Filled Out and Signed

Prior to checking credit, the application must be filled out and signed by the prospective tenant (see Chapter 7, Figure 7-8).

Residence Information

Include present and past residences and previous managers' phone numbers. Call and check housing references, especially the one prior to where the tenant is now living. Unfortunately, sometimes the present landlord will give a favorable reference to get rid of a bad tenant. Previous landlords are more likely to give truthful responses as they do not benefit from the renter's vacancy.

Employment History

The application should include present and past employment history and Social Security number, which is needed to do a credit check. As time is of the essence, it is difficult to check with large employers who respond only to written requests. A quick shortcut is to have the prospect show a recent paycheck stub. If a listed employer is a small firm, the manager should check the phone book to see if there really is such a business. This eliminates the friend or relative who answers the phone, "Joe's Carpet Shop."

Vehicle and Driver's License Number

What kind of car is the prospect driving? Does it look clean and well cared for? Or is it, as Ed Kelley, the distinguished CPM, author, and lecturer, says, "a Bonjo Tank"? Compare the name, signature, address, and picture on the driver's license to the information the tenant wrote on the credit application.

Credit Reporting Agencies

Agencies such as *TRW* can give the manager a verbal credit report in a matter of a few hours for less than $15. Additional reports are available to see if the tenant has ever been evicted. In Southern California, the *Unlawful Detainer Registry* (UDR) can provide such reports within hours by phone. Local apartment associations many times offer these services at low rates to their members.

Bank Account Verification

It is easy to verify a bank balance by using a little subterfuge. Call the bank branch at which the account is held and ask if a check for the amount the tenant says is in the account is good. The property manager may also request a rating on the account at this time. As we do not accept checks for the first month's rent, we usually ask the prospect for a blank deposit slip which has the bank address and account number imprinted. This prevents errors when transcribing account numbers onto the printed application and also double-verifies the existence of the account and the prospect's address.

In Case of Emergency

Emergency names and phone numbers can also be used to track down tenants to collect judgments after eviction.

Permission to Check Credit

The permission to check credit clause allows the manager to check the prospect's credit. It is an invasion of privacy and against the law to do so without written permission. The manager *cannot* discriminate on the basis of race, religion, creed, national origin, marital status, sex, age, or handicap. The manager *can* discriminate on the basis of the prospective tenant's financial ability to pay rent. The same questions should be asked of *all* tenants, not just those to whom the manager doesn't want to rent. Credit criteria must be applied equally.

Consumer Credit Reporting Law

On July 1, 1993, Civil Code Section 1785.2 went into effect. If the manager or the landlord relies on information from a credit report to deny rental, the manager must:

1. Provide the prospective renter with written notice of denial.

2. Provide the prospective renter with the name, address, and phone number of the credit reporting agency.

3. Provide notice to the prospective renter of the right to a free credit report within 60 days and that information given may be disputed by the prospective renter.

If information for rental denial is from a former employer, landlord, or creditor, then the prospective renter must be advised of the right of full disclosure from that party, and the name, address, and phone number of the source must be given to the prospective renter.

Summary

The property manager is often involved in the leasing function either as the leasing agent or by supervising the leasing agent. The types of leases, lease clauses, and terms are items the property manager should be familiar with and have a working knowledge of.

There are four basic types of leasehold estates; Estate for Years (specific termination date), Estate at Sufferance (holdover), Estate from Period to Period (month to month), and Estate at Will. The most common is periodic tenancy (Estate from Period to Period) which is the basic residential month-to-month agreement.

There are three basic types of leases: gross lease (tenant pays one fixed amount), net lease (tenant pays minimum rent plus share of taxes, insurance, and maintenance), and percentage rent (tenant pays percentage of gross sales each month). Lease and rental agreements vary, but valid leases should contain at least the following: description of property, names of parties, signature, term of duration, rental rate, legal purpose, and competent parties.

Commercial lease clauses are numerous and very detailed due to the fact that these leases are for long periods and must specify what happens under certain conditions in order to protect both parties. Rent acceleration (CPI index increases) is a very common clause. Renewal options by the tenant should specify the time to exercise, rental rate, and length of option. The assignment and sublet clause has usually been held by the courts to restrict the owner/manager from "unreasonable withholding" of permission. The use clause specifies the particular use allowed the tenant under the lease. Other common clauses include: radius, exclusive use, condemnation, common area maintenance, sign restrictions, and merchants association.

Residential agreements cannot waive or deprive tenants of their rights. Credit applications should be filled out and signed, with information verified before renting. Credit reporting agencies can provide fast, inexpensive credit reports for the owner/manager.

In conclusion, the property manager should review the lease and leasing procedures as to their effects on the subject property. On legal questions, consult a competent attorney who specializes in real estate law.

Chapter 3 Review Questions

1. *The most common type of commercial lease is:*

   a. Estate for Years.
   b. Estate at Sufferance.
   c. Estate From Period to Period (Periodic Tenancy).
   d. Estate at Will.
   e. none of the above.

2. *The most common type of residential lease is:*

   a. Estate for Years.
   b. Estate at Sufferance.
   c. Estate From Period to Period (Periodic Tenancy).
   d. Estate at Will.
   e. none of the above.

3. *Basic types of commercial leases include:*

   a. gross.
   b. net.
   c. percentage.
   d. all of the above.
   e. none of the above.

4. *Percentage leases are most often used in:*

   a. office.
   b. retail.
   c. residential.
   d. industrial.
   e. none of the above.

5. *Requirements of a valid lease include:*

   a. term.
   b. rental rate.
   c. names of parties.
   d. all of the above.
   e. only a and c.

6. *In an assignment, the former lessee is:*

    a. no longer responsible.
    b. still responsible.
    c. responsible only in the event of default.
    d. none of the above.

7. *The radius clause protects the:*

    a. lessee.
    b. lessor.
    c. lender.
    d. merchant.
    e. none of the above.

8. *The condemnation clause protects the:*

    a. lessee.
    b. lessor.
    c. city.
    d. lender.
    e. none of the above.

9. *Waiver of residential tenant rights is permissible:*

    a. if the tenant signs the lease.
    b. if the tenant verbally agrees.
    c. if the tenant is over 18 years of age.
    d. never.

10. *Lease terms should be reviewed by:*

    a. a real estate agent.
    b. a CPA.
    c. an attorney.
    d. a doctor.

Chapter 3
Selected Additional References and Readings

Black's Office Leasing Guide (Annual)
McGraw-Hill Informational Systems Co.
P.O. Box 2090
Red Bank, NJ 07701

Commercial Lease Law Insider (Monthly)
Brownstone Publishers
P.O. Box 4167
Grand Central Station
New York, NY

Gale, Jack L., *Commercial Investment Brokerage*, National Association of Realtors, Chicago, IL, 1979.

Kusnet, J. and R. Lepatin, *Modern Real Estate Leasing Forms*, Warren, Gorham & Lamont, Inc., Boston, MA, 1986.

Real Estate Leasing Report (Monthly)
Federal Reserve Press
210 Lincoln Street
Boston, MA

Real Estate Record and Builder's Guide (Weekly)
475 Fifth Avenue
New York, NY 10017

Real Estate Times (Twice Monthly)
Galla Publications
1515 Broadway
New York, NY 10036

NOTES

Chapter 4

THE
MANAGEMENT CLIENT

Key Terms

Fee management
Sole proprietorship
Partnership
Corporation
Management
  agreement
REIT
Cash flow
Tax benefits
Leverage
Trust account

Food for Thought

"Be sure you love people and use things. Don't use people and love things."

Will Rogers

The Management Client

Introduction

The property manager must manage the property according to the owner's objectives and goals. A feeling of mutual understanding, requiring a coordinated effort between both agent and owner, should develop. This chapter will deal with types of ownerships, owner's goals and objectives, the management agreement, fiduciary responsibility, and the establishment of management fees.

Principal/Agent

In the principal/agent relationship, the property manager acts as the go-between for the owner in relation to other parties. The property manager has the power to represent the owner for the purpose of making decisions and contracts on the owner's behalf. This agency arrangement, if it is for over one year, must be governed by a written agreement (management contract, see Chapter 14). Under California Agency Law, the property manager, as the agent for the owner, discloses this fact to other parties, such as tenants and vendors.

Under the principal/agent relationship, the property manager should possess a California Real Estate License if he or she acts as an agent for the owner. This is commonly known as "fee management."

Section 10131 of the Business and Professions Code defines a real estate *broker (or salesperson, per Business and Profession Code Section 10132) as any person "who, for a compensation or in expectation of a compensation, does or negotiates to do, one or more of the following acts for another or others: . . . (b) leases or rents or solicits for prospective tenants or negotiates the sale, purchase or exchanges of leases on real property or on a business opportunity, or collects rents from real property, or improvements thereon, or from business opportunities."* Since showing and leasing properties and collecting rents are among the most fundamental duties of a property manager, it is clear that property managers must normally be real estate licensees. This licensing requirement is plainly consistent with the position of responsibility and trust held by the property manager. From the owner's perspective, the license requirements indicate that the manager has met the State's standards of education and good moral character.

There can be situations in which the property manager need not hold a real estate license. These exceptions to the licensing requirements are contained in Business and Professions Code Section 10133, which exempts ". . . anyone who directly performs any of the acts within the scope of this chapter with reference to his own property or, in the case of a corporation which, through its regular officers receiving no special compensation therefor, performs any of the acts with reference to the corporation's own property . . ." This is a quotation from *Real Estate Law* published by the California Department of Real Estate. Other exemptions would be an onsite resident manager, and unlicensed rental hosts or hostesses who, as defined under AB 2242:

1. Show units to tenants.

2. Provide assistance in completing rental applications.

3. Accept rents and deposits.

4. Quote rental rates.

5. Accept and execute leases and rental agreements.

The above acts must be under the supervision and control of a licensed Real Estate Broker.

As a rule, the property manager will be licensed by the Department of Real Estate. This means, as in the case of any other licensed activity, that the employing broker will be held responsible for the activities of his or her agents. All trust fund records and other important documents and agreements must be kept on file for three years and will be subject to Department of Real Estate audit. Any violations of the real estate law or the Regulations of the Real Estate Commissioner could result in revocation or suspension of the agent's or broker's license.

Employer/Employee

The employer/employee situation exists when the property manager works directly for the owner and is on salary. Examples are property managers working for banks, insurance companies, and corporations.

Forms Of Ownership

Sole Proprietorship

A sole-proprietorship investor usually has other businesses (i.e., a medical practice) or employment and owns properties as investments. Since the investor or owner does not have the time or expertise to collect rents, lease, and handle management, a professional property manager is hired. Title of this type of ownership is usually held in the form of joint tenants, tenants in common, severalty, or as community property.

Advantages

1. Simplicity and ease to establish and dissolve.

2. Fewer organizational and legal restrictions.

3. Lowest cost to organize and operate.

4. Less disclosure and more secrecy.

5. More self-satisfaction and ego gratification for owners.

Disadvantages

1. Unlimited liability.

2. Less counsel and professional input on decisions.

3. Lack of survivorship — depends on health of owner.

4. More difficult to raise funds.

General Partnership

Advantages

1. Capital contributions and loans easier to obtain than for sole proprietorship.

2. Spreads risk and liabilities among more individuals.

3. Ease of formation and operation.

Disadvantages

1. Death, insanity, or bankruptcy of one partner may affect the partnership.

2. Needs mutual agreement (divided authority).

3. Unlimited liability of partners.

4. Transferring of ownership interest is difficult.

Limited Partnership

<u>Advantages</u>

1. Limited liability to limited partners.

2. No personal involvement or effort by limited partners.

<u>Disadvantages</u>

1. Unlimited liability of general partner.

2. Transferring of ownership interest is difficult.

3. Success depends mainly on performance of general partner.

Corporation

A corporation has perpetual life and operates under a charter granted by the California State Department of Corporations. It is a legal entity and may enter into contracts, leases, sales, etc. The stock (ownership) is held by its shareholders who are limited in liability to the cost of their stock. A board of directors is elected to run the company and appoint its officers (president, treasurer, secretary, etc.). Most large businesses are corporations, except in real estate due to double taxation of profits. Corporate profits are taxed at the company level and then the dividends distributed to the stockholders are taxed as personal (portfolio) income. If managing for a corporation, the property manager should make sure there is a corporate resolution and that authorized corporate officers have signed the management agreement.

<u>Advantages</u>

1. Ease of transfer and marketability — sell stock on exchange.

2. Limited liability.

3. Perpetual life.

4. Easier to raise money by selling more stock or bonds.

<u>Disadvantages</u>

1. Formation and operation of corporation is costly.

2. Security laws and regulations are cumbersome.

3. Double taxation.

Real Estate Investment Trust (REIT)

A Real Estate Investment Trust allows investors to share in ownership and profits without being involved in the management or operations of the property. The trust issues shares of ownership to investors that can be bought and sold much like stock. This allows for quick liquidity which is usually not found in real estate investments.

The trust is also able to use depreciation write-off to reduce taxable income and gives special tax benefits by not being taxed as dividends if 95% of the profits are distributed to the investors each year. These trusts are usually large and supervised by the California Department of Corporations, and by the Security and Exchange Commission if they operate in more than one state. The property manager should, as with corporations, verify which officers are authorized to sign the management agreement.

Government Agencies

Several local, state, and federal agencies hire professional property managers to manage and lease their facilities. Contracts are usually let on a bid basis with stiff requirements for both insurance and reporting by the manager. Examples would be right-of-way lands, Veterans Administration foreclosures, etc.

Owner's Goals and Objectives

While it is true that owner goals vary, it is possible for the property manager to categorize these goals and then set priorities to meet the requirements of the client.

Figure 4-1.

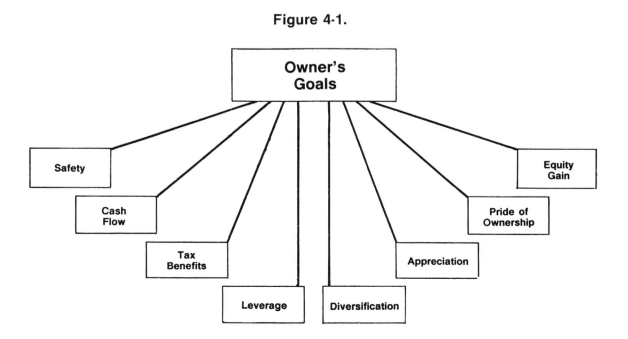

Cash Flows

Most investors prefer a positive cash flow, but often they will purchase property at too high a price or with too low a down payment, resulting in expenses and mortgage payments exceeding rental income. This is called a "negative cash flow" or an "alligator" since it needs to be constantly fed by additional owner funds. Investors who are retired and/or on a fixed income are necessarily very concerned with cash flow. Astute investors today are insisting upon reasonable cash flow at least comparable to other forms of investments such as stocks and bonds.

Tax Benefits

Through depreciation (phantom loss) the owner can reduce the profit on property for income tax purposes. This write-off may reduce personal income tax up to a maximum of $25,000 per year, if the taxpayer makes less than $100,000 annually and is active in its management. This loss is described as passive income under the Tax Reform Act of 1986, as discussed in Chapter 2. In other words, large losses from real estate may not be deductible in the year of loss, but may have to be carried over to year of sale. As tax laws change, tax benefits for real estate seem to be on a trend toward curtailment with fewer depreciation write-offs in the future.

The Omnibus Budget Reconciliation Act of 1993 was of mixed benefit to real estate. It lengthens the depreciation schedule while easing the rules on passive losses.

Leverage

Most investments (stocks, bonds, etc.) require that the investor pay in full for their purchase. In real estate, one can make a 10-30% down payment and purchase property by borrowing the balance. This is known as leverage (Figure 4-2). In other words, others' funds are used to acquire a larger investment than possible with an "all cash" purchase. This strategy works well in times of rising real estate values, but may result in foreclosures during hard times. For example:

Sale price	$1,000,000
Down payment (10%)	100,000
Loans (first trust deed)	900,000

If the inflation rate is 10%, the investor's profit (10% of $1 million) would be $100,000. If the same investor put the same funds (down payment) of $100,000 in a bank at 10% simple interest, the return would be only $10,000. In this case, the investor's additional gain is $90,000 the first year.

Figure 4-2. Leverage

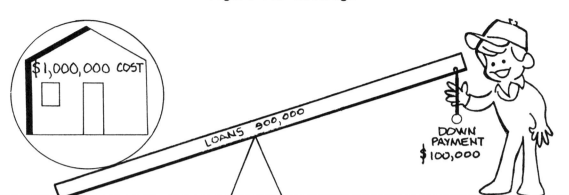

Appreciation

All investors want the property to increase in value during the ownership period. Some investors' — sometimes referred to as speculators — primary motivation is to buy, hold, and sell the property, making a profit through appreciation. Speculators usually have a short holding period of one to three years and are willing to incur negative cash flow. In periods of high inflation, speculators have seen the sale price more than double in a few years, and many investors easily become millionaires. As in most high-stakes investment strategies, however, the risks are considerable. The property manager should ensure that sufficient funds are available to cover expenses, especially those relating to habitability of the property. Government agencies have gone to court and have named the management company as defendant in some cases where repairs could not be made due to lack of funds.

Pride of Ownership

Pride of ownership is an important factor for investors who want to drive by their property with relatives, friends, and associates to show it off. The curb appeal should be high on the property management priority list when managing this type of property. People like to see, feel, and touch their investment. Seeing a well-manicured strip center on a busy street in a prestigious area would be an example of pride of ownership.

Safety and Sense of Security

Investors who purchase high-grade bonds, blue chip stocks, or have money in federally-insured certificates of deposit have more liquidity and safety than with a real estate investment. An office building in Houston, Texas, with its high vacancy rate and depressed value, is not as secure as high-grade bonds. A conservative investor would feel uncomfortable with the risky office building, preferring a safer investment at a lower yield.

Equity Build-Up

Equity build-up is really the power of loan pay-down. At some point the loan will be paid off and the NOI (net operating income) will equal the cash flow. The most basic example is the purchase of a single-family rental house each year for ten years, starting at the investor's age of 25. If at the time of purchase the rents of $1,000 per month equal the mortgage payment on a 30-year loan, when the investor is 65 he could retire with $10,000 per month income assuming all other factors remain constant.

Diversification

Diversification of their investment portfolio is the goal of some real estate investors. A balance of investments — stocks, bonds, real estate, etc. — is desirable to protect the value in total during times of decreasing value of one investment.

Knowing Your Client

Net Worth Statement

In order to better understand and assist your client, it is helpful to examine the net worth statement, a snapshot of the client's financial position (Figure 4-3). The difference between assets and liabilities, net worth, is a measure of the client's wealth. This statement will reveal existing loans, equity, and cash on hand. If the client's loans to equity is 80% (high) and there are few cash assets on hand, the property manager will probably have a difficult time obtaining more funds from the owner for major rehabilitation projects and must prepare the owner for major capital expenditures such as a new roof well in advance of the expenditure.

Figure 4-3. Sample Net Worth Statement

SAMPLE
NET WORTH STATEMENT

Assets		Liabilities & Net Worth	
Liquid Assets		**Short-Term Liabilities**	
Cash in bank	$ 10,000	Credit cards	$ 5,000
CD certificate	40,000	Installment loans	6,000
Money market fund	10,000	Personal loans	10,000
Total liquid assets	$ 60,000	Borrowing — life insurance	4,000
		Accrued income tax	
Investment Assets		Total short-term liabilities	$ 25,000
Notes receivable	$ 50,000		
Stocks and bonds	10,000	**Long-Term Obligations**	
IRA/retirement	15,000	Mortgage loans — R.E.	$ 600,000
Real estate (Market Value)	950,000	Mortgage — residence	100,000
Total investment assets	$1,025,000	Loans — personal assets	5,000
		Loans — investments	8,000
		Other	
Personal Assets		Total long-term obligations	$ 713,000
Residence	$ 250,000		
Furnishings	50,000	Total Liabilities	$ 738,000
Vehicle	20,000		
Other	10,000		
Total personal assets	$ 330,000	Net Worth	$ 677,000
Total Assets	$1,415,000	Total Liabilities & Net Worth	$1,415,000

Assets	$1,415,000
Liabilities	−738,000
Net Worth	$ 677,000

The Management Agreement

Statute of Frauds law requires agreements of more than one year to be in writing. The professional property manager will insist on a contract which spells out his or her responsibilities, duties, authority, and fees. Figure 4-4 is an example of such an agreement.

Essential Clauses

1. *Description of property.*

2. *Term.*

3. *Fees and special costs.*

4. *Authority to operate: collect rent, pay bills, etc.*

5. *Spending limit by property manager without owner approval other than normal operating expenses (i.e., new roof).*

6. *Hold harmless clause (indemnification).*

7. *Additionally insured where the client's insurance company covers the agent along with the owner. Cost is usually negligible and protects the interests of the property manager.*

Fiduciary Responsibility

Trust Accounts

California requires that the funds collected by the property manager be deposited into a trust account. The question is often asked as to whether a separate trust account is needed for each owner. The answer is no, but a separate accounting of each owner's funds must be maintained. Interest cannot be collected, however, unless passed on to the owner. Broker's personal property cannot be kept in the trust account. Only real estate agents can sign on the account unless other designated individuals are bonded for an amount in excess of the entire trust account.

Trust Account Procedures

1. All trust accounts must be maintained in accordance with standard accounting procedures. (10 California Admin. Code § 2831). Business and Professions Code 10145(a) requires the real estate broker to have a trust account as follows:

    a. Client accounts must be balanced daily.

    b. Dates and amounts of funds deposited.

    c. Dates, amounts, and check numbers of checks written.

2. Trust account records must be kept for three years.

3. Trust funds must be kept in a federally-insured bank, savings and loan, or thrift. The amount for any one client cannot exceed $100,000, which is the

maximum amount of the federal insurance. The master trust account balance may exceed the $100,000 limit in total.

4. The account should be opened and labeled as a "trust account" with the broker named as trustee.

5. Funds must be deposited the next working day after receipt. (This requirement is sometimes difficult for the property manager to meet.)

6. Bank reconciliation should be done at least on a monthly basis and will be checked by the Department of Real Estate during spot audits of property management firms.

7. Owner or property name and address, or code, should identify each transaction.

8. Broker is only allowed to have $100 of his own money as "slush funds" in the account for extra bank charges or miscellaneous items. The broker or his/her salespersons cannot deposit rents on their personal (principal) properties into the trust account, but must open a separate account even if a management fee is charged for their own properties' management. This also applies to any limited partnerships a broker or agent may be involved in.

Master Trust Account (All Funds Collected)

Advantages:

1. Easier and faster to record and deposit funds.

2. Computerized check-writing and statements.

Disadvantages:

1. More difficult to reconcile bank balances.

2. More complicated.

Separate Trust Accounts (Individual Checking Accounts)

Advantages:

1. Mistakes limited to one checkbook.

2. Gives a greater sense of security to the owner.

Disadvantages:

1. More difficult for computerization.

2. More time-consuming paperwork.

Figure 4-4.

MANAGEMENT AGREEMENT

Parties	In consideration of the covenants hereto contained,

_____ (Owner) _____

and _____ (Agent) _____

Exclusive Agency

1. The owner hereby employs the Agent exclusively to rent, lease, operate and manage the property whose address is _____ upon the terms hereinafter set forth beginning on the ____ day of _____ 19___ and continuing until either party gives a 30-day notice of cancellation in writing. Said agreement shall be for a minimum of one year.

Renting of Premises

2. The Agent accepts the employment and agrees:

Monthly Statements

> a) To use due diligence in the management of the premises for the period and upon the terms herein provided, and agrees to furnish the services of its organization for the renting, leasing, operating and managing of the herein described premises.

Separate Owner's Funds

> b) To render monthly statements of receipts, expenses and charges. In the event the disbursements shall be in excess of the rents collected by the Agent, the Owner herby agrees to pay such excess promptly upon demand of the Agent.

Advertising and Signs

> c) To deposit all receipts collected for Owner (less any sums properly deducted as otherwise provided herein) in an Account, separate from Agent's personal account. However, Agent will not be held liable in event of bankruptcy or failure of a depository.

3. The Owner hereby gives to the Agent the following authority and powers and agrees to assume the expenses in connection herewith:

Collection of Rent

> a) To advertise the availability for rental of the herein decribed premises, and to display signs thereon, to sign, renew and/or cancel leases for the premises, to collect rents due or to become due and give receipts therefore, to terminate tenancies and to sign and serve in the name of the Owner notices as are deemed needful by Agent; to institute and prosecute actions, to evict tenants and to recover possession of said premises; to sue for in the name of the Owner and recover rents and other sums due; and when expedient, to settle, compromise, and release such actions or suits or reinstate such tenancies.

Repairs

> b) To make or cause to be made and supervise repairs and alterations and to do decorating on said premises; to purchase supplies and pay all bills. The Agent agrees to secure the approval of the Owner on all expenditures in excess of $ _____ for any item, except monthly or recurring operating charges and/or emergency repairs in excess of the maximum, if in the opinion of the Agents such repairs are necessary to protect the property from damage or to maintain services to the tenants as called for by their tenancy.

Employees

> c) To hire, discharge and supervise all labor and employees required for the operation and maintenance of the premises; it being agreed that all employees shall be deemed employees of the Owner and not the Agent, and that the Agent may perform any of its duties through its attorneys, agents or employees and shall not be responsible for their acts, defaults or negligence if reasonable care has been excercised in their appointment and retention. The Agent shall not be liable for any error in judgment or for any mistake of fact of law, or for anything which it may do or refrain from doing hereafter, except in cases of willful misconduct or gross negligence.

Figure 4-4. (Continued)

Service
Contracts

     d) To make contracts for utilities, and other services as the Agent shall deem advisable; the Owner to assume the obligation of any contract so entered into at the termination of this agreement.

     e) Owner is aware and acknowledges that all repairs and services of the building are performed by J.D. Maintenance & Construction Co., a subsidiary of J.D. Property Management. J.D. charges 10% of subcontractors bill.

4. The Owner further agrees

     a) To save the Agent harmless from all damage suits in connection with the management of the herein described property and from liability from injury suffered by any employee or other person whomsoever, and to carry, at his own expense, necessary public liability and workmen's compensation insurance adequate to protect the interests of the parties hereto, which policies shall be so written as to protect the Agent in the same manner and to the same extent they protect the Owner. The Agent shall be added as additional insured to his policy.

Interest and
Tax Payments,
Insurance

     b) To advise the Agent in writing if payment of mortgage indebtedness, property or employee taxes or special assessments, or the placing of fire, liability, steam boiler, pressure vessel or any other insurance is desired.

Agent's
Compensation

     c) To pay the Agent each month:

For Management _____

For rental of each vacancy _____

     d) Owner agrees to deposit with Agent _____ per unit to open Owners bank account

     e) In the event that owner sells the building while managed by J.D. Property Management, Owner shall pay a three (3) month management fee penalty based on the last month's fee. Management company is authorized to withdraw said penalty funds from the Owner's account prior to closing account. This condition is waived if new Owner retains J.D. Property Management as managing Agent.

This Agreement shall be binding upon, the successors and assigns of the Agent, and the heirs, administrators, executors, successors and assigns of the Owner.

_____   _____
Owner's Name   Agent

_____   J.D. PROPERTY MANAGEMENT COMPANY
Signature   P.O. Box 1438

_____   Costa Mesa, CA 92626
Signature   (714) 751-2787

_____
Address

_____
City, State and Zip

_____ _____
Phone Work   Phone Home

_____
Date

Secret Profit

Secret profit by the management company could occur if the management company owning a part of the landscaping or maintenance company doing work on the property fails to inform the owner of this relationship. Ownership of such entities is permissible and may be advantageous to the owner, but must be disclosed before the fact.

Commingling

Commingling occurs when one client's funds are used to pay another client's bills. Daily balance reconciliation must be part of any utilized computer program in order to avoid inadvertent commingling. It also occurs when the broker has mixed client funds with his/her own funds.

Conversion

Conversion is illegally using or misappropriating client funds for the property manager's own interests (i.e., payment of rent on the management office).

Offset of Monies Due

Even if the licensee has a valid civil claim, trust funds held may not be used as an offset to pay debts, unless written authorization is given by the owner of the funds.

Establishing the Management Fee

The management company, like the owner, wants to make a profit. If the property manager prices services too low, the firm will go out of business. This is an area of weakness with many good property managers. The real estate law in most states says that management fees are negotiable. The property manager should know his/her costs and bid services accordingly.

Kinds of Fees

1. *Flat Amount.* A flat amount per month for management services provided to the property; i.e., $500 per month.

2. *Per Door.* A unit fee which is a certain dollar figure for each unit managed; i.e., a 36-unit apartment building at $14 per unit would equal $504 per month.

3. *Percentage of Collected Income.* This is the method in most common usage (i.e., if rents are $15,500 per month and your management percentage is 5% of gross income collected, the management company's income would be $775 per month). Sometimes there is a flat-fee minimum versus percentage, whichever is greater. Owners and managers prefer this method as it gives incentives to collect and increase rents. Fees are usually based on collected income and not on security deposits which must be returned and thus are not considered income.

4. *Lease or Re-Rent Fees.* Extra charges that would be made to the owner when performing specified rental services.

Determining the Cost of Management

In order for the property manager to intelligently bid services, a monthly profit and loss statement should be prepared for the management company. From this statement, using percentages, it will be seen that salary is the largest expense, consuming over 40% of the fee income. A standard "bid sheet" should be prepared so that, when asked to quote, the property manager need only fill in the appropriate blanks and total the figures (see Figure 4-5). Additional management company expenses are discussed in Chapter 13.

Ethics

Ethics is an important aspect in the property manager's daily activity. The owner must have trust and confidence in the property manager in order to have a successful relationship. The definitions of ethics are many and varied. Webster's Dictionary — "Principles of conduct governing an individual or group." Dr. Albert Schweitzer, the Nobel Prize humanitarian — "Ethics is the name we give to our concern for good behavior. We feel an obligation to consider not only our own personal well-being, but also that of others and of human society as a whole."

Unethical acts by the property manager would include: cash or expensive gifts from vendors, billing for work not performed, not reporting all the rents, etc. The Institute of Real Estate Management (IREM) has a code of ethics (Figure 4-6) to which all Certified Property Managers (CPMs) must adhere. The National Association of Realtors has a code of ethics for its realtors and the California Department of Real Estate, under Business and Professions Code Sections 10176 and 10177, has a code of ethics to which all California real estate licensees must adhere.

Figure 4-5. Management Fee Bid Sheet

```
                           MANAGEMENT FEE
                             BID SHEET


Property address_____ City_____
Date_____ Miles from office_____ No. of units_____
Sq. ft._____ Age_____ Condition_____ Gross rents_____


Owner's name_____ Phone no._(___)_____
Address_____ City_____ State_____

                                                    Total
MANAGEMENT SERVICES      No.     Hours    Rate     Hours       Cost

Inspections:
  Property supervisor   _____  _____  _____  _____    _____
  CPM                   _____  _____  _____  _____    _____

Association meetings:
  Property supervisor   _____  _____  _____  _____    _____
  CPM                   _____  _____  _____  _____    _____

Improvement supervision:
  Property supervisor   _____  _____  _____  _____    _____
  CPM                   _____  _____  _____  _____    _____

Management review:
  Property supervisor   _____  _____  _____  _____    _____
  CPM                   _____  _____  _____  _____    _____

Travel expense:
  Property supervisor   _____ miles x _____¢ per mile  =  _____
  CPM                   _____ miles x _____¢ per mile  =  _____

ADMINISTRATION AND ACCOUNTING                      SUBTOTAL  _____

Computer input         _____  _____  _____  _____    _____
Disbursements          _____  _____  _____  _____    _____
Payroll                _____  _____  _____  _____    _____
Monthly statements     _____  _____  _____  _____    _____
Computer expense       _____  _____  _____  _____    _____
Extra reports          _____  _____  _____  _____    _____


                                                   SUBTOTAL  _____

OVERHEAD ON PERSONNEL                              _____%
OVERHEAD FOR POSTAGE, COPYING, RENT, ETC.          _____%
PROFIT & CONTINGENCIES                             _____%
                                                   SUBTOTAL  _____

TOTAL MONTHLY FEE                                            _____

Fee per unit: $_____ fee ÷ no. of units $_____ = $_____ per unit
% management fee: $_____ fee ÷ gross rents $_____ = _____%
Received management at _____%   Competitor_____ bid %_____

Prepared by_____
```

Figure 4-6. Code of Ethics

Institute of Real Estate Management
Code of Professional Ethics of the CERTIFIED PROPERTY MANAGER®

Introduction

To establish and maintain public confidence in the honesty, integrity, professionalism, and ability of the professional property manager is fundamental to the future success of the Institute of Real Estate Management and its members. This Code and performance pursuant to its provisions will be beneficial to the general public and contribute to the continued development of a mutually beneficial relationship among CERTIFIED PROPERTY MANAGER®s, CANDIDATES, REALTORS®, clients, employers, and the public.

The Institute of Real Estate Management, as the professional society of property managers, seeks to work closely with all other segments of the real estate industry to protect and enhance the interests of the public. To this end, members of the Institute have adopted and, as a condition of membership, subscribe to this Code of Professional Ethics. By doing so, they give notice that they clearly recognize the vital need to preserve and encourage fair and equitable practices and competition among all who are engaged in the profession of property management.

Those who are members of the Institute are dedicated individuals who are sincerely concerned with the protection and interests of those who come in contact with the industry. To this end, members of the Institute have subscribed to this Professional Pledge:

I pledge myself to the advancement of professional property management through the mutual efforts of members of the Institute of Real Estate Management and by any other proper means available to me.

I pledge myself to seek and maintain an equitable, honorable, and cooperative association with fellow members of the Institute and with all others who may become a part of my business and professional life.

I pledge myself to place honesty, integrity, and industriousness above all else; to pursue my gainful efforts with diligent study and dedication to the end that service to my clients shall always be maintained at the highest possible level.

I pledge myself to comply with the principles and declarations of the Institute of Real Estate Management as set forth in its bylaws and regulations and the CPM® Code of Professional Ethics.

1. Fiduciary Obligation to Clients

A CERTIFIED PROPERTY MANAGER® shall at all times exercise the utmost business loyalty to the interests of his or her clients and shall be diligent in the maintenance and protection of the clients' properties. In order to achieve this goal, a CERTIFIED PROPERTY MANAGER® shall not engage in any activity which could be reasonably construed as contrary to the best interests of the client or the client's property. The CERTIFIED PROPERTY MANAGER® shall not represent personal interests divergent or conflicting with those of the client, unless the client has been previously notified in writing of the actual or potential conflict of interest, and has also in writing assented to such representation. A CERTIFIED PROPERTY MANAGER®, as a fiduciary for the client, shall not receive, directly or indirectly, any rebate, fee, commission, discount or other benefit, whether monetary or otherwise, which has not been fully disclosed to and approved by the client.

2. Disclosure

A CERTIFIED PROPERTY MANAGER® shall not disclose to a third party confidential information which would be injurious or damaging concerning the business or personal affairs of a client without prior written consent of the client, except as may otherwise be required or compelled by applicable law or regulation.

3. Accounting and Reporting

A CERTIFIED PROPERTY MANAGER® shall at all times keep and maintain accurate accounting records concerning the properties managed for the client, and such records shall be available for inspection at all reasonable times by each client. A CERTIFIED PROPERTY MANAGER® shall cause to be furnished to the client, at intervals to be agreed upon with the client, a regular report in respect to that client's properties.

4. Protection of Funds and Property

A CERTIFIED PROPERTY MANAGER® shall at all times exert due diligence for the protection of client's funds and property in the possession or control of the CERTIFIED PROPERTY MANAGER® against all reasonably foreseeable contingencies or losses.

5. Relations with Other Members of the Profession

A CERTIFIED PROPERTY MANAGER® shall not make, authorize, or otherwise encourage any unfounded derogatory or disparaging comments concerning the practices of another CERTIFIED PROPERTY MANAGER®. CERTIFIED

PROPERTY MANAGER®s subscribing to this Code shall not exaggerate or misrepresent the services offered by him or her as compared with competing CERTIFIED PROPERTY MANAGER®s. Nothing in this Code, however, shall restrict legal and reasonable business competition by and among CERTIFIED PROPERTY MANAGER®s.

6. Contract

The contract, if any, between a CERTIFIED PROPERTY MANAGER® and his or her client shall provide for the specific terms agreed upon between the parties and shall be in clear and understandable terms, including a general description of the services to be provided by and responsibilities of the CERTIFIED PROPERTY MANAGER®.

7. Duty to Firm or Employer

A CERTIFIED PROPERTY MANAGER® shall at all times exercise the utmost loyalty to his or her employer or firm and shall be diligent in the maintenance and protection of the interests and property of the employer or firm. The CERTIFIED PROPERTY MANAGER® shall not engage in any activity or undertake any obligation which could reasonably be seen as contrary to the obligation of loyalty and diligence owed to his or her employer or firm, and shall not receive, directly or indirectly, any rebate, fee, commission, discount or other benefit, whether monetary or otherwise, which could reasonably be seen as producing a conflict with the interests of his or her employer or firm. A CERTIFIED PROPERTY MANAGER® shall at all times exercise due diligence for the protection of the funds of his or her employer or firm against all reasonably foreseeable contingencies or losses and shall as agent of his or her employer or firm exercise the highest degree of responsibility for the safekeeping and preservation of these funds.

8. Preserving and Protecting Property of the Client

It shall be the duty of the CERTIFIED PROPERTY MANAGER® as a skilled and highly trained professional, to competently manage the property of the client with due regard for the rights, responsibilities and benefits of the tenant. A CERTIFIED PROPERTY MANAGER® shall manage the property of his or her clients in a manner which takes due regard for his or her obligations to conserve natural resources and to maximize the preservation of the environment.

9. Duty to Former Clients and Former Firms or Employers

All obligations and duties of the CERTIFIED PROPERTY MANAGER® to clients, firms, and employers as specified in this Code shall also apply to relationships with former clients and former firms and employers. The CERTIFIED PROPERTY MANAGER® shall conduct himself or herself in the highest professional manner when, for whatever reason, relationships are terminated between the CERTIFIED PROPERTY MANAGER® and clients and firm or employer. Nothing in this section, however, shall be construed to cause a CERTIFIED PROPERTY MANAGER® to breach obligations and duties to current clients and firm or employer.

10. Compliance with Laws and Regulations

A CERTIFIED PROPERTY MANAGER® shall at all times conduct his or her business and personal activities with knowledge of and in compliance with applicable federal, state, and local laws and regulations, and shall maintain the highest moral and ethical standards consistent with membership in and the purposes of the Institute of Real Estate Management.

11. Continuing Professional Education

A CERTIFIED PROPERTY MANAGER®, in order to assure the continued retention and further growth and development of his or her skills as a professional, shall utilize to the highest extent possible the facilities offered to him or her for continuing professional education and refinement of his or her management skills.

12. Incorporation of NATIONAL ASSOCIATION OF REALTORS® Code of Ethics

The Code of Ethics of the NATIONAL ASSOCIATION OF REALTORS®, as in effect from time to time, is incorporated by reference into this Code and in relevant parts shall be binding on CERTIFIED PROPERTY MANAGER®s as other articles of this Code.

13. Enforcement

Any violation by a CERTIFIED PROPERTY MANAGER® of the obligations of this Code shall be determined in accordance with and pursuant to the terms of the Bylaws and Regulations of the Institute of Real Estate Management. Disciplinary action for violation of any portion of this Code shall be instituted by the Institute of Real Estate Management in accordance with the Bylaws and Rules and Regulations established by the Governing Council of the Institute. The result of such disciplinary action shall be final and binding upon the affected CERTIFIED PROPERTY MANAGER® and without recourse to the Institute, its officers, councillors, members, employees or agents.

Figure 4-7. Mini Management Plan

MINI MANAGEMENT PLAN

Owner: _____ Date: _____

Building Address: _____ Type: _____

_____ Units: _____

Owner Goals: _____ Holding Period: _____

_____

Prepared By: _____

1. Regional Analysis:

2. Neighborhood Analysis:

3. Property Analysis:
   a. Physical:

   b. Fiscal (Budget):

   c. Operational (Policies & Procedures):

4. Market Analysis:
   a. Rent Survey Summary:

   b. Vacancy Rate:

5. Analysis of Alternatives:

6. Proposed Plan Performance:
   a. Physical:

   b. Implementation & Timing:

   c. Fiscal:

   d. Operational:

7. Financing Needed:
   a. Capital Budget Needed in Dollars $ _____
   b. Expenses to Rental Income Ratio: _____ %

8. Valuation Comparison:
   a. Present Status:
      (1.) Dollar Value _____
      (2.) Cap Rate _____
      (3.) Gross Multiplier _____

   b. Projected Status:
      (1.) Dollar Value _____
      (2.) Cap Rate _____
      (3.) Gross Multiplier _____

9. Recommendations & Conclusion:

Approved By: _____

Real Estate Market Facts and Figures

Real Estate Ownership

1. Total U.S. real estate stock as estimated by an Arthur Anderson & Co. study in 1990 was $8.777 trillion.

> Individuals own $5.088 trillion
> Corporations own $1.699 trillion
> Partnerships own $1.011 trillion
> Non-Profit & Gov. own $.965 trillion

2. Foreign ownership is relatively small at $35.8 billion, even though it gets a disproportionate amount of attention.

3. Commercial properties account for $2.655 trillion, or 30% of total inventory.

> Retail value is $1.115 trillion (13%)
> Office value is $1.009 trillion (11%)
> Manufacturing is $308 billion (3.5%)
> Warehouse is $223 billion (2.5%)

4. Residential properties account for $6.122 trillion or 70% of total, with 107.6 million housing units.

> Single-family homes, 67.3 million units (63%), $3.857 trillion
> Multi-family conventional, 24.9 million units (23%), $1.4 trillion
> Other (HUD, condo, mobile home), 15.4 million units (14%),
> $86 billion

5. Size of U.S. residential properties is small. Only 14% of housing structures have 50 or more units. Most units, therefore, are located in small complexes.

Summary

The property manager should manage the property according to the owner's goals and objectives. The property manager may be an agent for the owner, acting as an intermediary between the owner and other parties. The property manager, if he or she manages for more than one owner, must possess a real estate license. A written management agreement outlining the duties and responsibilities should also have been signed. In some instances, the property manager works as an employee for the owner, or may be the owner of the building. Forms of ownership include: sole proprietorship, which is the most popular due to its ease to establish and dissolve; partnerships can be either general or limited; corporations offer limited liability but incur double taxation; and REITs are usually large in size and distribute 95% of their income each year to stockholders, but avoid double taxation.

The goals of the owner are varied and differ from owner to owner. Cash flow is a goal that owners of fixed income frequently favor; tax benefits are a goal that has been diminished by the 1986 Tax Reform Act; leverage is used by investors who foresee high inflation; appreciation is one of the goals of most investors; pride of ownership, safety and security, and diversification are additional goals of some owners.

The management contract spells out the responsibilities, duties, authority, and fees of the property manager. Some essential clauses would be description of the property, term, fees, authority, spending limits, hold harmless clause, and additional insured.

The property manager in California, if managing for others, needs a real estate license and must establish and maintain a trust account. The client's account must be balanced daily and the trust account reconciled on a monthly basis with the bank balance. These funds must be kept in a federally-insured institution and money deposited by the next working day after receipt. The files must be kept for a minimum of three years. Management fees are negotiable and vary according to type, size, and location of property. The four basic kinds of fees are: flat amount, per door, percentage of collected income, lease or re-rent fees. The property manager should determine the company costs so that a profit can be achieved on each property managed.

In conclusion, the property manager should view the property as a business entity and run it in accordance with the goals and objectives of the owner. The main function of the property manager is to increase the income stream, thereby increasing the NOI and the value of the property. There should be rapport and feedback between the owner and property manager in order to develop a long-term business relationship.

Chapter 4 Review Questions

1. *In a principal/agent relationship, the property manager would:*

   a. need a real estate license.
   b. need to be an attorney.
   c. not need a license.
   d. need to be a CPA.

2. *Types of real estate ownership would include:*

   a. corporation.
   b. REIT.
   c. partnership.
   d. all of the above.

3. *A prudent property manager would insist on:*

   a. a written management agreement.
   b. a free company car.
   c. a large office.
   d. an oral agreement.

4. *An increase in value refers to which benefit of ownership?*

   a. Tax benefits.
   b. Pride of ownership.
   c. Appreciation.
   d. Leverage.

5. *A management agreement for longer than what period of time needs to be in writing?*

   a. Six months.
   b. One year.
   c. Three months.
   d. Five months.

6. *The management agreement should include:*

    a. term.
    b. fees.
    c. both a and b.
    d. the management company's profit projection.
    e. all of the above.

7. *Which of the following is required?*

    a. Separate bank account for each client.
    b. Separate accounting for each owner.
    c. Trust funds may be held only in large banks.
    d. Secret profit is acceptable.

8. *Comingling is:*

    a. one client's funds used to pay the bills of another.
    b. non-disclosure of interest to owners.
    c. using client funds for broker's own use.
    d. none of the above.

9. *What is the management fee in dollars if the gross collected rents equal $20,000 and the management fee is 6%?*

    a. $1,000.
    b. $1,200.
    c. $1,500.
    d. None of the above.

10. *Which of the following is usually the most desirable fee structure?*

    a. Minimum and/or percentage fee, whichever is higher.
    b. Fixed amount.
    c. Percentage.
    d. Per door.

Chapter 4
Selected Additional Reference and Reading

California Department of Real Estate, *Real Estate Law*, Sacramento, CA, 1988.

California Department of Real Estate, *Reference Book; A Real Estate Guide*, Sacramento, CA, 1988.

Commercial Investment Real Estate Journal (Bimonthly)
430 N. Michigan Avenue
Chicago, IL 60611

Hallman, Victor, and Jerry Rosenbloom, *Personal Financial Planning*, 3rd Edition, McGraw-Hill, New York, NY, 1983.

Jarchow, Steven, *Real Estate Investment Trusts*, John Wiley & Sons, Somerset, NJ, 1988.

O'Connell, Daniel, *Apartment Building Valuation, Finance and Investment Analysis*, John Wiley & Sons, Somerset, NJ, 1982.

The Partnership Strategist (Monthly)
Newsletter Management Corporation
10076 Boca Entrada Boulevard
Boca Raton, FL 33433

The Real Estate Briefing (Quarterly)
Arthur Young and Company
One Post Street, Suite 3100
San Francisco, CA 94104

Real Estate Insight (Monthly)
Laventhol and Horwath
919 Third Avenue
New York, NY

Real Estate Investment Journal (Bimonthly)
P.O. Box 19564
Irvine, CA 92713

Real Estate Review (Bimonthly)
Touche Ross & Company
1 Maritime Plaza
San Francisco, CA 94111

Realtor (Monthly)
National Association of Realtors
430 N. Michigan Avenue
Chicago, IL 60611

The REIT Report (Bimonthly)
National Association of Real Estate Investment Trusts, Inc.
1101 Seventeenth Street, N.W., Suite 700
Washington, D.C. 20036

NOTES

Chapter 5

PERFORMANCE OBJECTIVES OF THE PROPERTY MANAGER

Key Terms

Increase revenue
Minimize expenses
Rent roll
Check register
Appearance
Demographics
Security deposit
  report
Vacancy report
Delinquency report
Marketing survey
Location
Tenant mix

Food for Thought

"The difference between crazy and eccentric is net worth."

Performance Objectives of the Property Manager

Introduction

Property management has been described and defined in many different ways over the years. The *California Department of Real Estate Reference Book* describes it as "a branch of the real estate business involving the marketing, operation, maintenance, and day-to-day financing of rental properties." Our definition is "the management, by an independent agent, of a property to maximize net operating income (NOI) while protecting and enhancing appreciation." NOI can be increased by three basic methods or a combination of these methods.

1. *Increase revenues (rents)*

   a. Rental surveys

   b. Addition of amenities; i.e., ceiling fans, etc.

   c. Good curb appeal; i.e., landscaping, facade

   d. Good onsite management

   e. Rental contracts; i.e., laundry, soda machines

2. *Minimize expenses*

   a. Budgeting of expenses

   b. Centralized and volume purchasing

   c. Energy-saving techniques

      1) Insulate water pipes
      2) Insulation in attic area

      3) Hot water heater blanket

      4) Solar power

    d. An effective preventive maintenance program

  3. *Protect the Asset.*

    a. Proper insurance coverage

    b. Adequate lighting for safety

Reporting to the Owner

The property manager, like any other type of manager, must give status reports to the client or boss. In property management these not only have to be accurate, since they concern other people's money, but timely as well. Nothing is more distressing than getting a statement or report too late to address the issue. See Figure 5-1.

Figure 5-1. Reports To Owners

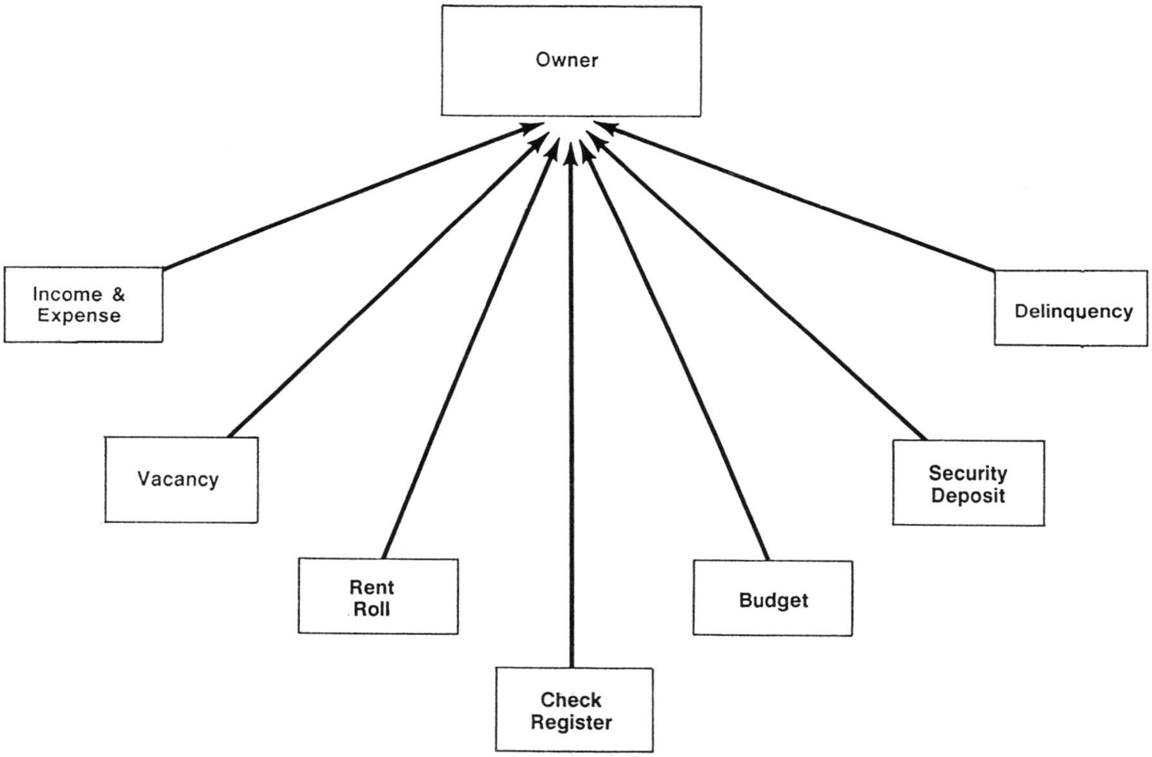

Types of Reports

Income and Expense Reports

This type of report (Figure 5-2) shows a summary of rents collected and operating expenses by category (plumbing, insurance, etc.). The difference is

Figure 5-2. Statement of Income and Expense

STATEMENT OF INCOME & EXPENSE
FOR THE 12 MONTH(S) ENDED DECEMBER 31
3341

INCOME	CURRENT MONTH	%	YEAR TO DATE	%
OPERATING INCOME				
RENTAL INCOME	5,300.00	97.54	67,481.63	97.89
WASHER/DRYER INCOME	133.50	2.46	1,551.70	2.25
PREVIOUS RENT	0.00	0.00	(99.04)	(0.14)
TOTAL OPERATING INCOME	5,433.50	100.00	68,934.29	100.00
TOTAL INCOME	5,433.50	100.00	68,934.29	100.00
OPERATING EXPENSES				
G&A EXPENSE				
APPLIANCES	0.00	0.00	460.00	0.67
BUILDING REPAIRS	(1.83)	(0.03)	3,253.93	4.72
CARPETS/CARPET CLEANING	0.00	0.00	245.00	0.36
CLEANING	(40.00)	(0.74)	65.00	0.09
DRAPES	196.10	3.61	285.25	0.41
ELECTRIC	101.43	1.87	919.32	1.33
ELECTRICAL REPAIRS	0.00	0.00	97.95	0.14
FLOOR REPAIRS	0.00	0.00	417.37	0.61
GAS	296.89	5.46	3,545.95	5.14
GLASS/SCREENS	40.78	0.75	187.45	0.27
HEATING/COOLING	0.00	0.00	492.12	0.71
INSURANCE	0.00	0.00	899.00	1.30
LANDSCAPE MAINTENANCE	75.00	1.38	1,081.03	1.57
LEGAL	0.00	0.00	(8.00)	(0.01)
LICENSES	0.00	0.00	25.00	0.04
LIGHTING REPAIRS	0.00	0.00	184.81	0.27
LOCKS/KEYS	40.00	0.74	143.16	0.21
LOAN PAYMENT	1,696.00	31.21	20,352.00	29.53
MANAGEMENT FEES	265.00	4.88	3,369.14	4.89
MANAGERS SALARY	243.43	4.48	1,576.77	2.29
MISCELLANEOUS	0.00	0.00	150.00	0.22
PAINTING	(56.50)	(1.04)	913.17	1.32
PAYROLL TAXES	0.00	0.00	194.52	0.28
PEST CONTROL	54.00	0.99	450.00	0.65
PLUMBING	84.71	1.56	3,203.29	4.65
PROPERTY TAXES	1,593.87	29.33	3,143.21	4.56
ROOFING	0.00	0.00	975.00	1.41
RUBBISH COLLECTION	140.50	2.59	1,407.13	2.04
SUPPLIES	0.00	0.00	45.09	0.07
WATER	280.50	5.16	2,074.55	3.01
TOTAL OPERATING EXPENSES	5,009.88	92.20	50,148.20	72.75
NET PROFIT OR LOSS	423.62	7.80	18,786.09	27.25
OPENING TRUST BALANCE	(4,025.00)			
MONIES TO/FROM OWNER	0.00		(18,122.47)	
CLOSING TRUST BALANCE	(3,601.38)			
CASH IN BANK (DEPOSITS)	3,905.00			
TOTAL CASH BALANCE	303.62			

called net operating income (NOI). If a loan payment is included, as in Figure 5-2, it becomes a cash flow statement. It should be pointed out that only the interest and not the principal of a mortgage payment is deductible on income taxes, so a "13th month" adjustment must be made after the December statement, breaking down loan expense into principal and interest. Cash flow is "pocket income," money that can be sent to the owner each month. This report also includes year-to-date summaries and comparison percentages of expense items to income collected.

Rent Roll

The rent roll (Figure 5-3) is part of the cash flow statement and is also sent to the client. A rent roll shows the unit numbers as well as receipts and disbursements for each unit. In our example, which is for a 12-unit building, it's easy to see whether all tenants paid their rent and the amounts of their individual rents. In Figure 5-3 we see one vacancy in Unit 914-4. When all the rents are added up, they equal the amount under the rental income category of the cash flow statement.

Check Register

The check register (Figure 5-4) is also part of the cash flow statement. It allows the client to see the amount of each check, date written, check number, and purpose. If each payment under electrical is totaled, that total would equal the electrical expense category in the cash flow statement shown in Figure 5-2. This is not only an invaluable control tool for the client, but also a security check that allows the client to easily see how the money was spent.

Security Deposit Balance

The security deposit balance is also shown on the check register. For accounting purposes, only the security deposit balance is reported separately from the client's balance, although the client has use of the funds until they need to be returned to a vacating tenant — thus the negative amount in the client's balance (Figure 5-4).

Total Cash Balance

The total cash balance in Figure 5-2 is the difference between the closing security deposit balance and the closing client balance, which in our illustration is $303.62.

Figure 5-3.   Rent Roll

J. D. PROPERTY MANAGEMENT
P.O. Box 1438, Costa Mesa, CA 92626
(714) 751-2787

PROPERTY MANAGEMENT STATEMENT

IMPORTANT: RETAIN FOR INCOME TAX RETURNS

FOR: 3341.1

DATE: 31 DEC

PROPERTY: SANTA ANA, CA. 92703

DATE	CHECK NO OR DATE PAID TO	RECEIPTS	DISBURSEMENTS	TRANSACTION DESCRIPTION	UNIT DESIGNATION
13 DEC 85	01 JAN 86	475.00		RENT	908-1
13 DEC 85		55.00		SD RECEIPT/REFUND	908-2
13 DEC 85	01 JAN 86	475.00		RENT	908-2
13 DEC 85	01 JAN 86	475.00		RENT	908-3
13 DEC 85	01 JAN 86	475.00		RENT	908-4
13 DEC 85	01 JAN 86	475.00		RENT	914-1
13 DEC 85	01 JAN 86	475.00		RENT	914-2
13 DEC 85	01 JAN 86	475.00		RENT	914-3
13 DEC 85	21336.1		338.50	SD RECEIPT/REFUND SD	914-4
12 DEC 85		40.00		CLEANING 6430	914-4
12 DEC 85		76.50		PAINTING	914-4
12 DEC 85		10.00		LOCKS/KEYS	914-4
12 DEC 85		10.00		BUILDING REPAIRS	914-4
12 DEC 85			136.50	SD RECEIPT/REFUND SD	914-4
13 DEC 85	01 JAN 86	475.00		RENT	920-1
13 DEC 85	01 JAN 86	465.00		RENT	920-2
13 DEC 85	01 JAN 86	475.00		RENT	920-3
01 DEC 85	01 DEC 85	560.00		RENT	920-4
01 DEC 85	M3708		20.00	PAINTING	
10 DEC 85	21279.1		1593.87	PROPERTY TAXES-REAL	
13 DEC 85	21346.1		243.43	MANAGERS SALARY	
16 DEC 85	21379.1		1696.00	LOAN PAYMENT	
17 DEC 85		119.50		WASHER/DRYER INCOME	
17 DEC 85		14.00		WASHER/DRYER INCOME	
18 DEC 85	21498.1		39.30	ELECTRIC	
18 DEC 85	21498.1		32.27	ELECTRIC	
18 DEC 85	21498.1		29.86	ELECTRIC	
18 DEC 85	21454.1		107.50	RUBBISH COLLECTION	
18 DEC 85	21491.1		84.71	PLUMBING	

DEPOSIT BALANCE			
PREVIOUS BALANCE	RECEIPTS	DISBURSED	CLOSING BALANCE

CLIENTS BALANCE			
PREVIOUS BALANCE	RECEIPTS	DISBURSEMENTS	CLOSING BALANCE

HERITAGE BUSINESS FORMS—(714) 859-1667   684333

Figure 5-4.   Check Register

J.D. PROPERTY MANAGEMENT
P.O. Box 1438, Costa Mesa, CA 92626
(714) 751-2787

PROPERTY MANAGEMENT STATEMENT

IMPORTANT: RETAIN FOR INCOME TAX RETURNS

FOR:
3341.1

DATE: 31 DEC

PROPERTY: SANTA ANA, CA. 92703

DATE	CHECK NO OR DATE PAID TO	RECEIPTS	DISBURSEMENTS	TRANSACTION DESCRIPTION	UNIT DESIGNATION
18 DEC 85	21451.1		8.17	BUILDING REPAIRS	
18 DEC 85	21451.1		50.00	LOCKS/KEYS	
19 DEC 85	21524.1		27.00	PEST CONTROL	
19 DEC 85	21524.1		40.78	GLASS/SCREENS	
20 DEC 85	21690.1		27.00	PEST CONTROL	
23 DEC 85	21696.1		75.00	LANDSCAPE MAINTENANC	
23 DEC 85	21562.1		280.50	WATER	
23 DEC 85	21562.1		33.00	RUBBISH COLLECTION	
23 DEC 85	21574.1		196.10	DRAPES	
23 DEC 85	21595.1		94.74	GAS	
23 DEC 85	21595.1		145.33	GAS	
23 DEC 85	21595.1		56.82	GAS	
31 DEC 85	18197		265.00	MANAGEMENT FEES MGMT	

DEPOSIT BALANCE

PREVIOUS BALANCE	RECEIPTS	DISBURSED	CLOSING BALANCE
4325.00	55.00	475.00	3905.00

CLIENTS BALANCE

PREVIOUS BALANCE	RECEIPTS	DISBURSEMENTS	CLOSING BALANCE
-4025.00	5570.00	5146.38	-3601.38

Figure 5-5.   Security Deposit Report

RESIDENT	NAME	ADDRESS	RENT	SECURITY DEPOSIT
3920.1.1	MANUEL CORTEZ MARTINEZ	1141 POPLAR SO. #1 SANTA ANA, CA 92704	400.00	375.00
3920.1.10	G. CHAVEZ/D. ARMAS	1143 POPLAR SO. #2 SANTA ANA, CA 92704	430.00	375.00
3920.1.11	MARIO DE JESUS GUARDADO	1143 POPLAR SO. #3 SANTA ANA, CA 92704	430.00	390.00
3920.1.12	CONSUELA ALCARAZ	1143 POPLAR SO. #4 SANTA ANA, CA 92704	430.00	75.00
3920.1.13	B. ALBERTO/G. BELMONTES	1143 POPLAR SO. #5 SANTA ANA, CA 92704	430.00	290.00
3920.1.14	ANGEL GUZMAN	1143 POPLAR SO. #6 SANTA ANA, CA 92704	450.00	425.00
3920.1.15	MARY IBARRA	1143 POPLAR SO. #7 SANTA ANA, CA 92704	430.00	380.00
3920.1.16	VACANT	1143 POPLAR SO. #8 SANTA ANA, CA, 92704		
3920.1.2	MARTHA HERNANDEZ	1141 POPLAR SO. #2 SANTA ANA, CA 92704	390.00	390.00
3920.1.3	IRMA CASTRO/SIMON D'CAMPO	1141 POPLAR SO. #3 SANTA ANA, CA 92704	430.00	380.00
3920.1.4	EFREN CORTEZ	1141 POPLAR SO. #4 SANTA ANA, CA 92704	430.00	380.00
3920.1.5	ARMANDO GARCIA	1141 POPLAR SO. #5 SANTA ANA, CA 92704	430.00	360.00
3920.1.6	MARIA RUIZ	1141 POPLAR SO. #6 SANTA ANA, CA 92704	430.00	290.00
3920.1.7	ARTURO DIAZ/RACINDO AMBRIZ	1141 POPLAR SO. #7 SANTA ANA, CA 92704	400.00	495.00
3920.1.8	HECTOR AGUSTO	1141 POPLAR SO. #8 SANTA ANA, CA 92704	430.00	340.00
3920.1.9	JOSE OTIZ	1143 POPLAR SO. #1 SANTA ANA, CA 92704	430.00	250.00

[405] 16 ITEMS LISTED

Budget Comparison Statement

This type of report is an expanded cash flow report which includes a budget and variances from budget (see Chapter 10, Figure 10-2). This is used when more sophisticated reports are needed, such as for syndicates and institutions.

Vacancy Report

The vacancy report can be generated for each property on a weekly basis or daily for problem properties. In many cases a project marketing summary report is prepared.

Delinquency Report

Delinquency reports (Figure 5-6) are usually generated by the fifth of the month to begin the eviction process on tenants who have not paid their rent. Some computer programs print out 3-Day Pay or Quit Notices from the delinquency list in a matter of minutes.

Monthly Summary

The monthly summary (Figure 5-7) is a narrative report that goes along with the cash flow report and summarizes the events of the past month. It comments on vacancies, delinquencies, major expenditures, budget variances, and any major problems occurring on the property.

Bills to Owner

In many cases the property manager sends the client the paid bills each month. This relieves the property manager of the responsibility for storage and ensuing costs. Most states require that the property manager keep records for up to four years. The property manager should never give accounting advice, but should refer the client to a Certified Public Accountant.

The Marketing Survey

The success of a property in meeting the goals and objectives set forth by either the property manager or owner depends primarily on the quality of the tenants occupying the building. Each building is unique and will attract different types of tenants. The property manager must examine the property to determine its strengths and weaknesses before a management plan can be written for operating the building (Figure 5-8).

Figure 5-6. Delinquency Status Report

J.D. PROPERTY MANAGEMENT

DELINQUENCY STATUS REPORT
28 FEB

RES NO	SURNAME	UNIT DESIG	CHARGE	PRIOR BALANCE	AMOUNT BILLED	AMOUNT RECEIVED	CURRENT BALANCE	TOTAL DUE	PAID TO DATE
1 3		8916	EST CAM		71.73	71.73			03-01
			RENT		974.81	974.81			
			85 CAM	20.03			20.03	20.03	
1 5		8920	EST CAM		52.00	52.00			03-01
			RENT		660.00	660.00			
				287.21			287.21	287.21	
1 11		8932	EST CAM		105.00	105.00			03-01
			RENT		800.00	800.00			
			85 CAM	586.80			586.80	586.80	
1 12		8944	EST CAM		148.00		148.00		02-26
			RENT		1650.00	1650.00			
			85 CAM	818.27			818.27	966.27	
1 13		8948	EST CAM		540.00		540.00		02-26
			RENT		5265.00	5265.00			
			85 CAM	999.84		999.84		540.00	
1 15		8956	EST CAM		346.00		346.00		02-01
			RENT		4025.00		4025.00		
			85 CAM	1902.12			1902.12	6273.12	
1 16		8960	EST CAM		904.80	904.80			03-01
			RENT		7062.30	7062.30			
			85 CAM	283.05			283.05	283.05	
1 17		8962	EST CAM		233.36	233.36	233.36		02-01
			RENT	2865.64	2806.97	2865.64	2806.97	3040.33	
1 21		8976	EST CAM		110.00		110.00		02-01
			RENT		1212.75		1212.75		
			85 CAM	599.36		96.32	503.04	1825.79	
1 22		8978	RENT	740.00	1617.00	2280.00	77.00		02-25
			EST CAM		148.00		148.00		
			85 CAM	926.99			926.99	1151.99	
1 25		8988	RENT	2950.00	1840.90	1519.73	3271.17		01-07

Figure 5-7. Monthly Summary

 J.D. PROPERTY MANAGEMENT, INC.
3520 Cadillac Ave., Suite B, Costa Mesa, CA 92626
(714) 751-2787

Shelton Terrace Monthly Summary -- December

    Vacancies -- one
    Deliquencies -- none

1. Property Taxes of 1,593 were paid this month which is the main reason
       for the low profit margin this month.

2. Rental of apartment 914-4 was at $560.00. It was completed after state-
       ment was run and doesn't show this month.

3. Repairs were minor replacements with no major problems.

4. Year End Comments:
       A. The rental income increased 8.2% this year vs. last year. We
          hope to achieve at least 7% in the coming year.
       B. Repairs were down 1% over last years and we don't anticipate
any major projects in the coming year.

BRANCH OFFICES
4075 MAIN STREET, SUITE 455, RIVERSIDE, CA 92501 (714) 369-1103
2105 W. GENESEE ST., SUITE 210, SYRACUSE, NY 13219 (315) 468-0556

LICENSED REAL ESTATE BROKER CALIFORNIA AND NEW YORK

Figure 5-8. Project Marketing Survey

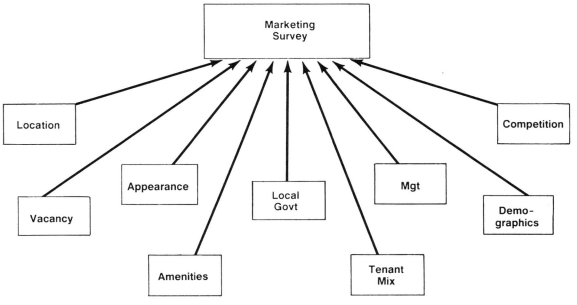

Location

Location is always paramount in real estate. If an office building is near the courthouse, it will attract attorneys as clients. A hospital-proximate medical building has a distinct advantage in attracting physician tenants. An apartment building in a high-crime area will have trouble attracting affluent renters.

Appearance

Appearance, or curb appeal, is important as people like to live and work in nice surroundings. Banks and institutions like to be located in prestigious, high-image buildings. An apartment building that has weeds and no landscaping will not attract renters who can afford to pay more for a "nice" place to live.

Government

Restrictive zoning or stiff parking requirements for office/retail use could deter potential tenants. On the other hand, being next to a well-used bus line or in a city which has good police, fire protection, and schools is a plus.

Demographics

Where are your tenants coming from? If near a freeway interchange, your office building will attract sales-oriented businesses or companies which need easy transportation access for their employees. If an apartment building is located in a depressed area, it will be difficult to attract middle-class tenants.

Competition

Who and where is your competition? What are their rental rates and giveaway programs (i.e., free rent, free parking)?

Vacancy Rate

What is the vacancy rate in your area? The Federal Home Loan Bank, using information generated by the Postal Service, compiles these data.

Amenities

Does your apartment building provide drapes? Does it have garages, fireplaces, extra bathrooms? Rental rates can't be compared without taking a survey to determine how your amenities stack up compared to those of the competition. Refer back to Figure 5-8.

Tenant Mix

The tenant mix is important in retaining and attracting new tenants. Renting to a veterinarian, for example, in a medical building might hurt the building image (see Chapter 8-11). The property manager must be careful, however, not to discriminate on the basis of race, age, religion, color, creed, or national origin.

Management

Potential tenants are attracted to a well-managed building. Are the lobbies, elevators, and restrooms clean? Are you responsive to tenant questions and problems?

Summary

The definition of property management varies with no widely accepted description. This book defines the role of the property manager as being three-fold:

1. Increase net operating income

   a. Increase rents; i.e., amenities, good management

   b. Minimize expenses; i.e., energy-saving techniques

2. Enhance value; i.e., curb appeal, increased sale price

3. Protect the asset; i.e., adequate insurance

The property manager needs to give adequate and timely reports to the owner on the operation of the building. Typical reports may include: income and expense, vacancy, rent roll, check register, budgets (operating and proforma), security deposit, and delinquency reports. These reports may be weekly or monthly depending on owner reporting requirements. In many instances, the client also receives the paid bills each month to keep for his/her files.

The property manager should conduct a market survey of the property to determine its strengths and weaknesses. This is very important in order to determine how the property manager will meet the owner's goals and objectives. Areas to examine in the marketing survey include: location, vacancy, appearance, government, demographics, competition, amenities, tenant mix, and management.

In conclusion, we have defined property management and covered the methods of increasing net operating income and we discussed the different reports to the owner and the market survey.

Chapter 5 Review Questions

1. *The property manager can increase revenues by:*

    a. adding amenities.
    b. good curb appeal.
    c. neither a nor b.
    d. both a and b.

2. *The property manager can minimize expenses by:*

    a. installing energy-saving devices.
    b. raising rents.
    c. adding washers and dryers.
    d. painting the building.

3. *The goal of the property manager is to:*

    a. increase revenues.
    b. minimize expenses.
    c. protect future value.

d. all of the above.
e. only increase revenues.

4. *Rent roll statements should be prepared:*

a. weekly.
b. monthly.
c. annually.
d. bimonthly.

5. *Security deposit records should be kept:*

a. only when the tenant vacates.
b. only when the tenant rents.
c. at all times during the tenant's residency.
d. only if the tenant requests that they be kept.

6. *Reports to the owner:*

a. should maximize use of only one page.
b. should be timely and accurate.
c. should be submitted only once a year.
d. should include tax returns prepared by the property manager.
e. none of the above.

7. *Location is important for which type of real estate?*

a. Apartments.
b. Office buildings.
c. Neither a nor b.
d. Both a and b.

8. *Local government controls:*

a. interest rates.
b. zoning and parking.
c. tenant selection.
d. all of the above.
e. none of the above.

9. *Demographics deals with:*

    a. interest rates.
    b. zoning and parking.
    c. population and income characteristics.
    d. all of the above.
    e. none of the above.

10. Tenant mix allows the property manager to discriminate on the basis of:

    a. color.
    b. race.
    c. national origin.
    d. none of the above.
    e. only b and c.

NOTES

Chapter 5

Case Study

Introduction

To enhance your understanding of property management while learning to apply in practice the principles discussed in this book, we have developed a case study to complement the practical application of each chapter. This somewhat humorous case study concerns a 20-unit apartment building, called "Whiskey Manor," located in Orange County, California. The study will address rental rates, vacancy, maintenance and repair, and property performance improvement techniques. The student will be asked to develop solutions and management strategies. Since property management is both an art and a science, there is no absolute answer. A possible solution will be offered to help guide the student, with the answers in the back of the book. Case study questions will be located at the end of several chapters.

"Whiskey Manor" Fact Sheet

Regional Information

Whiskey Manor is located in Orange County, California, which has a rapidly growing population, now over two million people. Most of the employment in the county is moving from manufacturing toward the service industry. Wages are $5-12/hour with low unemployment (less than 4%). The area has several minority groups comprising in total nearly 50% of the population. These minorities tend to earn lower wages. The climate is one of the world's best, with moderately warm summers and mild winters (no snow). The area has a major regional shopping center (five miles away), several colleges, and cultural and recreational facilities within a 30-mile radius. The area is served by several newspapers, but the main ones are the *Los Angeles Times* and *The Register*. *The Register* is best for advertising vacant apartments because of its "local paper" reputation.

Figure 5-9. Whiskey Manor Typical Month

```
Scheduled income                                              $9,500

  Vacancies and delinquencies    ($2,700)

  Actual income                             $6,800
  Washer/dryer                                 110
  Total income                                                 6,910

Operating expenses:

  Advertising                             $    0
  Building repairs                           385
  Carpets/carpet cleaning                     24
  Electricity                                 82
  Gas                                        282
  Insurance                                   76
  Landscaping                                  0
  Legal                                       24
  Loan payment                             4,900
  Management fees                              0
  Manager's salary                           400
  Property taxes                             623
  Repairs:
    Painting                                  77
    Plumbing                                  79
    Electrical                                 0
  Rubbish                                    154
  Water                                      231
  Miscellaneous                               13
  Total operating expenses                                     7,350

Cash flow (negative)                                        ($  440)
```

Neighborhood Information

The property is located in a central city of the county and has a population of approximately 80,000. A large contingent of immigrants from Southeast Asia has settled in the area. Most employment in the immediate area is service-related, with an average wage of $6–9/hour. Shopping, schools, parks, and churches are all available nearby. The most immediate neighbor is a Catholic church. A bus stop is four blocks away. The apartment building overlooks the city civic center, administration building, and police station. The area vacancy rate is 3–4%.

Figure 5-10.

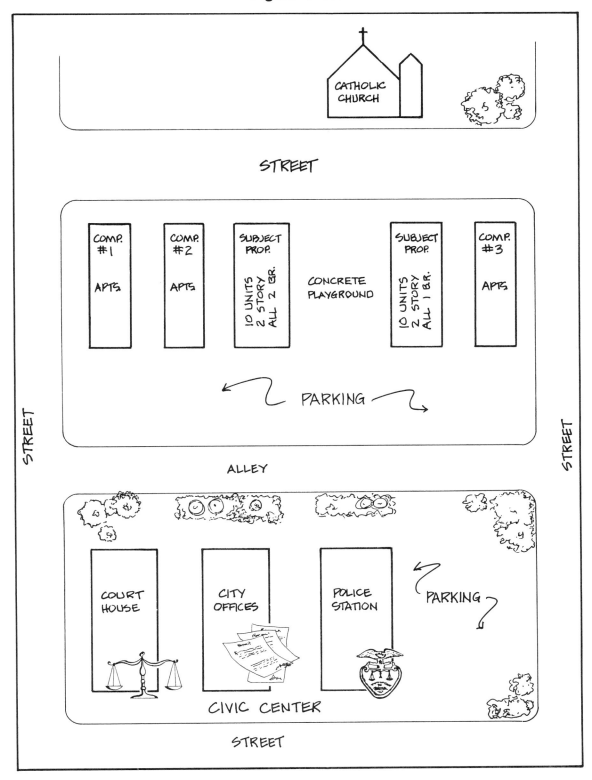

Comparable Rental Rates

Amenities	Subject Property	Comp. #1	Comp. #2	Comp. #3
1 bedroom	$450	$530	$525	$535
2 bedrooms	$500	$570	$575	$565
Fireplace	No	No	No	Yes
Utilities	Partial	No	Yes	Partial
Pool	No	No	Yes	Yes
Garage	No	Yes	Yes	No
Spa	No	No	Yes	No
Age	20 years	15 years	New	10 years
Condition	Fair	Good	Good	Good
Location	Good	Fair	Good	Good
Play area	Yes	No	No	No

The Property

1. *Age*: 20 years.

2. *Construction*: Two-story wood frame with stucco.

3. *Number of units*: 10 one-bedroom, approx. 650 s.f.
   10 two-bedroom, approx. 750 s.f.

4. *Heating* is gas wall units; stoves are gas.

5. *Utilities*: Electricity paid by tenant; gas and water paid by owner.

6. *Amenities*: No pool, but large concrete play area; coin laundry facilities. No air-conditioning.

7. *Parking*: One space per apartment

8. *Landscaping*: Non-existent

9. *Condition of units*: Fair, but has plumbing problems; has new roof

10. *Layout*: Two buildings facing each other across a courtyard which is part parking and part play area.

History of Units

The complex was formerly owned for several years by "Big Bertha," the neighborhood "madam," who had a "red light" on at the manager's apartment for her clients. She was shot and killed by a dissatisfied customer. The present owners, Pete and Mary Scrooge, purchased the units at an estate sale.

Operating Policies

1. *Office hours:* Whenever.

2. *Pet deposit:* $200 plus $25/month for a cat, no dogs.

3. *Late charge:* $100 (never collected).

4. *Deposits:* First and last month's rent, no security.

5. *Rental term:* Month to month (verbal).

6. *Rental agreement:* None.

Operating History

Vacancies: Three one-bedroom, two two-bedroom units.

Delinquencies: Four.

The manager takes tenants to Small Claims Court for eviction after they have been delinquent for two months. The new owners have had both vacancy and delinquency problems since purchasing the apartment building.

The Management

The onsite manager is Judy Lovelace, who used to work for Bertha. She tries hard to please, but doesn't collect the rent on time and her paperwork is never correct. Because of her friendly personality, she is a good leasing agent.

The Owners

Husband Pete is an aerospace engineer and wife Mary is a college librarian. They bought the complex as a tax shelter and to become millionaires through real estate investments. They are both too busy with their careers to have time to be involved in management. They also don't like to put money into the complex to cover the negative on a monthly basis, nor do they want to correct deferred maintenance.

Chapter 5
Selected Additional References and Reading

Boardroom Reports (Biweekly)
    330 W. 42nd Street
    New York, NY 10036

The Cash Flow Letter (Monthly)
    Impact Publishing Company
    2110 Omega Road, Suite A
    San Ramon, CA 94583

Crittenden Bulletin (Monthly)
    Crittenden Research, Inc.
    P.O. Box 1150
    Novato, CA 94948

The Goodkin Report (Monthly)
    Sanford R. Goodkin Research Corporation
    23041 Friar Street
    Woodland Hills, CA 91367

Huber, Walt, *California Real Estate Principles,* Educational Textbook Company, Covina, CA, 1987.

Institutional Investor (Monthly)
    Institutional Investor, Inc.
    488 Madison Avenue
    New York, NY 10022

Klink, James, *Real Estate Accounting and Reporting,* John Wiley & Sons, Somerset, NJ, 1985.

McKenzie, Dennis, Lowell Anderson, Frank Battino, and Cecilia Hopkins, *California Real Estate Principles,* 3rd Edition, John Wiley & Sons, New York, NY.

National Real Estate Investor
    P.O Box 28965
    Atlanta, GA 30358

Southern California Real Estate Journal (Bi-Weekly)
    3450 Wilshire Blvd., Suite 310
    Los Angeles, CA 90010

Chapter 6

THE MANAGEMENT PLAN

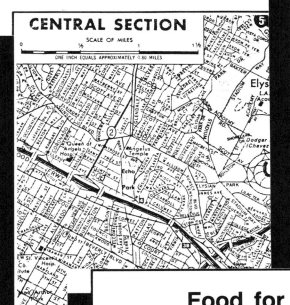

Key Terms

Regional analysis
Neighborhood analysis
Infrastructure
Property analysis
Modernize
Pro forma analysis
Operating history
Measurement of
   market
Comparable analysis
Alteration
Areas of analysis
IRR

Food for Thought

"There are two things to aim at in life: First, to get what you want; and after that to enjoy it. Only the wisest of mankind achieve the second."
Logan Pearsall Smith

The Management Plan

Introduction

One of the most important property management tools is the *management plan*. It establishes management objectives for the property and the blueprint by which to achieve those objectives. The management plan is formulated by gathering, analyzing, and interpreting all information pertaining to the property. It is important that the owner, property manager, and onsite manager understand the game plan the property manager uses to manage and operate the building.

The management plan format is divided into seven sections. Each section will be analyzed separately to simplify the subject matter. After identifying trends and factors in the regional, neighborhood, property, and market analysis, the manager analyzes and organizes the material to help determine the strengths and weaknesses of the property. A recommended plan is then prepared with financing and return on investments projected along with final recommendations for operation and management of the property.

Scope of the Plan

The scope of the management plan will include financing, staffing, occupancy, tenant mix, marketing and leasing policies, income and expenses of the property, physical inspections, and policies and procedures. Some of these areas will be interrelated. For example, deferred maintenance will affect the vacancy factor which affects net operating income on the subject property. Basic assumptions, limitations, terminology, and time frame should be outlined along with the qualifications of the preparer. The plan cost and payment schedule for the client should also be referenced.

Format of the Plan

The plan should start with a title page including identification of the property, address, and description of the project. The page should also contain the owner name and address as well as the preparer of the plan. The proposed completion date and a photograph of the property should be included. A table of contents that outlines the format of the plan and provides page references should be the second page. The third page should be a letter of transmittal including summary of observations, conclusions, and recommendations. The plan should contain pictures, charts, graphs, and source references of where the data were obtained.

Regional Analysis

The region encompasses the metropolitan area in which the property is located. The property manager should try to use one of the 64 Standard Metropolitan Statistical Areas (SMSA) compiled by the Bureau of the Census. This makes it easier for the property manager to obtain statistical data for:

1. *Population characteristics and growth, past and projected trends*

2. *Demographics of the area*

3. *Industrial base*

4. *Transportation facilities*

5. *Educational facilities*

6. *Real estate market data*

7. *Political and social climate and trends*

Additional sources of data can include:

1. *Trade associations*
   a. Institute of Real Estate Management (IREM) (Figure 6-11)
   b. International Council of Shopping Centers (ICSC)
   c. Building Owners and Managers Institute International (BOMI)

2. *Local and state governments*
   a. Redevelopment agencies

3. *Local Chamber of Commerce*

4. *Local banks and savings and loans*

5. *Local utility companies*

Figure 6-1

Management Plan

For

Whiskey Manor

1000 Civic Center Drive

Garden Grove, CA

This is a 20-unit, garden-style (two-story) apartment building

picture

Prepared For:

Peter and Mary Ross
200 Highland
Los Angeles, CA 92712

Date: January 15, 19 ___

Prepared By:

JD Property Management, Inc.
3520 Cadillac Ave., Ste. B
Costa Mesa, CA 92626
(714) 751-2787

Figure 6-2

TABLE OF CONTENTS
FOR
WHISKEY MANOR MANAGEMENT PLAN

Figure 6-3. Letter of Transmittal

J.D. PROPERTY MANAGEMENT, INC.
3520 Cadillac Ave., Suite B, Costa Mesa, CA 92626
(714) 751-2787

January 10, 19____

Peter and Mary Ross
200 Highland
Los Angeles, CA 92712

RE: Management Plan for Whiskey Manor

Dear Peter and Mary:

Pursuant to your assignment in your letter of December 12th, I have prepared a comprehensive management survey of your subject property located at 1000 Civic Center Drive, Garden Grove, CA.

After three personal inspections of the subject property and three selected properties in the rental area, plus analyzing the immediate neighborhood and region, and analyzing your financial data, I am prepared to answer your specific questions and make the following recommendations.

The management plan to be implemented calls for correction of deferred maintenance, both exterior and interior, replacing the present onsite manager, and increasing the rental rates through a planned marketing approach. The present operation functions with a $6,000 negative cash flow and a decline in value of the property due to deteriorated condition and poor management policies. The proposed improvements and operational plan will produce a positive cash flow - and increase the value almost $200,000.

The estimated costs of the improvements are $50,000. A detailed analysis with cost breakdown is located in this report. Our survey of the region indicates that growth will increase over 17% by 1995, creating a need for housing. An analysis of the neighborhood shows that it is a lower-income, blue-collar area with a large contingent of immigrants from Southeast Asia that will continue to grow. The income level of the area is also rising and is sufficient to afford the proposed new rental rates of the operational plan. In other words, the demand is already present for upgrading Whiskey Manor.

Sincerely,

BRANCH OFFICES
4075 MAIN STREET, SUITE 455, RIVERSIDE, CA 92501 (714) 369-1103
2105 W. GENESEE ST., SUITE 210, SYRACUSE, NY 13219 (315) 468-0556

LICENSED REAL ESTATE BROKER CALIFORNIA AND NEW YORK

Figure 6-4. Sources of Information

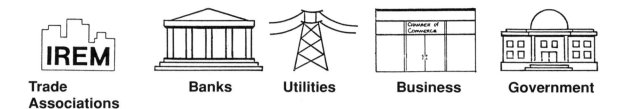

Trade Associations   **Banks**   **Utilities**   **Business**   **Government**

Neighborhood Analysis

Under the regional analysis we were looking to see if trends were positive. We are looking for positive trends in the 3- to 5-mile neighborhood analysis of the subject property.

1. *Population characteristics and trends*

   a. Family size
   b. Neighborhood life cycle (improving, static, deteriorating)
   c. Age level
   d. Population increasing or decreasing

2. *Economic characteristics*

   a. Employment levels going up or down
   b. Types of industry or business
   c. Rental rates and sale prices

3. *Infrastructure*

   a. Transportation
      1) Bus lines
      2) Freeways
   b. Government and political attributes (favorable or unfavorable)
   c. Amenities
      1) Schools
      2) Shopping

4. *Measurement of neighborhood*

   a. Square miles
   b. Major streets or freeways
   c. Natural boundaries (i.e., rivers, mountains)

Figure 6-5.

RESIDENTIAL INCOME PROPERTY
(MULTI-FAMILY UNITS)
VACANCY RATE SURVEY

| | | TOTAL UNITS | VACANT | | | | | | UNDER CONSTRUCTION | |
| | | | ------USED------ | | ------NEW------ | | ------TOTAL------ | | | |
			Number	Percent	Number	Percent	Number	Percent	Number	Percent
Anaheim	92801	9,519	243	2.6%	0	0.0%	243	2.6%	84	0.9%
	92802	5,733	138	2.4%	0	0.0%	138	2.4%	0	0.0%
	92804	11,505	428	3.7%	0	0.0%	428	3.7%	82	0.7%
	92805	5,320	104	2.0%	24	0.5%	128	2.4%	49	0.9%
	92806	5,563	288	5.2%	0	0.0%	288	5.2%	48	0.9%
	92807	2,143	34	1.6%	0	0.0%	34	1.6%	93	4.3%
	Total Anaheim	39,783	1,235	3.1%	24	0.1%	1,259	3.2%	356	0.9%
Costa Mesa	92626	6,845	217	3.2%	130	1.9%	347	5.1%	148	2.2%
	92627	9,213	89	1.0%	20	0.2%	109	1.2%	24	0.3%
	Total Costa Mesa	16,058	306	1.9%	150	0.9%	456	2.8%	172	1.1%
Garden Grove	92640	4,616	217	4.7%	78	1.7%	295	6.4%	78	1.7%
	92641	2,811	49	1.7%	0	0.0%	49	1.7%	0	0.0%
	92643	3,687	42	1.1%	11	0.3%	53	1.4%	0	0.0%
	92644	3,111	80	2.6%	0	0.0%	80	2.6%	28	0.9%
	92645	362	0	0.0%	0	0.0%	0	0.0%	0	0.0%
	Total Garden Grove	14,587	388	2.7%	89	0.6%	477	3.3%	106	0.7%
Huntington Beach	92646	4,198	104	2.5%	35	0.8%	139	3.3%	0	0.0%
	92647	8,274	296	3.6%	16	0.2%	312	3.8%	4	0.0%
	92648	6,597	109	1.7%	0	0.0%	109	1.7%	4	0.1%
	92649	4,818	193	4.0%	35	0.7%	228	4.7%	60	1.2%
	Total Hunt. Beach	23,887	702	2.9%	86	0.4%	788	3.3%	68	0.3%

Source: Federal Home Load Bank of San Francisco

Property Analysis

We must now develop a physical profile of the property which would include:

1. *Physical*

    a. Age
    b. Number of units
    c. Layout of complex
    d. Condition
       1) Roof
       2) Elevators
       3) Plumbing and electrical
       4) Mechanical (i.e., air-conditioning)
    e. Obsolescence
       1) Functional
       2) Economic

2. *Desirability of property*

    a. Curb appeal
    b. Tenant mix
    c. Attractiveness of units
       1) Layout and size
       2) View
       3) Fixtures and appliances
    d. Condition of public areas
       1) Laundry facilities
       2) Halls
       3) Parking lot
    e. Amenities and their condition

3. *Management of property*

    a. Vacancy rate (Figure 6-5)
    b. Onsite staff
    c. Records and files
    d. Screening procedures
    e. Tenant relations
    f. New building checklist (Figure 6-7)

4. *Financial data*

    a. Debt service
    b. Real estate taxes
    c. Insurance
    d. Operating history — expenses and income

5. *Policies and procedures* — a policies and procedures manual should be compiled into one body of records. This "Standard Operating Procedures" manual is the plan of operation for the property. It is a guideline for both onsite managers and supervisors. It details the objectives of operating the property and describes the jobs and skills needed to carry out the plan. The basis for the manual is:

    a. What is to be done
    b. Who is to do it
    c. How it is to be done
    d. When it is to be done
    e. Why it is to be done

A proper manual describes every activity that could, would, or should happen at a property (Figure 6-6).

Figure 6-6. SOP Manual

PROCEDURES MANUAL

TABLE OF CONTENTS

Appraisal Reports

Although the property manager does not usually prepare appraisal reports, he/she should be familiar with the format. The property manager is often involved in refinance, selling, or purchasing property which involves appraisal reports. On August 10, 1990, California enacted an Appraisal Standards system to comply with Federal appraisal requirements for most institutional real estate loans. The Office of Real Estate Appraisers (OREA) is part of the State of California Business, Transportation & Housing Agency. There are two basic licensing categories: Certified Residential and Certified General, each with different educational and experience factors.

Certified Residential Criteria

This category is for appraisers whose practice entails one to four family residential units. Appraisers with this license cannot do complex non-residential appraisals. The requirements as of January 1, 1994, include:

Category	Education	Experience
Licensed	75 hours	2,000 hours over any time period
		Non-complex, one to four units residential, less than $1 million transaction value; complex, one to four units residential, less than $250,000 transaction value.
Certified Residential	105 hours	2,000 hours with no more than 1,000 in any 12-month period
		All one- to four-unit residential without regard to transaction value or complexity.
Certified General	165 hours	2,000 hours with 50% in non-residential (more than four units work)
		All real estate transactions without regard to value or complexity.

Property Taxes

In California, property tax bills are split into two equal payments:

November 1st   — Due
December 10th — Delinquent

February 1st   — Due
April 10th   — Delinquent

Assessments are mailed to property owners in July for the coming tax year. If the owner disagrees, an appeal must be filed by September 15th. Under Proposition 13, passed in 1978, the property taxes can increase only 2% per year unless the property is sold, an addition is made, or a bond proposal passes by 2/3 vote. If the property is sold, the new tax will be 1% of sale or market price plus any existing bond or special assessments. For example, an apartment building is purchased for $1,000,000. The tax would be 1% plus the local bond assessment of .25%, or 1.25%:

$1,000,000   — Property Value
  × .0125   — Tax Rate
$ 12,500   — Tax Due

Market Analysis

The market analysis determines the rental, leasing, and vacancy rates in the market served by the subject building.

1. *Measurement of the market*

    a. Sub-market (apartment buildings)
        1) Multi-story (high-rise)
        2) Mid-rise (four-story)
        3) Low-rise (two-story)
        4) Garden apartments
    b. Size and characteristics of the market
        1) Age of units in the area
        2) Number of units in the area
        3) Size of units (i.e., one bedroom, 650 square feet)
        4) Rental rates
            a. Monthly rent (residential)
            b. Cost per square foot (commercial)
        5) Vacancy level

2. *Comparable analysis*

    a. Conduct market survey. Compare and contrast to subject property — is your building better or worse?

    b. Location analysis
      1) Freeways and transportation
      2) Prestige area

3. *Obtain Cost Data*

    a. Local contractors and vendors should be contacted for cost estimates; i.e., carpet is usually quoted by price per yard plus padding, plus installation. Cost may range from $8-10 per yard.

    b. Consult reference books that contain cost data broken down by item such as a garbage disposal. One such reference is *Means Repairs and Remodeling Cost Data — Commercial Residential*, published by the R.S. Means Co. Another reference is Marshall and Swift.

    c. Cost of supervision, usually 10-15%, should be added to these estimates. In some cases the property manager will be the supervisor and will be paid the fee. At other times a general contractor will be hired.

Analysis of Alternatives

In the alternatives analysis, the building is reviewed not only for its present use "as is," but also for the "highest and best use" of the property. A pro-forma analysis showing projected rents, expenses, and increased net return to the owner should be prepared for each alternative considered.

1. *Alteration*

    a. Change of use
      1) Condominium conversion
      2) Convert to retail or office use (consider city zoning and use ordinances)

    b. Change of unit mix
      1) Converting bachelor and one-bedroom units to two- or three-bedroom units; converting two- or three-bedroom units to one-bedroom or bachelor units.

2. *Modernize and rehabilitate*

    a. Replace original equipment (i.e., air-conditioning, carpets)

    b. Upgrade or replace building facade

    c. Correct deferred maintenance

Figure 6-7. New Building Checklist

NEW BUILDING CHECKLIST   Managed by _____

STREET & NUMBER _____

MANAGEMENT COMMISSION RATE _____ STARTING DATE _____

OWNER'S SOC. SEC. # OR I.D. # _____

WHO GETS A COPY OF THE MONTHLY STATEMENT:

       Name _____ Address _____

       Phone _____   _____

If more than one owner, or add'l copies needed, use reverse side.

WHO GETS PAID BILLS WITH MONTHLY STATEMENT _____

DISTRIBUTE FUNDS MONTHLY OR KEEP A BALANCE? _____

IF TITLE TO BUILDING IS IN TRUST, WHO HOLDS TITLE? (Bank & Trust #)

_____

PREVIOUS AGENT

       Company _____ Person _____

       Address _____ Phone _____

       Copy of previous month's statement _____

PAYROLL

       Do we handle? _____ Employer name

       Employer I.D. # _____ (as listed with gov't) _____

       If new, do we file? _____

       If previous employer, collect prior quarter returns.

JANITOR

       Name _____ Address _____

       Phone _____ Date began on bldg. _____

       Monthly Salary _____ Married or single? _____

       Number of dependents _____ Anything extra w/h from salary? _____

LEASES

       Collect current leases _____ Show how many rooms on lease.

       Last decorated? _____ Security deposits _____

Units   Apartments _____ Stores _____ Office _____

       Garages _____ Total number of units _____

REAL ESTATE TAXES & MORTGAGE

       Permanent Index No. _____ Volume _____

       Do we handle payment or do we handle direct? _____

       Do we charge a monthly reserve? _____ Amount _____

       Attorney for tax protest _____

       Is there a mortgage? _____ With whom? _____

       Loan # _____

       Does mortgage have a tax reserve? _____

INSURANCE

       Current agent? _____ Phone _____

       OLT. AMOUNT _____ WC. AMOUNT _____ FIRE & EC AMT. _____

       Endorsement needed to add our name _____

       Copy of policies needed for our files _____

       Upon expiration, shall we write? _____

MAINTENANCE

       Fuel _____ Type _____

       Exterminator _____ Scavenger _____

       Hardware _____ Decorator _____

       Plumber _____ Electrician _____

GUARANTEES:

       Roof _____

       Boiler _____

Figure 6-8. Market Survey

MARKET SURVEY WORKSHEET

Complex Name: _____ Cross Streets: _____

Address: _____ Map Page: _____

City: _____ State: _____ Zip: _____

Manager Name: _____ Phone: _____

Owner Name: _____ Phone: _____

Description of Complex

_____ one-story   _____ two-story   _____ three-story   _____ other

No. of one-bedrooms: _____   No. of baths: _____

No. of two-bedrooms: _____   No. of baths: _____

No. of three-bedrooms: _____   No. of baths: _____

No. other: _____   No. of baths: _____

Total Units: _____

Location of Complex

_____ Superior   _____ Equal   _____ Inferior   _____ Other: _____

Curb Appeal

_____ Superior   _____ Equal   _____ Inferior   _____ Other: _____

Special Features (i.e., Ocean View)

_____ Superior   _____ Equal   _____ Inferior   _____ Other: _____

Age of Project

_____ Newer   _____ Equal   _____ Inferior   _____ Year Built

Amenities in Complex

_____ A/C	_____ Exercise Room	_____ Refrigerator
_____ Cable TV	_____ Fireplace (wood/gas)	_____ Sauna
_____ Carpeting	_____ Garages	_____ Security gate
_____ Covered Carports	_____ Microwave	_____ Stove
_____ Dishwashers	_____ Laundry Facilities	_____ Trash comp.
_____ Disposals	_____ Parking spaces	_____ Util. incl.
_____ Drapes	_____ Pool	_____ gas
_____ Elevators	_____ Recreation Room	_____ electric

RENTAL ANALYSIS

Type	No. Baths	Sq.Ft.	Mo. Rent	Vacancy	Price per Sq. Ft.
Bachelor	_____	_____	_____	_____	_____
1 bedroom	_____	_____	_____	_____	_____
2 bedroom	_____	_____	_____	_____	_____
3 bedroom	_____	_____	_____	_____	_____
Other	_____	_____	_____	_____	_____

Prepared by: _____ Date: _____

Figure 6-9. Comparison Worksheet

COMPARISON WORKSHEET

Subject Property	Comparison Property
Complex Name: _____	Complex Name: _____
Address: _____	Address: _____
No. Units: _____	No. Units: _____

	Subject		Comparable	
	Present Condition	After Rehabilitation	Present Condition	After Rehabilitation

Exterior

Accessibility	_____	_____	_____	_____
Age	_____	_____	_____	_____
Curb appeal	_____	_____	_____	_____
Exterior	_____	_____	_____	_____
Grounds	_____	_____	_____	_____
Laundry	_____	_____	_____	_____
Location	_____	_____	_____	_____
Parking (gar.)	_____	_____	_____	_____
Pool	_____	_____	_____	_____
Rec room	_____	_____	_____	_____
Other:	_____	_____	_____	_____

Interior

Carpet	_____	_____	_____	_____
Closets	_____	_____	_____	_____
Dishwasher	_____	_____	_____	_____
Disposal	_____	_____	_____	_____
Drapes	_____	_____	_____	_____
Fireplace	_____	_____	_____	_____
Range	_____	_____	_____	_____
Refrigerator	_____	_____	_____	_____
Size of units	_____	_____	_____	_____
Utilities				
Gas	_____	_____	_____	_____
Electric	_____	_____	_____	_____
Other:	_____	_____	_____	_____

Area Amenities

Access roads	_____	_____	_____	_____
Churches	_____	_____	_____	_____
Image	_____	_____	_____	_____
Public trans.	_____	_____	_____	_____
Schools	_____	_____	_____	_____
Shopping	_____	_____	_____	_____
Other:	_____	_____	_____	_____

Present Rents:	_____	_____	_____	_____
Rents per s.f.:	_____	_____	_____	_____
Rent change:	_____	_____	_____	_____
New rents:	_____	_____	_____	_____
New rent per s.f.	_____	_____	_____	_____

Figure 6-10.

PRO FORMA BUDGET

	Last Year	Current year	Projected As Is	Projected After Rehab.
Gross Potential Income				
Laundry				
Other income				
Vacancy loss				
Effective Gross Income				
Operating Expense				
Repair				
Painting				
Plumbing				
Electrical				
Building				
Supplies				
Utilities				
Water				
Electric				
Gas				
Trash				
Management				
Onsite				
Offsite				
Legal & Accounting				
Taxes				
Insurance				
Capital Improvements				
Roof				
Appliances				
Other:				
Subtotal Expenses				
Net Operating Income				

Figure 6-11. Median Income and Operating Expenses

GARDEN TYPE BUILDINGS UNFURNISHED — MEDIAN INCOME AND OPERATING COSTS — SELECTED METROPOLITAN AREAS U.S.A.

SAN DIEGO, CA — 40 BUILDINGS — 3,274 APARTMENTS — 2,715,428 RENTABLE SQUARE FEET

SAN FRANCISCO, CA — 12 BUILDINGS — 1,748 APARTMENTS — 1,451,096 RENTABLE SQUARE FEET

	BLDGS.	% OF GPTI MED	LOW	HIGH	$/SQ.FT. MED	LOW	HIGH	BLDGS.	% OF GPTI MED	LOW	HIGH	$/SQ.FT. MED	LOW	HIGH
INCOME														
RENTS-APARTMENTS	(40)	98.2%	97.1%	98.8%	7.41	6.87	8.02	(12)	99.0%	98.6%	99.3%	11.30	9.58	12.20
RENTS-GARAGE/PARKING	(7)	.9			.06			(2)	.4			.03		
RENTS-STORES/OFFICES	( )							( )						
GROSS POSSIBLE RENTS	(40)	98.5%	97.5%	98.9%	7.41	6.87	8.02	(12)	99.1%	98.9%	99.3%	11.30	9.58	12.20
VACANCIES/RENT LOSS	(40)	5.3	3.3	7.6	.43	.22	.63	(12)	4.9	3.6	5.8	.56	.37	.68
TOTAL RENTS COLLECTED	(40)	92.4	88.9	95.1	6.85	6.49	7.53	(12)	94.8	92.4	95.2	10.75	8.90	11.49
OTHER INCOME	(37)	1.6	1.2	2.8	.12	.09	.21	(12)	1.0	.7	1.1	.11	.07	.12
GROSS POSSIBLE INCOME	(40)	100.0%	100.0%	100.0%	7.54	6.97	8.08	(12)	100.0%	100.0%	100.0%	11.34	9.71	12.23
TOTAL COLLECTIONS	(40)	95.0	92.4	96.7	7.00	6.65	7.62	(12)	95.2	94.2	96.4	10.78	9.04	11.52
EXPENSES														
MANAGEMENT FEE	(39)	4.5	3.6	5.0	.34	.26	.40	(10)	4.7			.57		
OTHER ADMINISTRTVE.**	(33)	4.3	2.5	5.6	.33	.20	.43	(11)	3.2	2.9	4.0	.37	.32	.49
SUBTOTAL ADMINIST.	(40)	7.8%	5.7%	9.9%	.61	.44	.76	(12)	7.7%	6.2%	8.8%	.94	.58	1.03
SUPPLIES	(35)	.5	.1	1.0	.04	.01	.07	(12)	.5	.2	.7	.06	.02	.08
HEATING FUEL-CA ONLY*	(8)	2.0			.12			(1)	.4			.03		
CA & APTS.*	(1)	.7			.07			(1)	3.0			.29		
ELECTRICITY--CA ONLY*	(35)	1.5	1.3	2.2	.12	.09	.15	(12)	1.5	.8	1.6	.15	.08	.18
CA & APTS.*	(4)	1.6			.16			( )						
WATER/SEWER--CA ONLY*	(1)	2.0			.17			( )						
CA & APTS.*	(38)	2.4	1.8	3.3	.18	.14	.23	(12)	2.3	2.0	2.4	.26	.22	.28
GAS----------CA ONLY*	(22)	1.9	1.0	2.3	.13	.09	.17	(7)	1.3			.14		
CA & APTS.*	(8)	2.1			.17			(1)	1.5			.19		
BUILDING SERVICES	(32)	1.5	.9	3.1	.11	.07	.20	(10)	1.7			.16		
OTHER OPERATING	(26)	1.6	.6	2.1	.12	.04	.16	(8)	1.2			.12		
SUBTOTAL OPERATING	(40)	8.6%	6.5%	11.1%	.71	.52	.82	(12)	7.5%	5.6%	7.8%	.73	.68	.89
SECURITY**	(13)	.5	.4	1.9	.04	.03	.14	(6)	.6			.06		
GROUNDS MAINTENANCE**	(40)	2.4	1.5	3.3	.20	.11	.25	(12)	2.8	1.4	3.0	.25	.14	.32
MAINTENANCE-REPAIRS	(40)	4.8	2.4	6.8	.37	.19	.53	(12)	2.6	1.5	3.7	.32	.16	.35
PAINTING/DECORATING**	(38)	2.1	1.1	3.2	.16	.08	.25	(11)	1.4	1.2	1.8	.16	.12	.18
SUBTOTAL MAINTENANCE	(40)	9.8%	6.4%	13.4%	.76	.47	1.01	(12)	7.6%	6.4%	8.2%	.80	.72	.87
REAL ESTATE TAXES	(40)	4.5	2.9	7.2	.33	.22	.57	(12)	5.8	4.0	7.1	.56	.39	.71
OTHER TAX/FEE/PERMIT	(35)	.1	.0	.2	.01	.00	.01	(7)	.1			.01		
INSURANCE	(40)	2.0	1.6	3.0	.15	.11	.22	(12)	2.2	1.3	3.2	.24	.12	.40
SUBTOTAL TAX-INSURNCE	(40)	7.6%	5.7%	9.4%	.54	.40	.75	(12)	9.1%	6.9%	10.5%	.93	.87	1.26
RECREATNL/AMENITIES**	(13)	.5	.4	1.0	.04	.03	.08	(5)	.9			.09		
OTHER PAYROLL**	(21)	3.5	.8	4.4	.26	.06	.32	(7)	2.0			.18		
TOTAL ALL EXPENSES	(40)	36.0%	32.1%	41.1%	2.80	2.45	3.11	(12)	33.9%	30.3%	34.7%	3.71	3.30	3.85
NET OPERATING INCOME	(40)	56.8%	52.2%	62.4%	4.11	3.64	5.13	(12)	61.3%	59.1%	64.1%	6.93	5.74	7.26
PAYROLL RECAP**	(31)	5.0	3.7	5.8	.37	.26	.43	(11)	5.0	4.2	5.6	.51	.48	.63

FOOTNOTE: For a description of Utility Expense (*) and Payroll Cost (**) reporting, and an explanation of the report layouts and method of data analysis, refer to the sections entitled *Guidelines for the Use of this Data* and *Interpretation of a Page of Data*. For definitions of the income and expense categories, refer to the Appendix. Copyright © 1987, Institute of Real Estate Management.

Investment Analysis

Figure 6-12. Investment Analysis

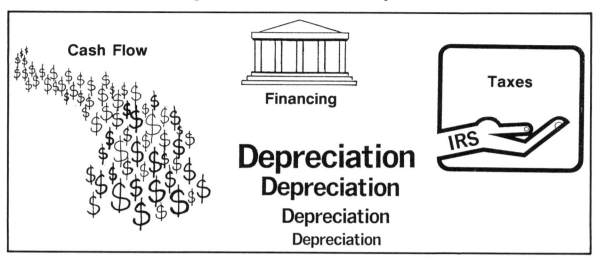

After analyzing the projection of income and expenses of the proposed property upgrade alternatives, an investment analysis of the property from the client's perspective must be made. This may be time-consuming and the property manager may not have the expertise or background to provide an investment analysis. Consultation with a Certified Public Accountant (CPA) or attorney may be required.

1. *Areas of analysis*

    a. Cash flow calculations (5-year IRR)
       1) Presently existing building
       2) After improvements
    b. Depreciation benefits
    c. Valuation of building (capitalization rate)
       1) Presently existing building
       2) After improvements
    d. Financing costs, sources, and methods
    e. Tax ramifications
       1) Income
       2) Property

Recommendations and Conclusions

The property manager should have supporting documentation for the recommendations. A five-year pro-forma cash flow projection must be devised based on the internal rate of return (IRR) both before and after taxes, considering:

1. *Complete cost estimates as supplied by contractors*

2. *A method to finance and cost thereof*

3. *A market study to support the increased rental income*

Be prepared to defined your recommendations, but remember that it is the client's property and money and the client will make the final decision.

Financial Calculations

In order to be able to determine whether an investor should proceed with rehabilitation of a property, an analysis of the present operating income and expenses must be made. These figures must be projected on a pro-forma basis into the future. The same process must take place on projected income and expenses for the proposed rehabilitation alternative. If the investor can get a higher return and greater cash flow, he/she will probably decide to proceed. The property manager should be familiar with how to make the necessary calculations.

HP12C Calculator

The Hewlett-Packard 12C Financial Calculator is commonly used in the real estate industry. This small, hand-held calculator has four registers and is programmable.

Figure 6-13. HP12C Calculator

HP19BII Calculator

The Hewlett-Packard 19BII Business Calculator, faster than the HP12C and menu-driven, is now used exclusively in both CPM courses and the CCIM courses. It is advisable to take a one-day class on how to operate both calculators. If students would like solutions to these problems using the HP19BII, please send a self-addressed envelope to JD Seminars, 3520-C Cadillac Ave., Costa Mesa, CA 92626.

For the examples in this book we utilize the HP12C.

Loan Constants

In order to compare which loan is more advantageous when the interest rates and length of the loan differ, we need to convert to a loan constant. For example, which is the best loan for an investor?

Loan Information	Loan Constant	
10.5% for 25 years	.1133	
11% for 30 years	.1143	
9.5% for 20 years	.1119	← Best Loan

The loan with the lowest loan constant, which is comprised of the interest and principal, is usually the best loan. If there were a balloon payment (all due and payable) after the fifth year on the 9.5% loan, the investor might choose a loan with a longer life.

Keystrokes			Display
f 4		=	.0000
1 CHS PV		=	−1.000
10.5 g i		=	.8750 interest rate per month
25 g n		=	300 months
PMT		=	.0094 monthly constant
12 X		=	.1133 annual constant

Calculation of Loan Payment

It used to be necessary to use tables to calculate loan payments, which is time-consuming and sometimes not readily available. Using the HP12C, it is relatively easy. For example, what is the monthly and annual loan payment for the following loan?

> 25 years — term of the loan
> 10.5%   — interest rate
> $650,000 — amount of the loan

Keystrokes			Display
f 2		=	.00
10.5 g i		=	.88 interest rate per month
25 g n		=	300 months
650,000 PV		=	$650,000 amount of loan
PMT		=	$6,137.18 payment per month
12 X		=	$73,646.17 payment per year

Loan Balance

It is necessary to know the loan balance during the term of the loan in order to logically determine the financial implications of the rehabilitation project. The process starts with determining the loan payment as previously shown. We now add some steps to determine the loan balance at the end of five years:

> Loan amount — $650,000
> Term   — 25 years
> Interest   — 10.5%

Keystrokes				Display
10.5	g	i	=	.88 interest rate per month
25	g	n	=	300 months
650,000	PV		=	$650,000 amount of loan
PMT			=	$6,137.18 payment per month
60	f	n	=	$332,944.88 interest — 5 yrs.
	x≷y		=	$35,285.92 principal — 5 yrs.
RCL	PV		=	$614,714.08 loan bal — end of fifth year

Rate of Return

The investor, when comparing the different alternative solutions, needs to know the return on investment (ROI), payback period (how many years to get the extended funds back), and the internal rate of return (IRR). We use the IRR where the amount of the cash flow is not the same from period to period. The IRR is used to determine the return rate. This formula is complex and not used very often by the property manager. We will outline the basic keystrokes for those who want to do the calculations:

Example: purchased building for $650,000 and sold it for $1,100,000 five years later. You had cash flows as follows:

1st year	—	<25,000>
2nd year	—	<10,000>
3rd year	—	5,000
4th year	—	20,000

What is the IRR for the 5 years?

Keystrokes					Display
f	CLX				.00
650,000	CHS	g	CFo	=	–650,000
25,000	CHS	g	CFj	=	–25,000
10,000	CHS	g	CFj	=	–10,000
5,000		g	CFj	=	5,000
20,000		g	CFj	=	20,000
1,100,000		g	CFj	=	1,100,000
f	IRR			=	10.63 Internal Rate of Return

Follow-Up and Implementation

When the management plan finally emerges, one of three things can happen to it:

1. The owner, property manager, and onsite manager breathe a sigh of relief, put the plan in a binder, and let it collect dust.

2. The management plan becomes sacred — and adjusting it becomes impossible; i.e., it is etched in stone.

3. The management plan emerges as a working tool. Assumptions and projections are monitored and changed when necessary.

The purpose of developing the management plan should be the third scenario. It is the "game plan" on how the property is to be operated.

Summary

In this chapter, the management plan, sometimes called the blueprint to manage the property, was discussed and outlined. The actual format of a plan starting with the title page, followed by the table of contents and the letter of transmittal, was explained and examples provided. The actual plan was divided into six sections: regional analysis, neighborhood analysis, property analysis, marketing analysis, analysis of alternatives, and recommendations and conclusions.

Under regional analysis, areas covered were population characteristics and growth, demographics, industrial base, transportation and educational facilities, and political and social trends. These data can be obtained from trade associations, chambers of commerce, banks, utility companies, as well as government agencies such as the Census Bureau. The next step in developing the management plan is to analyze the neighborhood in which the subject property is located, usually comprised of three to five miles. As in the regional analysis, we are looking for characteristics and trends in population, employment, types of businesses in the neighborhood, rental rates and sales prices, adequate transportation system, and local government attitudes (it may not be desirable to do a rehabilitation in a rent-controlled community that looks unfavorably upon landlords, such as the "People's Republic of Santa Monica").

The next step is to analyze the subject property. Questions that need to be answered include: What is the physical condition, age, number of units, layout, and both functional and economic obsolescence? What is the desirability of the property, which would include curb appeal, tenant mix, amenities, vacancy, tenant relations, management, and financial data such as taxes, insurance, repair costs, and debt? Does the property have a standard operating procedure (SOP) manual? Are there deficiencies in any of the above areas? Can these problems be corrected and at what cost?

The next area we turn to is the market analysis, in which a rental survey is done on similar properties. The subject property is compared and contrasted to the comparable and an indicated rent is determined both before and after rehabilitation. Cost estimates are obtained from contractors and reference books such as R.S. Means and Marshal and Swift, in order to prepare pro-forma budgets, valuations, and cash flow projections. The next step is recommendations and conclusions where the property manager will point out the rehabilitation benefits of increased cash flow, higher resale value, and payback period of the rehabilitation costs to the owner. In some cases, the regional or neighborhood analysis will bring to the surface factors that *may not* make rehabilitation a viable alternative. The rate of return, payback period, and increase in value may also be insufficient to warrant a recommendation to proceed.

The last step is follow-up and implementation of the management plan. It should be used as a working tool or the "game plan" for operation of the property.

Conclusion

It can be seen that the management plan should be prepared for all types of properties: apartments, offices, retail, or industrial. The length and depth of the plan depend upon property size, financial condition, owner goals, etc. Most property managers charge an extra fee on an hourly basis for anything other than a short, simple plan. A full-scale management plan can run up to 150 pages including pictures, charts, illustrations, references, and supporting data.

Chapter 6 Review Questions

1. *The management plan:*

    a. establishes objectives and goals for the property.
    b. is used for tax assessments.
    c. is used for tax depreciation.
    d. establishes the value of the property.

2. *Regional analysis would consider:*

    a. population.
    b. demographics.
    c. both a and b.
    d. neither a nor b.

3. *Sources of regional information would include:*

    a. trade associations.
    b. country clubs.
    c. the local PTA.
    d. all of the above.
    e. none of the above.

4. *Neighborhood analysis would consider:*

    a. employment levels.
    b. rental rates.
    c. both a and b.
    d. neither a nor b.

5. *Boundaries for the neighborhood could include:*

    a. major streets or freeways.
    b. natural boundaries such as rivers.
    c. both a and b.
    d. neither a nor b.

6. *Property analysis would consider:*

   a. the unemployment rate.
   b. physical condition.
   c. family size.
   d. all of the above.
   e. none of the above.

7. *Financial data in the property analysis would include:*

   a. debt service.
   b. insurance.
   c. both a and b.
   d. neither a nor b.

8. *Considerations under size and characteristics of the market would include:*

   a. age of the units.
   b. the number of units in the area.
   c. rental rates.
   d. all of the above.
   e. none of the above.

9. *Modernization could include:*

   a. replacing original equipment.
   b. upgrading the building facade.
   c. correcting deferred maintenance.
   d. all of the above.
   e. none of the above.

10. *Pro-forma cash flow projections are used for:*

    a. real estate tax assessors.
    b. federal income tax returns.
    c. projecting profits before and after improvements.
    d. all of the above.
    e. none of the above.

Chapter 6 Case Study Problem

1. Do you feel that "Whiskey Manor" is located in a good regional area in which to rehab an apartment complex?

2. Do you feel that "Whiskey Manor" is a desirable neighborhood area in which to own and/or manage an apartment complex?

3. How do the amenities of "Whiskey Manor" compare to those of comparable properties?

4. Describe the desirability (i.e., curb appeal) to prospective tenants.

5. Would you recommend to the owners that they let the complex continue its present course or that they pay a CPM to develop a comprehensive management plan? Justify your answer.

Chapter 6
Selected Additional References and Reading

American Institute of Real Estate Appraisers, *1988 Directory of Members*, Chicago, IL, 1988.

American Institute of Real Estate Appraisers, *The Uniform Residential Appraisal Report*, Chicago, IL, 1987.

Coffin, Chris and Ted Wadman, *An Easy Course in Using the HP12C Calculator*, Grapevine Publications, Corvallis, OR, 1984.

Crane, Eric, *The HP12C Made Easy*, Eric Crane Seminars, La Canada, CA, 1984.

Demographic Profiles Service
    Donnelly Marketing Information Systems
    70 Seaview Avenue
    Stamford, CT 06904

Downs, James, *Principles of Real Estate Management*, Institute of Real Estate Management, Chicago, IL, 1980.

Institute of Real Estate Management, *Expense Analysis: Apartments*, Chicago, IL, 1988.

Kyle, Donald and Frank Baird, *Property Management*, 3rd Edition, Real Estate Education Company, Chicago, IL.

Means Co., *Means Repair and Remodeling Cost Data — Commercial and Residential*, Chicago, IL.

Residential Income Property Vacancy Rate (Annual)
    Federal Home Loan Bank of San Francisco
    P.O. Box 7948
    San Francisco, CA 94120

United States Bureau of the Census, *Statistical Abstract of the United States, 1987*, U.S. Government Printing Office, 1987.

Chapter 7

RESIDENTIAL MANAGEMENT

Key Terms

Garden apartments
Mid-rise
Curb appeal
Signage
Normal wear and
   tear
CPA
Delinquency rate
Rental agreement
Pricing apartments
"Shopping"
Break-even vacancy
Base rent
Last month's rent
CBS
Security deposit

Food for Thought

"He who is always right may be left."

Chapter 7

Residential Management

Introduction

In this chapter we will examine the largest area of property management: residential property management. We will interweave the case study of "Whiskey Manor" which was outlined in Chapter 5. During this case study you will be acting as the property manager and will be expected to make decisions on the operation of the property. Possible answers can be found in the back of the book.

The property manager must take into consideration that local and state laws may vary and are constantly changing and being revised (rent control and eviction, for example). Discussion, then, will be in general terms based on present laws within the state. The property manager should routinely consult with local attorneys, apartment associations, and government officials to fully understand the laws in the geographic area.

Classification of Multi-Family Buildings

Garden Apartments

Garden apartments are usually spread-out, low-rise (two-story), walk-up apartments containing one- and two-bedroom apartments. They are of low density (25 units per acre) and located mostly in the suburbs due to lower land costs. Main characteristics include amenities such as pools, tennis courts, ample parking, recreation room, extensive landscaping, central laundry, and individual air-conditioning. Garden apartments are usually individually metered.

Mid-Rise

Mid-rise apartments are usually found on the edge of urban areas and are of medium density. These apartments usually have elevators and can be four to nine stories in height. More often, these buildings are now being developed in the suburbs, increasing in density as land costs rise. The main characteristics of the mid-rise include parking structures, central lobby area, pool, recreation or exercise rooms, and central air-conditioning.

High-Rise

High-rise apartments are usually found in major metropolitan areas where land costs are very high and high density is a resulting necessity. They have the highest density per acre. The main characteristics of the high-rise include elevators, central air-conditioning, security, pools, etc. The size can exceed 25 stories. Prestigious locations and views are extremely important as many of these buildings are marketed as luxury apartments.

Other Types

There are also duplexes, triplexes, walk-up apartments, and single-family rental houses. On these types of properties there is typically no onsite manager due to cost considerations. Management is therefore difficult and time-consuming.

Government-Assisted Housing

This requires specialized training of the property manager due to special demands such as verification of eligibility, rental increases, evictions, and government reports (see Chapter 11 for further discussion).

Market Analysis

The property manager and onsite manager must know their product, geographic area, competition, schools, transportation, population, and income statistics. We discussed these under the management plan in Chapter 6. Rental value — except in areas of rent control — is determined by supply and demand. Supply and demand is determined by ascertaining the vacancy rate within the market area. The vacancy factor can be obtained through the Federal Home Loan Bank which compiles rates broken down by zip code (Figure 7-1). Under uninfluenced supply and demand, rents will increase until prospective renters can find a cheaper form of housing (i.e., purchase, doubling up with family or friends, etc.). Shopping competitive properties is one of the best methods of analyzing the market.

Apartment Marketing Strategies

The property manager and onsite manager can help create demand and desirability for their units, resulting in increased rental rates.

Figure 7-1. Vacancy Survey

	ZIP CODE	TOTAL UNITS	VACANT USED Number	USED Percent	VACANT NEW Number	NEW Percent	VACANT TOTAL Number	TOTAL Percent	UNDER CONSTRUCTION Number	CONSTRUCTION Percent
Newport Beach	92660	3,006	187	6.2%	0	0.0%	187	6.2%	0	0.0%
	92661	436	20	4.6%	0	0.0%	20	4.6%	0	0.0%
	92662	391	16	4.1%	0	0.0%	16	4.1%	0	0.0%
	92663	4,452	165	3.7%	0	0.0%	165	3.7%	46	1.0%
Total Newport Beach		8,285	288	3.5%	0	0.0%	388	4.7%	46	0.6%
Orange	92665	1,572	26	1.7%	0	0.0%	26	1.7%	0	0.0%
	92666	1,800	33	1.8%	0	0.0%	33	1.8%	100	5.6%
	92776	3,030	42	1.4%	0	0.0%	42	1.4%	0	0.0%
	92668	3,914	112	2.9%	0	0.0%	112	2.9%	0	0.0%
	92669	1,818	41	2.3%	24	1.3%	65	3.6%	0	0.0%
Total Orange		12,134	254	2.1%	24	0.2%	278	2.3%	100	0.8%
Santa Ana	92701	6,928	163	2.4%	122	1.8%	285	4.1%	199	2.9%
	92703	1,770	44	2.5%	22	1.2%	66	3.7%	451	25.5%
	92704	6,746	211	3.1%	0	0.0%	211	3.1%	0	0.0%
	92705	2,454	31	1.3%	0	0.0%	31	1.3%	0	0.0%
	92706	3,106	78	2.5%	0	0.0%	78	2.5%	90	2.9%
	92707	5,236	170	3.2%	0	0.0%	170	3.2%	2	0.0%
	92708	3,097	82	2.6%	0	0.0%	82	2.6%	184	5.9%
	92709	293	0	0.0%	0	0.0%	0	0.0%	0	0.0%
	92714	6,313	72	1.1%	324	5.1%	396	6.3%	0	0.0%
	92715	5,137	0	0.0%	0	0.0%	0	0.0%	67	1.3%
	92720	1,324	20	1.5%	0	0.0%	20	1.5%	0	0.0%
Total Santa Ana		42,404	871	2.1%	468	1.1%	1,339	3.2%	993	2.3%

Definition of terms: *Multi-Family Units* — housing units in the same building, attached to each other along the side(s), floor, and/or ceiling; includes apartment buildings and high rise condominiums.

Source: Federal Home Loan Bank of San Francisco. The survey is conducted under an inter agency agreement between the U.S. Postal Service and the Federal Home Loan Bank. The data is supplied by individual mail carriers of residential delivery routes under supervision of local postmaster.

Merchandising

There is an old adage, "Merchandise well displayed is half sold." What is the appearance (curb appeal) of your building? Is it well-landscaped? Are grounds neat and clean? Are old junk cars parked in the parking lot? Have the vacancies been cleaned and made ready to show to prospects?

A model apartment should be cheerful and tastefully decorated, but not so fancy that a prospective tenant won't be able to identify with it. (Hint: Use of mirrors on walls makes units seem larger.)

Signage and Graphics

The signage, building graphics, letterhead, and brochures should be coordinated in type style, color, theme, and logo. Signage should always look crisp, clean, new, and be simple to read. Colors should be warm and friendly. Flowers and landscaping around posts will enhance the signage (Figures 7-2, 7-3, and 7-4).

The name of the complex should complement the area. If there is a mountain in view, the complex could be called "Mountain View Terrace." A name such as "Whiskey Manor" for a complex located across from a church is offensive. Residential units which do not contain an elevator must post

Figure 7-2. Good Signage

Figure 7-3. Billboard Signage

Figure 7-4. Poor Signage

ownership/management signs including an emergency phone number in two separate and conspicuous locations under CC (1962.5(2). Examples of locations could be next to mailboxes, laundry room, or entrances to the complex.

Advertising

Advertising creates traffic and brings prospects to your complex. An ad should answer three questions:

1. *What am I going to get?* One- or two-bedroom apartment and amenities. Can I have a pet? Do I pay for utilities?

2. *What is it going to cost?* Placing the rental rate in the ad eliminates wasted calls by residents who can't afford the unit. A converse opinion, for times of poor rental, is that deleting the rate from the ad broadens your market to those tenants who have set a figure in mind while being able, in actuality, to pay more.

3. *How can I find you?* Telephone number and/or address. In display ads, a simple map to the property may be appropriate.

Newspapers are the most common form of media. Frequently, smaller (local) newspapers with a good circulation in the market area will pull in more prospects than larger, more expensive and prestigious papers.

1. *Classified ads* (Figure 7-5) usually produce the best results per dollar of advertising cost.

Figure 7-5. Classified Ad

CIVIC CENTER TERRACE
Lg., spacious 1 bdrm., newly decorated, ready for immediate occupancy, only $595. Pets OK. 20 Civic Center Dr., (714) 751-2787. Ask for Sue.

2. *Display ads* (Figure 7-6) are more expensive and require artwork. Display ads are frequently used for large complexes, new projects, or in times of high vacancy.

3. *Magazines* are good for institutional ads, but due to long lead time prior to printing are not timely. They are a useful medium mostly for large, prestigious complexes.

Figure 7-6. Display Ad

OPEN HOUSE
1 & 2 Bedroom Apartments

Beautiful new townhomes, now available for rent.

$595 +UTILITIES

- Underground Heated Garage
- Wall to Wall Carpet
- Storage/Laundry Facilities in Building
- Heat and Hot Water Included
- $300 Security Deposit
- 1st Month Rent Free
- Health Club Facilities Available

SATURDAY DECEMBER 14 10am–4pm
SUNDAY DECEMBER 15 11am–4pm

THE
VILLAGE HIGHLANDS 451-7142
5-1 Avon Parkway, Liverpool (Off Morgan Rd.)

4. *News releases* on unique features of your complex or tenants may be helpful. For example, a "Clothing Optional" apartment complex would be newsworthy.

5. *Apartment Guides* are magazines listing apartment communities, showing a picture, amenities, rental range, address, and phone number. The publications are distributed through a variety of conventional outlets including supermarkets, convenience stores, banks and savings associations, restaurants, newsstands, hotels and motels, airports, car rental agencies, corporate personnel departments, chambers of commerce, and high-traffic retail locations.

Depending on local market conditions, these guides are published annually/quarterly/monthly. Some are very high-quality publications featuring full-color pictures on glossy paper.

Marshall's *THE Apartment MAP AND VIDEO™*, headquartered in Irvine, California, is a pioneer in both the directory format and more recently the large fold-out map format, which pinpoints apartment location, lists outstanding features, and includes full-color pictures of each apartment.

Their company also produces and distributes videotaped tours of local apartments (short showing of several apartments on a single videotape) so prospective tenants can review several communities at once (in the comfort of their own home or office) before deciding which to actually visit. These services are not only time-saving, but a major advantage to those relocating into the area from other parts of the nation/world. The MAP™ publication and VIDEO TOURS™ are available at major hotels/motels, corporate personnel offices, retail outlets, relocation companies, and video rental stores.

Sales Presentation

The onsite manager's appearance should be neat, clean, and businesslike. First impressions are very important. The manager should know the product and the community. (Is there a church nearby? Schools?) A good onsite manager will develop rapport with the prospect, helping the prospect relax. Care should be exercised in prequalifying the tenant to avoid actual or perceived discrimination. A traffic list is usually kept to check prospects coming through the complex. A rule of thumb is for the manager to close (rent) one out of every three prospects.

Onsite managers are not born good salespeople, and in many cases have to be properly trained. Training firms such as *Dorothy Gourley & Associates* in Newport Beach, California, will visit (shop) the complex, grading the manager's sales presentation for the property manager. Such firms will then set up a training session to correct the manager's weak areas, followed by another "shop" to see if the manager is following through on learned skills. A good property manager will "spot-check" managers through phone calls to ascertain that onsite personnel are following procedures regarding sales presentation and avoiding discrimination.

A good salesperson helps the prospect make decisions by asking positive questions: "Would you prefer the brown carpet or the gray?" "Would you like to move in on the first or the fifteenth?" The key is to ask questions which elicit a response, not just a yes or no answer. What is the prospect's hot button? By learning the prospect's objections, they can be overcome by emphasizing other positive amenities. To overcome objections the manager should never argue, but switch to a positive benefit. For example, if the tenant complains that the bathtub is too small, the manager might say, "Most of our residents like this model, and we do have a spa next to the pool." If, however, the prospect insists on a large bathtub, a salesperson should never promise something that can't be delivered, as an owner normally will not bear this unnecessary cost. In the same vein, selling doesn't stop when the renter moves in. Renewals and referrals by existing residents are the best way to achieve a high occupancy rate. Be courteous and responsive to tenant requests. Sometimes the manager forgets that the renter is the customer. Without the renter, the property manager would not have a job and the owner would not have a business.

Another marketing training tool is a day-long seminar developed by Mitch Cazier of Santa Ana, California. Mitch brings together 20 or 30 of his onsite managers at a particular complex. The morning session is devoted to role-playing with some managers acting as prospective tenants while others act as monitors and still others attempt to rent an apartment. Objects such as smelly, half-eaten sandwiches are left in a cupboard to create a problem to which the manager must respond. Discussion of these responses is held during a roundtable session at the end of the role-playing. The afternoon session is devoted to policies and procedures and their implementation. An example is keeping rental tools available in one packet prior to the prospect's arrival. These tools include credit application, rental agreement, brochures, etc.

Pricing an Apartment

Some property managers think all similar units in a complex need to have the same rental rate. Astute managers charge higher prices based on amenities (view and desirability) and usually charge existing renters slightly less than incoming renters, the rate for new tenants being constantly increased with each vacancy. Annual or semi-annual increases are given existing residents to keep them at market. Increasing the rents for new tenants also tests the market.

Aggressive Rents vs. Vacancies

If there is never a vacancy, rents are probably too low. Conversely, if rents are too high, a serious vacancy problem will occur. For example, let's examine a 50-unit building with no vacancies with the idea of raising rents. The property manager needs to determine how high the vacancy factor can increase before vacancy losses exceed additional rental income. The following example, while increasing the vacancy factor, shows the ensuing income and valuation increase after an appropriate rent increase.

No Increase

Before increase: 50 units @ $550/month = $27,500/month

Rent Increase

After increase ($50/month, or a 9% increase): 50 units at $600/month = $30,000/month

Zero vacancy: monthly income $27,500	5% vacancy: monthly income $28,500 Additional income: $1,000/month
Annual income $330,000	Annual income $342,000
Assume 30% operating expense: $99,000	Assume 30% operating expense: $102,600
NOI: $231,000	NOI: $239,400
Assume cap. rate of 10%	Assume cap. rate of 10%
Valuation: $2,310,000	Valuation: $2,394,000
	Increased value: $84,000

The *"break-even"* vacancy rate in this example would be approximately 8.5%.

The example shows that by raising rent approximately 9% ($50/month), the monthly income will increase by $1,000/month with the vacancy rate increasing from zero to 5%. The vacancy rate must increase to 8.5% before losses from vacancy would exceed the additional income. The property manager, as exemplified by a 10% cap. rate, has also increased the value of the complex by $84,000. This value increase is over four times more than the typical management fee. "Good management doesn't cost, it pays" should be the motto of the property manager.

Determining Base Rent

Since not all apartments are alike, a property manager has to compare apples with apples. This can be done through the use of a comparison guide. Information is collected by using the Rental Survey Form discussed in Chapter 5. By combining the property manager's knowledge of the market area, including factors such as neighborhood vacancy rate and income data, an indicated rent is determined. This is accomplished by comparing by grid similar properties to the subject property after making adjustments for differences such as amenities, age, unit size, etc. The grid sometimes makes it confusing as to whether to add or subtract. If the property manager remembers the following formula, he/she should have no problem.

Subject property better = add (+) to comparable rent

Subject property poorer = subtract (–) from comparable rent

By using the above formulas, rents can be adjusted on the comparable properties. In the example below of 2-bedroom, 1-bath units, Comparable #1 does not have a fireplace and it is determined that renters would pay $5.00 per month in rent for this amenity. Thus, we add $5.00 to the comparable's rent to determine rent comparison for the subject property.

Many times students are confused when to add or subtract on the comparables. Remember that all the additions (+) and subtractions (–) are made to the comparable property and not to the subject property. Some formulas to help you remember would be:

SBA — Subject better, add to comparable

SPS — Subject worse, subtract from comparable

Comparable #2 has a fireplace, as does the subject property, thus there is no advantage and the grid is marked 0, which indicates equal comparison.

If the adjustments are added to and subtracted from present rents, the indicated subject property rent as compared to Comparable #1 is $525 per month, and $510–520 per month by Comparable #2. Since the subject property rent is only $475 per month, the property manager should consider raising the rent to the $515-520 rental range.

Figure 7-7. Comparison Grid

Amenities	Subject (Your Property)	Comparable #1 (Competition)		Comparable #2 (Competition)	
Pool	Yes	No	+ 10	No	+ 10
Fireplace	Yes	No	+ 5	Yes	0
Garage	No	Yes	– 10	No	0
Utilities	No	No	0	Yes	– 30
		Total:	+ 5	Total:	– 20
Current Rents	$475	$520		$530	
		+ 5		– 20	
Adjusted indicated rents:		$525		$510	
Proposed rental rates: $515 for subject building					

Resident Selection

Prudent property managers know that poor selection is the root of most tenant problems. If the vacancy rate is 5% and the delinquency rate is 7%, the loss rate is 12% per month (financial vacancy loss). Eviction cases are in many instances more costly than having the unit vacant as the tenant uses utilities, creates wear and tear, and causes legal costs to be incurred by the owner. Winning in court, if the tenant is indigent or unemployed, is a hollow victory as the property manager seldom collects the judgment. Remember, the primary purpose of an eviction proceeding is to regain control of the unit.

No car dealer would give the keys to a new $50,000 Mercedes without thoroughly checking the buyer's credit. Likewise, a prudent manager should not give the keys to a $50,000 apartment unit to a prospective tenant without doing a proper credit check.

In Chapter 3 (Leases), residential credit-checking procedures to ensure proper tenant screening were reviewed. CAR Form RA-14 is preferred by the author as it has both credit application (Figure 7-8) and rental agreement (Figure 7-11) on one sheet of paper (front and back).

Questions to Ask Prospects

Gleaning information from the tenant application (Figure 7-8), the property manager should try to spot "red flags" or inconsistencies. Sample questions follow.

1. *"Our company policy is to thoroughly check references with past landlords and employers as well as TRW and UDR credit reports. Is there anything you would like to tell me that might show up as unfavorable?"* Many prospects find an excuse to leave ("My wife needs to fill out the application") when this question is asked. It is a great pre-screening technique to eliminate the professional "deadbeat." (See Figure 7-12.)

2. *"Do you have your own telephone? What is the number?"* A telephone is no longer a luxury but a necessity. Prospects without a phone frequently have been cut off by "Ma Bell."

3. *"Our company policy is that the rent shouldn't exceed 30% of the prospect's gross income."* FHA and VA lenders use similar qualifying criteria. Using this basic criterion, a person who earns $2,000 per month could rent a $600 apartment. If this person rented a $1,000 apartment, only 50% of his/her income would be left for food, clothing, transportation, medical, etc. The prospect would probably be a poor credit risk or would have to bring in friends to share the rent, thus overcrowding the apartment. Recurring expenses also have to be taken into consideration. Even if the rent does not exceed 30% of the prospect's income, the rent might be too high if the prospect has an overabundance of car loan or other installment payments.

4. *"Your credit history doesn't qualify you for this apartment. Can you get a parent or relative to co-sign the lease and sign a personal guarantee?"* This allows renting, if so desired, to younger renters, single heads of household, and welfare families who otherwise would not qualify because of credit history or low income. The credit of the "personal guarantor" should also be checked.

These are only a few questions to ask. Points can be given for each question with a cutoff level determined to help rank prospective tenants. Credit criteria must be applied equally to all prospects to avoid actual or perceived discrimination.

This author has the philosophy that 95% of renters are good and will pay their rent. That leaves only 5% who are "deadbeats." (This 5% is usually evicted every three months (four times a year), so that 5% multiplied by four equals 20%.) Through careful selection these "deadbeats" will gravitate to property managers and owners who do not properly check credit or read this book.

Skip-Tracing

"Skip-tracing" is the art of tracking down deadbeat tenants who leave owing unpaid rent. Start the process with the information contained in the rental application. Some additional hints include:

1. DMV — if you have a driver's license number, a copy of a person's DMV file can be ordered which may contain a current address.

2. Post office — send a blank letter and write on the envelope the phrase "do not forward — address correction requested." For a small fee the new address can be obtained at the post office.

3. County Tax Assessor's Office — if the tenant owns some real property, check the assessor's records for a listed address.

4. Voter registration — call the County Registrar's office to obtain the registered address.

5. Credit bureau checks — you have the tenant's social security number and an authorization for a credit check on the rental application the tenant signed when initially applying to rent. Run another check to find a current address.

6. Hanes-Polk XX Directories — lists phone numbers, addresses, and sometimes place of employment and is updated regularly. Available at public libraries.

7. State agencies — was the tenant a real estate licensee, beautician, contractor, etc.? These professions require a state license.

8. Employer — ask for new address or new work number.

Additionally, several collection bureaus will accept tenant delinquency for collection. Credit bureau collection charges are about 15% to 50% of the amount collected, depending on the difficulty of the case.

Security Deposits

The most common dispute between the property manager and renters is the handling of security deposits. In many cases the manager/owner does not realize that the "deposit" is rightfully the resident's if all the conditions (such as proper notice and cleaning of the apartment) are met.

What is the Law?

California Civil Code Section 1950.5 covers the handling of security deposits. Some of its highlights are as follows:

1. *Maximum Amount of Security Deposit*

   a. Unfurnished = 2 months rent

   b. Furnished = 3 months rent

2. *Refundable.* All deposits are refundable, and it is unlawful — regardless of what it is called — to have a non-refundable deposit. Example: $200 move-out or move-in charge, cleaning deposit, key deposit, etc. must all be refundable.

3. *Returning of Deposit.* By law, the former resident is entitled to an accounting of all deductions. Refund of the balance must be made within 21 days of the resident's moving out.

4. *Penalties.* If the owner/manager in bad faith fails to provide an accounting or return the deposit, the renter can receive up to $600 statutory damages in Small Claims Court.

5. *What is Deductible?* "Normal wear and tear" is not deductible. Non-payment of rent, tenant-caused holes in walls, unreturned keys, or a dirty apartment are just a few of the items that can be charged to the renter. Deductibility is, however, a gray area that judges interpret differently. The prudent property manager should resolve these deposit disputes before he goes to court in order to reduce hassle and save time. Strict interpretation of the deductibility law could lead to a residents' grapevine passing the word that the property manager will always find a speck of dust on a window sill and charge for a full clean-up. If the residents have no hope of getting back their security deposit, they may automatically leave the apartment a mess, resulting in a longer turnaround time and an increased vacancy rate. This author's best advice is to use the Golden Rule: Treat the tenant as you yourself would want to be treated.

Move-In/Move-Out Form

In order to reduce conflicts and misunderstanding, the property manager should use a move-in/move-out form (Figure 7-9). This is similar to the walk-through form realtors use when selling a house. When the apartment is first rented, the onsite manager and tenant go through the move-in checklist and mark down any problems; i.e., "hole in master bedroom door." The form is dated, signed by both resident and manager, and a copy given to the resident. The manager puts the original in the resident's file.

Figure 7-8. Tenant Application*

APPLICATION TO RENT AND RENTAL DEPOSIT
CALIFORNIA ASSOCIATION OF REALTORS® (CAR) STANDARD FORM

Application to rent property at _____

Full name of applicant _____	Co-applicant/spouse _____
Phone (____) ____ Date of birth ___/___/___	Phone (____) ____ Date of birth ___/___/___
Present address _____	Present address _____
City/State/Zip _____	City/State/Zip _____
Name of current landlord/manager _____	Name of current landlord/manager _____
Landlord/manager's phone (____)	Landlord/manager's phone (____)
How long at present address _____	How long at present address _____
Reason for leaving _____	Reason for leaving _____

If present address is less than one year, list prior address and indicate landlord/managers name and phone number: _____

Name(s) of all other occupant(s) and relationship to applicant: _____

An application to rent is required for any occupant 18 years of age or over.

Pet(s) (number and type) _____

Applicant: Soc. Sec. No. _____ Driver's license no. _____ State ____ Expires ____

How long with this employer _____

Present employer _____

Employer's address _____ City _____ Zip _____ Phone (____)

Gross income $ _____ per _____

Position or title _____

Other income $ _____ per _____ Source _____

Auto make _____ Model _____ Year _____ License no. _____ State _____ Color _____

If present employment is less than one year, list immediate prior employment information: _____

Co-applicant: Soc. Sec. No. _____ Driver's license no. _____ State ____ Expires ____

How long with this employer _____

Present employer _____

Employer's address _____ City _____ Zip _____ Phone (____)

Gross income $ _____ per _____

Position or title _____

Other income $ _____ per _____ Source _____

Auto make _____ Model _____ License no. _____ State of registry _____ Color _____

If present employment is less than one year, list immediate prior employment information: _____

Do you plan to use liquid filled furniture? ☐ No ☐ Yes Type _____

Has either applicant been a party to an unlawful detainer action or filed bankruptcy within the last seven years? ☐ No ☐ Yes

If yes, explain _____

In case of emergency, person to notify _____ Relationship _____

Address _____ City _____ Zip _____ Phone (____)

Credit Information

Appl./Co-appl.	Name of creditor	Account number	Monthly payment	Balance Due

Bank Account Information

Appl./Co-appl.	Name of bank	Address/branch	Account number	Type of account

Applicant(s) represent(s) the above information to be true, correct and complete and hereby authorize(s) verification of the information provided, including obtaining credit report(s) at the actual cost of $_____ to be paid by applicant(s). The cost of the credit report is not a deposit or rent, and will not be applied to future rent or refunded, even if the application to rent is declined. Applicant(s) understand(s) that the landlord may terminate any rental agreement entered into for any misrepresentation made above.

Date _____ Time _____	Date _____ Time _____
Applicant _____ Phone (day) _____ Phone (eve.) _____	Co-applicant _____ Phone (day) _____ Phone (eve.) _____

Applicant(s) has/have deposited the Sum of _____ Dollars $_____

evidenced by: ☐ Cash ☐ Cashier's Check ☐ Personal Check ☐ or _____, to be held uncashed until approval of the application to rent, as deposit

to _____ at a monthly rent of $_____ .

on the property located at _____

The property to be occupied only by the person(s) named in the application. In the event the application to rent is not approved within _____ days, this deposit shall be returned to applicant(s). If approved, the ☐ month-to-month rental, ☐ lease, or ☐ other _____

shall commence on _____, 19___. Additional Terms: _____

TOTAL SUMS DUE PRIOR TO OCCUPANCY:

Rent for the period _____ to _____	$_____	
Security deposit (not applicable toward last months rent)	$_____	
Other _____	$_____	
Other _____	$_____	
Total	$_____	
Less amount received above	$_____	
Balance due, on or before _____, 19___	$_____	

In addition to the above, applicant(s) has/have paid $_____ for the credit report(s) and agree(s) to execute the lease or rental agreement on the reverse. The undersigned has/have read the foregoing and acknowledges receipt of a copy.

_____ _____ | _____ _____
Applicant | Date | Co-applicant | Date

Figure 7-9. Move-In/Move-Out Form

RESIDENCE CONDITION CHECK LIST

Residence_____ Apt. #_____

	MOVE-IN	MOVE-OUT		MOVE-IN	MOVE-OUT
LIVING & DINING ROOMS			BEDROOMS		
Carpets			Closet		
Drapes			Doors		
Windows			Carpet		
Screens			Drapes		
Light fixtures			Windows		
Walls/Ceilings			Screens		
Doors			Misc.		
Misc.					
KITCHEN			PATIO/BALCONY		
Cabinets			Weed Free		
Sink			Fence/Rails		
Counter Tops			Patio doors		
Drawers			Screens		
Floors			Clean		
Dishwasher			Misc.		
Garbage Disposal			HALL		
Refrigerator			Closets		
Range/oven/burners			Carpets		
Hood/fan/filters			Misc.		
Misc.			SMOKE DETECTOR		
BATHROOM(s)			LOCKS & HINGES		
Tub					
Track			MOVE-IN REMARKS:_____		
Shower door					
Medicine Cabinet					
Toilet					
Sinks					
Towel Racks			MOVE-OUT REMARKS:_____		
Counter					
Floor					
Drains					
Misc.					

MOVE-IN DATE _____

_____   _____
MANAGER   RESIDENT

MOVE-OUT DATE _____

_____   _____
MANAGER   RESIDENT

FORWARDING ADDRESS _____

_____

_____

_____

J.D. PROPERTY MANAGEMENT, INC.
P. O. BOX 1438
COSTA MESA, CA. 92626

Figure 7-10.

```
          RESIDENT REFUND AND LIABILITY STATEMENT


NAME: _____     RESIDENT ADDRESS: _____

FORWARDING ADDRESS: _____   _____

_____  RESIDENT NUMBER: _____

_____  RESIDENT NAME: _____

TODAY'S DATE: _____    MOVE OUT DATE: _____
```

INITAL SECURITY DEPOSIT PAID $ _____	COMPUTER INPUT ONLY:
CHARGES TO TENANT:	PORTION TO REFUND TO TENANT WITH CHECK
Apartment cleaning (_____)	
Carpet cleaning (_____)	A. Debit Ck-Amt Credit Ck-Amt
Drapery cleaning (_____)	
Painting (_____)	2003 1103
Carpet (_____)	
Drapery (_____)	
Exterminating (_____)	
Glass/screens (_____)	PORTION TO REDISTRIBUTE TO CLIENT
Other ~ (_____)	
Legal (_____)	
_____ (_____)	B. Debit Tot.Dist.Amt.Credit Tot.Dist.
_____ (_____)	
Utilities (_____)	2003 1103
TOTAL CHARGES ($ _____)	
	DISTRIBUTION AGAINST EXPENSES
TOTAL DEPOSIT REFUND OR	
BALANCE DUE (circle one) $ _____	C. Debit Exp. Amt. Credit Exp. Amt.
LESS RENT DUE: (insufficient	1002
30 day notice) $ _____	
_____ days @ _____ $ _____	
PLUS RENT REFUND:	
_____ days @ _____ $ _____	
(rent paid through _____)	
TOTAL CHECK OR BALANCE DUE: $ _____	COMPUTER INPUT NOTES:
(circle correct item) Ck. No. _____	
	A + B must equal amount of total S.D.
REMARKS: _____	The total distribution of C must equal
_____	the amount of B.
_____	If manual check has been written for
_____	S.D. refund use B & C only and in C
_____	credit 6540 for amount that was refunde·
	(Manual check should Dr. 6540)
J.D. PROPERTY MANAGEMENT, INC.	
P. O. BOX 1438	
COSTA MESA, CA. 92626	

Upon move-out, the apartment is reinspected by both parties and the form is again dated and signed. Without this form, especially if the renting manager is no longer with the complex, there is no way to disprove the renter's claim of existing damage when he/she initially moved in.

Deposit Return Form

The manager prepares the resident refund and liability statement (Figure 7-10) from the move-in/move-out form. This disposition must be prepared and mailed within 21 days of move-out to the forwarding address given by the renter. If no forwarding address was left, the disposition may be mailed to the renter's last known address (i.e., the apartment itself). A check for any monies to be returned should accompany the form.

Security Deposit vs. Last Month's Rent

These terms are often confusing to both property managers and renters. The prudent manager should use only the term "security deposit" as it is more inclusive and can be used for unpaid rent, cleaning, damage, improper notice, etc. If the property manager collects the last month's rent, it can be used only for the last month's rent. The amount of the security deposit should be different from the monthly rent to avoid confusion. For example, if the rent is $500 the security deposit could be $475. This also avoids the problem of having to increase the "last month's rent" each time there is a rental increase. In addition, it helps the tenant understand the difference between "last month's rent" and a security deposit. When determining the maximum security deposit, the last month's rent is included.

Interest on Security Deposits

At present, state law in California does not require payment of interest to a tenant on security deposits. However, some localities within the state do have this requirement.

Residential landlords failing to properly account for security deposits within 21 days after a tenant vacates will thereafter be liable for up to $600 in damages and the portion of the security deposit due, plus monthly interest at 2% (Civil Code 1950.5 [k]).

Rental Agreement

As with credit applications, we recommend CAR (California Association of Realtors) Form RA-14 for the rental agreement (Figure 7-11). Both credit application and rental agreement are printed on the same 8-1/2 x 14" sheet. The rental

Figure 7-11. Rental Agreement

RESIDENTIAL MONTH-TO-MONTH RENTAL AGREEMENT
THIS IS INTENDED TO BE A LEGALLY BINDING AGREEMENT — READ IT CAREFULLY.
CALIFORNIA ASSOCIATION OF REALTORS® (CAR) STANDARD FORM

_____, California _____ 19____
_____, Landlord, and
_____, Tenant, agree as follows:

1. **PROPERTY:** Landlord rents to Tenant and Tenant hires from Landlord the "premises" described as: _____
_____. Inventory of personal property, if any, to be attached.

2. **TERM:** The term shall commence on _____ 19____, and shall continue from month to month. This rental agreement may be terminated at any time by either party by giving written notice 30 days in advance.

3. **RENT:** Tenant agrees to pay $ _____ rent per month, payable in advance, on the _____ day of each month and
$_____ representing prorated rent from _____, 19____ to _____, 19____ .

4. **LATE CHARGE:** Tenant acknowledges that late payment of rent may cause Landlord to incur costs and expenses, the exact amount of such costs being extremely difficult and impractical to fix. Such costs may include, but are not limited to, processing and accounting expenses, late charges that may be imposed on Landlord by terms of any loan secured by the property, costs for additional attempts to collect rent, and preparation of notices. Therefore, if any installment of rent due from Tenant is not received by Landlord within _____ calendar days after date due, Tenant shall pay to Landlord an additional sum of $ _____ as a late charge which shall be deemed additional rent. The Parties agree that this late charge represents a fair and reasonable estimate of the costs that Landlord may incur by reason of Tenant's late payments. Acceptance of any late charge shall not constitute a waiver of Tenant's default with respect to the past due amount, or prevent Landlord from exercising any other rights and remedies under this agreement, and as provided by law.

5. **PAYMENT:** The rent shall be paid at _____ .

6. **SECURITY DEPOSIT:** $_____ as a security deposit has been received. Landlord may use therefrom such amounts as are reasonably necessary to remedy Tenant's default in the payment of rent, to repair damages caused by Tenant, or by a guest or a licensee of the Tenant, to clean the premises, if necessary, upon termination of tenancy, and to replace or return personal property or appurtenances exclusive of ordinary wear and tear. If used toward rent or damages during the term of tenancy, Tenant agrees to reinstate said total security deposit upon five days written notice delivered to Tenant in person or by mail. No later than two weeks after the Tenant has vacated the premises, the Landlord shall furnish the Tenant with an itemized written statement of the basis for, and the amount of, any security received and the disposition of the security and shall return any remaining portion of the security to the Tenant.

7. **UTILITIES:** Tenant agrees to pay for all utilities and services based upon occupancy of the premises and the following charges: _____
_____
except _____ which shall be paid for by Landlord.

8. **CONDITION:** Tenant has examined the premises and all furniture, furnishings and appliances if any, and fixtures including smoke detector(s) contained therein, and accepts the same as being clean, and in operative condition, with the following exceptions: _____
_____

9. **OCCUPANTS:** The premises are for the sole use as a residence by the following named persons **only:** _____
_____

10. **PETS:** No animal, bird or pet shall be kept on or about the premises without Landlord's prior written consent, except _____

11. **USE:** Tenant shall not disturb, annoy, endanger or interfere with other Tenants of the building or neighbors, nor use the premises for any unlawful purposes, nor violate any law or ordinance, nor commit waste or nuisance upon or about the premises.

12. **RULES & REGULATIONS:** Tenant agrees to comply with all CC&R's, Bylaws, reasonable rules or regulations, decisions of owners' association which are at any time posted on the premises or delivered to Tenant, or adopted by owners' association, and to be liable for any fines or charges levied due to violation(s).

13. **MAINTENANCE:** Tenant shall properly use and operate all furniture, furnishings and appliances, electrical, gas and plumbing fixtures and keep them as clean and sanitary as their condition permits. Excluding ordinary wear and tear, Tenant shall notify Landlord and pay for all repairs or replacements caused by Tenant(s) or Tenants invitees' negligence or misuse. Tenant's personal property is not insured by Landlord.

14. **ALTERATIONS:** Tenant shall not paint, wallpaper, add or change locks or make alterations to the property without Landlord's prior written consent.

15. **KEYS:** Tenant acknowledges receipt of_____ keys to premises and_____ .
At Tenant's expense, Tenant may re-key existing locks and shall deliver duplicate keys to Landlord upon installation.

16. **ENTRY:** Upon not less than 24 hours notice, Tenant shall make the premises available during normal business hours to Landlord, authorized agent or representative, for the purpose of entering to (a) make necessary or agreed repairs, decorations, alterations or improvements or supply necessary or agreed services, or (b) show the premises to prospective or actual purchasers, mortgagees, tenants, or contractors. In an emergency, Landlord, authorized agent or representative may enter the premises, at any time, without prior permission from Tenant.

17. **ASSIGNMENT & SUBLETTINGS:** Tenant shall not let or sublet all or any part of the premises nor assign this agreement or any interest in it.

18. **POSSESSION:** If Tenant abandons or vacates the premises, Landlord may terminate this agreement and regain lawful possession.

19. **ATTORNEY FEES:** In any action or proceeding arising out of this agreement, the prevailing party shall be entitled to reasonable attorney's fees and costs.

20. **WAIVER:** The waiver of any breach shall not be construed to be a continuing waiver of any subsequent breach.

21. **NOTICE:** Notice to Landlord may be served upon Landlord or Manager at_____ .

22. **ESTOPPEL CERTIFICATE:** Within 10 days after written notice, Tenant agrees to execute and deliver an estoppel certificate as submitted by Landlord acknowledging that this agreement is unmodified and in full force and effect or in full force and effect as modified and stating the modifications. Failure to comply shall be deemed Tenants acknowledgement that the certificate as submitted by Landlord is true and correct and may be relied upon by a lender or purchaser.

23. **ADDITIONAL TERMS AND CONDITIONS:** _____ .

24. **ENTIRE CONTRACT:** Time is of the essence. All prior agreements between the parties are incorporated in this agreement which constitutes the entire contract. Its terms are intended by the parties as a final expression of their agreement with respect to such terms as are included herein and may not be contradicted by evidence of any prior agreement or contemporaneous oral agreement. The parties further intend that this agreement constitutes the complete and exclusive statement of its terms and that no extrinsic evidence whatsoever may be introduced in any judicial or other proceeding, if any, involving this agreement.

25. **ACKNOWLEDGEMENT:** The undersigned have read the foregoing prior to execution and acknowledge receipt of a copy.

Landlord _____ Tenant _____
(or authorized agent)
Landlord _____ Tenant _____

FORM RA-14

OFFICE USE ONLY
Reviewed by Broker or Designee _____
Date _____

SF-Dec-87

agreement lists the parties, terms, and conditions of the rental. It has clauses such as No. 16 which states that the renter shall, upon 24 hours advance notice during normal business hours, allow the property manager or his/her agent to enter the premises. The rental agreement should be signed and dated with a copy given to the resident. Waiver of residents' rights is prohibited by California Civil Code Section 1953, and even if included in the agreement is invalid. Residential landlords must retain rental applications and eviction records for two years. Also, landlords must retain rental records until final determination of any discrimination case has been made (Government Code 12940 and 12942). The property manager, however, must keep records for three years in compliance with Department of Real Estate regulations.

Rent Control

Rent control dates back to World War I. In 1942, the "Emergency Price Control Act" froze rents. In New York City, many of the city's rental units remain under rent control while units added later are covered under rent stabilization. Currently, approximately 200 United States cities have residential rent control, representing 12% of the 30 million units in the nationwide rental market. In California, about half of the state's renters are covered under rent control, including the two major cities of Los Angeles and San Francisco. Many other surrounding cities such as Santa Monica, West Hollywood, and San Jose have even more stringent rent control laws. The social policy that fosters rent control is to: (1) preserve low- and middle-cost housing which, due to the high cost of land in California, has increased new construction costs, (2) prevent displacement due to evictions or not being able to afford the local increased rental rate.

Rent control has traditionally been a local concern ignored by state and federal governments. The City of Santa Monica, in order to help the majority of its elderly residents, *could not* regulate the price of groceries, clothes, gasoline, etc., but had the power to regulate rents. The federal government in 1981 spent $27 billion on low-cost housing, but only $11 billion in 1986. This decrease adds more pressure for rent control and passes the burden on to the local government and the private sector (the landlord).

In areas of non-rent control, the landlord has benefited as many lenders and builders have curtailed building more apartments due to the threat of rent control, thus increasing existing rents. Many units that have been under rent control for ten or more years (such as New York City), have been abandoned, which reduces the existing rental stock.

Two major United States Supreme Court decisions (see Chapter 14) have upheld a city's powers to regulate rents. Only state and/or federal intervention will repeal rent control and this will have to involve spending large sums of money to transfer the housing problem back to society as a whole rather than singling out the landlord.

Rent Control Terms

Since each city may have its own rent control ordinance, the property manager should obtain a copy and become thoroughly familiar with all codes where apartments are managed.

Rental rate decontrol — when a tenant willingly moves, the owner may raise the rent to current market rates.

Annual increases — amount of increase allowed each year.

Enforcement — which agency handles enforcement.

Coverage — what types of units are covered; i.e., single-family houses may be exempt.

Managing Small Properties

Small properties are defined as single-family rentals of one to four units. There are over 10 million single-family rentals in the United States, or about 30% of the total number of rental units. Managing small properties is more time-consuming and management-intensive as there is no onsite manager and the central office must deal directly with tenants and vendors. This can take up a great deal of time and disrupt the other property management operations in an office. In order to be successful, a separate division or operation should be established to centralize the single-family operations, headed by an experienced property manager. Some areas to include are:

Rental or leasing — who will handle showing and leasing the houses? Will you charge separate rental fees?

Maintenance — will outside vendors or in-house maintenance personnel be used?

Accounting — centralized computer operation, but who will collect the rent? Or will rents be mailed to the main office?

Management fees — will they be high enough to offset the additional personnel and costs?

Paying of bills — many times the rent check does not cover the expenses and mortgage. How and when will the owner send you additional funds?

Statements to owner — should include rent roll, check register, and monthly profits, if any.

These are a few of the questions that need to be answered to successfully manage smaller properties. A book published by the Institute of Real Estate Management, *Managing Single-Family Homes* by Barbara Holland, CPM, is a good reference source.

Figure 7-12. Credit Profile

Summary

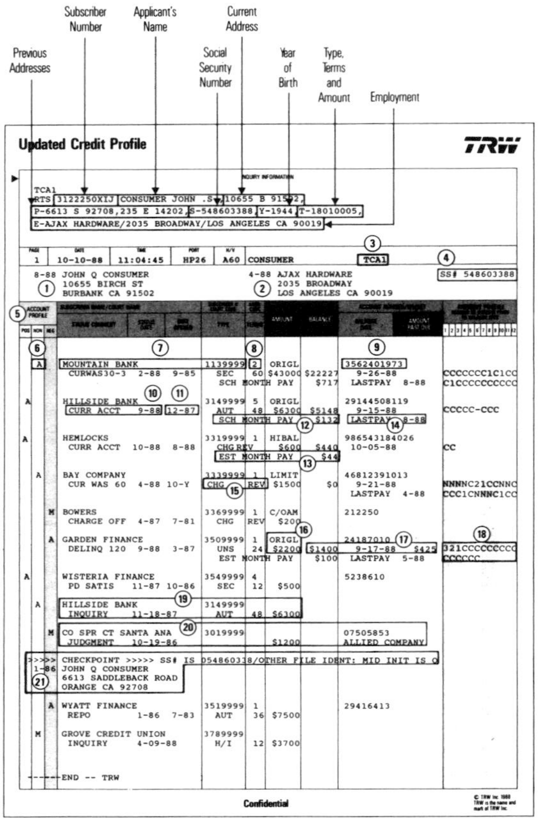

The largest area within the property management field is residential. Federal, state, and local laws that affect the property manager are varied and constantly changing. The property manager needs to consult with attorneys, CPAs, government officials, and organizations such as IREM or local apartment associations to keep abreast of new changes in the law. The classification of multi-family buildings falls into five areas: garden apartments (3-story); mid-rise (4- to 9-story); high-rise (high-density); other (fourplexes); and government-assisted housing (HUD). The property manager, in order to create demand and desirability for an apartment community or building, should be aware of different marketing strategies. These include merchandising, signage and graphics, pricing, advertising, and effective sales presentations.

The property manager needs to balance vacancies versus lower rent. If the complex has no vacancies, rents may be too low and should be increased. When determining base rents, a grid should be completed by comparing similar properties to the subject property. If the subject property is better than the comparable property, add to the rent of the comparable property to determine the rental value of the subject property. If the subject property is poorer than the comparable property, subtract from the rent of the comparable property to determine the rental value of the subject property. For example, if the subject property has a pool with tenant value of $10.00 per month and the comparable property does not, you would add $10.00 to the comparable property rent to determine the rental value of the subject property.

When screening prospective tenants, a credit application should be completed by the applicant. A consumer credit bureau report should be obtained and employment, references, and income level verified. The time and money spent qualifying tenants will reduce delinquencies and save the owner money as well as grief and aggravation in the long run. If a tenant leaves without paying the rent, there are skip-tracing procedures available to locate the tenant's new address. These include: Department of Motor Vehicles, Post Office, voter registration, credit bureaus, Hanes-Polk XX Directory, and current or past employers.

Security deposit laws (California Civil Code 1950.5) require that all deposits be refundable. Within 21 days after move-out, the tenant is entitled to an accounting and return of the balance of the deposit which was not used for unpaid rent or damage caused by the tenant. The property manager should remember the tenant cannot be charged for "normal wear and tear" such as painting if a tenant has lived in the apartment over a year in most instances. A move-in/move-out form should be used, dated and signed by the tenant and manager. It is better to call the security deposit a security deposit, rather than breaking it down into key deposit, last month's rent, cleaning, etc., as these deposits can be used only for that specific purpose. The more generalized term "security deposit" can cover all of these items.

In conclusion, we have examined residential management, the largest single area in the property management field. We have analyzed the types of buildings and their characteristics, market analysis, marketing strategies, sales presentations, pricing of apartments, determining base rent, resident selection, security deposits, and rental agreements. It would be a beneficial learning experience for the reader to answer the case study questions relating to "Whiskey Manor Apartments" at the end of this chapter and subsequent chapters to enhance the practical application of the material and to highlight the presented information and concepts in a "real world" perspective.

NOTES

Chapter 7 Review Questions

1. *The largest area in property management is:*

   a. office building management.
   b. shopping center management.
   c. residential management.
   d. none of the above.

2. *Classifications of multi-family buildings include:*

   a. garden.
   b. mid-rise.
   c. high-rise.
   d. all of the above.
   e. none of the above.

3. *Marketing strategies include:*

   a. merchandising, signage, and advertising.
   b. DRE regulations.
   c. depreciation methods.
   d. all of the above.
   e. none of the above.

4. *In determining base rent, if the subject property is poorer you would:*

   a. add to comparable rent.
   b. subtract from comparable rent.
   c. add to subject rent.
   d. subtract from subject rent.

5. *If subject property has a garage worth $10.00 per month and comparable does not, you would:*

   a. add $10.00 to comparable rent to determine subject rent.
   b. subtract $10.00 from comparable rent.
   c. add $10.00 to subject rent to determine comparable rent.
   d. subtract $10.00 from subject rent.

6. *The prudent property manager should:*

   a. get a credit application filled out and signed.
   b. check with the resident's parents.
   c. check with the resident's best friend.
   d. do none of the above.

7. *The property manager cannot discriminate on the basis of:*

   a. religion.
   b. sex.
   c. color.
   d. age.
   e. all of the above.

8. *All security deposits are:*

   a. non-refundable.
   b. refundable.
   c. last month's rent.
   d. first month's rent.
   e. all of the above.

9. *The move-in/move-out form is used to:*

   a. qualify renters.
   b. evict renters.
   c. return security deposits.
   d. discriminate against renters.

10. *Which is more prudent for the property manager to request?*

    a. Key deposit.
    b. Last month's rent.
    c. Cleaning deposit.
    d. Security deposit.

Chapter 7 Case Study Problem

1. Would you have a model apartment?

2. What would you recommend to improve curb appeal?

3. Would you consider changing the name of the complex? Why or why not?

4. What would you choose for a new name?

5. Would you put up signage? Can you justify the cost?

6. Design a classified ad for apartment rental at "Whiskey Manor."

7. What would you do about the present onsite manager?

8. What training programs would you implement for present or new management?

9. Would you raise, lower, or keep the rents the same?

10. Determine the base rent of the 20-unit apartment complex which we will now call "Civic Center Terrace."

11. How would you change the present security deposit procedure?

12. Would you use a written rental agreement? Explain your reasoning.

Chapter 7
Selected Additional References and Reading

Baisle, Frank, CPM, *Back to Basics with Basile*, Charisma Publications, Indianapolis, IN, 1982.

Blumberg, Richard and James Grow, *The Rights of Tenants*, Avon Publishers, New York, NY, 1979.

California Apartment Association, *California Rental Housing Reference Book*, Sacramento, CA, 1985.

Glassman, Sidney, *New Guide to Residential Management*, National Multi-Housing Council, Washington, D.C., 1984.

Gomer, Duane, CPM, *Creative Apartment Management*, Calabasas, CA, 1978.

Harmon, James, *Apartment Owner/Manager Handbook*, Apartment News Publications, Los Angeles, CA, 1972.

Holco/Zimmerman Multifamily Investment Outlook (Quarterly)
P.O. Box 3000
Denville, NJ 07834

I.D. Checking Guide
Driver License Guide Co.
1492 Oddstad Drive, Department 87
Redwood City, CA 94063

Institute of Real Estate Management, *Income/Expense Analysis — Apartments*, Chicago, IL, 1988.

Kelly, Edward N., CPM: *Practical Apartment House Management*, Institute of Real Estate Management, Chicago, IL, 1980.

Landlord-Tenant Relations Report (Monthly)
CD Publications
100 Summit Building
8555 16th Street
Silver Spring, MD 20910

Moskovit, Myron, Ralph Warner, and Charles Sherman, *Tenants' Rights*, 4th Edition, Nolo Press, Berkeley, CA.

Professional Apartment Management (Monthly)
Brownstone Publications
P.O. Box 4164 Grand Central Station
New York, NY 10163

NOTES

Chapter 8

SHOPPING CENTER MANAGEMENT

Key Terms

Strip center
Neighborhood center
Regional center
Community center
   Percentage lease
Net lease
Trade area
Merchant
  association
Market share
Tenant mix
Tenant selection
Category killers
Kiosk
CAM charges
Robbins v. Pruneyard
Mini-billboards

Food for Thought

"When the going gets tough, the tough go shopping."

Shopping Center Management

Introduction

This chapter will examine and analyze shopping center classifications and characteristics, types of leases, merchant associations, trade area, tenant mix, tenant selection, and common area maintenance. As discussed in Chapter 1, shopping centers are a relatively new phenomenon and did not have a dominant presence until after World War II.

There are more than 35,000 shopping centers nationwide, which represents a 15-fold increase in the last three decades. Shopping center retail sales are approximately $700 billion per year and account for about 55% of all non-automotive retail sales. Leasable space totaled 4.2 billion sq. ft. which equates to 17 square feet of retail space for every U.S. resident. Shopping centers employed almost 10 million workers and generated $25 billion in state sales tax revenue.

Shopping Center Classifications

Strip Center

1. Small in size, consisting of several stores.

2 Usually laid out in a straight line, L, or U shape.

3. Trading area is usually the immediate neighborhood.

4. Convenience stores and 7-11 stores are typical anchor tenants.

5. The function of the strip center is to provide convenient and accessible one-stop shopping. The focus is strictly on location and community convenience.

Neighborhood Center

1. From 25,000 to 125,000 square feet in size.

2. Normally has one anchor (main) tenant such as a supermarket or discount store (Figure 8-1).

3. Trade area up to two miles.

Community Center

1. Size is 125,000 to 300,000 square feet.

2. Contains two or more anchors such as home improvement store, junior department store, discount store, variety store, or supermarket.

3. Trade area is over three miles.

Regional Center

1. Size is up to 1,000,000 square feet.

2. Contains apparel, jewelry, and one or two department stores.

3. Trade area is over five miles.

4. Is often an enclosed mall.

Figure 8-1. Neighborhood Center

Super-Regional Center

1. Size is over 1,000,000 square feet.

2. Is usually an enclosed mall.

3. Contains at least three department stores.

4. Contains specialty women's and men's apparel stores and specialty shops of all kinds.

5. Usually contains fast food locations and one or more restaurants.

6. May contain community or cultural centers; i.e., library, music center, etc.

7. Trade area is 15 miles or more.

Specialty Center

1. Usually small in size with a maximum of 100,000 square feet.

2. No anchor or large tenant.

3. Contains unique stores and boutiques.

4. May contain one or more restaurants.

5. Usually located near high-income areas or major tourist attraction centers.

Other Centers

Promotional, off-price, discount, factory outlet, and "power" centers which flourish through heavy advertising and low prices that produce high-volume-dollar sales are a growing trend.

"Hypermart" is a new retailing concept from France with its first store opening in Dallas, Texas, in 1988. The retail store, which claims to be the largest in the country at 222,000 square feet, is all on one floor. Merchandise ranges from bananas to refrigerators to fine jewelry, a deli, shoe repair shop, and 58 checkout stands. Sales clerks wear roller skates and the store philosophy is to undercut its competition on prices.

Future Trends

1. Anchorless strip centers.

2. Historic preservation theme — Ghirardelli Square in San Francisco.

3. Vertical shopping centers — Watertowner Center in Chicago.

4. Underground centers — Toronto, Canada.

5. Power centers — category killers like Toys 'R Us.

Types of Leases

In shopping centers, the net lease with annual increases is most prevalent. The percentage lease with a minimum base rent is the standard in larger centers and for national tenants. Both the merchant and the landlord want to maximize sales and work in closer harmony. See Chapter 3 for a review of these leases, terms, and clauses. Additional information can be obtained from *A Standard Manual of Accounting for Shopping Center Operations*, published by the Urban Land Institute. Depending on the size of the shopping center, the property manager may or may not do the leasing. Large regional centers usually have a separate leasing agent.

Percentage leases — what constitutes gross sales for percentage-lease purposes? Some additional sources of percentage rent over sales alone would include:

1. Services — such as a clothing store charging extra for alterations or gift wrapping.

2. Equipment set-up — store charges customer extra fees for setting up equipment (such as washing machine installation in the customer's home).

3. Labor charges — auto parts store that charges the customer extra for installing tires, batteries, etc.

4. Maintenance agreements — retail appliance store sells television maintenance contracts when televisions are purchased.

5. Service center charges — retail store does repair work in the customer's home.

Types of percentage leases include:

1. *Percentage-Only:* the amount of rent is pegged to sales. There is no base or minimum rent. A percentage-only lease may be a good option for attracting socially conscious, quality tenants in depressed areas. The negative is that if the business does poorly, there is no minimum rent guarantee.

2. *Variable-Scale:* there is no base rent. The percentage scale may increase or decrease by various conditions. This lease is adaptable to the planning and rehab phases of "turnaround" projects for distressed or problem properties.

3. *Minimum Percentage:* a minimum rent is established that, when added to all other base rents for the property, should cover all ownership expenses. A percentage of sales over a base amount serves as "overage" rent to provide the owner with net additions to annual cash flow and to serve as a hedge against inflation.

4. *Maximum Percentage:* a minimum rent is negotiated. The percentage clause for overage rent may be straight or variable. However, a ceiling or maximum rent is also stipulated. Anchor tenants or franchises with bargaining leverage may pursue or insist upon this type of lease. They may also wish to tie the maximum to an index.

Break Point

The point at which the percentage clause kicks in; the lessor gets a certain percentage of income from sales over the break point. The natural break point is determined by dividing the total base rent by the percentage. For example, if lease space is 1,000 s.f. at $25/s.f. versus 5% percentage clause, the natural break point would be $25,000 ÷ .05, or $500,000.

Merchants Association

Many leases require that the tenant belong to the merchants association. The purpose of the association is to help promote and advertise the merchants collectively and/or centerwide events in order to increase the center's traffic. The owner will usually contribute money and the property manager or staff will help run the association. The property manager must be careful, however, not to allow association meetings to turn into a gripe session. The merchants association is controlled and managed by the store owners. Usually the property manager acts only in an advisory capacity. In larger centers the association may be run by a marketing director whose background is in advertising and public relations. Marketing funds are replacing merchants associations in some regional centers because the marketing director administers the fund with complete control and responsibility, without the need for getting approvals from store managers and owners who may not understand marketing.

Marketing Retail Space

The marketing of a new center, especially a regional center, must start at project conception. Prospective anchor (key) tenants must be convinced that the proposed or existing site will offer sufficient retail sales potential. Unless commitments from anchor tenants are obtained prior to development, financing the project will be difficult.

Trade Area

The trade area is the area from which 70-80% of the typical retail sales will be attracted. A regional center usually needs a primary trade area of at least 150,000 population. Driving time must usually be less than 20 minutes, depending on the proximity to competing centers and customer loyalty to certain stores.

Figure 8-2.

```
                    SUMMARY OF PERCENTAGE RENT DUE


             For the Month of:  _____



Gross Cash Sales                      $ _____
Gross Credit Sales                      _____
Other Gross Receipts                    _____
      Total Gross Receipts for month          $ _____
Less:   cash refunds/rebates          $ _____
          credit losses                 _____
          sales and use taxes           _____
      Adjusted Gross Receipts for month       $ _____
      Percentage Rent Rate                    x_____%
      Percentage Rent                         $ _____


      Less Minimum Rent Paid                  $ _____

Percentage Rent Due:                          $ _____



I certify that the above information is true and correct to the best
of my knowledge and belief.


_____    _____    _____
By                                Title           Date
```

Topographical factors, including natural barriers such as rivers, mountains, airports, and railroad tracks, may be a barrier to the trade area. A major center may also have a secondary trade area from which customers are attracted. This area may extend 30-50 miles and having a driving time of up to almost one hour. See Figure 8-3.

Rental Rates

Rental rates for retail commercial space vary depending on location. Location of retail enterprises depends on the need for traffic, either foot or vehicular. For example, it has been customary for banks to be located in the high-rent, prime space of the first floor. In today's society, with the advent of checks and credit cards, the majority of banking transactions are done by mail, courier, phone, or computer and no longer require physical pedestrian traffic to a bank. Thus, some banks are locating in less desirable locations, such as the second floor of downtown office buildings, in order to reduce rental costs.

A recent survey shows that E. 57th (New York City) has the highest ground-floor retail rents in the world, at $425 per square foot per year. In second place is Tokyo's Ginza at $400 per square foot. Third is Fifth Avenue (New York City) at $375 per square foot per year. An active leasing program may involve tasteful signage, "cold calling" existing desirable local merchants in other locations, soliciting broker assistance, contacting other property managers who may have good tenants

Figure 8-3. Trade Area

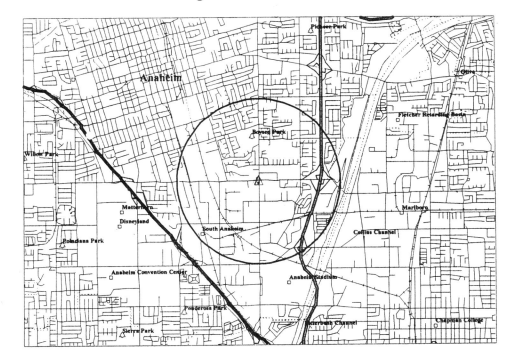

Figure 8-4. Computerized Data

```
DEMOGRAPHIC TRENDS: 1980-90-95          URBAN DECISION SYSTEMS, INC.
ANAHEIM,CA:EAST BALL RD & STATE COLLEGE
1.0 MILE RING


                          1980 Census      1990 Est.      1995 Proj.
POPULATION                     13646          14275          14564
   In Group Quarters              51             62             64

HOUSEHOLDS                4861    %      4968    %      5012    %
   1 Person                925   19.0   1146   23.1   1230   24.5
   2 Person               1610   33.1   1660   33.4   1684   33.6
   3-4 Person             1699   34.9   1678   33.8   1681   33.5
   5+ Person               628   12.9    484    9.7    418    8.3
Avg Hshld Size            2.80           2.86           2.89

FAMILIES                  3631           3520           3427
                                 %              %              %
RACE: White              12713   93.2  12585   88.2  12477   85.7
      Black                156    1.1    231    1.6    282    1.9
      Amer. Indian         108    0.8    204    1.4    252    1.7
      Asian/Pacific Islndr  540   4.0   1015    7.1   1255    8.6
      Other*               128    0.9    241    1.7    297    2.0
SPANISH/HISPANIC          1608   11.8   2324   16.3   2727   18.7

                                 %              %              %
AGE:   0 -  5              859    6.3    901    6.3    801    5.5
       6 - 13            1518   11.1   1270    8.9   1168    8.0
      14 - 17            1126    8.3    839    5.9    831    5.7
      18 - 20             955    7.0    807    5.7    813    5.6
      21 - 24            1061    7.8   1033    7.2   1020    7.0
      25 - 34            2158   15.8   2340   16.4   2118   14.5
      35 - 44            1838   13.5   2341   16.4   2387   16.4
      45 - 54            1865   13.7   2119   14.8   2619   18.0
      55 - 64            1456   10.7   1533   10.7   1601   11.0
      65 +                810    5.9   1092    7.6   1204    8.3
   Median Age             30.8           34.8           37.2

MALES                     6777    %     7153    %     7325    %
       0 - 20             2255   33.3   1944   27.2   1844   25.2
      21 - 44             2559   37.8   2964   41.4   2899   39.6
      45 - 64             1647   24.3   1785   25.0   2066   28.2
      65 +                 316    4.7    460    6.4    516    7.0

FEMALES                   6869    %     7123    %     7239    %
       0 - 20             2203   32.1   1874   26.3   1769   24.4
      21 - 44             2497   36.4   2751   38.6   2626   36.3
      45 - 64             1674   24.4   1867   26.2   2154   29.8
      65 +                 494    7.2    631    8.9    688    9.5

HOUSING UNITS             5007    %
   Owner-Occupied         3147   62.9   3097           3069
   Renter-Occupied        1714   34.2   1870           1944

*1980 other race modified to current Census Bureau definition

Source: 1980 Census, Apr. 1,1990 US Census & UDS Est.     123674 (DTA)
-------------------------------------------------------------------
Urban Decision Systems/PO Box 25953/Los Angeles, CA 90025/(800) 633-9568
```

Figure 8-5. Computerized Data

```
DEMOGRAPHIC TRENDS: 1980-90-95        URBAN DECISION SYSTEMS, INC.
ANAHEIM,CA:EAST BALL RD & STATE COLLEGE
1.0 MILE RING


                       1980 Census     1990 Est.      1995 Proj.

POPULATION                    13646         14275          14564
   In Group Quarters             51            62             64

HOUSEHOLDS             4861    %    4968    %    5012    %
   1 Person             925  19.0   1146  23.1   1230  24.5
   2 Person            1610  33.1   1660  33.4   1684  33.6
 3-4 Person            1699  34.9   1678  33.8   1681  33.5
 5+ Person              628  12.9    484   9.7    418   8.3
Avg Hshld Size          2.80         2.86         2.89

FAMILIES                      3631          3520           3427
                       %             %              %
RACE: White           12713  93.2  12585  88.2  12477  85.7
      Black             156   1.1    231   1.6    282   1.9
      Amer. Indian      108   0.8    204   1.4    252   1.7
      Asian/Pacific Islndr 540 4.0  1015   7.1   1255   8.6
      Other*            128   0.9    241   1.7    297   2.0
SPANISH/HISPANIC       1608  11.8   2324  16.3   2727  18.7

                       %             %              %
AGE:   0 -  5           859   6.3    901   6.3    801   5.5
       6 - 13          1518  11.1   1270   8.9   1168   8.0
      14 - 17          1126   8.3    839   5.9    831   5.7
      18 - 20           955   7.0    807   5.7    813   5.6
      21 - 24          1061   7.8   1033   7.2   1020   7.0
      25 - 34          2158  15.8   2340  16.4   2118  14.5
      35 - 44          1838  13.5   2341  16.4   2387  16.4
      45 - 54          1865  13.7   2119  14.8   2619  18.0
      55 - 64          1456  10.7   1533  10.7   1601  11.0
      65 +              810   5.9   1092   7.6   1204   8.3
   Median Age           30.8         34.8         37.2

MALES                  6777    %    7153    %    7325    %
       0 - 20          2255  33.3   1944  27.2   1844  25.2
      21 - 44          2559  37.8   2964  41.4   2899  39.6
      45 - 64          1647  24.3   1785  25.0   2066  28.2
      65 +              316   4.7    460   6.4    516   7.0

FEMALES                6869    %    7123    %    7239    %
       0 - 20          2203  32.1   1874  26.3   1769  24.4
      21 - 44          2497  36.4   2751  38.6   2626  36.3
      45 - 64          1674  24.4   1867  26.2   2154  29.8
      65 +              494   7.2    631   8.9    688   9.5

HOUSING UNITS          5007    %
   Owner-Occupied      3147  62.9   3097          3069
   Renter-Occupied     1714  34.2   1870          1944

*1980 other race modified to current Census Bureau definition

Source: 1980 Census, Apr. 1,1990 US Census & UDS Est.    123674 (DTA)
---------------------------------------------------------------------
Urban Decision Systems/PO Box 25953/Los Angeles, CA 90025/(800) 633-9568
```

seeking opportunities to expand, and advertising in local and trade publications. Calling prospects from the Yellow Pages can also be appropriate. Attending ICSC (International Council of Shopping Centers) conventions, regional idea exchanges, and deal-making sessions is an ideal way to meet national and sometimes regional chains.

Market Research

Most property managers divide the trade area into census tracts in order to expedite information gathering.

Population and Income Data

Population multiplied by per-capita income equals total income for each census tract. Adding up the census tracts in the trade area gives total area income.

Retail Sales and Income

Because there normally is a close correlation between personal income and the percentage of income spent in retail sales, total retail sales are derived by multiplying trade area income by the ratio of retail sales to personal income.

This demographic analysis can sometimes be misleading. Psychographic analysis may determine, for example, that the trade area is a well-established, conservative, "old money" community that spends less than normal ratios for retail merchandise. Also, proximity to a tourist attraction or vacation resort may contribute many additional shoppers not reflected in demographic studies of permanent residents.

Market Share

The market share should be based on estimates of both existing and projected competition. New centers usually do not create increased buying power, but reallocate expenditures among existing businesses.

Sales Potential of Department Stores

The sales potential of department stores is calculated by using retail trade area statistics to convert dollar expenditures for department stores for census tracts in a trade area to a percentage of total retail sales. Multiplying this percentage times total potential retail sales in the area gives total sales potential for all department stores in the trade area (Figure 8-6).

Figure 8-6.

Type of Revenues	Annual Sales PSF Department Stores	Gross Margin	Annual Sales PSF Mass Merchandisers/ Variety Stores/ Specialty Shops	Gross Margin
RETAILER PRODUCTIVITY BREAKDOWN CHART				
Home Textiles	$116	40%	$120	34%
Toys	166	35	208	25
Housewares Non-Electric	150	30	142	16
Housewares Electric	195	22	242	16
Home Office/Stationery	114	41.4	148	37.8
Photo/Camera	227	18	545	16
Health/Beauty Aids	312	40	110	24
Sewing/Crafts	30.50	40	55	31
Sporting Goods	77	33.4	120	25.2
Home Furnishings	124	36.7	80	29.7
Consumer Electronics	235	19.6	247	15.0

Source: Chain Store Age

Tenant Mix

Shopping centers, even more than office buildings, need to have a balanced, predetermined tenant make-up. The three things that matter most to owners and tenants in a shopping center are traffic, traffic, and more traffic. A good tenant mix helps attract and retain customers. The goal of good tenant mix is having a variety of stores that work well together to enhance the performance of the entire center as well as the success of each individual store. The key is determining what types of tenants work well and have a symbiotic relationship.

When determining the mix, the property manager starts with location, competition, and customer base. These factors determine the center's orientation and the property manager then pursues appropriate anchor and satellite stores that complement each other. For example, with a neighborhood center which has a supermarket as the anchor tenant, desirable satellite tenants would include a florist, stationery or gift store, barber or beauty shop, dry cleaner, pizza parlor, etc. This would be called a "needs-based" center. Research shows that clothes shopping is usually done on a separate shopping trip from needs. In a "fashion center," complementary stores would include shoe stores, men's and women's apparel, children's stores, and accessory stores.

In most instances, the anchor tenant, such as a supermarket, department store, etc., establishes the profile of the center, with the satellite stores adapting to its lead.

Research by Jodi Greenspan of the Knover Management Company showed that putting an athletic shoe store (usually found in a fashion-oriented center) into a need-based center anchored by a supermarket was not successful. A better choice would have been a photo shop or quick printer.

For a regional center with a major department store as the anchor, desirable complementary tenants would include women's and men's apparel stores, jewelry stores, specialty gift shops, etc. The rental rate per square foot is usually higher in a regional center than in a smaller center, so in addition to being complementary the tenants must have either higher markups on their goods or higher sales volumes in order to afford mall space. Regional centers tend to focus on fashion and apparel. Specialty businesses such as furniture stores may wish to cluster together to benefit from a wider draw. While two florists in a center would vie for business, certain retail uses benefit from proximity to one another.

Tenant Selection

Tenant selection is an area that will be discussed again in more depth in Chapter 9. If tenant selection is poor, it will not only cost the center money in lost rents but also in goodwill and image. Empty or boarded-up stores which have gone bankrupt or out of business can stigmatize other merchants. Additional information can be obtained from *Dollars and Cents of Shopping Centers*, published by the Urban Land Institute.

Layout of Shopping Centers

When a center is designed, the physical layout should reflect the types of merchants and customers it hopes to attract. Shopping should be a fun, exciting, convenient event. The developer, owner, and property manager should try to instill that feeling into the center.

Colors

Colors should be bright and cheerful. Use of banners, awnings, and flags which can be changed periodically to create a new and exciting atmosphere is desirable. Sodium vapor lamps are very bright and long lasting, while relatively inexpensive to operate. On the other hand, their eerie yellow light can be unnerving and has become associated with high-crime areas. The new sodium vapor lights have improved color-correction and are now virtually indistinguishable from other parking lot lights, while retaining their cost and illumination benefits.

Figure 8-7. Layout of Center

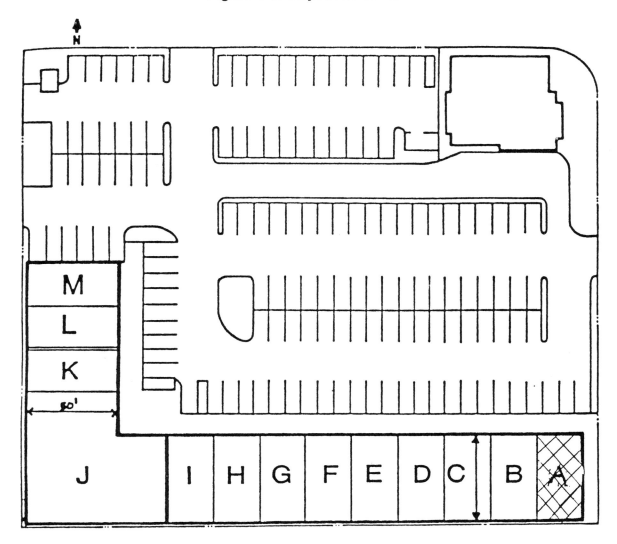

Power Centers

A recent trend is toward power centers in which each retailer is a dominant merchant in its merchandising area. These are called *category killers* and would include such names as Toys 'R Us, Build & Save, and Circuit City. There may be four or five large anchors and only a few small tenants. The term power center comes from the ability to attract customers from a much wider radius than similarly-sized community shopping centers.

Space Planning

Undesirable "bowling alley" centers exist when the developer tries to maximize floor space by making long, narrow retail spaces. Such designs eliminate the large window display space desired by tenants and usually create wasted space in the rear of the stores.

Hide-and-seek spaces located around corners or behind columns are undesirable to the merchant, and confusing and frustrating for the customer.

Enclosed malls are very desirable, and almost a necessity for the regional center today. Lighting, flooring, and decor should be coordinated to make the mall cheerful and bright.

Additional Profit Centers

1. *Kiosks* are free-standing shops (booths) located within a mall or center. Uses include custom signs, keys, costume jewelry, lettered T-shirts, etc. and command a high rental rate per square foot (see Figure 8-8).

2. *Wall shops* are used in older centers that have long, blank walls. They are very shallow stores (ten feet deep) that liven up the center while at the same time producing income (see Figure 8-9).

Figure 8-8. Kiosk

Figure 8-9. Wall Shop

3. *Seasonal holiday tenants* such as a Christmas gift-wrapping booth or a cheese and jam gift center operate within open mall space. The property manager should check existing leases and receive permission if necessary prior to implementing any of the above profit center strategies.

4. *Mini-billboards* within the shopping center (see Figure 8-10).

5. *Outparcels* such as fast food outlets may also be built in the parking lot.

6. *Push carts* can add charm and are space-intensive, with the average size being only 4' x 6'.

7. *Car care malls* offer one-stop shopping for your car. Services include auto parts, tire sales, mufflers, brakes, transmission service, tune-ups, oil and lube, auto sound systems, and gasoline.

Layout Measurements

Space is usually measured from the center wall to the center wall, except that free-standing spaces are measured to the outside of the outer wall. Some developers measure from the end of the eaves or overhang, so the property manager should be familiar with the space sizes and how they were measured.

Figure 8-10. Mini Billboard

Common Area Maintenance

Common area maintenance (CAM) costs are charges for maintaining, improving, and supplying common areas in a retail strip or mall. These costs include taxes, insurance, repairs, landscaping, utilities, etc. and are charged back to the tenant. The concept for CAM is that the manager and tenant need to act in a partnership with each other in order for both to be successful. Each tenant relies on other tenants and a clean, cheerful center to generate consumer traffic and contribute to the overall success of the shared environment. CAM costs can range from $.10 per square foot to over $1.00 per square foot per month. It is important for the tenant to be aware and budget for these costs which are added to the base rent. From the owner's position, being able to pass on these CAM costs and any increases ensures profitability on the lease.

Calculation

A clause allowing additional rent must be included in the lease in order to charge tenants for common area maintenance (CAM) costs.

Pro-ration of costs is usually based on the pro-rated square footage of the space in relation to total rentable area. For example, if the merchant's space is 1,200 square feet and the total center is 100,000 square feet, his share would be 1.2% of the total amount of the CAM bills.

The billing cycle may be monthly, quarterly, or yearly depending upon lease terminology. This author prefers monthly billing based on an annual budget, with year-end adjustments. This improves the owner's cash flow while keeping the merchant's payments equal so he does not get hit with one large bill.

The most desirable and fastest method of calculation is through a computer program designed for the property manager. The hand format (Figure 8-11) is time-consuming. The totals across the bottom must equal the totals from top to bottom as a double-check. The computer format (Figure 8-12) is much faster and easier for the property manager to calculate.

Cost of Calculation

The cost of calculation and CAM supervision is usually charged back to the tenant, if permitted, in the lease, at a percentage of total CAM charges. Supervisory charges such as this range from 5% to 15%. The property manager usually retains these charges for his/her efforts if the management agreement so permits.

Additional CAM Items

1. *Security*. Security should include adequate lighting in both the center and parking lots. Security guards are usually employed in larger centers to protect both customers and merchants.

2. *Insurance*. Insurance policies should have a high liability amount to protect against injury in common areas. Each merchant should have insurance for his own store's contents and interior liability. The property manager should require Certificates of Additionally Insured on both the owner's and tenants' policies.

The property manager must periodically review the entire center and eliminate or minimize every "risk" exposure. Frequently, insurance company representatives are willing to inspect and share their observations and insight. Risk avoidance or management is an important part of every property manager's job.

3. *Real Estate Taxes*. The lease should specify who pays the increased taxes if a property is sold, as the reassessment may increase astronomically the amount included in the CAM expenses and also the building taxes if allocated back to the tenant.

Figure 8-11. CAM Hand Calculation

MONTH _____ YEAR _____

COMP #	RENT	SQ. FT.	KWH	ELECT	GAS	WATER	TRASH	CAM	TAX	INS	TOTAL CAM EXP.	% OF CAM for ADMIN.	MISC.	TOTAL
AMOUNT														
(1)														
(7)		2000												
(2)		925												
(3)		1500												
(4)		1050												
(5)		1200												
(6)		1200												
(7)		1200												
(9)		1200												
(10)		1380												
(11)		1110												
(12)		2400												
(13)		1200												
(14)		1200												
(15)		1200												
(16)		1200												
(17)		1200												
(18)		1580												
(19)		2960												
(8)		1200												
(20)		1000												
(21)		1027												
(22)		973												
(23)		3000												
(24)		3100												
		36005												

Comments:

Figure 8-12. CAM Computer Calculation

BILLING SUMMARY FOR PROPERTY 60001   FROM 12/01/   TO 12/31/

STORE NAME NUMBER		RENT	SQ FT	KWH	ELECT	GAS	WATER	TRASH	CAM	TAX	INS	CAM TOTAL	CAM PCT	CAM CHARGE	SPECIAL ASSESS	TOTAL CHARGE
BILLED AMOUNT:				40183	3777.60	110.82	101.46	368.06	2135.20	1023.83	255.00				945.50	
RATIO:					.09401	.00354	.00282	.01119	.05930	.02844	.00708				.02626	
	(24)	3861.00	3100	0	0.00	0.00	8.74	0.00	183.83	88.16	21.95	302.68	30.26	214.09	81.41	4275.35
2037 10	(7)	0.00	2000	970	91.19	7.08	5.64	22.38	118.60	56.88	14.16	315.93	31.59	150.19	52.52	400.04
2093-95 10	(2)	555.00	925	840	78.97	3.27	2.61	10.35	54.85	26.31	6.55	182.91	18.29	73.14	24.29	780.49
2097 10	3)	1200.00	1500	1985	186.61	5.31	4.23	16.79	88.95	42.66	10.62	355.17	17.75	106.70	39.39	1612.31
2099 5	(4	700.00	1050	2720	255.71	3.72	2.96	11.75	62.27	29.86	7.43	373.70	37.37	99.64	27.57	1138.64
2101 10	(5)	699.61	1200	1635	153.71	4.25	3.38	13.43	71.16	34.13	8.50	288.56	28.85	100.01	31.51	1048.53
2103 10	(6)	900.00	1200	1830	172.04	4.25	3.38	13.43	71.16	34.13	8.50	306.89	30.68	101.84	31.51	1269.08
2105 10	(7)	1105.95	1200	1465	137.72	4.25	3.38	13.43	71.16	34.13	8.50	272.57	27.25	98.41	31.51	1437.28
2107 10	(9)	750.60	1200	1790	168.28	4.25	3.38	13.43	71.16	34.13	8.50	303.13	30.31	101.47	31.51	1115.55
2109 10	(10)	925.00	1380	1070	100.59	4.89	3.89	15.44	81.83	39.25	9.77	255.66	25.56	107.39	36.24	1242.46
2111 10	(11)	666.00	1110	1785	167.81	3.93	3.13	12.42	65.82	31.57	7.86	292.54	29.25	95.07	29.15	1016.94
2113 10	(12)	1422.14	2400	0	0.00	8.50	6.77	26.86	142.32	0.00	16.99	201.44	10.07	152.39	63.02	1696.67
2115-17 5	(13)	698.00	1200	4695	441.38	4.25	3.38	13.43	71.16	34.13	8.50	576.23	28.81	99.97	31.51	1334.55
2119 5	(14)	780.00	1200	2425	227.97	4.25	3.38	13.43	71.16	34.13	8.50	362.82	36.28	107.44	31.51	1210.61
2121 10	(15)	540.00	1200	1950	183.32	4.25	3.38	13.43	71.16	34.13	8.50	318.17	31.81	102.97	31.51	921.49
2123 10	(16)	540.00	1200	2510	235.97	4.25	3.38	13.43	71.16	34.13	8.50	370.82	37.08	108.24	31.51	979.41
2125 10	(17	591.82	1200	0	0.00	4.25	3.38	13.43	71.16	34.13	8.50	134.85	6.74	77.90	31.51	764.92
2127 5	(18)	700.00	1580	0	0.00	0.00	4.46	17.68	93.69	0.00	0.00	115.83	11.58	105.27	41.49	868.90
2129 10	(19)	1861.80	2960	2955	277.80	10.48	8.35	33.12	175.53	84.18	20.96	610.42	61.04	236.57	77.73	2610.99
2131-5 10	(8)	500.00	1200	1020	95.89	4.25	3.38	13.43	71.16	34.13	8.50	230.74	23.07	94.23	31.51	785.32
2137 10	(20)	575.30	1000	1395	131.14	3.54	2.82	11.19	59.30	28.44	7.08	243.51	24.35	83.65	26.26	869.42
2139 10	(21)	610.28	1027	920	86.49	3.64	2.90	11.49	60.90	29.21	7.27	201.90	20.19	81.09	26.97	859.34
2141 10	(22)	685.00	973	905	85.08	3.44	2.74	10.89	57.70	27.67	6.89	194.41	19.44	77.14	25.55	924.40
2143 10	(23)	0.00	3000	0	0.00	10.62	8.46	33.57	177.90	0.00	0.00	230.55	11.52	189.42	78.78	320.85
2145 5																
		20867.50	36005	34865	3277.67	110.92	101.50	368.23	2135.09	825.49	222.53	7041.43	629.23	2764.32	945.47	29483.63

SQ FT FOR GAS RATIO = 31325	OTHER CAM EXPENSES...... 1635.26	TAX DIFFERENCE........ 198.34
SQ FT FOR WATER RATIO = 36005	+ ELECTRICAL DIFFERENCE... 499.94	+ INSURANCE DIFFERENCE.. 32.47
SQ FT FOR TRASH RATIO = 32905	= TOTAL CAM BILLED AMOUNT 2135.20	= ABSORBED BY OWNER..... 230.81

Legal Considerations

A U.S. Supreme Court decision in *Robbins v. Pruneyard* said that shopping centers — even if privately owned — are quasi-public and must allow solicitors such as religious groups and cults as well as Girl Scout cookie sales. The property manager can, however, set forth reasonable rules, regulations, and insurance requirements to be observed by these groups.

In *Kendall v. Ernest Pestana*, a 1985 California Supreme Court decision, the court said a commercial lessor cannot withhold consent to assignment of a lease if the landlord has the right to approve said assignment unless there is a commercially reasonable objection to assignee or the proposed use. A lease can prohibit certain types of assignments and call for increased rents at time of assignment if such a clause is freely negotiated at the time of signing.

Commercial Rent Control

Effective January 1, 1988, the Costa-Keene-Seymour Commercial Investment Act (SB 692) prohibits local governments from imposing rent control regulations on commercial buildings. The only California city with such an ordinance was Berkeley, but the authors of the bill were afraid other cities in the state would pass commercial rent control ordinances. Unfortunately, this bill excludes from its provisions residential dwellings, residential hotels, and mobile home parks.

Bankruptcy Law Amendments

The "Leased Management Amendment of the Bankruptcy Amendments and Federal Judgeship Act of 1984" made changes in the handling of unexpired nonresidential leases. The debtors-in-possession or trustees must assume or reject a lease within 60 days from filing the case. The court may grant more time if the request is made within the 60-day period. On rejection, either by choice or when the 60-day period expires, the lessee must immediately surrender the property to the lessor. If the lease is assumed, a subsequent breach will elevate the lessor's claim to the cost of administration of the estate. This receives the highest payment priority, rather than becoming an unsecured claim. Pending decision on whether to assume the lease, all obligations and payment of rent and CAM charges must be made in accordance with the lease.

When assuming or assigning an unexpired lease, the revised Bankruptcy Amendment states the lessee's financial and operating statements must be at least equal to the present tenant's and that all provisions such as percentage rent, radius, and use clauses are applicable to the new tenant. Any lease that expires before or during the bankruptcy period is not part of the estate.

Summary

After World War II, with the advent of the automobile and the creation of suburbia, a major shift in retailing occurred. Stores moved out of downtown to shopping centers in suburban areas to be closer to their customers. The different classifications of shopping centers include: strip, neighborhood, community, regional, super-regional, and specialty. Leases in shopping centers are usually percentage or net leases. Merchants associations were formed to help promote and advertise the merchants collectively in the center and to increase customer traffic. The trade area of the center varies according to its classification. A strip center, for example, is for convenience shopping and draws from the immediate neighborhood. At the other end of the spectrum, the super-regional center trade area may extend 30 to 50 miles in radius.

Market research uses demographics to obtain data on income, age, home ownership, etc., as there is a close correlation between personal income and percentage of income spent in retail sales. Market share compares the number of people who shop at competing centers. The sales potential of department stores is calculated by using retail trade area statistics to convert dollar expenditures for department stores for census tracts in a trade area to a percentage of total retail sales. Tenant mix is very important in a shopping center so the center will have a wide selection of goods and bring in customers who will shop at more than one store on their trip (cross-shop). When leasing, tenant selection is very important so they complement each other in a symbiotic relationship.

The physical layout of the center should reflect the types of merchants and customers the developer/owner hopes to attract. Shopping should be made a fun, exciting, convenient event. Colors should be bright and cheerful. Long, narrow stores and hide-and-seek spaces should be avoided. Additional profit centers would be kiosks, wall shops, and holiday tenants. Common area maintenance (CAM) costs such as taxes, insurance, maintenance, utilities, etc. are billed back to the merchant on a pro-rata share depending on what percentage of the total space each merchant has in the center. Rental rates vary from area to area and where in the center the store is located. The trend is toward high-margin retailers, for example Gucci's replacing traditional ground-floor tenants such as banks in prime downtown locations in major cities. The Robbins v. Pruneyard U.S. Supreme Court decision classified shopping centers as quasi-public that must allow groups to solicit. The manager can establish rules, regulations, and insurance requirements.

In conclusion, it can be seen that shopping center management is distinctly different from residential management, requiring unique skills and specialized knowledge. The consequences of poor judgment can affect the center for many years. Unlike residential property, where most agreements are month to month, shopping center leases may be long-term, costing the owner "mega-bucks" for a bad decision. Shopping centers are a new phenomenon that has changed the shopping habits of America. The customers have moved from downtown to the outlying sub-urbs. The property manager has to be informed not only about his center's trade area, but about trends in retailing so he can correctly select the best tenant mix to make a success of the center. The center owner and merchant are truly a partner-ship. A successful merchant will contribute to a successful center and vice versa.

Chapter 8 Review Questions

1. *Which of the following is usually the smallest-size shopping center?*

   a. Community center.
   b. Strip center.
   c. Super-regional center.
   d. Regional center.

2. *Which of the following is usually the largest-size shopping center?*

   a. Community center.
   b. Strip center.
   c. Super-regional center.
   d. Regional center.

3. *Specialty centers usually have how many anchor tenants?*

   a. One.
   b. Two or more.
   c. None.
   d. Five or more.

4. *A lease in which the merchant pays a portion of gross sales as rent is:*

   a. percentage.
   b. gross.
   c. net.
   d. industrial.

5. *Merchants associations are made up of:*

   a. tenants.
   b. attorneys.
   c. CPMs.
   d. CSMs.

6. *Regional center trade areas usually have a population of at least:*

   a. 50,000.
   b. 100,000.
   c. 150,000.
   d. 500,000.

7. *An anchor tenant for a neighborhood shopping center would be:*

   a. a large department store.
   b. a supermarket.
   c. an office building.
   d. a florist shop.

8. *Additional profit areas for a shopping center would include:*

   a. kiosks.
   b. wall shops.
   c. seasonal tenants.
   d. all of the above.
   e. only b and c

9. *Items in common area maintenance include:*

   a. taxes.
   b. insurance.
   c. parking lot maintenance.
   d. all of the above.
   e. only a and b.

10. *The U.S. Supreme Court decision establishing that shopping centers are quasi-public is:*

    a. Robbins v. Pruneyard.
    b. Costa Mesa v. DRE.
    c. De Carlo v. McLelland.
    d. Kendall v. Ernest Pestana.

Chapter 8
Selected Additional References and Reading

Andrew Report (Monthly)
P.O. Box 80209
Indianapolis, IN 46208
Chain Store Executive (Monthly)
305 Madison Avenue, Suite 535
New York, NY 10164
Crittenden Retail Space News (Biweekly)
Crittenden Business Publications
P.O. Box 1150
Novato, CA 94948
Directory of Major Malls
P.O. Box 2
Suffern, NY 10901
Institute of Real Estate Management, *Managing the Shopping Center*, Chicago, IL, 1983.
International Council of Shopping Centers, *The Competitive Edge*, New York, NY, 1988.
International Council of Shopping Centers, *Food Courts*, New York, NY, 1986.
International Council of Shopping Centers, *Leasing Opportunities*, New York, NY.
International Council of Shopping Centers, *The Legal Edge*, New York, NY, 1986.
International Council of Shopping Centers, *The Operating Edge*, New York, NY, 1987.
National Mall Monitor (Bimonthly)
National Mall Monitor, Inc.
2280 U.S. 19 North, Suite 264
Clearwater, FL 33575
Retail Leasing Reporter (Twice Monthly)
P.O. Box 248
Kendall Park, NJ 08824
Retail Tenant Directory (Annual)
National Mall Monitor
1351 Washington Boulevard
Stamford, CT 06902
Shopping Center Directory (*West*) (Annual)
National Research Bureau
310 S. Michigan Avenue, Suite 1150
Chicago, IL 60664
Shopping Centers Today (Monthly)
International Council of Shopping Centers
665 Fifth Avenue
New York, NY 10022

Stores (Monthly)
    NRMA Enterprises, Inc.
    100 W. 31st Street
    New York, NY 10001
Sugarman, A.D., R.F. Cushman, and A.D. Lipman, *The Commercial Real Estate Tenant's Handbook*, John Wiley & Sons, Somerset, NJ, 1987.
Urban Land Institute, *Dollars and Cents of Shopping Centers*, Washington, D.C.
Urban Land Institute, *Shopping Center Development Handbook*, Washington, D.C., 1982.
Urban Land Institute, *Smart Building and Technology — Enhanced Real Estate*, Volumes I and II, Washington, D.C., 1985.
Western Real Estate News (WREN) (Twice Monthly)
    3057 17th Street
    San Francisco, CA 94110

Chapter 9

THE OFFICE BUILDING

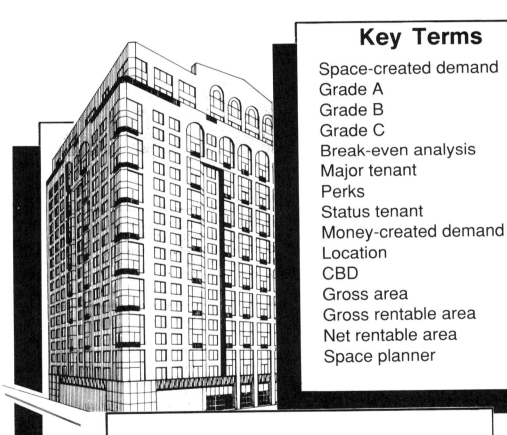

Key Terms

Space-created demand
Grade A
Grade B
Grade C
Break-even analysis
Major tenant
Perks
Status tenant
Money-created demand
Location
CBD
Gross area
Gross rentable area
Net rentable area
Space planner

Food for Thought

"Use not only all the brains you have — but all you can borrow."

The Office Building

Introduction

An office building can be defined as a property which provides facilities (space) to a tenant engaged in services (legal, accounting) rather than a location where goods are sold (shopping center) or manufactured (industrial building). As we discussed in Chapter 2, the United States economy has been moving away from manufacturing due to competition from countries such as Japan and Korea where production costs are lower. These countries can export their products to the United States more cheaply than our domestic manufacturers can produce them. This trend — unless tariffs are imposed — will continue into the next century.

Developers build office space dependent on two types of demand:

1. *Space-created demand* — typically, developers build only when the vacancy rate drops below 7% or when they anticipate vacancy will decline.

2. *Money-created demand* — developers build because the lenders (banks, savings and loans) have money to lend. The availability of money for their projects encourages developers to proceed with development. This results in high vacancy rates as it ignores basic principles of supply and demand. The reason for this imbalance is that real estate has become a favorite investment for pension funds, banks, insurance companies, and syndicators. With the long holding ability of such institutional investors, oversupply vacancies are not as negative a factor to lenders as they would be to other "cash-poor" customers. Bankers lend because they obtain large loan transaction fees (points) and they feel real estate investors are more favorable borrowers than other customers such as Third World countries and farmers. Syndicators and insurance companies like the favorable tax shelter benefits. In conclusion, lenders and investors may only be fooling themselves, as chronic overbuilding will reduce rents and values of both new and used (older) office buildings.

Size

Sizes range from small, one-story buildings to the enormous Sears Tower of 110 stories and 1,454 feet in height in Chicago (one of the world's tallest buildings). As was discussed in Chapter 1, new technological advances in elevators, design, and energy management allow for the construction of skyscrapers. Initially, skyscrapers were all constructed in central business districts (CBDs), but have now moved into the suburbs as well.

Desirability

Why are some office buildings at full occupancy with high rental rates while others are half empty at bargain basement rents? The answer is "desirability." Desirability is divided into four categories, or grades, as discussed in *Principles of Real Estate Management* (Institute of Real Estate Management, Chicago, 1980, Pg. 234). See Figure 9-2.

Figure 9-1. Location Benefits

Figure 9-2. Location Desirability

GRADE	LOCATION	RENTAL RATE	TENANTS
A	*Best*	*Highest*	*Most Prestigious*
B	Second best	Slightly less than A	Good, solid
C	Older area	Below A & B	Lower income
D	Near CBD	Lowest	Not usually maintained

The grades are achieved by ranking 12 criteria:

1. *Location:* Based more on prestige than geographic area.

2. *Neighborhood:* Based on appearance and upkeep of other buildings in the surrounding area.

3. *Transportation:* Are freeways and rapid transit convenient?

4. *Prestige of Building:* Does the reputation of the tenants enhance the building and vice versa?

5. *Appearance:* Does the building have an attractive facade and entrance (so-called "curb appeal") which enhances an older building?

6. *Lobby:* Is it clean, neat, and cheerful; is the directory neat and organized?

7. *Elevators:* Are they conveniently located; are they clean; are they high-speed?

8. *Corridors:* Are the colors and design coordinated; are they cheerfully decorated and well-lighted?

9. *Office Interiors:* Do they have window views, good column spacing, sufficient ceiling height?

10. *Management:* Are common areas and restrooms clean?

11. *Tenant Mix:* What is the reputation of the tenants (i.e., attorneys, CPAs, etc.)? Are they compatible uses?

12. *Tenant Services:* Are the janitorial and security services of high quality? Does the building have built-in telecommunications?

Office Building Statistics

The Institute of Real Estate Management (IREM) publishes an annual report entitled *Income and Expense Analysis: Office Buildings*. This publication compares building types, age groups, rental range, and building size. Using IREM

Figure 9-3. Institute of Real Estate Management Experience Exchange Report: Office Buildings

METROPOLITAN ANALYSIS BY RENTAL RANGE   SUBURBAN

SUBURBAN OFFICE BUILDINGS   RENTAL RANGE ORANGE COUNTY, CA $16.00 AND ABOVE

CHART OF ACCOUNTS	$/GROSS AREA OF ENTIRE BLG. BLGS SQ. FT. (10000)	MED.	RANGE LOW	HIGH	$/GROSS RENTABLE OFFC. AREA BLGS SQ. FT. (10000)	MED.	RANGE LOW	HIGH	$/NET RENTABLE OFFC. AREA BLGS SQ. FT. (10000)	MED.	RANGE LOW	HIGH
INCOME												
OFFICES	12	112	18.59	17.25 20.90	5	23	20.99		12	104	19.64	17.99 22.04
GROSS POSSBLE INCOME	12	112	21.87	18.68 23.64	5	23	22.41		12	104	22.97	20.75 23.64
VACANCY/DELIN.RENTS	12	112	2.72	1.22 2.99	5	23	3.20		12	104	2.85	1.29 3.32
TOTAL COLLECTIONS	12	112	19.62	14.30 21.51	5	23	19.62		12	104	20.60	16.35 22.52
EXPENSES												
SUBTOTAL UTILITIES	12	112	1.89	1.36 2.24	5	23	1.75		12	104	1.98	1.53 2.37
JAN.PAYROLL/CONTRACT	12	112	.53	.48 .56	5	23	.56		12	104	.55	.50 .59
SUBTOT JAN/MAINT/RPR	12	112	1.32	1.00 1.64	5	23	1.32		12	104	1.39	1.14 1.64
MANAGEMENT FEE	12	112	.60	.44 .99	5	23	.99		12	104	.69	.47 1.03
SUBTOTAL ADMIN/PAYRL	12	112	.88	.63 1.20	5	23	1.51		12	104	.92	.72 1.65
INSURANCE	12	112	.33	.13 .44	5	23	.47		12	104	.35	.15 .47
SUBTOTAL INSUR/SRVCS	12	112	.66	.46 .79	5	23	.78		12	104	.69	.53 .83
NET OPERATING COSTS	12	112	5.00	4.28 5.43	5	23	5.43		12	104	5.24	4.48 5.63
REAL ESTATE TAXES	12	112	1.11	.73 1.30	5	23	1.10		12	104	1.15	.83 1.50
TOTAL OPERATNG COSTS	12	112	5.71	5.48 6.48	5	23	6.52		12	104	6.01	5.92 6.67

criteria, the property manager can compare a building to a sample of over 11,000 buildings, divided by national, regional, and metropolitan areas. These figures, used as benchmarks, make analysis and comparison of the property manager's operation and performance more meaningful (Figure 9-3).

Measuring the Building

The two most common methods of measuring a building are those developed by BOMI and IREM. This chapter will use the IREM method.

Gross Area of Entire Building

This is the total sum of the areas of each floor, including lobbies and corridors, within the outside faces of the exterior walls.

Gross Rentable Area

The gross rentable area includes all areas within the outside walls, less pipe shafts, vertical ducts, elevator shafts, balconies, and stairs.

Net Rentable Area

The net rentable area is computed by deducting the following from gross rentable area: public corridors, washrooms, janitor and electrical closets, air-conditioning rooms, and other rooms or areas not available to the tenant and the tenant's employees.

The property manager should be sure that figures are accurate and truthful in order to avoid confusion and lawsuits. In describing the space, the lease document should contain language such as "Suite 300, which is approximately 3,000 sq. ft." As a rule of thumb, the higher the loss or "load factor" (unusable space), the lower the rent, because the tenant receives less usable space. For example, if the net rentable area is 80,000 s.f., but only 70,000 s.f. are usable due to corridors, the load factor is:

$$\frac{10,000}{80,000} \text{, or } 12.5\%$$

Measuring the Building

	gross area of entire building
−	shafts, ducts, balconies, and stairs
=	rentable area (tenant pays rent on)
−	public corridors, restrooms, mechanical rooms
=	usable area (tenant occupies)

In the United States and Canada, there are three additional methods of measuring rentable area in office buildings. All three measure total square footage.

1. *International Association of Building Owners and Managers* — from the inside of the outside wall (or in new buildings, from the glass line) to the outside of the inside wall (or hall wall) and center to center on the division walls. Columns are included.

2. *General Services Administration* — same as above except all columns, division walls, service closets, etc. are excluded from calculation of net usable space. In negotiating leases with the federal government, this method must be used. After October 1993 the General Services Administration will require federal government leases to be in metric and not square footage.

3. *So-Called New York Method* — space is measured right across the floor from glass line to glass line, subtracting only elevator shafts and stairwells. In the case of multiple occupancy on one floor, the common space, usable and nonusable, is apportioned among the tenants according to the size of their respective areas.

Usable Area

Any area in a given floor that could be used by the tenant. This area includes a point from the perimeter glass line to demising walls; it also includes column areas within such a space.

Although these are the most commonly used methods, there are other methods that may be encountered; i.e., drip line (the rentable area includes that portion outside the building that is within the area whose perimeter is defined by a line formed by the water dripping off the roof or canopy).

Setting the Rent Schedule

When setting the rent schedule, the property manager must take into account the 12 criteria for ranking the building, additional amenities, general economic conditions, and the owner's break-even point.

Market Survey

The property manager should conduct a market survey of the competition. A form similar to the one used for a residential market survey can be used, and at least three comparable properties should be analyzed. The rental rate measure most commonly used is "cost per square foot." On the West Coast this is usually quoted on a monthly basis, but in other parts of the country it is annualized. For example, if the rent is $4,000 per month on 2,500 square feet of space, on the West Coast the quoted rate would be $1.60 per square foot per month. The rate in the East would be 12 months times $1.60, or an annualized rate of $19.20 per square foot. The cost is really the same; the only difference is the semantics.

Break-Even Analysis

A "break-even analysis" determines the minimum rent needed to pay all of the building's expenses, costs, and expected return. The formula to calculate the break-even rent is as follows:

$$\text{B/E Rent} = \frac{\text{Expenses} + \text{Mortgage} + \text{Return}}{\text{Rentable area of building in square feet}}$$

For example:

Rentable space = 50,000 s.f.

Expenses = $291,258

Owner's equity = $1,000,000

Owner's rate of return = 10% = $100,000

Mortgage payment = $568,742

Mortgage = $4,500,000

Therefore:

$$\text{B/E Rent} = \frac{\$291,258 + \$568,742 + \$100,000}{50,000 \text{ s.f.}} = \frac{\$960,000}{50,000 \text{ s.f.}} = \$19.20/\text{s.f.}$$

Thus we can see from the above example that the minimum rent we can charge is $19.20/s.f./year, or $1.60/s.f./month, to cover all of the building's expenses, costs, and owner's return.

Tenant Selection

The selection of commercial tenants is different and much more important than the selection of residential tenants due to the length of time leases may run and the large rental sums therefore involved. A mistake can be very expensive.

Major Tenants

Major tenants can be checked by using Dun & Bradstreet (D&B) reports and ratings, contacting the tenant's bank account manager, and checking with the tenant's vendors and landlords at other locations. Also, copies of tenant financial statements can be obtained and analyzed. See Figure 9-4 for a D&B rating report.

Small Tenants

Small tenants such as "*Ma and Pa*" merchants are not usually rated and may not have other locations. With smaller tenants, look more to the individuals than to the business. Run credit reports (TRWs) on their personal credit history. Also contact their bank and vendors. Additionally, ask for a business plan (verbal or written) as to their goals and objectives. To ensure rent payment, the property manager should in some cases ask for a "*personal guarantee*," much as a bank does, if the entity is a corporation. The property manager should obtain written permission from the prospective tenant before checking credit to avoid violating privacy laws.

In summary, a conscientious effort by the property manager in tenant selection will save considerable time, expense, and aggravation in the future.

Figure 9-4. D&B Ratings and Symbols

D&B Rating System

The D&B Rating System is a widely used tool that uses a two-part code to represent a firm's estimated financial strength and composite credit appraisal. A Rating may be based on a book financial statement or on an estimated financial statement submitted by the company.

	Estimated Financial Strength			Composite Credit Appraisal			
				High	Good	Fair	Limited
Estimated financial strength, based on an actual book financial statement.	$50,000,000	and over	**5A**	1	2	3	4
	$10,000,000	to $49,999,999	**4A**	1	2	3	4
For example, if a company has a Rating of "3A3," this means its financial strength is between $1,000,000 and $9,999,999 and	$1,000,000	to $9,999,999	**3A**	1	2	3	4
	$750,000	to $999,999	**2A**	1	2	3	4
its composite credit appraisal is "fair."	$500,000	to $749,999	**1A**	1	2	3	4
Copyright 1991.	$300,000	to $499,999	**BA**	1	2	3	4
Dun & Bradstreet, Inc.	$200,000	to $299,999	**BB**	1	2	3	4
All Rights Reserved.	$125,000	to $199,999	**CB**	1	2	3	4
Reprinted With Permission.	$75,000	to $124,999	**CC**	1	2	3	4
	$50,000	to $74,999	**DC**	1	2	3	4
Estimated financial strength, based on either an actual book financial statement or an estimated financial statement.	$35,000	to $49,999	**DD**	1	2	3	4
	$20,000	to $34,999	**EE**	1	2	3	4
	$10,000	to $19,999	**FF**	1	2	3	4
	$5,000	to $9,999	**GG**	1	2	3	4
		up to $4,999	**HH**	1	2	3	4
Estimated financial strength, based on an estimated financial statement (when an actual book financial statement is not available to us).	$125,000	and over	**1R**		2	3	4
	$50,000	to $124,999	**2R**		2	3	4

Symbols in the Rating column — what do they mean?

-- (Absence of a Rating)

A Business Information Report is available on this business, and other information products may be available as well. However, a D&B Rating has not been assigned. A "--" symbol should not be interpreted as indicating that credit should be denied. It simply means that the information available to Dun & Bradstreet does not permit us to classify the company within our Rating key and that further inquiry should be made before reaching a credit decision.

In many cases, a "--" symbol is used because a current financial statement on the business is not available to us. Some other reasons for using a "--" symbol include:

☐ Unavailability of the source and amount of starting capital — in the case of a new business
☐ A deficit net worth ☐ Bankruptcy proceedings ☐ A critical financial condition

ER (Employee Range)

Certain lines of business, primarily banks, insurance companies and other service-type businesses, do not lend themselves to classification under the D&B Rating System. Instead, we assign these types of businesses an Employee Range symbol based on the number of people employed. No other significance should be attached to this symbol.

For example, a Rating of "ER7" means there are between 5 and 9 employees in the company.

"ERN" should not be interpreted negatively. It simply means we don't have information indicating how many people are employed at this firm.

Key to Employee Range	
1000 or more employees	ER 1
500 to 999	ER 2
100 to 499	ER 3
50 to 99	ER 4
20 to 49	ER 5
10 to 19	ER 6
5 to 9	ER 7
1 to 4	ER 8
Not available	ER N

Questions? Please call your D&B Customer Service Center at 1-800-234-DUNS (1-800-234-3867). Our Customer Service Representatives will be happy to help you interpret the D&B Rating System and other symbols.

Attracting Tenants

In order to screen and obtain commercial tenants, they need to be made aware of the property. The cost (rental rate) is not always the deciding factor. Creativity and hard work are important in finding prospective tenants. For example, because image is important, a small office building which has interior courtyards may be named "The Courtyards." A project that has a pond or overlooks water may be named "The Lakes." The name gives the building an identity.

The most productive forms of advertising are shown in Figure 9-5.

Figure 9-5. Marketing Strategies

Newspaper Advertisements

Place advertisements in newspapers and magazines that business people will read; e.g. the *Wall Street Journal* has separate editions for different parts of the country.

Direct Mail

Direct mail can be an effective tool if you select your targeted markets properly. Word processors can be used to send individual personalized letters to prospects.

Publicity

Arrange for grand openings and open houses for prospective tenants and other leasing agents. Write articles for newspapers about unique building features or tenants.

Signage

Signage is very important, especially for a new building. The sign should include the name of the building, address, and phone number of the leasing contact.

Brochures

Brochures should create excitement about the building, location, amenities, and features. It should have pictures and a map of how to get to the building.

Miscellaneous Media

Radio and television are expensive and not as effective as printed media. They target a mass market rather than an individual market. Advertising medical building space in a medical association magazine is a very effective tool.

Perks

Perks are items such as free rent, extra tenant improvements (TI's), and amenities such as free parking and exercise rooms. Most popular as perks for existing tenants are lunches and Christmas parties (Figure 9-6). One of the newer perks is addition of a "concierge" in an office building to help busy executives.

Figure 9-6. Existing Tenant Perks

Tenant Happy Factor*	Action	Frequency	(Unit Cost) Annual Cost	Cost/Sq. Ft.	Annual % Return on Investment
☺☺☺☺☺	Lunches/Meals	[monthly] 12	($50) $600	$.09	16,922%
☺☺☺	Flowers/Plants	[quarterly] 3	($40) $120	$.02	85,011%
☺☺☺☺	Christmas Party	[annual] 1	$500	$.07	20,326%
☺	Holiday Cards	[bi-annual] 2	($2) $4	$.0005	2,553,219%
☺☺	Cookies/Candy	[quarterly] 3	($10) $30	$.004	340,343%
	TOTAL		$1254	$.18	8,045%

* Tenant Happy Factor — Amount of good will generated by the different tenant relations activities, with five smiles the high and one smile the low.

Leasing Considerations

Onsite vs. Offsite

The question of whether there should be an onsite leasing agent is often asked. *The answer depends on the size* of the building and its vacancy level. For a new 250,000-square-foot office building, an onsite leasing agent is desirable. If the building is 96% occupied after one year, however, an onsite agent is not needed.

Property Management vs. Leasing Agents

Should the property manager and leasing agent be the same person from the same firm or should they be from different companies? The answer again depends on size, location, other duties of the property manager, time, etc. The leasing agent's job is usually complete when the tenant signs the lease; the property manager will live with the lease for its entire term. As a result, the property manager may be *more diligent* in looking at the long-term benefits of the lease.

Small vs. Large Leasing Firms

Is it best to hire a small, local leasing firm or a large, national company? We recommend compromise. A large firm, due to its national exposure, will be retained to solicit and lease major anchor tenants for large rental spaces (over 2,500 square feet). A small, local firm is usually more effective in renting smaller stores and offices attractive to "*Ma and Pa*" type tenants. Attention should be paid not only to the reputation of the leasing company, but also to that of the individual leasing agent. The agent will be the "man on the spot" and it will be primarily his efforts that get results.

Leasing Techniques

Some leasing techniques have been covered under tenant selection, but additional techniques need to be discussed. An empty building does not make for good rapport with the owner. The importance of leasing *cannot* be over-emphasized.

Cold-Calling

Cold-calling by the property manager on the telephone and through personal visits is important. Again, the market should be targeted to achieve the best results. Cold-calling is difficult for the property manager due to the high rate of rejection, but it can often be a very effective tool for reaching certain potential tenants.

Space Planner

A space planner should be available to help potential tenants design an office to meet their needs. Space planning can be done in a computerized format, helping the tenant lower costs by better utilization of space. Well-planned but smaller space at higher rental rates can benefit both owner and tenant. In the past each employee averaged 250 square feet of work space, but due to telecommuting (computer and fax) it is estimated in a study by Link Resources Corp. that 8 million employees use phone technology to work from home. The latest guestimate is down to an average of 200 square feet per employee.

Existing Tenants

Retention is the best tool for maintaining high occupancy rates. Find out existing tenant concerns and problems well before leases expire.

High-Status Tenants

High-status tenants can attract other tenants to your building. A rent concession to draw family practitioners and pediatricians can be beneficial for leasing to specialists who hope to obtain referrals from these general practitioners.

Comparison of Buildings

The property manager should, from time to time, compare his/her buildings to those of competitors. This information can be useful for planning, refinancing, prospecting, or sale.

Objective Data — ownership, total square footage, name of management company, name of leasing agent, quoted rent range, names of tenants, tenant mix, vacancies, floor plans, financing, and type of construction. Sources for these data would be the assessor's office, realty trade associations, chamber of commerce, government agencies.

Subjective Data — actual rents and lease terms, renewal data and options, concessions or incentives being given, condition of building, effectiveness of management, and any management or ownership changes that are anticipated. Sources for this information would include tenants, management company, brokers, onsite personnel, contractors, vendors, and other owners and managers.

Maintenance

When high vacancy rates are being experienced in the office rental market, keeping existing tenants happy so they will renew their leases is imperative. BOMI, in addition to the RPA designation, has a Systems Maintenance Administrator (SMA) designation for those who must operate and maintain today's complex commercial buildings systems. The candidate must complete eight courses ranging from heating and air-conditioning to electrical systems, building design, energy management, control systems, and supervision.

After World War II, central air-conditioning was installed in most new buildings, but temperature is still the major source of complaints. It is difficult to satisfy everyone when it comes to temperature. Some buildings are airtight and have few or no drafts, space locations vary within the building, construction materials differ, and climates differ — so common sense must be used to establish ideal temperatures for each building.

Standard Temperature Guidelines		
	Temperature	Humidity
Summer	73–79 degrees	20–60%
Winter	68–74 degrees	30–70%
Ideal	75 degrees	50%
Air velocity	15 feet per minute	

Source: Skylines (December 1987)

Smart (Intelligent) Buildings

A buzz word being used today in office building management and development is "smart" or "intelligent" buildings. The factors for comparing intelligent building features are the amount of automation, communication, and information-processing technologies present within the building. The higher the intelligence, the more desirable the building will be to most tenants.

Five Classifications of Smart Buildings

Level Zero — has no intelligent amenities and doesn't qualify.

Level One — provides infrastructural core, including computerized energy management, HVAC, elevators, and security and life safety systems.

Level Two — provides Level One capabilities, plus shared conference space, photocopying, and word-processing centers.

Level Three — provides Level Two capabilities, plus telecommunications services utilizing building cabling system.

Level Four — provides Level Three capabilities, plus sophisticated office automation and information-processing services. This level is sometimes called an "Einstein" building.

Commercial Building Organizations

Intelligent Building Institute (IBI) is an international trade association established in 1986 to serve the needs of all sectors involved in advanced technologies used in commercial, institutional, and industrial buildings.

IBI Headquarters
2101 L Street, N.W., Suite 300
Washington, D.C. 20037

International Facilities Management Association (IFMA) offers a Certified Facilities Manager (CFM) designation. This designation involves education, work experience, and an examination.

IFMA
1 E. Greenway Plaza, 11th Floor
Houston, TX 77046

Figure 9-7. Office Building

Sick Buildings

A recent *Wall Street Journal* report stated more office workers are filing lawsuits, claiming they were made ill by indoor air pollution from such things as insect sprays, industrial cleaners, cigarette smoke, and fumes from new carpets, drapes, and copiers. Most of the suits involve airtight, energy-efficient buildings. No plaintiff has yet won a major suit, but there have been several out-of-court settlements. The most frequent targets of suits are landlords, architects, contractors, building product manufacturers, and real estate managers.

Summary

The office building provides space for tenants to engage in services such as legal, accounting, etc. Since our economy is moving away from production and toward service, office buildings have experienced overdevelopment so that many areas have an abundance of space and a high vacancy rate. The two main reasons for new developments are space-created and money-created demand. During periods of high vacancy, the availability of money causes developers to create office buildings built on speculation without being pre-leased to tenants.

There are four grades of office buildings, with Grade A being the best and having the highest rents. Grade D is the poorest and not usually well-maintained, in less desirable areas, and with the lowest rental rates. Statistics for office buildings can be obtained from the Institute of Real Estate Management annual report entitled *Income and Expense Analysis: Office Buildings* as well as from BOMI.

The measurement of gross and net rentable area varies, so the property manager should double-check measurements before quoting to tenants. When establishing the rent schedule, a market survey should be made of competing buildings. On the West Coast, rental rates are quoted per square foot per month rather than per square foot per year. A break-even analysis is made to determine the minimum rent needed to pay all building operating and debt-service expenses. When screening tenants for financial ability to pay rent, the major (larger) tenant rating can be found in Dun and Bradstreet (D&B). Smaller "Ma and Pa" type tenants should be checked out personally much like a residential tenant, as described in Chapter 7. Bank references, financial statements, and income tax returns may be checked.

When marketing space in an office building, the property manager or leasing agent may use newspaper ads, direct mail, publicity, signage, brochures, media, and perks. Some leasing considerations are onsite vs. offsite leasing agent, property manager vs. leasing agent, small vs. large leasing firms. Leasing techniques include cold-calling, space planner, existing tenants, and prestige tenants.

Property maintenance in an office building can help reduce vacancy by having proper temperature settings so tenants are comfortable and satisfied. Newer "smart buildings" have built-in features for automation, communications, and information processing.

In conclusion, office buildings are a growth area in property management as our society moves from an industrial goods manufacturing base to a society which is service-oriented. We discussed the size, characteristics, and grading criteria of office buildings. There followed an analysis of how the property manager measures space and sets rental rates. Finally, we discussed break-even analysis, tenant selection, attracting tenants, and concluded with leasing considerations and techniques.

Chapter 9 Review Questions

1. *The most desirable office building category is:*

    a. Grade A.
    b. Grade B.
    c. Grade C.
    d. Grade D.
    e. None of the above.

2. *Criteria for ranking office buildings include:*

    a. location.
    b. appearance.
    c. tenant mix.
    d. management.
    e. all of the above.

3. *Compatible tenant mix would include:*

    a. CPAs and attorneys.
    b. CPAs and a massage parlor.
    c. CPAs and a second-hand store.
    d. all of the above.
    e. none of the above.

4. *Net rentable space includes:*

    a. A/C rooms.
    b. washrooms.
    c. public corridors.
    d. all of the above.
    e. none of the above.

5. *Usable area usually means:*

    a. the gross area of the building.
    b. the area the tenant occupies.
    c. the area for which the tenant pays rent.
    d. the gross area plus the parking lot.

6. *Commercial tenant screening is usually checked by use of:*

   a. CPA.
   b. DRE.
   c. D&B.
   d. TRW.

7. *Methods of attracting tenants include:*

   a. newspaper.
   b. signage.
   c. brochures.
   d. direct mail.
   e. all of the above.

8. *Onsite leasing agents for commercial buildings are usually:*

   a. required at all times.
   b. never needed.
   c. needed for large buildings with high vacancy rates.
   d. required by law.

9. *Leasing techniques include:*

   a. cold-calling.
   b. model offices.
   c. space planning.
   d. existing tenants.
   e. all of the above.

10. *The best source of tenants is:*

    a. status tenants.
    b. existing tenants.
    c. anchor tenants.
    d. prestige.

Chapter 9 Home Study Problem (HP12C)

The nominal rent rate is reduced by the amount of free rent and any concessions. The property manager needs to be able to calculate the real or effective rental rate in order to compare competing lease offers. For example, does the lease proposal meet the owner's objectives of $1.50/s.f. effective monthly rent?

Case Study: A medical office building located near a hospital is well-managed and has only one 10,000 s.f. vacancy out of 30,000 s.f. in the entire building. The current contract rate is $1.75/s.f. or $17,500/month (triple net). The owner has a required rate of return of 7% and wants a minimum of $1.50/s.f.

Term	5 years
Rental Rate	$1.75/s.f. or $17,500/month
Free Rent	12 months
Tenant Improvements	$50,000
Required Rate of Return	7%
Owner Minimum Rent	$1.50/s.f.

Keystrokes	Display
[f] [REG]	0.00
50,000 [CHS] [g] [CFO]	– $50,000 tenant improvements
7 [g] [i]	.58 discount rate
0 [g] [cfj]	0.00 free rent
12 [g] [nj]	
17,500 [g] [cfj]	$17,500 rental rate
48 [g] [nj]	48 months of paid rent (1 year free rent)
[f] [NPV]	$631,535 present value

TO FIND MONTHLY EFFECTIVE RENT

Keystrokes	Display
[f] [FIN]	$631,535
[CHS] [PV]	$631,535 present value

7	$\boxed{g}$	$\boxed{i}$	.58 discount rate
5	$\boxed{g}$	$\boxed{n}$	60 months term of lease
$\boxed{PMT}$			$12,505 effective monthly rent
10,000	$\boxed{\div}$		$1.25 effective monthly rent per s.f.

Contract (stated) rent was $1.75 and owner minimum monthly objective rent was $1.50/s.f. Since $1.25 is lower than $1.50, the lease offer will be rejected.

Chapter 9
Selected Additional References and Reading

Alexander, Alan and Richard Muhlebach, *Managing and Leasing Commercial Properties*, John Wiley & Sons, Colorado Springs, CO, 1990.

BOMA, *The Changing Office Workplace*, Washington, D.C., 1983.

BOMA, *Experience Exchange Report*, Washington, D.C., 1983.

BOMA, *Leasing Concepts: A Guide to Leasing Office Space*, Washington, D.C., 1983.

Buildings (Monthly)
Stamats Communications, Inc.
427 Sixth Street, S.E.
Cedar Rapids, IA 52406

Commercial Investment Journal (Quarterly)
National Association of Realtors
430 N. Michigan Avenue
Chicago, IL 60611

Institute of Real Estate Management, *Managing the Office Building*, Chicago, IL, 1981.

Northern California Real Estate Journal (Biweekly)
44 Montgomery Street, Suite 785
San Francisco, CA 94104

Real Estate Times (Bimonthly)
Gralla Publications
1515 Broadway
New York, NY 10036

Skylines (Monthly)
BOMI
1250 Eye Street, N.W., Suite 200
Washington, D.C. 20005

Smith, Charles, *A Guide to Commercial Management*, BOMA, Washington, D.C., 1983.

Southern California Real Estate Journal (Biweekly)
3450 Wilshire Boulevard, Suite 310
Los Angeles, CA 90010

Urban Land Institute, *Office Development Handbook*, Washington, D.C.

Chapter 10

CONDOMINIUM MANAGEMENT

Key Terms

Condominium
Cooperative
Townhouse
Association
CAI
By-laws
Board of Directors
PUD
CC&Rs
Per diem fee
Committee
Rules and
regulations

Food for Thought

"Let everyone sweep in front of his own door, and the whole world will be clean."

Condominiums

Community Associations

The nature of community association types of ownership and operations, whether residential or commercial, is an area of much confusion. This chapter will examine these issues with a concentration on residential condominiums, co-ops, and planned unit developments (PUDs). Special emphasis will be placed on these types of ownership as well as the special problems inherent in their management.

Definition of Terms

1. *Condominium.* A condominium is a property in which there is separate fee ownership of individual units (by grant deed) and an assigned interest in common with all other owners in the "common elements" (e.g., lawns, parking lots, pool, etc.). The owner of the "condo" unit owns an "interest in space" within the walls of the unit. Any maintenance problems with internal fixtures, such as a broken garbage disposal, are the owner's responsibility.

The owner has a separate mortgage and tax bill, but pays a monthly association fee to cover common area expenses. Common area expenses may include, but are not limited to, landscape maintenance, pool repairs and maintenance, common area utilities, management, exterior building maintenance, etc. Insurance of the building for common area liability is usually included in the association fee, while interior liability and contents insurance is carried separately by the owner.

2. *Cooperative (Co-Op).* A cooperative is a stock corporation which owns the building(s) and land. The buyer is issued a share of stock and a long-term proprietary lease for the unit. For example, in a 100-unit building there would be 100 shares; therefore, each owner would have 1/100th interest.

In some cases, separate tax bills and mortgages are issued. This form of ownership has not been as desirable as that of a condo due to difficulties in financing, since the purchaser is not issued a grant deed.

3. *Planned Unit Development (PUD).* In a planned unit development, the person owns the living unit plus the land underneath, with an undivided interest in the common areas. Typically, there are no units above or below another in a PUD.

4. *Timeshare.* The owner typically buys an interest in time in a building. Fee title may or may not be involved. For example, the buyer would have the right to occupy a unit for a week each year. Timeshare ownership is associated primarily with resort property.

5. *Townhouse.* Townhouses are a type of architecture (usually two-story), not a form of ownership.

Size of the Condo Market

Due to increased land costs, PUDs and condos are an attractive way for a developer to obtain the highest and best use of the land. In the United States there are approximately 30 million residents living in 12.5 million units in over 140,000 community associations. The average size is 95 units per association.

California alone has over 25,000 associations, with a median size of approximately 43 units per association, accounting for over 2 million units in the state.

According to a research study sponsored by the California Department of Real Estate entitled *Common Interest Homeowner's Association Management Study*, 44% of associations are self-managed (usually the smaller complexes), 16% have onsite management, and 40% have offsite management.

Government of Condos

The condominium development is usually formed into a non-profit corporation governed by a Board of Directors based on Articles of Incorporation, CC&Rs, By-Laws, and Rules and Regulations.

The homeowners association is created by the previously mentioned documents and is responsible for operation of the community. The community's Board of Directors establishes and enforces rules and regulations, fees, collection procedures, budgets, and an overall management policy for the community.

The homeowners elect members to the Board of Directors in much the same manner as a city elects its City Council. The number can vary depending on the Articles of Incorporation, but five or seven is most typical. The property manager is selected by and reports to the Board of Directors.

The Board usually elects its own officers, which typically include President, Vice-President, Secretary, and Treasurer.

Government of the Board

Rights and duties of the Board of Directors and homeowners are set forth in the following:

1. *Articles of Incorporation* — establish the corporation.

2. *By-Laws* — provide procedures for operation of the corporation; i.e., election procedures.

3. *CC&Rs* — Covenants, Conditions, and Restrictions; provide land use and deed restrictions.

4. *Grant Deed* — A mechanism which conveys ownership interest.

5. *Rules and Regulations* — everyday rules to guide the conduct of owners and/or their tenants; i.e., pool hours, parking, pets, etc.

Election of Officers

The association by-laws normally set forth the notice period, date, time, place, and general nature of the business to be discussed. Corporations Code Section 7511 mandates notices not less than 10 days nor more than 90 days before date of a meeting where members are permitted to take action such as elections. A written notice must be sent by first class mail. Nomination procedures must include:

a. *Reasonable means of nominating persons.*

b. *Reasonable opportunities for nominee to communicate to members.*

c. *Reasonable opportunity for all nominees to solicit votes.*

d. *Reasonable opportunity for all members to chose among the nominees.*

The by-laws usually provide for a nominating committee to select candidates and also for written nominations and nominations from the floor. If a proxy is used, it *should not* be confused with a mail-in ballot, which is not permitted by law. The proxy giver vests the proxy holder with the power to vote at the meeting in a pre-determined manner. The election ballots should not be issued until the meeting date. All members who register at the meeting should be given a ballot for themselves and proxies. Most by-laws allow for cumulative voting. For example, if a member owns one unit and there are five directors to be elected, the member has one vote for each director or a total of five votes. The member may then accumulate those votes, casting them all for any one director or some for one and some for another. The by-laws also set forth the way a quorum is determined. For example, 50% of the homeowners must cast ballots. If a quorum is not attained, 25% would constitute a quorum in the second election.

Fiscal Reporting

The property manager is usually responsible for supplying the Board of Directors with the financial statements and an annual budget, in which the income, expenses, and reserves for the following year need to be projected (see Figure 10-1). Financial reports to the homeowners must also be sent, usually on a yearly basis (see Figure 10-2). Actual income and expenses are compared with the projected budget; the differences are called variances. A negative variance in income would be bad, and a variance in expenses over budget would be undesirable. If dealing with several large condo associations, the assistance of computerization is essential to streamline bookkeeping and reduce costs for the property manager. Individual median annual expenses for condominiums can be found in IREM Expense Analysis — Condominiums (Figure 10-3).

An association must, according to Civil Code Section 1365.5, prepare a financial statement and distribute it to its members not less than 45 and no more than 60 days prior to the beginning of the association's fiscal year. The budget must include:

1. *An estimate of revenue and expenses on accrual basis.*

2. *Identification of total cash reserves set aside.*

3. *Identification of estimated remaining life and method of funding to defray future repairs.*

4. *A general statement addressing the procedure for establishing and calculating reserves.*

5. *A statement describing association lien rights or other remedies of default.*

6. *Review on at least a quarterly basis a reconciliation of reserve, operating accounts, and bank statements.*

7. *A statement comparing actual reserve account revenue against budget reserves.*

8. *Signatures of at least two board members to withdraw reserve funds.*

Assessment Increases

In addition to any limitations placed on the board by the governing documents, the maximum levy cannot exceed 20%, according to Civil Code 1365.

Figure 10-1. Condo Budget

```
                COAST TERRACE HOMEOWNERS ASSOCIATION          ** 08-Aug-    **


                      BUDGET/MO        BUDGET/UNIT       BUDGET/YR
                                           256

400 Monthly Dues          35,990              N/A          431,880
401 Interest                 450             1.76            5,400
405 Delinquency Fees         100             0.39            1,200
410 Other Income             200             0.78            2,400
415 Laundry                1,300             5.08           15,600
      TOTAL INCOME                 38,040  148.59          456,480

500 Landscape-Basic        2,000             7.81           24,000
501 Sprinkler Repairs        150             0.59            1,800
505 Landscape-Extra          100             0.39            1,200
510 Pool-Basic               330             1.29            3,960
515 Pool-Extra               300             1.17            3,600
516 Pest Control-Basic       225             0.88            2,700
517 Pest Control-Termites     75             0.29              900
520 Common Area Repairs      775             3.03            9,300
523 Salaries-Cash          1,500             5.86           18,000
525 Street Sweeping          275             1.07            3,300
526 Plumbing Repairs       1,200             4.69           14,400
527 Sewer Service            100             0.39            1,200
530 Common Area Supplies     400             1.56            4,800
545 Roof Maintenance          75             0.29              900
546 Security Expense       2,200             8.59           26,400
547 Security Gate Repair     150             0.59            1,800
      TOTAL MAINTENANCE              9,855   38.50          118,260


550 *  Gas                 4,860            18.98           58,320
550 Gas (Common)           1,215             4.75
555 Electric               1,850             7.23           22,200
560 *  Water               1,480             5.78           17,760
560 Water (Common)           370             1.45
565 Trash                  1,900             7.42           22,800
570 Telephone                 50             0.20              600
      TOTAL UTILITIES               11,725   45.80          140,700

600 Management Fee         1,400             5.47           16,800
610 Accounting               175             0.68            2,100
620 Taxes & Permits           50             0.20              600
630 Printing & Postage       375             1.46            4,500
640 Bad Debts                                0.00                0
645 Legal & Collection       600             2.34            7,200
646 *  Insurance (Property) 4,141           16.18           49,692
646 Insurance (Liability)  1,784
      TOTAL ADMINISTRATIVE           8,525   33.30          102,300

      RESERVES
705 Air Conditioners          15             0.06              180
706 *  Water Heaters         325             1.27            3,900
707 Decking                  975             3.81           11,700
710 *  Painting            1,415             5.53           16,980
715 *  Roofing             1,625             6.35           19,500
720 Driveways                325             1.27            3,900



** PAGE 1 **
```

Figure 10-1 (Cont'd). Condo Budget

```
                    COAST TERRACE HOMEOWNERS ASSOCIATION          ** 08-Aug-    **


724 Carpet                          30                  0.12            360
725 Recreation Facil. (Pool)       780                  3.05          9,360
726 Furnishings                     50                  0.20            600
728 Playground Equipment            65                  0.25            780
730 Fences                         325                  1.27          3,900
731 Iron Fences                     25                  0.10            300
732 Security Gates                  45                  0.18            540
745 Other (Contingency)            585                  2.29          7,020
761 Irrigation System               65                  0.25            780
765 Tree Trimming                  540                  2.11          6,480
775 Lighting                       745                  2.91          8,940
    TOTAL RESERVE ALLOCATION              7,935        31.00         95,220


TOTAL COSTS                             38,040        148.59        456,480

NET INCOME                                   0          0.00              0


ASSESSMENT BREAKDOWN

Total Prorated Expenses     13,846 (Designated with an " * ")
   Flat Expense             24,194
   less Other Income         2,050
Total Equal Share           22,144

TOTAL                       35,990


UNITS    RATIO    PRORATED FLAT RATE      LAST YEAR       NEW
                  AMOUNT   AMOUNT         ASSESSMENT      ASSESSMENT

    12  0.00290    40.15    86.50          107.79         126.65
    32  0.00356    49.29    86.50          114.46         135.79
    44  0.00357    49.43    86.50          114.74         135.93
    44  0.00382    52.89    86.50          117.34         139.39
    32  0.00385    53.31    86.50          117.66         139.81
    80  0.00427    59.12    86.50          122.06         145.62
     6  0.00509    70.48    86.50          130.78         156.98
     6  0.00513    71.03    86.50          131.24         157.53
    ----------
    256
                                                          ** PAGE 2 **
```

Figure 10-2. Condo Profit and Loss Statement

	CURRENT MONTH ACTUAL	CURRENT MONTH BUDGET	CURRENT MONTH VARIANCE*	YEAR-TO-DATE ACTUAL	YEAR-TO-DATE BUDGET	YEAR-TO-DATE VARIANCE*	ANNUAL BUDGET	ANNUAL VARIANCE*
INCOME								
OPERATING INCOME								
4110 ASSESSMENT INCOME	4,341.18	3,851.50	489.68	7,905.08	7,703.00	202.08	46,218.00	(38,312.92)
4122 INTEREST INCOME	193.94	226.50	(32.56)	406.47	453.00	(46.53)	2,718.00	(2,311.53)
TOTAL OPERATING INCOME	4,535.12	4,078.00	457.12	8,311.55	8,156.00	155.55	48,936.00	(40,624.45)
TOTAL INCOME	4,535.12	4,078.00	457.12	8,311.55	8,156.00	155.55	48,936.00	(40,624.45)
OPERATING EXPENSES								
G & A EXPENSE								
6205 GROUNDS UPKEEP		50.00	50.00		100.00	100.00	600.00	600.00
6212 PAINTING		41.67	41.67		83.34	83.34	500.04	500.04
6213 PLUMBING		25.00	25.00		50.00	50.00	300.00	300.00
6217 HEATING/COOLING	187.26	135.00	(52.26)	187.26	270.00	82.74	1,620.00	1,432.74
6220 ROOFING		83.33	83.33		166.66	166.66	999.96	999.96
6221 TAXES		50.00	50.00		100.00	100.00	600.00	600.00
6222 MISCELLANEOUS REPAIRS	136.41	83.33	(53.08)	1,242.64	166.66	(1,075.98)	999.96	(242.68)
6224 WATER		108.33	108.33	220.37	216.66	(3.71)	1,299.96	1,079.59
6225 GAS	25.94	25.00	(0.94)	48.23	50.00	1.77	300.00	251.77
6226 ELECTRIC	386.66	433.33	46.67	718.24	866.66	148.42	5,199.96	4,481.72
6230 LANDSCAPE MAINTENANCE	503.00	375.00	(128.00)	2,060.00	750.00	(1,310.00)	4,500.00	2,440.00
6233 RUBBISH COLLECTION		91.67	91.67	78.40	183.34	104.94	1,100.04	1,021.64
6246 TELEPHONE		16.67	16.67		33.34	33.34	200.04	200.04
6249 SECURITY SERVICE	150.00	65.00	(85.00)	225.00	130.00	(95.00)	780.00	555.00
6250 ACCOUNTING		108.33	108.33		216.66	216.66	1,299.96	1,299.96
6255 SIDEWALK CLEANING		100.00	100.00		200.00	200.00	1,200.00	1,200.00
6272 MANAGEMENT FEE	500.00	500.00		1,000.00	1,000.00		6,000.00	5,000.00
6273 MISCELLANEOUS	260.00	83.33	(176.67)	251.77	166.66	(85.11)	999.96	748.19
6290 INSURANCE		250.00	250.00		500.00	500.00	3,000.00	3,000.00
6296 JANITORIAL SUPPLIES		12.50	12.50		25.00	25.00	150.00	150.00
6305 JANITORIAL	450.00	333.33	(116.67)	1,350.00	666.66	(683.34)	3,999.96	2,649.96
6325 ELEVATOR MAINT	187.07	191.67	4.60	374.14	383.34	9.20	2,300.04	1,925.90
6345 ANSWERING SERVICE	53.51	75.00	21.49	138.46	150.00	11.54	900.00	761.54
6350 FIRE EXTINGUISHERS		8.33	8.33		16.66	16.66	99.96	99.96
6375 CARPET REPAIRS		41.67	41.67		83.34	83.34	500.04	500.04
6905 WINDOW WASHING		41.67	41.67		83.34	83.34	500.04	500.04
TOTAL G & A EXPENSE	2,839.35	3,329.16	489.81	7,894.51	6,658.32	(1,236.19)	39,949.92	32,055.41
RESERVE ALLOCATIONS								
6256 CONTINGENCY RESERVE	70.83	76.00	5.17	141.66	152.00	10.34	912.00	770.34
6274 PAINTING RESERVE	172.00	100.00	(72.00)	344.00	200.00	(144.00)	1,200.00	856.00
6275 ROOF RESERVE	285.00	100.00	(185.00)	570.00	200.00	(370.00)	1,200.00	630.00
6383 PARKING AREA & ROAD RES	86.25	86.00	(0.25)	172.50	172.00	(0.50)	1,032.00	859.50
6394 BUILDING MAINTENANCE RE	154.00	100.00	(54.00)	308.00	200.00	(108.00)	1,200.00	892.00
6680 ELEVATOR RESERVE	45.00	45.00		90.00	90.00		540.00	450.00
TOTAL RESERVE ALLOCATIONS	813.08	507.00	(306.08)	1,626.16	1,014.00	(612.16)	6,084.00	4,457.84
TOTAL OPERATING EXPENSES	3,652.93	3,836.16	183.23	9,520.67	7,672.32	(1,848.35)	46,033.92	36,513.25
NET PROFIT OR LOSS	882.19	241.84	640.35	(1,209.12)	483.68	(1,692.80)	2,902.08	(4,111.20)

Collection

The property manager is usually responsible for collecting dues, banking, and sending late notices. The bank account is normally in the name of the association. Reserves are usually put into interest-bearing savings accounts. Each member of the Board of Directors is given an accounting of the cash balances in the different accounts, usually on a monthly basis.

In the past, associations were subject to the "one action rule" which required the holder of the lien to first foreclose the lien and prohibit filing personal action against the delinquent owner until the lien rights were first exhausted. Civil Code 1367 now allows the association to sue for personal money judgments. If the owner has little equity in a unit, this might be an advisable course of action.

Late Charges

Condominium Law (AB 314) allows for a late charge of $10.00 or 10%, whichever is greater, after 15 days for late dues.

Paying the Bills

The property manager usually solicits bids for work to be done and gains approval from the Board of Directors for large amounts (typically $500 and over, except for routine monthly bills such as utilities). The bills are coded according to a chart of accounts, and amounts are checked for accuracy and further verified against purchase orders. The checks are then drawn up by the property manager and given to the designated Board member(s) to sign. It is customary to have the books of the association audited at least annually and to have the tax return prepared by a CPA.

Insurance

The property manager is usually responsible for obtaining bids and making recommendations on insurance coverages to the Board of Directors. A prudent property manager will enlist the assistance of a competent insurance broker to ensure proper coverage and also comply with coverage requirements set forth in the By-Laws and CC&Rs. A more in-depth analysis of insurance will be made in Chapter 13, but the following coverages are usually recommended:

1. *Fire Insurance*

2. *General Liability*

3. *Worker's Compensation on employees*

Figure 10-3.

CONDOMINIUM ANALYSIS

LOS ANGELES, CA — MEDIAN ANNUAL EXPENSES – CONDOMINIUMS LOW RISE 25 UNITS+ — BY METROPOLITAN AREA

EXPENSES	\$ DOLLARS PER UNIT					SALEABLE FLOOR AREA DOLLARS PER SQ. FOOT				
	PROJECTS	UNITS	MED	LOW	HIGH	PROJECTS	SQ.FT.	MED	LOW	HIGH
ADMINISTRATIVE EXP.										
OFFICE SALARIES	7	1,481	171.74	41.48	176.13	2	379,400	.29	.05	.29
OFFICE EXPENSE	27	2,859	15.98	12.13	25.77	8	869,258	.02	.02	.03
MANAGEMENT FEE	29	2,978	114.00	101.47	126.00	9	964,258	.11	.10	.12
LEGAL, AUDIT	27	2,887	18.84	12.75	41.32	8	913,001	.03	.01	.03
OTHER	9	1,017	16.11	9.36	19.37	3	397,316	.02	.00	.02
SUBTOTAL ADMINIST.	29	2,978	186.37	148.98	223.06	9	964,258	.16	.14	.26
OPERATING EXPENSES										
ELEVATOR	20	1,775	27.39	23.29	39.73	6	465,101	.03	.03	.04
HEATING FUEL	1	263	30.12	30.12	30.12					
ELECTRICITY	29	2,978	110.50	80.51	180.68	9	964,258	.14	.09	.24
WATER/SEWER	29	2,578	92.15	66.38	120.26	9	964,258	.13	.08	.14
NATURAL GAS	29	2,978	141.36	97.97	209.56	9	964,258	.14	.11	.19
EXTERMINATING	26	2,852	10.94	8.00	15.48	8	913,001	.01	.01	.02
RUBBISH REMOVAL	29	2,978	40.00	32.31	56.33	9	964,258	.04	.03	.06
WINDOW WASHING										
MISCELLANEOUS	8	1,055	23.95	9.23	30.18	5	603,716	.01	.01	.02
SUBTOTAL OPERATING	29	2,978	443.03	362.77	542.41	9	964,258	.49	.39	.54
REPAIR AND MAINT.										
SECURITY	24	2,709	31.15	13.55	69.20	6	764,001	.07	.02	.18
GROUND MAINTENANCE	29	2,978	97.06	73.88	124.09	9	964,258	.11	.06	.15
CUSTODIAL	26	2,600	111.06	47.73	158.16	8	700,758	.17	.07	.18
GENERAL MAINTENANCE	29	2,978	122.94	78.21	155.74	9	964,258	.10	.07	.12
HEAT/AC/VENT	8	1,153	6.77	1.81	10.85	3	309,716	.01	.01	.01
PAINT-INT CA ONLY	2	228	21.86	5.48	21.86	2	231,657	.02	.01	.02
PAINT-EXTERIOR	2	530	43.49	.60	43.49	1	180,400	.04	.04	.04
RECREATIONAL	27	2,898	28.59	19.06	39.38	9	964,258	.03	.02	.04
OTHER	14	1,554	27.30	16.38	40.13	3	178,385	.02	.01	.02
SUBTOTAL REP/MAINT.	29	2,978	385.55	333.90	525.75	9	964,258	.39	.34	.44
FIXED EXPENSES										
REAL ESTATE TAX	25	2,501	7.76	2.71	22.91	5	642,400	.01	.00	.01
OTHER TAX	28	2,939	114.30	83.74	146.23	9	964,258	.13	.13	.17
INSURANCE	29	2,978	123.13	86.45	156.38	9	964,258	.14	.13	.17
SUBTOTAL FIXED EXP.										
TOTAL ALL EXPENSES	29	2,978	1206.22	959.92	1510.83	9	964,258	1.11	1.09	1.33
GROUND RENT										
REPLACEMENT RESERVE	26	2,548	200.00	118.18	294.78	7	649,501	.14	.12	.19
AMENITIES										
POOL	26	2,865	28.59	19.06	37.69	8	914,758	.03	.02	.03
REC BUILDING	3	671	3.69	2.17	3.69	1	180,400	.01	.01	.01
OUTDOOR REC FACILITY	1	52	19.23	19.23	19.23	1	51,257	.02	.02	.02
OTHER	2	362	3.15	1.85	3.15	2	314,757	.00	.00	.00

FOOTNOTE: For an explanation of the report layouts and method of data analysis, refer to the sections entitled "Guidelines for Use of this Data" and "Interpretation of a Page of Data". For definitions of the expense categories, refer to the Appendix. Copyright 1986, Institute of Real Estate Management.

4. *Fidelity Bond to protect from embezzlement*

5. *Directors and Officers Liability (D&O Coverage) to protect the Board of Directors if they become personally liable due to an "act, error, or omission in their performance."*

Liability of Associations

A condominium owner's unit was burglarized. The owner requested the association to install better lighting, but the Board of Directors refused. The owner then installed her own lighting, but the Association removed it as a violation of the CC&Rs. The owner, after removal of the lights, was sexually assaulted and subsequently sued the association for failure to have prevented (with better lighting) the crime which caused her injury. (Frances T. v. Village Green Owner's Association)

The California Supreme Court ruled that when an association is aware of hazards or potential injury and fails to take reasonable steps to prevent them, the association, like the landlord, is liable.

Role of the Property Manager

Even though a community association is a non-profit entity, it is big business. A 300-unit complex with association fees of $100 per month would have an annual income of $360,000. The elected members of the Board of Directors usually hold non-paying positions, and the operation of management is complex, time-consuming, and requires expertise and training. This is where the property management team comes into play, with its computerized systems and procedures to professionally run the business. In many instances condos are purchased as an investment and the owners live offsite, renting the units to tenants. The ratio of tenants to owners has surpassed 50% in some complexes, leading to problems between onsite owners and tenants.

Resident Relations

Resident relations are more difficult in community association management since each "tenant" is also usually an owner. In a 300-unit complex, the property manager may feel there are 300 bosses rather than just the Board of Directors. The property manager should be familiar with the CC&Rs, By-Laws, and Rules and Regulations, as well as the management agreement, so that decisions made are within the scope and guidelines of the property manager's authority. Newsletters prepared by the association and published on a regular basis are a good way to transmit official notices and rule changes, as well as to promote a feeling of togetherness and camaraderie.

The leading sources of problems, according to the Department of Real Estate study, were "parking violations, followed by late payments, pet violations, rules for common areas, unauthorized changes in dwellings, and noise and disorderly conduct."

Maintenance and Security

The property manager is responsible for supervising maintenance of the common areas and outside walls (i.e., landscaping, parking lot repairs, exterior painting, etc.) to preserve and enhance the value of the complex. The budget and priorities of maintenance must be decided by the Board of Directors, but the property manager is responsible for implementation. The property manager should avoid showing favoritism among the homeowners.

Proper outside lighting and security precautions must also be considered to protect the homeowners and prevent undue liability exposure to the association.

Association Meetings

Many associations hold regular monthly meetings of the Board of Directors which are open to homeowners. The property manager usually prepares the agendas and provides income and expense reports, delinquency reports, bank balances, etc. The property manager also usually sets up and coordinates elections of the Board of Directors.

Committees

Most associations have several committees such as Finance, Social, Architectural, Rules, Ground, Nominating, etc., which report back to the Board of Directors with their recommendations. The property manager will oftentimes coordinate and help facilitate these efforts. See Figure 10-4.

Employees

Someone must hire, fire, supervise, and train employees for office work, housekeeping, maintenance, etc. They must be paid at least minimum wage and have deductions such as income tax and Social Security withheld from their pay. In many instances this is the responsibility of the property manager.

Figure 10-4. Organizational Chart

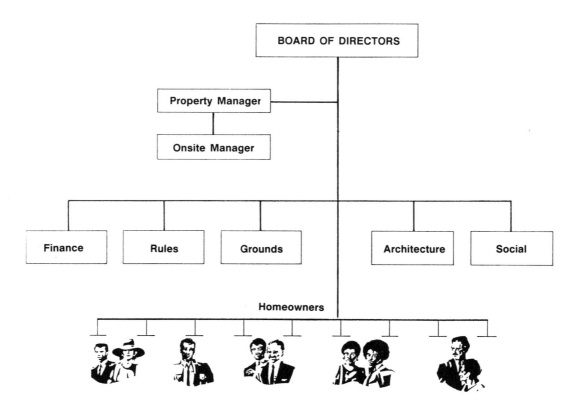

Rentals

Theoretically, there are no rentals in a condo complex since the owners are residents. In actuality, however, almost *half* of some complexes are rented. Rules, regulations, and procedures governing such rentals must be established. In some instances, for an additional fee the property manager will handle rentals to ensure the quality of the tenants. The association can suggest credit and qualifying criteria so long as such criteria are not discriminatory.

Restriction of Children

The Federal Amendments Act of 1988 prohibits discrimination in rules and regulations restricting children unless the rules are reasonable and other facilities are available. Some associations may qualify as "senior complexes" and would be exempt from these regulations.

Commercial Condo Associations

Office and industrial buildings may also be condo associations. The individual units are either owner/user-occupied or the unit owner may lease out the unit. A major difference from residential associations is that if rented the lessee usually pays a triple net lease. Also, there is no statutory limit on the increase percentage for commercial association dues.

The Management Contract

The property manager should have a *signed management agreement*, although this is not required by law if the term is less than one year. The agreement should spell out the term in years, fees, and duties of management. Duties should be detailed as specifically as possible. A hold harmless clause covering both parties is essential. Additionally, a spending limit should be established for the property manager. Extra charges to the association should be stated, such as copying, postage, transfer fees, etc. Additional meetings the property manager is required to attend, other than regular monthly meetings, are often charged to the association at an hourly rate or a flat charge per meeting. By explicitly stating the authority and responsibilities of the property manager, the management agreement (Figure 10-5) should eliminate future misunderstandings.

Management Fee Structure

Traditionally, the fee structure has been low and *usually based on a cost per door (unit)*; i.e., $10 per unit times 100 units equals $1,000 per month. Management companies thus need to handle several thousand units (a high volume) in order to make a profit.

The management company should disclose all interests it may have in vendors, such as landscaping, plumbing, etc., in writing. Non-disclosure would be considered "secret profit." The management company may in some cases act strictly as a bookkeeping operation or a paid consultant, with the association being self-managed. This is especially true for associations under 100 units.

Choosing the Management Company

Maintaining clients is difficult for condo management companies as Boards of Directors frequently change and new directors want to make their own selections. Choosing the property manager is also a difficult task for the association, as this facet of the management industry is still relatively new. The background, reputation, and references of the property manager should be checked. Does the firm employ CPMs or PCAMs? Does the firm belong to the Community Association

Figure 10-5. Condo Management Agreement

This Management contract (the "Agreement") is being entered into by and between a Sole Proprietorship, ("Manager") and _____

_____

(The "Association"), to provide for Manager's performance of various management functions with respect to that certain _____ development known as _____

located in _____

(the "Project"), under the following terms and conditions:

A.   BOOKKEEPING & ACCOUNTING - Manager shall perform the following:

   1.   Collect all Association fees and provide residents with a statement of account or precoded coupon books which cover twelve (12) months, together with return envelopes, in accordance with the CC&Rs, By-Laws and Rules and Regulations of the Association. Collections shall be made on a ____monthly____ basis. A charge will be made to the homeowner for processing each "insufficient funds" or "closed account" check. Said charges will be deposited to the Association Account and paid to DBC Management Co. on an Association check.

   2.   Bank all receipts in a separate "Association Trust Account" in a bank selected by the Manager unless the Association Board requests otherwise. Banks shall be FDIC insured and Savings and Loans shall be insured by the FSLIC. Association Board members will be on signature cards of banking institutions. Only Board of Directors shall sign check and there must be at least two (2) signatures on each check.

   3.   Pay all approved bills out of said Association Trust Account.

   4.   Establish and fund _____ an account for long term replacement and contingency reserves. This shall be a separate account from the Association Trust Account.

   5.   Association attorney will handle all liens and filing of said notices for the Association.

   6.   Render on a ____monthly____ basis a "Profit & Loss" Statement. Said Statement shall be in a "Budget Comparison - Actual" and "Year to Date" format.

   7.   Render a ____monthly____ "Check Register" itemizing all disbursements.

   8.   COMPENSATION OF THE MANAGER

      1.   The compensation which the Manager shall be entitled to receive for all services performed under this Agreement, with the exception of the additional services or fees specified herein, shall be a fee payable monthly in an amount of _____
Such compensation shall be paid in advance monthly to the Manager on or before the fifth (5th) day of each month during the term of this Agreement.

Figure 10-5 (cont'd). Condo Management Agreement

9. TERMS AND TERMINATION OF AGREEMENT

    1. This Agreement shall be in effect for one (1) year from _____ _____, to _____ At the end of this original term, this Agreement may be renewed by the mutual agreement of the Parties for successive one (1) year periods.

    2. This Agreement may be terminated without cause by either Party upon ninety (90) days written notice to the other Party or with cause here-under, including any breach of this Agreement by either Party or their respective bankruptcy, insolvency or similar event upon thirty (30) days written notice.

    3. This Agreement shall be considered automatically renewed at the end of this original term unless either Party has given notice to the other Party in accordance with paragraph 2. above. An addendum to the Agreement will be provided to the Board for signature to confirm such automatic renewal acceptance if the Board deems it necessary.

    4. In the event termination notice is given mid-month, the thirty (30) day or ninety (90) day notice goes into effect the first (1st) of the following month, thereby allowing ample time to reconcile bank accounts, compile all records and documentation for a timely and thorough turnover to the succeeding management company.

10. Clauses 10-20 are omitted from this sample agreement.

21. This agreement shall not be amended or modified in any respect except with the written consent of Manager and the Association, or by addendum hereto.

22. All capitalized words used herein shall have their meanings defined in the recorded Declaration of Covenants, Conditions and Restrictions for the Association.

THE PARTIES HERETO have read and understand the foregoing Agreement. Modi-fication may have been made to this Agreement and attached as Addendum "A", having been signed and dated by the Parties hereto.

AGREED TO this _____ day of _____ 19_____

_____

_____

By:_____   By:_____

Its:_____   Its:_____

_____

_____

        (address)   (address)

Witnesses: _____

Institute (CAI)? What accounts does it presently manage? How do the firm's present clients rate the firm? Does the management firm have a real estate license? Does it have a trust account in a federally-insured bank or savings and loan?

Additional Information

Additional information may be obtained through:

Institute of Real Estate Management (IREM)
430 N. Michigan Avenue
Chicago, IL 60611

Community Associations Institute (CAI)
1423 Powhatan, #7
Alexandria, VA 22314

community
associations
institute

Education

Reports

The Community Associations Institution (CAI) publishes a series of monographs — GAP Reports (Guide for Association Practitioners). Professionals and homeowner experts throughout the country are authors of these comprehensive and detailed guidebooks. These detailed GAP Reports provide needed information for persons involved in the community association industry including association managers, property managers, lenders, homeowners, association board members, etc. Some selected topics of the GAP Reports available include:

GAP #1 — Association Management

GAP #2 — Architectural Control

GAP #3 — Transition from Developer's Control

GAP #4 — Insurance

GAP #5 — Association Collections; Legal Remedies

GAP #6 — Property TAX and HOA's

GAP #7 — Drafting Association Rules

GAP #8 — Choosing a Management Company

GAP #9 — Bid Specification & Contract Negotiation

GAP #10 — Assessment Collection; Creating a System

Designations

1. *PCAM (Professional Community Association Manager)* is a designation for managers of condominiums, cooperatives, or homeowners associations who are interested in career growth. This program honors association managers who demonstrate an advanced degree of skills and knowledge.

2. *Operations and Management Program* offers intensive coursework on complexities of association operation and management. This program is for board members, developers, and managers who want to have a solid understanding of responsibility, liability, and authority.

3. *Professional Management Development Program* is a comprehensive educational program with over 100 hours of instruction. Courses included in the program are legal basis of community associations, communications and meetings, operations, asset protection, and management practices.

These reports can be obtained by contacting the Community Associations Institute, whose address is on the previous page.

Marketing of Condos

The sale of individual condos is similar to that of single-family homes. In California, the agent must have agency forms AD-11 and AC-6 completed and signed (Figures 10-6, 10-7). These agency forms were required as of January 1, 1988, on sales of four or fewer residential units.

Even though commercial properties are exempt, it may be prudent to use these forms on all transactions to reduce the liability risk. Use of a preprinted deposit receipt form such as the California Association of Realtors Form DLF-14 is also advisable, as it covers the conditions, terms, and disclosures involved in the sale (Figure 10-8).

Unique marketing conditions in the sale of a condo include:

1. Posting of For Sale signs in compliance with the CC&Rs.

2. Holding of open houses and showing the condo in security-gated complexes where access is limited.

3. In the sale of a new condo, a pink and white paper (approved by the Department of Real Estate) must be given to the buyer.

4. Copies of the By-Laws, CC&Rs, current budget, and reserve study must be given to buyer prior to close.

Figure 10-6. Agency Disclosure Form AD-11

DISCLOSURE REGARDING
REAL ESTATE AGENCY RELATIONSHIPS
(As required by the Civil Code)
CALIFORNIA ASSOCIATION OF REALTORS© (CAR) STANDARD FORM

When you enter into a discussion with a real estate agent regarding a real estate transaction, you should from the outset understand what type of agency relationship or representation you wish to have with the agent in the transaction.

SELLER'S AGENT
A Seller's agent under a listing agreement with Seller acts as the agent for the Seller only. A Seller's agent or a subagent of that agent has the following affirmative obligations:
To the Seller:
   (a) A Fiduciary duty of utmost care, integrity, honesty, and loyalty in dealings with the Seller.
To the Buyer & the Seller:
   (a) Diligent exercise of reasonable skill and care in performance of the agent's duties.
   (b) A duty of honest and fair dealing and good faith.
   (c) A duty to disclose all facts known to the agent materially affecting the value or desirability of property that are not known to, or within the diligent attention and observation of, the parties.

An agent is not obligated to reveal to either party any confidential information obtained from the other party which does not involve the affirmative duties set forth above.

BUYER'S AGENT
A selling agent can, with a Buyer's consent, agree to act as agent for the Buyer only. In these situations, the agent is not the Seller's agent, even if by agreement the agent may receive compensation for services rendered, either in full or in part from the Seller. An agent acting only for a Buyer has the following affirmative obligations:
To the Buyer:
   (a) A fiduciary duty of utmost care, integrity, honesty, and loyalty in dealings with the Buyer.
To the Buyer & Seller:
   (a) Diligent exercise of reasonable skill and care in performance of the agent's duties.
   (b) A duty of honest and fair dealing and good faith.
   (c) A duty to disclose all facts known to the agent materially affecting the value or desirability of the property that are not known to, or within the diligent attention and observation of, the parties.

An agent is not obligated to reveal to either party any confidential information obtained from the other party which does not involve the affirmative duties set forth above.

AGENT REPRESENTING BOTH SELLER & BUYER
A real estate agent, either acting directly or through one or more associate licensees, can legally be the agent of both the Seller and the Buyer in a transaction, but only with the knowledge and consent of both the Seller and the Buyer.

In a dual agency situation, the agent has the following affirmative obligations to both the Seller and the Buyer:
   (a) A fiduciary duty of utmost care, integrity, honesty and loyalty in the dealings with either Seller or the Buyer.
   (b) Other duties to the Seller and the Buyer as stated above in their respective sections.

In representing both Seller and Buyer, the agent may not, without the express permission of the respective party, disclose to the other party that the Seller will accept a price less than the listing price or that the Buyer will pay a price greater than the price offered.

The above duties of the agent in a real estate transaction do not relieve a Seller or a Buyer from the responsibility to protect their own interests. You should carefully read all agreements to assure that they adequately express your understanding of the transaction. A real estate agent is a person qualified to advise about real estate. If legal or tax advice is desired, consult a competent professional.

Throughout your real property transaction you may receive more than one disclosure form, depending upon the number of agents assisting in the transaction. The law requires each agent with whom you have more than a casual relationship to present you with this disclosure form. You should read its contents each time it is presented to you, considering the relationship between you and the real estate agent in your specific transaction.

This disclosure form includes the provisions of article 2.5 (commencing with Section 2373) of Chapter 2 of Title 9 of Part 4 of Division 3 of the Civil Code set forth on the reverse hereof. Read it carefully.

I/WE ACKNOWLEDGE RECEIPT OF A COPY OF THIS DISCLOSURE.

BUYER/SELLER_____ Date_____ TIME_____ AM/PM

BUYER/SELLER_____ Date_____ TIME_____ AM/PM

AGENT _____ By_____ Date_____
    (Please Print)   (Associate Licensee or Broker-Signature)

A REAL ESTATE BROKER IS QUALIFIED TO ADVISE ON REAL ESTATE. IF YOU DESIRE LEGAL ADVICE, CONSULT YOUR ATTORNEY.

This form is available for use by the entire real estate industry. The use of this form is not intended to identify the user as a REALTOR®. REALTOR® is a registered collective membership mark which may be used only by real estate licensees who are members of the NATIONAL ASSOCIATION OF REALTORS® and who subscribe to its Code of Ethics.

Copyright© 1987, CALIFORNIA ASSOCIATION OF REALTORS®
525 South Virgil Avenue, Los Angeles, California 90020   FORM AD-11

OFFICE USE ONLY
Reviewed by Broker or Designee _____
Date _____

EQUAL HOUSING OPPORTUNITY

SF-Oct-87

Figure 10-7. Agency Confirmation Form AC-6

CALIFORNIA ASSOCIATION OF REALTORS®

CONFIRMATION
REAL ESTATE AGENCY RELATIONSHIPS
(As required by the Civil Code)
CALIFORNIA ASSOCIATION OF REALTORS® (CAR) STANDARD FORM

Subject Property Address _____.

The following agency relationship(s) is/are hereby confirmed for this transaction:

LISTING AGENT: _____

is the agent of (check one):

☐ the Seller exclusively; or

☐ both the Buyer and Seller

SELLING AGENT: _____
(if not the same as Listing Agent)

is the agent of (check one):

☐ the Buyer exclusively; or

☐ the Seller exclusively; or

☐ both the Buyer and Seller

I/WE ACKNOWLEDGE RECEIPT OF A COPY OF THIS CONFIRMATION.

Seller _____ Date _____ By _____ Buyer _____ Date _____

Seller _____ Date _____ By _____ Buyer _____ Date _____

Listing Agent _____ By _____ Date _____
(Please Print)   (Associate Licensee or Broker-Signature)

Selling Agent _____ By _____ Date _____
(Please Print)   (Associate Licensee or Broker-Signature)

A REAL ESTATE BROKER IS QUALIFIED TO ADVISE ON REAL ESTATE. IF YOU DESIRE LEGAL ADVICE, CONSULT YOUR ATTORNEY.

This form is available for use by the entire real estate industry. The use of this form is not intended to identify the user as a REALTOR®. REALTOR® is a registered collective membership mark which may be used only by real estate licensees who are members of the NATIONAL ASSOCIATION OF REALTORS® and who subscribe to its Code of Ethics.

FORM AC-6

────── OFFICE USE ONLY ──────

Reviewed by Broker or Designee _____

Date _____

EQUAL HOUSING OPPORTUNITY

SF-Jan-88

Figure 10-8. Deposit Receipt

CALIFORNIA ASSOCIATION OF REALTORS

REAL ESTATE PURCHASE CONTRACT AND RECEIPT FOR DEPOSIT
(LONG FORM — WITH FINANCING CLAUSES)
THIS IS MORE THAN A RECEIPT FOR MONEY. IT IS INTENDED TO BE A LEGALLY BINDING CONTRACT. READ IT CAREFULLY.
CALIFORNIA ASSOCIATION OF REALTORS® (CAR) STANDARD FORM

_____, California, _____, 19____

Received from _____

herein called Buyer, the sum of _____ Dollars $ _____

evidenced by ☐ cash, ☐ cashier's check, ☐ personal check or ☐ _____, payable to _____

_____, to be held uncashed until acceptance of this offer as deposit on account of purchase price of

_____ Dollars $ _____

for the purchase of property, situated in _____, County of _____ California,

described as follows: _____

1. FINANCING: The obtaining of Buyer's financing is a contingency of this agreement.

A. DEPOSIT upon acceptance, to be deposited into _____ $ _____

B. INCREASED DEPOSIT within_____ days of Seller's acceptance to be deposited into _____ $ _____

C. BALANCE OF DOWN PAYMENT to be deposited into _____ on or before _____ $ _____

D. Buyer to apply, qualify for and obtain a NEW FIRST LOAN in the amount of .... $ _____
payable monthly at approximately $_____ including interest at origination not to exceed
_____ %, ☐ fixed rate, ☐ other _____ all due _____ years from date of
origination. Loan fee not to exceed _____ Seller agrees to pay a maximum of _____
FHA/VA discount points. Additional terms_____

E. Buyer ☐ to assume, ☐ to take title subject to an EXISTING FIRST LOAN with an approximate balance of ... $ _____
in favor of_____ payable monthly at $_____ including interest
at_____% ☐ fixed rate, ☐ other _____
Fees not to exceed_____ . Disposition of impound account _____
Additional Terms _____

F. Buyer to execute a NOTE SECURED BY a ☐ first, ☐ second, ☐ third DEED OF TRUST in the amount of $ _____
IN FAVOR OF SELLER payable monthly at $_____ ☐ or more, including interest at_____% all due
_____ years from date of origination, ☐ or upon sale or transfer of subject property. A late charge of
_____ shall be due on any installment not paid within_____ days of the due date.
☐ Deed of Trust to contain a request for notice of default or sale for the benefit of Seller. Buyer ☐ will, ☐ will not
execute a request for notice of delinquency. Additional terms_____

G. Buyer ☐ to assume, ☐ to take title subject to an EXISTING SECOND LOAN with an approximate balance of . $ _____
in favor of_____ payable monthly at $_____ including interest
at_____% ☐ fixed rate, ☐ other _____ . Buyer fees not to exceed _____
Additional terms _____

H. Buyer to apply, qualify for and obtain a NEW SECOND LOAN in the amount of .... $ _____
payable monthly at approximately $_____ including interest at origination not to exceed
_____% ☐ fixed rate, ☐ other _____
_____, all due_____ years from date of origination. Buyer's loan fee not to exceed_____ .
Additional Terms _____

I. In the event Buyer assumes or takes title subject to an existing loan, Seller shall provide Buyer with copies of
applicable notes and Deeds of Trust. A loan may contain a number of features which affect the loan, such as
interest rate changes, monthly payment changes, balloon payments, etc. Buyer shall be allowed_____ calendar
days after receipt of such copies to notify Seller in writing of disapproval. FAILURE TO NOTIFY SELLER SHALL
CONCLUSIVELY BE CONSIDERED APPROVAL. Buyer's approval shall not be unreasonably withheld.
Difference in existing loan balances shall be adjusted in ☐ Cash, ☐ Other_____

J. Buyer agrees to act diligently and in good faith to obtain all applicable financing. _____

K. ADDITIONAL FINANCING TERMS: _____

L. TOTAL PURCHASE PRICE.. $ _____

2. OCCUPANCY: Buyer ☐ does, ☐ does not intend to occupy subject property as Buyer's primary residence.

3. SUPPLEMENTS: The ATTACHED supplements are incorporated herein:
☐ Interim Occupancy Agreement (CAR FORM IOA-11)   ☐ _____
☐ Residential Lease Agreement after Sale (CAR FORM RLAS-11)   ☐ _____
☐ VA and FHA Amendments (CAR FORM VA/FHA-11)   ☐ _____

Buyer and Seller acknowledge receipt of copy of this page, which constitutes Page 1 of _____ Pages.
Buyer's Initials (_____) (_____)   Seller's Initials (_____) (_____)

THIS STANDARDIZED DOCUMENT FOR USE IN SIMPLE TRANSACTIONS HAS BEEN APPROVED BY THE CALIFORNIA ASSOCIATION OF REALTORS® IN FORM ONLY. NO REPRESENTATION IS MADE AS TO THE APPROVAL OF THE FORM OF ANY SUPPLEMENTS NOT CURRENTLY PUBLISHED BY THE CALIFORNIA ASSOCIATION OF REALTORS® OR THE LEGAL VALIDITY OR ADEQUACY OF ANY PROVISION IN ANY SPECIFIC TRANSACTION. IT SHOULD NOT BE USED IN COMPLEX TRANSACTIONS OR WITH EXTENSIVE RIDERS OR ADDITIONS.

A REAL ESTATE BROKER IS THE PERSON QUALIFIED TO ADVISE ON REAL ESTATE TRANSACTIONS. IF YOU DESIRE LEGAL OR TAX ADVICE, CONSULT AN APPROPRIATE PROFESSIONAL.

Copyright© 1986, 1987, CALIFORNIA ASSOCIATION OF REALTORS®
525 South Virgil Avenue, Los Angeles, California 90020
Revised 7/87

BROKER'S COPY

OFFICE USE ONLY
Reviewed by Broker or Designee _____
Date _____

EQUAL HOUSING OPPORTUNITY
SF-Apr-88

REAL ESTATE PURCHASE CONTRACT AND RECEIPT FOR DEPOSIT (DLF-14 PAGE 1 OF 4)

Figure 10-8 (cont'd). Deposit Receipt

Subject Property Address _____

4. **ESCROW:** Buyer and Seller shall deliver signed instructions to_____ the escrow holder, within _____calendar days from Seller's acceptance which shall provide for closing within_____ calendar days from Seller's acceptance. Escrow fees to be paid as follows: _____

5. **TITLE:** Title is to be free of liens, encumbrances, easements, restrictions, rights and conditions of record or known to Seller, other than the following: (a) Current property taxes, (b) covenants, conditions, restrictions, and public utility easements of record, if any, provided the same do not adversely affect the continued use of the property for the purposes for which it is presently being used, unless reasonably disapproved by Buyer in writing within _____ calendar days of receipt of a current preliminary report furnished at_____ expense, and (c) _____. Seller shall furnish Buyer at _____ expense a standard California Land Title Association policy issued by _____ Company, showing title vested in Buyer subject only to the above. If Seller is unwilling or unable to eliminate any title matter disapproved by Buyer as above, Buyer may terminate this agreement. If Seller fails to deliver title as above, Buyer may terminate this agreement; in either case, the deposit shall be returned to Buyer.

6. **PRORATIONS:** Property taxes, payments on bonds and assessments assumed by Buyer, interest, rents, association dues, premiums on insurance acceptable to Buyer, and _____ shall be paid current and prorated as of: ☐ the day of recordation of the deed; or ☐ _____. Bonds or assessments now a lien shall be ☐ paid current by Seller, payments not yet due to be assumed by Buyer; or ☐ paid in full by Seller, including payments not yet due; or ☐ _____. The _____ transfer tax County Transfer tax shall be paid by _____. **PROPERTY WILL BE REASSESSED UPON CHANGE OF** or transfer fee shall be paid by _____. **OWNERSHIP. THIS WILL AFFECT THE TAXES TO BE PAID.** A Supplemental tax bill will be issued, which shall be paid as follows: (a) for periods after close of escrow, by Buyer (or by final acquiring party if part of an exchange), and (b) for periods prior to close of escrow, by Seller. TAX BILLS ISSUED AFTER CLOSE OF ESCROW SHALL BE HANDLED DIRECTLY BETWEEN BUYER AND SELLER.

7. **POSSESSION:** Possession and occupancy shall be delivered to Buyer, ☐ on close of escrow, or ☐ not later than _____ days after close of escrow, or ☐ _____

8. **VESTING:** Unless otherwise designated in the escrow instructions of Buyer, title shall vest as follows: _____

(The manner of taking title may have significant legal and tax consequences. Therefore, give this matter serious consideration.)

9. **MULTIPLE LISTING SERVICE:** If Broker is a Participant of a Board multiple listing service ("MLS"), the Broker is authorized to report the sale, its price, terms, and financing for the publication, dissemination, information, and use of the authorized Board members, MLS Participants and Subscribers.

10. **LIQUIDATED DAMAGES: If Buyer fails to complete said purchase as herein provided by reason of any default of Buyer, Seller shall be released from obligation to sell the property to Buyer and may proceed against Buyer upon any claim or remedy which he/she may have in law or equity; provided, however, that by placing their initials here Buyer: (   ) Seller: (   ) agree that Seller shall retain the deposit as liquidated damages. If the described property is a dwelling with no more than four units, one of which the Buyer intends to occupy as his/her residence, Seller shall retain as liquidated damages the deposit actually paid, or an amount therefrom, not more than 3% of the purchase price and promptly return any excess to Buyer. Buyer and Seller agree to execute a similar liquidated damages provision, such as California Association of Realtors® Receipt for Increased Deposit (RID-11), for any increased deposits. (Funds deposited in trust accounts or in escrow are not released automatically in the event of a dispute. Release of funds requires written agreement of the parties or adjudication.)**

11. **ARBITRATION:** If the only controversy or claim between the parties arises out of or relates to the disposition of the Buyer's deposit, such controversy or claim shall at the election of the parties be decided by arbitration. Such arbitration shall be determined in accordance with the Rules of the American Arbitration Association, and judgment upon the award rendered by the Arbitrator(s) may be entered in any court having jurisdiction thereof. The provisions of Code of Civil Procedure Section 1283.05 shall be applicable to such arbitration.

12. **ATTORNEY'S FEES:** In any action or proceeding arising out of this agreement, the prevailing party shall be entitled to reasonable attorney's fees and costs.

13. **KEYS:** Seller shall, when possession is available to Buyer, provide keys and/or means to operate all property locks, and alarms, if any.

14. **PERSONAL PROPERTY:** The following items of personal property, free of liens and without warranty of condition, are included: _____

15. **FIXTURES:** All permanently installed fixtures and fittings that are attached to the property or for which special openings have been made are included in the purchase price, including electrical, light, plumbing and heating fixtures, built-in appliances, screens, awnings, shutters, all window coverings, attached floor coverings, T.V. antennas, air cooler or conditioner, garage door openers and controls, attached fireplace equipment, mailbox, trees and shrubs, and _____ except _____.

16. **SMOKE DETECTOR(S):** Approved smoke detector(s) shall be installed as required by law, at the expense of ☐ Buyer, ☐ Seller.

17. **TRANSFER DISCLOSURE:** Unless exempt, Transferor (Seller), shall comply with Civil Code Sections 1102 et seq., by providing Transferee(Buyer) with a Real Estate Transfer Disclosure Statement: a) ☐ Buyer has received and read a Real Estate Transfer Disclosure Statement; or b) ☐ Seller shall provide Buyer with a Real Estate Transfer Disclosure Statement within _____ calendar days of Seller's acceptance after which Buyer shall have three (3) days after delivery to Buyer, in person, or five (5) days after delivery by deposit in the mail, to terminate this agreement by delivery of a written notice of termination to Seller or Seller's Agent.

18. **TAX WITHHOLDING:** Under the Foreign Investment in Real Property Tax Act (FIRPTA), IRC 1445, *every* Buyer of U.S. real property *must,* unless an exemption applies, deduct and withhold from Seller's proceeds ten percent (10%) of the gross sales price. The primary exemptions are: No withholding is required if (a) Seller provides Buyer with an affidavit under penalty of perjury, that Seller is not a "foreign person," or (b) Seller provides Buyer with a "qualifying statement" issued by the Internal Revenue Service, or (c) if Buyer purchases real property for use as a residence and the purchase price is $300,000.00 or less and if Buyer or a member of Buyer's family has definite plans to reside at the property for at least 50% of the number of days it is in use during each of the first two twelve-months periods after transfer. Seller and Buyer agree to execute and deliver as directed, any instrument, affidavit and statement, or to perform any act reasonably necessary to carry out the provisions of FIRPTA and regulations promulgated thereunder.

19. **ENTIRE CONTRACT:** Time is of the essence. All prior agreements between the parties are incorporated in this agreement which constitutes the entire contract. Its terms are intended by the parties as a final expression of their agreement with respect to such terms as are included herein and may not be contradicted by evidence of any prior agreement or contemporaneous oral agreement. The parties further intend that this agreement constitutes the complete and exclusive statement of its terms and that no extrinsic evidence whatsoever may be introduced in any judicial or arbitration proceeding, if any, involving this agreement.

Buyer and Seller acknowledge receipt of copy of this page, which constitutes Page 2 of _____ Pages.
Buyer's Initials (_____) (_____)   Seller's Initials (_____) (_____)

OFFICE USE ONLY
Reviewed by Broker or Designee _____
Date _____

BROKER'S COPY

EQUAL HOUSING OPPORTUNITY
SF-Apr-88

REAL ESTATE PURCHASE CONTRACT AND RECEIPT FOR DEPOSIT (DLF-14 PAGE 2 OF 4)

Figure 10-8 (cont'd). Deposit Receipt

Subject Property Address _____

20. CAPTIONS: The captions in this agreement are for convenience of reference only and are not intended as part of this agreement.

21. ADDITIONAL TERMS AND CONDITIONS:
ONLY THE FOLLOWING PARAGRAPHS A THROUGH J *WHEN INITIALED BY BOTH BUYER AND SELLER* ARE INCORPORATED IN THIS AGREEMENT.

Buyer's Initials   Seller's Initials

____/____   ____/____   **A. PHYSICAL INSPECTION:** Within _____ calendar days after Seller's acceptance Buyer shall have the right, at Buyer's expense, to select a licensed contractor(s) or other qualified professional(s), to inspect and investigate the subject property, including but not limited to structural, plumbing, heating, electrical, built-in appliances, roof, soils, foundation, mechanical systems, pool, pool heater, pool filter, air conditioner, if any, possible environmental hazards such as asbestos, formaldehyde, radon gas and other substances / products. Buyer shall keep the subject property free and clear of any liens, indemnify and hold Seller harmless from all liability, claims, demands, damages or costs, and repair all damages to the property arising from the inspections. All claimed defects concerning the condition of the property that adversely affect the continued use of the property for the purposes for which it is presently being used shall be in writing, supported by written reports, if any, and delivered to Seller within_____ calendar days after Seller's acceptance. Buyer shall furnish Seller copies, at no cost, of all reports concerning the property obtained by Buyer. When such reports disclose conditions or information unsatisfactory to the Buyer, which the Seller is unwilling or unable to correct, Buyer may cancel this agreement. Seller shall make the premises available for all inspections. BUYER'S FAILURE TO NOTIFY SELLER SHALL CONCLUSIVELY BE CONSIDERED APPROVAL.

Buyer's Initials   Seller's Initials

____/____   ____/____   **B. GEOLOGICAL INSPECTION:** Within _____ calendar days after Seller's acceptance, Buyer shall have the right at Buyer's expense, to select a qualified professional to make tests, surveys, or other studies of the subject property. Buyer shall keep the subject property free and clear of any liens, indemnify and hold Seller harmless from all liability, claims, demands, damages or costs, and repair all damages to the property arising from the tests, surveys, or studies. All claimed defects concerning the condition of the property that adversely affect the continued use of the property for the purposes for which it is presently being used shall be in writing, supported by written reports, if any, and delivered to Seller within _____ calendar days after Seller's acceptance. Buyer shall furnish Seller copies, at no cost, of all reports concerning the property obtained by Buyer. When such reports disclose conditions or information unsatisfactory to the Buyer, which the Seller is unwilling or unable to correct, Buyer may cancel this agreement. Seller shall make the premises available for all inspections. BUYER'S FAILURE TO NOTIFY SELLER SHALL CONCLUSIVELY BE CONSIDERED APPROVAL.

Buyer's Initials   Seller's Initials

____/____   ____/____   **C. CONDITION OF PROPERTY:** Seller warrants, through the date possession is made available to Buyer: (1) property and improvements thereon, including landscaping, grounds and pool/spa, if any, shall be maintained in the same condition as upon the date of Seller's acceptance; (2) the roof is free of all known leaks and that water, sewer, plumbing, heating, air conditioning, if any, and electrical systems and all built-in appliances are operative, (3) _____ .

Buyer's Initials   Seller's Initials

____/____   ____/____   **D. SELLER REPRESENTATION:** Seller warrants that Seller has no knowledge of any notice of violations of City, County, State, Federal, Building, Zoning, Fire, Health Codes or ordinances, or other governmental regulation filed or issued against the property. This warranty shall be effective until the date of close of escrow.

Buyer's Initials   Seller's Initials

____/____   ____/____   **E. PEST CONTROL:** Within_____ calendar days from the date of Seller's acceptance Seller shall furnish Buyer, at the expense of ☐ Buyer, ☐ Seller, a current written report of an inspection by_____ , a licensed Structural Pest Control Operator, of the main building and all structures on the property, except_____

If no infestation or infection by wood destroying pests or organisms is found, the report shall include a written "Certification" as provided in Business and Professions Code 8519(a) that on the date of inspection "no evidence of active infestation or infection was found."

All work recommended in said report to repair damage caused by infestation or infection by wood-destroying pests or organisms found, including leaking shower stalls and replacing of tiles removed for repairs, and all work to correct conditions that cause such infestation or infection shall be done at the expense of Seller.

Funds for work to be performed shall be held in escrow and disbursed upon receipt of written Certification as provided in Business and Professions Code 8519(b) that the property "is now free of evidence of active infestation or infection".

Buyer agrees that any work to correct conditions usually deemed likely to lead to infestation or infection by wood-destroying pests or organisms, but where no evidence of existing infestation or infection is found with respect to such conditions is NOT the responsibility of Seller, and that such work shall be done only if requested by Buyer and then at the expense of Buyer.

If inspection of inaccessible areas is recommended by the report, Buyer has the option of accepting and approving the report or requesting further inspection be made at the Buyer's expense. If further inspection is made and infestation, infection, or damage is found, repair of such damage and all work to correct conditions that caused such infestation or infection and the cost of entry and closing of the inaccessible areas shall be at the expense of Seller. If no infestation, infection, or damage is found, the cost of entry and closing of the inaccessible areas shall be at the expense of Buyer.
Other _____ .

Buyer's Initials   Seller's Initials

____/____   ____/____   **F. FLOOD HAZARD AREA DISCLOSURE:** Buyer is informed that subject property is situated in a "Special Flood Hazard Area" as set forth on a Federal Emergency Management Agency (FEMA) "Flood Insurance Rate Map" (FIRM) or "Flood Hazard Boundary Map" (FHBM). The law provides that, as a condition of obtaining financing on most structures located in a "Special Flood Hazard Area," lenders require flood insurance where the property or its attachments are security for a loan.

The extent of coverage and the cost may vary. For further information consult the lender or insurance carrier. No representation or recommendation is made by the Seller and the Brokers in this transaction as to the legal effect or economic consequences of the National Flood Insurance Program and related legislation.

Buyer and Seller acknowledge receipt of copy of this page, which constitutes Page 3 of_____ Pages.
Buyer's Initials (_____) (_____)   Seller's Initials (_____) (_____)

┌─── OFFICE USE ONLY ───┐
Reviewed by Broker or Designee _____
Date _____

BROKER'S COPY

EQUAL HOUSING OPPORTUNITY
SF-Apr-88

REAL ESTATE PURCHASE CONTRACT AND RECEIPT FOR DEPOSIT (DLF-14 PAGE 3 OF 4)

Figure 10-8 (cont'd). Deposit Receipt

Subject Property Address _____

Buyer's Initials _____ Seller's Initials _____

G. SPECIAL STUDIES ZONE DISCLOSURE: Buyer is informed that subject property is situated in a Special Studies Zone as designated under Sections 2621-2625, inclusive, of the California Public Resources Code; and, as such, the construction or development on this property of any structure for human occupancy may be subject to the findings of a geologic report prepared by a geologist registered in the State of California, unless such a report is waived by the City or County under the terms of that act.

Buyer is allowed _____ calendar days from the date of Seller's acceptance to make further inquiries at appropriate governmental agencies concerning the use of the subject property under the terms of the Special Studies Zone Act and local building, zoning, fire, health and safety codes. When such inquiries disclose conditions or information unsatisfactory to the Buyer, which the Seller is unwilling or unable to correct, Buyer may cancel this agreement. BUYER'S FAILURE TO NOTIFY SELLER SHALL CONCLUSIVELY BE CONSIDERED APPROVAL.

Buyer's Initials _____ Seller's Initials _____

H. ENERGY CONSERVATION RETROFIT: If local ordinance requires that the property be brought in compliance with minimum energy Conservation Standards as a condition of sale or transfer, ☐ Buyer, ☐ Seller shall comply with and pay for these requirements. Where permitted by law, Seller may, if obligated hereunder, satisfy the obligation by authorizing escrow to credit Buyer with sufficient funds to cover the cost of such retrofit.

Buyer's Initials _____ Seller's Initials _____

I. HOME PROTECTION PLAN: Buyer and Seller have been informed that Home Protection Plans are available. Such plans may provide additional protection and benefit to a Seller or Buyer. California Association of Realtors® and the Broker(s) in this transaction do not endorse or approve any particular company or program:

a) ☐ A Buyer's coverage Home Protection Plan to be issued by _____ Company, at a cost not to exceed $ _____ , to be paid by ☐ Seller, ☐ Buyer; or

b) ☐ Buyer and Seller elect not to purchase a Home Protection Plan.

Buyer's Initials _____ Seller's Initials _____

J. CONDOMINIUM/P.U.D.: The subject of this transaction is a condominium/planned unit development (P.U.D.) designated as unit _____ and _____ parking space(s) and an undivided _____ interest in all community areas, and _____ . The current monthly assessment charge by the homeowner's association or other governing body(s) is $ _____ . As soon as practicable, Seller shall provide Buyer with copies of covenants, conditions and restrictions, articles of incorporation, by-laws, current rules and regulations, most current financial statements, and any other documents as required by law. Seller shall disclose in writing any known pending special assessment, claims, or litigation to Buyer. Buyer shall be allowed _____ calendar days from receipt to review these documents. If such documents disclose conditions or information unsatisfactory to Buyer, Buyer may cancel this agreement. BUYER'S FAILURE TO NOTIFY SELLER SHALL CONCLUSIVELY BE CONSIDERED APPROVAL.

22. **OTHER TERMS AND CONDITIONS:** _____
_____
_____
_____
_____

23. **AGENCY CONFIRMATION:** The following agency relationship(s) are hereby confirmed for this transaction:
LISTING AGENT: _____ is the agent of (check one):
☐ the Seller exclusively; or ☐ both the Buyer and Seller
SELLING AGENT: _____ (If not the same as Listing Agent) is the agent of (check one):
☐ the Buyer exclusively; or ☐ the Seller exclusively; or ☐ both the Buyer and Seller.

24. **AMENDMENTS: This agreement may not be amended, modified, altered or changed in any respect whatsoever except by a further agreement in writing executed by Buyer and Seller.**

25. **OFFER:** This constitutes an offer to purchase the described property. Unless acceptance is signed by Seller and the signed copy delivered in person or by mail to Buyer, or to _____ who is authorized to receive it, in person or by mail at the address below, within _____ calendar days of the date hereof, this offer shall be deemed revoked and the deposit shall be returned. Buyer has read and acknowledges receipt of a copy of this offer.

REAL ESTATE BROKER _____ BUYER _____
By _____ BUYER _____
Address _____ Address _____

Telephone _____ Telephone _____

ACCEPTANCE

The undersigned Seller accepts and agrees to sell the property on the above terms and conditions and agrees to the above confirmation of agency relationships. Seller agrees to pay to Broker(s) _____

compensation for services as follows: _____ .

Payable: (a) On recordation of the deed or other evidence of title, or (b) if completion of sale is prevented by default of Seller, upon Seller's default, or (c) if completion of sale is prevented by default of Buyer, only if and when Seller collects damages from Buyer, by suit or otherwise, and then in an amount not less than one-half of the damages recovered, but not to exceed the above fee, after first deducting title and escrow expenses and the expenses of collection, if any. Seller shall execute and deliver an escrow instruction irrevocably assigning the compensation for service in an amount equal to the compensation agreed to above. In any action or proceeding between Broker(s) and Seller arising out of this agreement, the prevailing party shall be entitled to reasonable attorneys fees and costs. The undersigned has read and acknowledges receipt of a copy of this agreement and authorizes Broker(s) to deliver a signed copy to Buyer.

Date _____ Telephone _____ SELLER _____
Address _____
SELLER _____

Real Estate Broker(s) agree to the foregoing.

Broker _____ By _____ Date _____
Broker _____ By _____ Date _____

This form is available for use by the entire real estate industry. The use of this form is not intended to identify the user as a REALTOR®. REALTOR® is a registered collective membership mark which may be used only by real estate licensees who are members of the NATIONAL ASSOCIATION OF REALTORS® and who subscribe to its Code of Ethics.

OFFICE USE ONLY
Reviewed by Broker or Designee _____
Date _____

SF-Apr-88

Page 4 of _____ Pages.

BROKER'S COPY

REAL ESTATE PURCHASE CONTRACT AND RECEIPT FOR DEPOSIT (DLF-14 PAGE 4 OF 4)

5. Statement from management company as to dues and any assessments owed and a change of ownership paperwork. A charge of $50 to $100 is usually made by the management company for supplying this information.

Condo Management Problems

Denise Arant, former Condo Association Board President, described ten problem types of condo owners:

1. *Veteran* — knows everything and wants to go back to the old ways.

2. *Cheapskate* — wants to hoard association funds and not maintain the complex.

3. *Time Burner* — places no value on time and wants to drag out meetings and get 100 bids on every project.

4. *Dictator* — wants rules for everything; i.e., no bicycles, no lit cigarettes on grounds, etc.

5. *Slob* — wants special permission to store washing machines and old furniture on balcony.

6. *Blamer* — accuses other residents of worse infractions.

7. *Melvin Belli* — threatens to sue on every little conflict.

8. *Party Animal* — plays loud music at 4 a.m. and is offended when people complain.

9. *Variance Freak* — wants to add extra room, windows, doors, etc.

10. *Bushwhacker* — confronts board members with earth-shattering issues such as burnt-out light bulbs, dog poop on lawn, etc.

Dispute Resolution Law

Effective January 1, 1994, with an amendment to California Civil Code Section 1354, property management disputes between condominium owners and homeowners associations are required to use dispute-resolution alternatives such as arbitration and mediation. Areas covered are CC&Rs (Covenants, Conditions, and Restrictions); for example, rules that govern individual outside design and landscaping of a unit. In the past the homeowner had to incur the expense of a lawsuit over arbitrary rules and enforcement on the height of bushes. A recent survey by UC Berkeley showed that over 40% of the 25,000 homeowners associations in California are involved in litigation. Hopefully, this law will improve and facilitate relations between homeowners associations and individual homeowners.

Summary

Condominiums are defined as separate fee ownership of an individual unit and an assigned interest in the common areas with other owners. In a cooperative, on the other hand, a stock corporation owns the building and the land, and the buyer is issued a share of stock and a long-term proprietary lease on a unit. A townhouse is often confused with a condominium, but in actuality is a type of architecture (usually two stories). The number of condominium associations is large with over 80,000 nationwide and 25,000 in California. A condominium association is governed by a Board of Directors based on Articles of Incorporation, CC&R's, By-Laws, and Rules and Regulations. The Board of Directors is elected by the homeowners, usually at annual elections, and the most common number of board members is five. The board usually meets once a month.

The property manager is responsible for preparing the fiscal reports and budgets for the Board of Directors. Collection of dues, payments of bills, and vendor selection are also usually assigned duties of the property manager. Other duties include resident relations, maintenance and security, and supervision of employees. The most frequent problems are parking violations, late payments, pet violations, common area rule violations, and unauthorized changes in the dwellings. The association usually has several committees which may include: finance, social, rules, architectural, and nominating.

Fees for condominium management have traditionally been low and unprofitable for many management firms. Prices are usually quoted per door or per unit; i.e., $6.00 per unit for a 200-unit complex equals a $1,200 management fee. Reasons for the low fees include high and frequent turnover of boards of directors and the fact that, in California, a real estate license is not required to manage condominiums, which eliminates the need for trust accounts and other consumer protection procedures required by the Department of Real Estate in other forms of management. This lack of control has led to missing and unaccounted for funds for some associations. The Institute of Real Estate Management (IREM) and the Community Associations Institute (CAI) have designations, educational programs, and books available to help better educate the property manager in condominium management.

In conclusion, we have analyzed the uniqueness of community association management. We have defined market size, community association governance, fiscal reporting, collections, bill payment procedures, insurance, the role of the property manager, the management agreement, and the management fee structure.

This is a large and specialized market which is very competitive since no license and little money are required to become established. It is, however, a service-intensive industry requiring that the property manager have not only excellent financial reporting skills, but a thorough knowledge of maintenance and public relations.

NOTES

Chapter 10 Review Questions

1. *In a condominium, the owner gets:*

   a. a life estate.
   b. a grant deed.
   c. stock ownership.
   d. a rental agreement.

2. *In a cooperative, the owner gets:*

   a. a life estate.
   b. a grant deed.
   c. stock ownership.
   d. a rental agreement.

3. *In a PUD, the person owns:*

   a. the living unit plus the land underneath.
   b. nothing, but has common interest.
   c. his unit only.
   d. the land only.

4. *Timeshare complexes are usually found in:*

   a. rural areas.
   b. urban areas.
   c. resort areas.
   d. depressed areas.

5. *The Board of Directors is:*

   a. elected by the homeowners.
   b. appointed by the Department of Real Estate (DRE).
   c. appointed by the City.
   d. appointed by the County.

6. *Condominiums are usually:*

    a. profit corporations.
    b. non-profit corporations.
    c. limited partnerships.
    d. general partnerships.

7. *Accounting and cash balance statements are usually given to the Board of Directors:*

    a. on an annual basis.
    b. when requested.
    c. only when required by law.
    d. on a monthly basis.

8. *Insurance provided by the homeowners association covers:*

    a. the inside of individual units.
    b. pools only.
    c. all common areas.
    d. liability inside the units.

9. *The property manager usually reports directly to:*

    a. each individual homeowner.
    b. the Board of Directors.
    c. the Department of Real Estate.
    d. the City Council.

10. *If the association pays a fee of $9 per door per month, what would be the monthly management fee for 200 units?*

    a. $900.
    b. $1,800.
    c. $18,000.
    d. $2,000.

Chapter 10
Selected Additional References and Reading

CAI News (Monthly)
  1423 Powhatan Street, Suite 7
  Alexandria, VA 22314

Common Ground
  CAI
  1423 Powhatan Street, Suite 7
  Alexandria, VA 22314

Condominium (Monthly)
  Robert W. Duff and Associates
  P.O. Box 1242
  Santa Ana, CA 92702

GAP Reports
  CAI
  1423 Powhatan Street, Suite 7
  Alexandria, VA 22314

Giese, Lester J. and Robert W. Kuehn, *Model Business Policies for Community Associations*, Condominium Management Maintenance Corporation, Clinton, NJ.

Holeman, Jack, *Condominium Management*, Prentice-Hall, Inc., Englewood Cliffs, NJ, 1980.

Hyatt, Wayne and Phillip Downer, *Condominium and Homeowners Association Litigation*, John Wiley & Sons, Somerset, NJ, 1987.

Institute of Real Estate Management, *The Condominium Community*, Chicago, IL, 1978.

Institute of Real Estate Management, *The Owner's and Manager's Guide to Condominium Management*, Chicago, IL, 1984.

Risky Business (Quarterly)
  Robert W. Little Insurance Agency
  11654 W. Pico Boulevard
  Los Angeles, CA 90064

Wade, J., *Condominiums: The Professional's Complete Manual and Guide*, Prentice-Hall, Inc., Old Tappan, NJ, 1983.

NOTES

Chapter 11

Other Types of Management

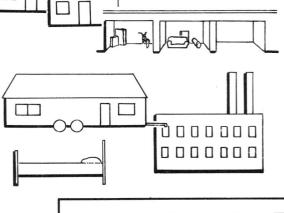

Key Terms

Multi-tenant
Parking requirements
Sale/leaseback
R&D building
  Medical building
"Keenager"
Mobile home park
Subdivision laws
Rating
SSSA
Retirement
  community
"Hot bedding"
"Key Money"
EIR

Food for Thought

"If you don't have the time to do things right—
    When will you have the time to do them over?"

Other Types of Management

Introduction

Professional property management encompasses a wide and diversified classification of properties. In this chapter we will discuss management as it relates to some of these, such as industrial research and development, mobile home parks, mini-storage facilities, medical buildings, retirement communities, and motel and resort rentals.

Each of these specialized areas embodies unique characteristics and customs, many of which can be learned only through years of experience. Therefore, for example, a successful property manager may be adept at managing shopping centers and yet have little experience related to the management of mini-storage facilities.

Industrial Building Characteristics

In previous chapters we have discussed the trend of the American economy away from manufacturing and more toward service-oriented industries. Even though industrial property includes all land and facilities used for heavy and light manufacturing, today's emphasis is related to storage and distribution of goods. Down through history, most industrial buildings have been owned and managed by the occupant manufacturer who endeavored to locate close to the source of the raw materials. (A good example of this is the steel industry in the Pennsylvania/Ohio area.)

As the trend away from the production of goods toward the producers of services became more apparent, the size of industrial buildings changed. Newer facilities became single-story as opposed to multi-storied. Locations were found closer to freeways and employee sources rather than to raw materials. Modern building layouts became more streamlined, and automated handling of goods by forklift and pallet became common practice. Many of the new buildings were conveniently located in industrial parks rather than on single-entity sites.

Types of Buildings

1. *Single-Tenant.* These buildings have increased in size and are usually leased on a long-term basis, with 5-10% of the space devoted to office functions.

2. *Multi-Tenant.* These are usually older multi-story buildings located in urban areas, such as in the garment industry area. A smaller portion of the space is devoted to office activities.

3. *Industrial Parks.* These are often located in the suburbs and include several tenants. They are frequently small (Ma and Pa) incubator users with short leases and usually experience a high business failure rate. The office space most often encompasses 10% of the total area.

Parking Requirements

Unlike office buildings where employees come and go at peak periods (7:30–9:30 a.m. and 3:30–5:30 p.m.), traffic flow for industrial buildings can be diversified utilizing two or three shifts. Using several shifts requires less machinery, space, and capital outlay per employee. This is especially true as manufacturers become more automated. Spacing work shifts means less traffic congestion and more lenient parking requirements than are necessary for office buildings and shopping centers.

TYPICAL PARKING REQUIREMENTS	
Building Type	*No. of Spaces Per 1,000 S.F.*
Industrial	3
Office	4
Medical building	6
Restaurant	10
Financial (banks)	5
Retail store	4
Furniture store	2

Location

Industrial buildings are usually located near sources of transportation. In the past, water and rail were the major transportation methods, but today modern highways and airports are emerging as the key elements.

Classification of Industry by Locational Orientation

There are six basic categories of industry:

1. *Market-Oriented* — finished products are sold directly to the consumers; i.e., food, beverages, electronics, and printing. Locations tend to be close to population centers to reduce transportation costs and perishability for some food products.

2. *Raw Materials and Resource-Oriented* — companies that fall into this category need to be close to sources of raw materials to reduce transportation costs; i.e., aluminum, steel, and grain elevators.

3. *Transportation-Oriented* — companies where freight, storage, and inventory costs are a major influence. An example would be oil refineries (near a seaport) and high-tech computer parts (near an airport).

4. *Labor Intensity-Oriented* — where labor rates and productivity are dominant factors. This can range from furniture assembly requiring cheap, unskilled labor to high-tech computer assembly requiring highly skilled technicians.

5. *Energy-Oriented* — companies that use large amounts of fuels such as electricity and coal tend to be located near their sources to reduce costs. Due to environmental concerns and constraints, energy and raw material-oriented companies have been leaving California for other states with fewer restrictions.

6. *Non-Descript-Oriented* — these are companies that do not fall into the other five categories. Transportation, labor costs, or raw materials are not dominant and these companies can locate in most areas. Such companies are sometimes lured by tax incentives to certain communities.

In California, most industry must be "clean" and not cause pollution or environmental problems. This precludes new, large manufacturing operations such as steel mills or auto plants from establishing. A detailed analysis of locational industry is covered starting on Page 41 of the book *Industrial Real Estate*, published by the Society of Industrial Realtors (4th Edition).

Management

Once industrial space is leased, it is one of the easiest types to manage and, as a result, management fees are usually lower than for other types of property.

Types of Leases

1. *Gross Lease:* A lease in which the tenant pays one flat rental amount. This type of lease is typical of older buildings in urban areas. These leases may have annual cost-of-living adjustments or increased cost "pass-throughs." The term is usually for several years with possible options due to the high expense of moving machinery.

2. *Net Lease or Triple Net Lease.* This is the most common type of lease. The tenant pays a base rent as well as a separate amount based on taxes, insurance, and maintenance. These leases almost always include cost-of-living increases. Like the gross lease, they are usually given for long periods of time. See Figure 11-1 for the first and last pages of a standard industrial net lease.

3. *Sale/Leaseback.* This is a new concept that allows the manufacturer to sell a building to an investor, thus freeing up the manufacturer's capital for use in the business. It benefits both parties as it gives the investor a tax shelter (depreciation) and a guaranteed income stream (lease) while the manufacturer has additional funds for operations.

Research and Development (R&D) Building Characteristics

R&D buildings are an offshoot of the industrial building and are considered to be a rapidly growing area in both development and property management.

1. *Location:* These buildings are often located near major highways, educational centers (universities), and in suburban areas.

2. *Employment:* They usually employ highly skilled and educated individuals.

3. *Building Layout:* They are usually two stories in height, with 50% or more of the area devoted to office space and/or laboratories.

4. *Rental Rates:* The rents are considerably higher than for industrial buildings, but lower than for office buildings.

5. *Trends:* The trend is for conversion of existing industrial buildings into research and development space.

Government Approvals

In California, before construction of a building, the environmental impact must be considered. The California Environmental Quality Act declares that "the long-term protection of the environment, consistent with the provision of a decent home and suitable living environment, for every Californian, shall be the guiding criterion in public decisions."

An assessment of a proposed project or activity must be made to determine whether it will have significant environmental effects on our man-made or natural environment. When no significant environmental impact will result, a "negative declaration" is submitted and signed by the city or county Planning Department instead of an Environmental Impact Report (EIR) on the proposed project. Some significant environmental effects would be as follows:

1. Displacing of existing homeowners or tenants (i.e., tearing down old homes inhabited by blue-collar workers and building luxury condominiums).

2. Altering or disrupting a scenic, recreational, or historical site (i.e., an Indian burial ground).

3. Altering or disrupting air or water quality (i.e., causing air pollution by building a steel mill).

4. Creating changes in land use or causing traffic congestion (i.e., converting farmland into a housing subdivision).

5. Threatening or endangering rare birds or plants (i.e., development on a bird sanctuary).

In order to comply with the California Environmental Quality Act, the developer will be required to undertake mitigation measures such as dedicating park land, building roads, or having an archaeologist onsite during grading.

Mobile Home Park Management

The "Mobile Homes Park Act" defines a mobile home park as "any area or tract of land where one or more mobile homes are rented or leased." A mobile home is actually a hybrid between a dwelling and a vehicle, and as larger and more attractive units are being built they have become more permanent and frequently are only moved once.

1. *Law Changes:* Since 1980, in California, new mobile homes are taxed as real and not personal property. Park jurisdiction falls under the State Department of Housing and Community Development. If the park has five or more lots, it is subject to the Subdivision Laws and Regulations.

2. *Evictions:* Evictions for mobile home parks are more difficult and take longer than for residential.

Figure 11-1. Standard Industrial Net Lease, First Page

STANDARD INDUSTRIAL LEASE — NET

AMERICAN INDUSTRIAL REAL ESTATE ASSOCIATION

1. Parties. This Lease, dated, for reference purposes only, _____ , 19 _____ , is made by and between _____

_____ (herein called "Lessor")

and _____

_____ (herein called "Lessee").

2. Premises. Lessor hereby leases to Lessee and Lessee leases from Lessor for the term, at the rental, and upon all of the conditions set forth herein, that certain real property situated in the County of _____ State of _____ ,

commonly known as _____

and described as _____

_____

_____

Said real property including the land and all improvements therein, is herein called "the Premises".

3. Term.

3.1 **Term.** The term of this Lease shall be for _____

commencing on _____ and ending on _____

unless sooner terminated pursuant to any provision hereof.

3.2 **Delay in Possession.** Notwithstanding said commencement date, if for any reason Lessor cannot deliver possession of the Premises to Lessee on said date, Lessor shall not be subject to any liability therefor, nor shall such failure affect the validity of this Lease or the obligations of Lessee hereunder or extend the term hereof, but in such case, Lessee shall not be obligated to pay rent until possession of the Premises is tendered to Lessee; provided, however, that if Lessor shall not have delivered possession of the Premises within sixty (60) days from said commencement date, Lessee may, at Lessee's option, by notice in writing to Lessor within ten (10) days thereafter, cancel this Lease, in which event the parties shall be discharged from all obligations hereunder; provided further, however, that if such written notice of Lessee is not received by Lessor within said ten (10) day period, Lessee's right to cancel this Lease hereunder shall terminate and be of no further force or effect.

3.3 **Early Possession.** If Lessee occupies the Premises prior to said commencement date, such occupancy shall be subject to all provisions hereof, such occupancy shall not advance the termination date, and Lessee shall pay rent for such period at the initial monthly rates set forth below.

4. Rent. Lessee shall pay to Lessor as rent for the Premises, monthly payments of $ _____ , in advance, on the _____

day of each month of the term hereof. Lessee shall pay Lessor upon the execution hereof $ _____ as rent for _____

_____

_____

Rent for any period during the term hereof which is for less than one month shall be a pro rata portion of the monthly installment. Rent shall be payable in lawful money of the United States to Lessor at the address stated herein or to such other persons or at such other places as Lessor may designate in writing.

5. Security Deposit. Lessee shall deposit with Lessor upon execution hereof $ _____ as security for Lessee's faithful performance of Lessee's obligations hereunder. If Lessee fails to pay rent or other charges due hereunder, or otherwise defaults with respect to any provision of this Lease, Lessor may use, apply or retain all or any portion of said deposit for the payment of any rent or other charge in default or for the payment of any other sum to which Lessor may become obligated by reason of Lessee's default, or to compensate Lessor for any loss or damage which Lessor may suffer thereby. If Lessor so uses or applies all or any portion of said deposit, Lessee shall within ten (10) days after written demand therefor deposit cash with Lessor in an amount sufficient to restore said deposit to the full amount hereinabove stated and Lessee's failure to do so shall be a material breach of this Lease. If the monthly rent shall, from time to time, increase during the term of this Lease, Lessee shall thereupon deposit with Lessor additional security deposit so that the amount of security deposit held by Lessor shall at all times bear the same proportion to current rent as the original security deposit bears to the original monthly rent set forth in paragraph 4 hereof. Lessor shall not be required to keep said deposit separate from its general accounts. If Lessee performs all of Lessee's obligations hereunder, said deposit, or so much thereof as has not theretofore been applied by Lessor, shall be returned, without payment of interest or other increment for its use, to Lessee (or, at Lessor's option, to the last assignee, if any, of Lessee's interest hereunder) at the expiration of the term hereof, and after Lessee has vacated the Premises. No trust relationship is created herein between Lessor and Lessee with respect to said Security Deposit.

6. Use.

6.1 **Use.** The Premises shall be used and occupied only for _____

_____

or any other use which is reasonably comparable and for no other purpose.

6.2 **Compliance with Law.**

(a) Lessor warrants to Lessee that the Premises, in its state existing on the date that the Lease term commences, but without regard to the use for which Lessee will use the Premises, does not violate any covenants or restrictions of record, or any applicable building code, regulation or ordinance in effect on such Lease term commencement date. In the event it is determined that this warranty has been violated, then it shall be the obligation of the Lessor, after written notice from Lessee, to promptly, at Lessor's sole cost and expense, rectify any such violation. In the event Lessee does not give to Lessor written notice of the violation of this warranty within six months from the date that the Lease term commences, the correction of same shall be the obligation of the Lessee at Lessee's sole cost. The warranty contained in this paragraph 6.2 (a) shall be of no force or effect if, prior to the date of this Lease, Lessee was the owner or occupant of the Premises, and, in such event, Lessee shall correct any such violation at Lessee's sole cost.

(b) Except as provided in paragraph 6.2(a), Lessee shall, at Lessee's expense, comply promptly with all applicable statutes, ordinances, rules, regulations, orders, covenants and restrictions of record, and requirements in effect during the term or any part of the term hereof, regulating the use by Lessee of the Premises. Lessee shall not use nor permit the use of the Premises in any manner that will tend to create waste or a nuisance or, if there shall be more than one tenant in the building containing the Premises, shall tend to disturb such other tenants.

6.3 **Condition of Premises.**

(a) Lessor shall deliver the Premises to Lessee clean and free of debris on Lease commencement date (unless Lessee is already in possession) and Lessor further warrants to Lessee that the plumbing, lighting, air conditioning, heating, and loading doors in the Premises shall be in good operating condition on the Lease commencement date. In the event that it is determined that this warranty has been violated, then it shall be the obligation of Lessor, after receipt of written notice from Lessee setting forth with specificity the nature of the violation, to promptly, at Lessor's sole cost, rectify such violation. Lessee's failure to give such written notice to Lessor within thirty (30) days after the Lease commencement date shall cause the conclusive presumption that Lessor has complied with all of Lessor's obligations hereunder. The warranty contained in this paragraph 6.3(a) shall be of no force or effect if prior to the date of this Lease, Lessee was the owner or occupant of the Premises.

(b) Except as otherwise provided in this Lease, Lessee hereby accepts the Premises in their condition existing as of the Lease commencement date or the date that Lessee takes possession of the Premises, whichever is earlier, subject to all applicable zoning, municipal, county and state laws, ordinances and regulations governing and regulating the use of the Premises, and any covenants or restrictions of record, and accepts this Lease subject thereto and to all matters disclosed thereby and by any exhibits attached hereto. Lessee acknowledges that neither Lessor nor Lessor's agent has made any representation or warranty as to the present or future suitability of the Premises for the conduct of Lessee's business.

7. Maintenance, Repairs and Alterations.

7.1 **Lessee's Obligations.** Lessee shall keep in good order, condition and repair the Premises and every part thereof, structural and non structural, (whether or not such portion of the Premises requiring repair, or the means of repairing the same are reasonably or readily accessible to Lessee, and whether or not the need for such repairs occurs as a result of Lessee's use, any prior use, the elements or the age of such portion of the Premises) including, without limiting the generality of the foregoing, all plumbing, heating, air conditioning, (Lessee shall procure and maintain, at Lessee's expense, an air conditioning system maintenance contract) ventilating, electrical, lighting facilities and equipment within the Premises, fixtures, walls (interior and exterior), foundations, ceilings, roofs (interior and exterior), floors, windows, doors, plate glass and skylights located within the Premises, and all landscaping, driveways, parking lots, fences and signs located on the Premises and sidewalks and parkways adjacent to the Premises.

7.2 **Surrender.** On the last day of the term hereof, or on any sooner termination, Lessee shall surrender the Premises to Lessor in the same condition as when received, ordinary wear and tear excepted, clean and free of debris. Lessee shall repair any damage to the Premises occasioned

© American Industrial Real Estate Association 1980   **NET**

Initials: _____

_____

Figure 11-1 (cont'd). Standard Industrial Net Lease, Last Page

39.2 Options Personal. Each Option granted to Lessee in this Lease are personal to Lessee and may not be exercised or be assigned, voluntarily or involuntarily, by or to any person or entity other than Lessee, provided, however, the Option may be exercised by or assigned to any Lessee Affiliate as defined in paragraph 12.2 of this Lease. The Options herein granted to Lessee are not assignable separate and apart from this Lease.

39.3 Multiple Options. In the event that Lessee has any multiple options to extend or renew this Lease a later option cannot be exercised unless the prior option to extend or renew this Lease has been so exercised.

39.4 Effect of Default on Options.

(a) **Lessee** shall have no right to exercise an Option, notwithstanding any provision in the grant of Option to the contrary, (i) during the time commencing from the date Lessor gives to Lessee a notice of default pursuant to paragraph 13.1(b) or 13.1(c) and continuing until the default alleged in said notice of default is cured, or (ii) during the period of time commencing on the day after a monetary obligation to Lessor is due from Lessee and unpaid (without any necessity for notice thereof to Lessee) continuing until the obligation is paid, or (iii) at any time after an event of default described in paragraphs 13.1(a), 13.1(d), or 13.1(e) (without any necessity of Lessor to give notice of such default to Lessee), or (iv) in the event that Lessor has given to Lessee three or more notices of default under paragraph 13.1(b), where a late charge has become payable under paragraph 13.4 for each of such defaults, or paragraph 13.1(c), whether or not the defaults are cured, during the 12 month period prior to the time that Lessee intends to exercise the subject Option.

(b) The period of time within which an Option may be exercised shall not be extended or enlarged by reason of Lessee's inability to exercise an Option because of the provisions of paragraph 39.4(a).

(c) All rights of Lessee under the provisions of an Option shall terminate and be of no further force or effect, notwithstanding Lessee's due and timely exercise of the Option, if, after such exercise and during the term of this Lease, (i) Lessee fails to pay to Lessor a monetary obligation of Lessee for a period of 30 days after such obligation becomes due (without any necessity of Lessor to give notice thereof to Lessee), or (ii) Lessee fails to commence to cure a default specified in paragraph 13.1(c) within 30 days after the date that Lessor gives notice to Lessee of such default and/or Lessee fails thereafter to diligently prosecute said cure to completion, or (iii) Lessee commits a default described in paragraph 13.1(a), 13.1(d) or 13.1(e) (without any necessity of Lessor to give notice of such default to Lessee), or (iv) Lessor gives to Lessee three or more notices of default under paragraph 13.1(b), where a late charge becomes payable under paragraph 13.4 for each such default, or paragraph 13.1(c), whether or not the defaults are cured.

40. Multiple Tenant Building. In the event that the Premises are part of a larger building or group of buildings then Lessee agrees that it will abide by, keep and observe all reasonable rules and regulations which Lessor may make from time to time for the management, safety, care, and cleanliness of the building and grounds, the parking of vehicles and the preservation of good order therein as well as for the convenience of other occupants and tenants of the building. The violations of any such rules and regulations shall be deemed a material breach of this Lease by Lessee.

41. Security Measures. Lessee hereby acknowledges that the rental payable to Lessor hereunder does not include the cost of guard service or other security measures, and that Lessor shall have no obligation whatsoever to provide same. Lessee assumes all responsibility for the protection of Lessee, its agents and invitees from acts of third parties.

42. Easements. Lessor reserves to itself the right, from time to time, to grant such easements, rights and dedications that Lessor deems necessary or desirable, and to cause the recordation of Parcel Maps and restrictions, so long as such easements, rights, dedications, Maps and restrictions do not unreasonably interfere with the use of the Premises by Lessee. Lessee shall sign any of the aforementioned documents upon request of Lessor and failure to do so shall constitute a material breach of this Lease.

43. Performance Under Protest. If at any time a dispute shall arise as to any amount or sum of money to be paid by one party to the other under the provisions hereof, the party against whom the obligation to pay the money is asserted shall have the right to make payment "under protest" and such payment shall not be regarded as a voluntary payment, and there shall survive the right on the part of said party to institute suit for recovery of such sum. If it shall be adjudged that there was no legal obligation on the part of said party to pay such sum or any part thereof, said party shall be entitled to recover such sum or so much thereof as it was not legally required to pay under the provisions of this Lease.

44. Authority. If Lessee is a corporation, trust, or general or limited partnership, each individual executing this Lease on behalf of such entity represents and warrants that he or she is duly authorized to execute and deliver this Lease on behalf of said entity. If Lessee is a corporation, trust or partnership, Lessee shall, within thirty (30) days after execution of this Lease, deliver to Lessor evidence of such authority satisfactory to Lessor.

45. Conflict. Any conflict between the printed provisions of this Lease and the typewritten or handwritten provisions shall be controlled by the typewritten or handwritten provisions.

46. Insuring Party. The insuring party under this lease shall be the _____

47. Addendum. Attached hereto is an addendum or addenda containing paragraphs _____ through _____ which constitutes a part of this Lease.

LESSOR AND LESSEE HAVE CAREFULLY READ AND REVIEWED THIS LEASE AND EACH TERM AND PROVISION CONTAINED HEREIN AND, BY EXECUTION OF THIS LEASE, SHOW THEIR INFORMED AND VOLUNTARY CONSENT THERETO. THE PARTIES HEREBY AGREE THAT, AT THE TIME THIS LEASE IS EXECUTED, THE TERMS OF THIS LEASE ARE COMMERCIALLY REASONABLE AND EFFECTUATE THE INTENT AND PURPOSE OF LESSOR AND LESSEE WITH RESPECT TO THE PREMISES.

IF THIS LEASE HAS BEEN FILLED IN IT HAS BEEN PREPARED FOR SUBMISSION TO YOUR ATTORNEY FOR HIS APPROVAL. NO REPRESENTATION OR RECOMMENDATION IS MADE BY THE AMERICAN INDUSTRIAL REAL ESTATE ASSOCIATION OR BY THE REAL ESTATE BROKER OR ITS AGENTS OR EMPLOYEES AS TO THE LEGAL SUFFICIENCY, LEGAL EFFECT, OR TAX CONSEQUENCES OF THIS LEASE OR THE TRANSACTION RELATING THERETO; THE PARTIES SHALL RELY SOLELY UPON THE ADVICE OF THEIR OWN LEGAL COUNSEL AS TO THE LEGAL AND TAX CONSEQUENCES OF THIS LEASE.

The parties hereto have executed this Lease at the place on the dates specified immediately adjacent to their respective signatures.

LESSEE   LESSOR

_____

By _____

Title _____

                                  _____

                                  By _____

                                  ATTEST:

                                  By _____

                                  Dated: _____

                                  APPROVAL RECOMMENDED:

                                  By _____

                                  APPROVED AS TO FORM:

                                  By _____

For these forms write or call the American Industrial Real Estate Association, 350 South Figueroa St., Suite 275, Los Angeles, CA 90071 (213) 657-9777

   a. A 60-day notice to vacate is required from the manager.
   b. Eviction for cause must be proved by the manager.
      1) Nonpayment of space rent.
      2) Willful and malicious violation of park rules and covenants.

3. Notices

   a. Rent increases require a 90-day notice.
   b. Park rules changes require six months' notice unless all residents agree. These involve pets, noise, speed limits, etc.

4. *Curing Delinquent Rent*

A mobile home tenant can cure a rent delinquency twice annually after a three-day notice. Any further delinquencies allow the lease to be terminated without a three-day notice (Civil Code 798.55 and 798.56 amended by AB 744).

5. *Residency Law Requirements*

Mobile home park managers must reference the "Mobile Home Residency Law" in rental agreements and provide a copy of the law to incoming residents (Civil Code 798.15) (Figure 11-2).

6. *Billings:* In addition to paying rent, the expenses of water, gas, and electricity are frequently metered and rebilled for payment by the tenants.

7. *Tenant Unions:* Many parks have tenant unions and the park manager must deal with them and their demands.

8. *Tenant Mix:* Senior citizens, many of whom are on fixed incomes, make up the majority of the tenants. Careful screening of new tenants by the property manager, similar to that in residential management (Chapter 7), is essential to good management.

9. *Ratings:* Parks are rated according to location, layout, amenities, etc., with a 5-star rating being the highest.

10. *Trends:* Prime locations of mobile home parks, such as nearness to the ocean, are being sold so that the land will become a more profitable venture. Many mobile home parks near the ocean are being converted to condominium developments.

11. *Management Opportunities:* This is a specialized area of management and one that shouldn't be entered into casually. It requires expertise in of its unique laws and regulations.

Figure 11-2.

MOBILEHOME PARK RENTAL AGREEMENT

For _____ , located at _____ , California.

THIS AGREEMENT is made as of the date specified below between _____ (herein the "Owner"), and those persons listed below on this Rental Agreement (the "Agreement") as the resident (the "Resident").

1. SPACE:
Owner rents to Resident and Resident rents from Owner Space No. _____
(herein the "Space") in above mentioned Park. _____
Resident's Initials

2. TERM:
2.1 Applicable Term (complete A or B)
A. The tenancy created under this Agreement shall be on a month-to-month basis and shall commence on _____ _____ ,19___. _____
Resident's Initials

B. The tenancy created under this Agreement shall be a period of _____ , (___) months and shall commence on _____ , 19___, and end on _____ ,19___ unless sooner terminated in accordance with the terms of this Agreement. _____
Resident's Initials

2.2 Resident acknowledges that Owner has offered Resident the Option of: a month-to-month rental agreement, a rental agreement having a term of twelve (12) months, a rental agreement having a term which is longer than a month-to-month tenancy but less than twelve (12) months in length, or a rental agreement having a term which is for more than twelve (12) months. Resident acknowledges his understanding that he may elect to accept any one of these four (4) options and that this election is solely at Resident's option. Resident further acknowledges that even though he has these four (4) options, he has voluntarily elected the term of tenancy set forth above. _____
Resident's Initials

3. RENT
3.1 Resident shall pay as rent to Owner without deduction or offset (without waiving Civil Code SS1942) and on the first day of each month: (1) The base rent (as it may be adjusted) as specified in Paragraph 3.2 below; (2) All utility charges billed to Resident by Owner during each month. (Please Note: Utility rates for utilities billed to Resident by Owner are set by the Public Utilities Commission and other governmental agencies. Therefore, charges for these utilities may be increased at any time in accordance with the rate established by these other parties and no advance notice of increases in these rates will be given to Resident by Owner.) (3) Owner may charge a reasonable fee for services relating to the maintenance of the land and premises upon which the mobilehome is situated in the event that resident fails to maintain such land or premises in accordance with the Rules and Regulations of the Park and the California Civil Code (SS 798.15) after written notication to the Resident and the failure of the Resident to comply within fourteen (14) days. (4) Charges for recreational vehicles and other vehicles, and charges listed after the title "Other Monthly Charges" may be increased upon sixty (60) days notice to Resident.

3.2 A. The base rent shall be _____ Dollars ($_____)
per month and it shall remain in effect until _____ , 19___ Effective _____ 1st, 19___, the base rent shall be increased by _____ Dollars ($_____) per month to a total of _____ Dollars ($_____) per month and it shall remain in effect until _____ , 19___

B. The base rent shall be _____ Dollars per month. This rent shall be increased pursuant to "Lease Supplement" which is incorporated by this reference.

Other Monthly Charges:
Recreational and extra vehicle storage charges are _____ Dollars ($_____) per vehicle per month.
Late charges are _____ Dollars ($_____) per month.
Returned Check charge is _____ Dollars ($_____)
The Security Deposit required for your Space is $_____
The current California Civil Code provisions known as the Mobilehome Home Residency Law is dated _____ _____ , 19___, and receipt of same is acknowledged.

Resident acknowledges that Park is/is not (circle one) operating pursuant to a zone or use permit subject to a renewal or expiration date. Permit number (if applicable): _____ ,
Expiration date (if applicable) _____ , or that Park is on leased ground (if applicable) and land lease expires _____

Other documents incorporated in this Agreement are: __(1) Park's current Rules & Regulations,__ _____

_____

Utilities provided by Park and included within rent:
____ Gas ____ Electricity ____ Cable T.V. ____ Rubbish ____ Sewer ____ Water
Utilities provided by Park to be billed as additional rent:
____ Gas ____ Electricity ____ Cable T.V. ____ Rubbish ____ Sewer ____ Water
Utilities Resident must obtain from suppliers:
____ Gas ____ Electricity ____ Cable T.V. ____ Rubbish ____ Sewer ____ Water
The minimum age limit for this park (if applicable) is _____
The following facilities and improvements are also provided by the Park:

_____

_____

This Agreement executed on the _____ day of _____ , 19___, in _____ , County of California.
THIS AGREEMENT INCLUDES PARAGRAPHS 3.3 THRU 30 ON REVERSE SIDE.

_____   _____   _____
Owner or Owner's Agent   Resident   Resident

WMHPM ●   WHITE — Park Office   YELLOW — Resident   PINK — Management Copy   GOLDENROD —
01PA

Figure 11-3.

Court Cases

Hall v. City of Santa Barbara (9th Cir 1988) overturned the Santa Barbara mobile home rent control ordinance requiring mobile home park owners to grant tenants (coach owners) leases of unlimited duration. The 9th Circuit Federal Court found that this ordinance effected a physical taking of property as it allowed the tenants a perpetual lease and to pay rents lower than market rates. Since this is a federal court case, it takes precedent over local and state laws.

City of Escondido v. Yee is a U.S. Supreme Court decision (9-0) which ruled that Fifth Amendment property rights are not infringed when rent is regulated. "Cities have broad powers to regulate the landlord-tenant relationship without paying compensation for all economic injuries that such regulation entails."

Federal Law

The Manufactured Home Construction and Safety Act (1976) established federal construction standards for design and installation of fire resistance and energy. This law also regulates installation and standards for plumbing, air-conditioning, heating, and electrical for mobile homes.

State Law

AB 925 (O'Connell) (1991) requires inspection of mobile homes and mobile home parks at least once every five years. Either the Department of Housing and Community Development (HCD) or the local enforcement agency will conduct the inspections. If violations are found, citations will be issued to either the homeowner or park owner, depending on who is the responsible party.

Association

Western Mobile Home Assoc. (WMA)
1760 Creekside Oaks Dr., Ste. 200
Sacramento, CA 95833

Mini-Storage Facilities Management

A recent phenomenon that began in the Southwest, but which has now spread nationwide, is the practice of using mini-storage or self-storage units. These facilities provide separate self-storage units of various sizes for individuals and businesses on a rental basis within one secure complex.

Layout

The typical layout consists of long, narrow buildings facing each other across large driveways (Figure 11-4). Units vary in size from 5' x 5' to 20' x 20' or larger. The average unit size is 113 square feet, with an average number of units per facility of approximately 400. The typical facility contains an average gross rentable space of 46,863 square feet. *Mini-Storage Messenger Magazine* reports that the typical facility for the western states is 11,673 square feet and the average number of units is 455. The occupancy rate for the western states was 89% in 1991 vs. the national rate of only 86.4%. Almost half of the facilities in the western states and U.S. maintained computerized records. (These figures were compiled by the Self-Service Storage Association, or SSSA, which is the trade association for mini-storage.) SSSA offers and seminars for property managers who need additional information in this area.

A good reference source for rental agreements and specific state laws is *The Self-Service Storage Rental Agreement: Handbook for Owners and Managers*, published by the Self-Service Storage Association.

According to a survey by the *Mini-Storage Messenger*, the four largest self-storage companies are U-Haul International, Public Storage, Colonial Storage Centers, and Shurguard Self Storage.

Figure 11-4. Mini-Storage Layout

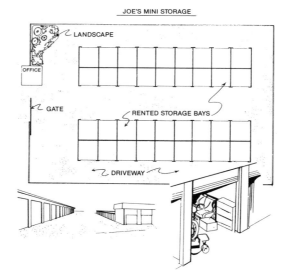

Onsite Management

The management team usually includes a resident onsite manager. Duties of the onsite manager include making collections, preparing reports, screening applicants, renting units, and taking care of maintenance.

Property Management

The property manager's responsibilities include marketing, providing 24-hour security, obtaining insurance, fiscal management, rent collection, supervision of the onsite manager, and responsibility for evictions.

Other Important Information

The customer base varies according to locality. The normal mix is 70% residential and 30% commercial. In areas near expensive office buildings, businesses utilize the majority of the storage space.

Security and safety are important, so mini-storage facilities often utilize closed-circuit cameras, gates, fences, and a method of screening visitors and customers for the successful operation of the complex.

Medical Building Management

Some investors consider office and medical building management as identical. There are, however, some major distinctions between the two and it takes a really professional property manager to properly manage in this unique area.

Location

The best location for a medical building is in *close proximity (within blocks) to a hospital*. This helps doctors keep in close communication with their patients. They are also able to capitalize on being near such services as radiology and laboratories of various kinds. Having quick access to equipment not in the doctor's office generates additional income for the practice.

Maintenance

This is of particular concern to the property manager. Lobbies and hallways must look and be clean. There must frequently be an emergency source of power (generator) to automatically kick in during power outages. Window washers should be scheduled on weekends to provide patient privacy during exams. Trash, such as contaminated needles, bandages, etc., is required in some areas to be segregated into separate containers for special disposal.

Tenant Mix

This is of *utmost* importance in a medical building. The most desirable arrangement is to have several general practitioners and pediatricians so they can refer patients to specialists such as orthopedists, plastic surgeons, etc.

Rental Rates

Rental rates are usually higher in a medical building than in an ordinary office building. A pharmacy off the main lobby, for example, will command premium rent, including *bonus or key money*. This is an amount paid at the beginning of the lease for the privilege of renting in a desirable location.

Retirement Community Management

By the year 2000, over 13% of the U.S. population will be over the age of 62, and by 2030 the figure will be over 21%. This is due to higher life expectancy rates and the maturing of "baby boomers." The names given to this older age group include senior citizens, Gray Panthers, elderly retirees, etc. This author prefers a more positive and youthful-sounding name such as "Keenagers." The housing for these people falls into three major categories:

1. *Independent living* — retirement residence communities.

2. *Semi-independent living* — meals provided.

3. *Supported living* — nursing homes.

The area on which we will concentrate is retirement communities such as "Leisure World" in which subdivisions, towns, and villages have been built expressly for the "Keenager." They are usually located near urban centers and cater to the middle and upper class. These communities include amenities such as pools, recreation halls, handicraft centers, and other facilities to give residents a self-contained and secure place to live (protected by security gates). The communities contain anywhere from 500 to 20,000 units and frequently require full-time management personnel to operate.

The management staff for these operations includes clerical personnel, gardeners, maintenance people, an onsite manager, security personnel, etc. The book *Housing for the Elderly* by Rosetta Parker (IREM, 1984) lists the property manager's duties. These include functioning as a community worker and organizer as well as the property supervisor who enforces policy, directs staff work, monitors costs, etc. As is very apparent, special skills of empathy and patience, along with expertise, knowledge, and experience in the area, are required of the property manager in order to be successful in the area of retirement community management.

Resort Rental Management

Managing resort rentals usually involves locations near beaches, mountains, or other resort areas. The term of the rental is usually short (days or weeks). The manager needs a housekeeping or maintenance crew to ensure that cleanup is done quickly and properly.

Reservation and referral systems are a must. The management fee is very high, often exceeding 25% of the gross rental.

An offshoot area of resort management is that of *timeshare complexes*. These complexes have onsite managers, but many times need sophisticated control systems to streamline operations. For example, a 100-unit complex sold for occupancy one week in the year would handle 5,200 requests in order to match available dates. Most timeshares are run by an elected Board of Directors much like for condominiums (Chapter 10).

Hospitality (Hotel) Management

In the language of today's hotel industry, a hotel is any facility that accommodates transient guests. From the downtown high-rise $750/room Hyatt Regency to the 11-room country bed and breakfast, all are included in the generic name — hotel.

While a hotel in the generic sense is any transient lodging facility, the terminology does get more specific. A "full-service hotel" has multi-stories, food, beverage, and other services, a lobby entrance, interior corridors, and remote parking. The word "motel" has disappeared from use, with a variety of more descriptive terms replacing it. Motor inn (exterior corridor, parking at the door) and motor hotel (interior corridor, parking at the building) are two of these.

Hotels are also distinguished by the price of the room, with full-service and luxury hotels having the highest prices, mid-market properties (usually motor hotels and motor inns) having mid-range prices, and economy the lowest. The fastest-growing segment of the hotel market is, and has been for the last five years, the economy segment.

While many hotels have no brand name (these are called "independents"), many more belong to franchise groups or membership organizations. The primary benefits of these are: 1) national and international reservations systems, and 2) group marketing and advertising programs.

The biggest of the franchising organizations are Holiday Inns, including Hampton Inns, and Choice International, which includes Quality Inns and Quality Suites, Clarion Hotels, Comfort Inns, Comfort Suites, Sleep Inns, Econolodge, Rodeway Inns, and Friendship Inns. In both cases the parent organization may own some of the facilities, but most are owned and operated by the franchisees.

By far the largest of the affiliation groups is Best Western International, with over 2,000 worldwide affiliates and an aggressive program for growth.

Each state has at least one trade association for hotel owners and managers. California has two, the California Lodging Industry Association (formerly the California Motel Association) and the California Hotel & Motel Association. CLIA is primarily a lobbying organization which also seeks to provide such membership services as group-discounted insurance rates.

CH&MA also emphasizes lobbying, but as an affiliate of the American Hotel & Motel Association has a broader perspective. At the national level the organization provides educational programs and the only professional designation available for hotel managers, Certified Hotel Administrator.

Federally-Subsidized Housing Programs — History and Background

Federal government involvement in housing was almost non-existent until 1918 when, after World War I, Congress created the U.S. Housing Corp. During the Depression years, the Federal Housing Authority (FHA) was created along with other programs to help provide more and better housing in the United States. During World War II, we saw the "Soldiers and Sailors Relief Act," which provided mortgage relief for servicemen. In 1942, the "Emergency Price Control Act" authorized federal rent control. The "Housing Act of 1949" established the federal government's commitment to housing by establishing a goal "of a decent home and a suitable living environment for every American family." This Act created grants for urban renewal. The "Housing Act of 1959" created new programs for elderly rental projects. In 1965, the Department of Housing and Urban Development (HUD) was created. It was also the beginning of a rent supplement program to assist lower-income tenants so that rent would not exceed 25% of income. The "Housing and Urban-Rural Recovery Act of 1983" reduced some of the rent supplements and created a voucher system.

Section 8 Program

Under this program, a low-income tenant pays rent equal to 30% of net income. The government pays the difference between that amount and the fair market rent. Both payments go directly to the landlord. HUD does rental surveys to establish guidelines for fair market value depending on size of the unit, utilities, etc. The landlord must accept this level and cannot request the tenant to pay any additional monies above the stated rent in the contract.

An inspection is also made to see if the unit meets HUD habitability standards. This program is voluntary and the landlord/manager does not have to participate. The program is based unit by unit and not on the entire building. For example, in a 20-unit building you may have any number of units rented to Section 8 tenants, but you need not rent them all in this manner. The lease term is usually for one year and is renegotiated annually. Tenants, in order to qualify for eligibility, must make no more than 80% of the area median income with adjustments for household size.

In California, many area median incomes exceed $40,000 per year, which means tenants earning up to $32,000 could qualify.

Public Housing Authority

A public housing project is built by a joint venture of local and federal governments using tax-exempt bonds. The bond debt service is paid by the federal government, and after the bonds are paid off federal subsidies are paid. The tenant pays no more than 30% of income for rent. In some cases, however, the tenant's income could make the rent negligible. A minimum rent of 5% of tenant's gross income or portion of welfare payment stipulated for housing, whichever is greater, will be paid. Tenant selection and rent increases are based on complex guidelines which make management very difficult and cumbersome.

Elderly Housing

In the United States today, more than 10% of the population is over the age of 65. According to the National Council of Senior Citizens, approximately one-third of our elderly are living below the poverty level. The "Housing Act of 1959," Section 202 Program, provides direct loans at below-market rates for up to 40-year loans for elderly housing. The Section 202 Program is also linked to Section 8, so that a tenant does not have to pay more than 30% of income for rent. Non-profit corporations, limited-dividend partnerships, consumer cooperatives, and public agencies can be Section 202 sponsors.

Another elderly program is Section 231, a mortgage insurance program in which one-half of the units must be rented to the elderly or handicapped. Under Section 232, HUD will insure loans on construction and rehabilitation of nursing homes.

Multi-Family HUD Programs:
Section 207 — loans for middle-income family housing projects.
Section 221(d)(3) — provided below-market-rate loans and direct subsidies. Replaced by Section 236, the Mortgage Interest Reduction Program.
Section 223(f) — allows owners to realize equity buildup by refinancing or sale of project in older, declining urban areas.
Section 213 — refers to cooperative programs.
Section 234 — refers to condominium programs.

The management of subsidized housing is very detailed and exacting. A property manager should not accept such projects without proper training and/or backup support. Projects are usually large with huge density and high maintenance costs. Property management is very intensive with high turnover, rent loss, and collection problems. Tenant unions and more vocal residents many times create management headaches. The Institute of Real Estate Management offers HUD-approved programs to train managers. There are computer programs to help compile the many reports, forms, and statistics necessary for compliance. One such program for an IBM PC is called Micro-HUD.

HUD Management

Congress passed the "Housing Act" in 1935. The act recognized the need for housing for low-income families and created programs to meet that need. The act has been amended many times over the years to accommodate housing needs as determined by Congress. Amendments to the act have created various programs for subsidizing mortgage interest rates while other programs subsidized the families themselves. Until the early 1980s, all of the various programs for family subsidies had their own sets of entrance requirements and paperwork/forms. In the early 1980s, many of the programs for family subsidies were phased out and converted to current programs, and the paperwork became uniform and streamlined.

Although HUD is not currently issuing subsidy contracts except for senior citizen housing, it has a huge inventory of properties that they must oversee. A large majority of properties are privately owned, federally subsidized, and managed by fee managers. The owners and management agents must be approved by HUD to own or manage property on a case-by-case basis.

When approved, the agent must manage the property within HUD guidelines. This translates into using the government charts of accounts, submitting monthly income and expense reports when required, and an annual certified audit. Of course, HUD has the right to inspect both the property and your records to ensure they are being properly maintained.

The key to success in dealing with HUD is to make sure the owner knows and will follow the guidelines as described in the Regulatory Agreement. This document, written in plain English, describes the things the owner can and cannot do. Most HUD-related problems occur when the owner disregards the guidelines.

Agents should be willing to adapt to some minor changes in their accounting, leases/rental forms, and management agreements. Agents should also recognize the fact that HUD has a real interest (either by way of mortgage insurance or other subsidy) in the property and its goals are the same as those of the manager, to manage the property to its best potential.

Dealing with tenants in subsidized properties is not vastly different from dealing with tenants in conventional properties. However, there are some differences in the management processes. The screening of the residents is much the same as for conventional management except that many more personal financial questions must be asked and documented. In many cases, the house rules are easier to enforce because of the possibility of eviction for noncompliance, in which case the tenant is aware he/she would not find other suitable housing at such low rates. Eviction proceedings require much more documentation than unsubsidized, but are not impossible. One vast difference is that there is virtually no need for marketing once a project is built as there is always a waiting list of people who want to move in.

As stated at the beginning of this chapter, managing different types of properties (i.e., commercial, mobile homes, etc.) has its own area of specialization, and HUD management is no different. In order to demonstrate the paperwork involved, some HUD forms follow in Figures 11-5 to 11-7: 1) Owner's Certification of Compliance with HUD's Tenant Eligibility and Rent Procedures, 2) Tenant Certification, and 3) Housing Owner's Certification and Application for Housing Assistance Payments.

Figure 11-5. Owner Certification

Owner's Certification of Compliance with HUD's Tenant Eligibility and Rent Procedures

U.S. Department of Housing and Urban Development
Office of Housing
Federal Housing Commissioner

Important: Read the Instructions in Appendix I of Handbook 4350.3 before completing this form.

OMB No. 2502-0204

Part I - GENERAL INFORMATION

1. Date this Form will be Effective. MM DD YY
2. Date Tenant Moved into this Project. MM DD YY
3. Project Name:
4. FHA/EH/Non-Insured Project No.:
5. Section 8 Project Contract Number:
6. Action Processed: *(See Instructions)*
   a. Always Enter One Code:
   1= Move-Ins
   2= Converted from: ________
   3= Initial Certification
   4= Annual Recertification
   5= Interim Recertification
   b. See Instructions:
   1= Correction to prior 50059
   2= Unit Transfer
   3= Gross Rent Change
   4= Rent Rebate
7. Type of Subsidy:
   a. Subsidy Tenant will receive (Enter One Code):
   1= Section 8
   2= Rent Supplement
   3= RAP
   4= Section 236
   5= BMIR
   6= HUD-owned
   b. Is this the type of subsidy the Family is NOW receiving? [ ] Yes [ ] No
8. Complete this item ONLY for Tenants who were already converted from Rent Supp. or RAP.
   8a. Date Code *(See Instructions)* [ ]
   8b. Was the Head or Spouse age 62 or older at time of conversion? [ ] Yes [ ] No
   8c. Has the Family received Section 8 continuously since being converted [ ] Yes [ ] No
9a. Race of Head of Household *(Enter One Code):*
   1= White
   2= Black
   3= American Indian or Alaskan Native
   4= Asian or Pacific Islander
9b. Ethnicity of Head of Household *(Enter One Code):*
   1= Hispanic
   2= Non-Hispanic
Use the Instructions to complete Items 10, 11, and 12.
10. Previous Housing Code *(For Move-Ins ONLY):*
11. Displacement Code: *(For Move-Ins ONLY):*
12. Preference Code *(For Move Ins or Initial Certifications ONLY):*

Part II - HOUSEHOLD COMPOSITION

13. Mbr. No.	14a. Last Name of Family Member	14b. First 8 Letters of First Name	14c. M. I.	15. Relationship to Head of Household	16. Sex	17. Date of Birth MM	DD	YY	18. Age	19. Spec Status Code
Head				Head of Household						
2										
3										
4										
5										
6										
7										
8										
9										

13. Mbr. No.	20. Social Security Number or Alien Registration Number	21. Elig. Code	22. Place of Birth	23. Family Member Occupation
Head				
2				
3				
4				
5				
6				
7				
8				
9				

24a. Number of Family Members
24b. Number of Foster Children and Live-in Attendants
25. Number of Dependents

Part III - NET FAMILY ASSETS AND INCOME
(Read instructions before completing this Chart.)

26a. Type of Assets	26b. C or I	26c. Cash Value of Assets	26d. Actual Yearly Income from Assets
TOTALS			

IF the Total in Column 26c exceeds $5,000, complete Item 27, Otherwise, enter "N.A." in Item 27 AND GO TO Item 28.

27. IMPUTED INCOME FROM ASSETS: *Enter the HUD-approved Passbook Rate here (%) and multiply the Total in Item 26c by that rate.* $

28. INCOME (USE ANNUAL AMOUNTS)
(Read Instructions before completing this Chart.)

28. Mbr. No.	28a. Care Code	28b. Employment or Business	28c. Social Security, Pensions, etc.	28d. Public Assistance	28e. Other Income
28f. Total Income from each source.					

29. Income from all sources except Assets *(Add all amounts on Line 28f above.)* . . . $
30. Income from Assets *(Enter the Greater of Item 27 or Total in Item 26d.)* . . $
31. ANNUAL INCOME *(Item 29 plus Item 30.)* . . . $
32. INCOME LIMITS:
   a. Lower . . . $
   b. Very Low $
33. Eligibility Universe *(See Instructions):* [ ] Pre-1981 [ ] Post 1981
34. Tenant's Current Income Status *(See Instructions):* [ ] Lower [ ] Very Low
35a. Did Tenant begin receiving Section 8 assistance on or after July 1, 1984 ? [ ] Yes [ ] No
35b. If "Yes", enter one of the exception codes listed in the instructions

Part IV - ALLOWANCES AND ADJUSTED INCOME

36. Allowance for Dependents *(Item 25 x $480)*. $
37. Child Care Allowance $
38. 3% of Annual Income *(.03 x Item 31)* . . $
39a. Total Handicapped Assistance Expenses . . . . . . $
39b. Allowance for Handicap Assistance *(See Inst.)* $
40a. Total Medical Expenses *(Elderly Households ONLY)* $
40b. Allowance for Medical Expenses *(See Instructions)* . . $
41. Elderly Household Allowance *(See Instructions.)* . . . $
42. Total Allowances *(Add Lines 36, 37, 39b, 40b and 41)*. $
43. ADJUSTED INCOME *(Line 31 minus Line 42.)*. $

Part V - PROJECT RENT INFORMATION (Use amounts that will be in effect on date shown in Item 1.)

44. CONTRACT RENT $
45. UTILITY ALLOWANCE $
46. GROSS RENT *(Line 44 plus Line 45.)* . . . . . . $

Part VI - FAMILY RENT & SUBSIDY INFORMATION (See Instructions)

47. WELFARE RENT $
48. HCDA percentage *(leave blank if BMIR)* [ ] 29% [ ] 30%
49. HUD-50059 Worksheet used *(See Instructions):*
50. TOTAL TENANT PAYMENT *(TTP)* $
51. TENANT RENT $
52. UTILITY REIMBURSEMENT $
53. ASSISTANCE PAYMENT *(Line 46 minus Line 50)* . . . $
54. Percentage of Adjusted Income Charged . . . . . . ____ %
55. Did the 1983 HURRA Rent Limitations affect the Tenant's Rent ? . . . [ ] Yes [ ] No

Part VII - UNIT ASSIGNMENT AND RECERTIFICATION INFORMATION

56. Date Next Annual Recertification Effective MM DD YY
57. Number of Bedrooms
58. Building Identification Code
59. Unit Number *(See Inst.)*

Part VIII - CERTIFICATIONS — SIGN ONLY AFTER READING THE STATEMENT THAT APPLIES TO YOU ON THE COVER FLAP.

Head of Household	*Date*
Spouse/ Co-Head	*Date*
Owner/Agent	*Date*

PREVIOUS EDITIONS OBSOLETE

HUD-50059 (10-84)
HB 4350.3

Figure 11-6. Tenant Certification

Form FmHA 1944-8 (Rev. 5-86)	USDA – FARMERS HOME ADMINISTRATION TENANT CERTIFICATION	FORM APPROVED OMB NO. 0575-0033

WARNING: Section 1001 of Title 18, United States Code provides, "Whoever, in any matter within the jurisdiction of any department or agency of the United States knowingly and willfully falsifies, conceals or covers up by any trick, scheme, or device a material fact, or makes any false, fictitious or fraudulent statements or representations, or makes or uses any false writing or document knowing the same to contain any false, fictitious or fraudulent statement or entry, shall be fined not more than $10,000 or imprisoned not more than five years, or both."

STATEMENT REQUIRED BY THE PRIVACY ACT:
The Farmers Home Adminstration (FmHA) is authorized by Title V of the Housing Act of 1949, as amended (42 U.S.C. 1471 et. seq.), to solicit the information requested on this form. Disclosure of the information requested is voluntary. However, failure to disclose certain items of information may result in a delay in the processing of your eligibility or rejection, except that it is unlawful for FmHA to deny eligibility because of the refusal to disclose the Social Security Account Number.

The principal purposes for collecting the requested information are to determine eligibility for occupancy in the FmHA financed rental project and to determine the amount of tenant contribution for rent. The information collected on this form may be released to appropriate Federal, State, and Local Agencies when relevant to civil, criminal or regulatory proceedings.

ALL MONETARY FIGURES SHOULD BE ROUNDED TO THE NEAREST DOLLAR

PART I — TENANT HOUSEHOLD INFORMATION

1. Household Member Name (Last, First and Middle Initial)	2. Sex	3. Date of Birth M M D D Y Y	4. Minor, Disabled or Handicapped	5. Elderly, Disabled or Handicapped	6. Race/National Origin of Tenant

(Complete this only when household member *is not* the Tenant or a Co-Tenant)

(Complete this only when household member *is a* Tenant or Co-Tenant)

(Check below when coded above)

1 - White, Non Hispanic
2 - Black, Non Hispanic
3 - Asian, Pacific Isld.
4 - American Indian Alaskan Native
5 - Hispanic

1.a. Number of Foster Children (if any) [ ]

Total (Line 4) [ ]   Elderly Status [ ]   Enter Race/National Origin Code [ ]

PART II — UNIT IDENTIFICATION

7. Unit Number [ ]   8. Unit Type [ ]

PART III — ASSET INCOME

9. Net Family Assets (NOTE: If Line 9 does not exceed $5,000, enter zero on Line 10.) $ [ ]

10. Imputed Income from Assets (Bank Passbook Savings Rate (•   ) x Line 9.) $ [ ]

11. Income from Assets $ [ ]

PART IV — INCOME CALCULATIONS

12. Income
a. Wages, Salaries, etc. $ [ ]
b. Soc. Sec., Pensions, etc. $ [ ]
c. Public Assistance $ [ ]
d. Income Contributed by Assets (Greater of Line 10 or Line 11) $ [ ]
e. Other $ [ ]
f. Annual Income [ ]

13. Adjustments to Income
a. $480 x total of Line 4 $ [ ]
b. $400 if elderly status $ [ ]
c. Medical (if elderly handicapped or disabled) $ [ ]
d. Child Care $ [ ]
e. Total Adjustments [ ]

14. Adjusted Annual Income (Line 12.f. minus 13.e.) $ [ ]

PART V — INCOME LEVELS

15. Number of Household Members [ ]

16. Current Eligibility Income Level (Enter Code) [ ]

17. Date of Initial Project Entry M M D D Y Y [ ]

18. Eligibility Income Level at Initial Project Entry (Enter Code) [ ]

PART VI — CERTIFICATION BY TENANT

I/we certify that the information in PARTS I through VI is true and correct to the best of my/our knowledge and belief. Inquiries may be made to verify this information.

a. Date: M M D D Y Y   b. Soc. Sec. No.   c. Tenant Signature

d. Date: M M D D Y Y   e. Soc. Sec. No.   f. Co-Tenant Signature

This form is used to certify tenant income, establish tenant eligibility, and assure compliance with Federal Regulations. The information is required as a condition to obtain a benefit. This statement is provided pursuant to P.L. 96-511.

Figure 11-6 (cont'd). Tenant Certification

PART VII — PRELIMINARY CALCULATIONS

19. Adjusted Monthly Income *(Line 14 ÷ 12)* a. $ [   ] × .30 = b. $ [   ]
20. Monthly Income *(Line 12.f. ÷ 12)* a. $ [   ] × .10 = b. $ [   ]

21. Designated Monthly Welfare Shelter Payment $ [   ]

22. Highest of Line 19.b., Line 20.b., or Line 21. $ [   ]

23. Gross Basic Rent
  a. Basic Rent $ [   ]
  b. Utility Allowance $ [   ]
  c. *(Line 23.a. + Line 23.b.)* $ [   ]

24. Gross Market Rent
  a. Market Rent $ [   ]
  b. Utility Allowance $ [   ]
  c. *(Line 24.a. + Line 24.b.)* $ [   ]

PART VIII — PRELIMINARY GROSS TENANT CONTRIBUTION (PGTC)

Decision: *(check one)*

☐ A. If tenant *Receives rental assistance (RA)* enter line 22 on line 25 below.

☐ B. If tenant *does not receive RA* and this project receives Plan II Interest Credit, enter the greater of line 22 or line 23.c. (but not to exceed line 24.c.) on line 25 below.

☐ C. If tenant *does not receive RA* and this project is a Plan I, Full Profit or Labor Housing project complete lines C.1. thru C.3. and enter C.3. on line 25.

  C.1. Enter line 24.c $ [   ]
  C.2. Add Plan I Surcharge *(if any)* $ [   ]
  C.3. Total *(enter on line 25)* $ [   ]

25. PGTC $ [   ]

PART IX — DOES PGTC BECOME FINAL GROSS TENANT CONTRIBUTION?

Decision: *(check one)* If you check Decision A, B, C, D, or E, Enter Line 25 on Line 26 Below

☐ A. Tenant initially occupied the project on or after October 1, 1986.

☐ B. You checked Decision B in PART VIII *and entered Line 23.c. on Line 25.*

☐ C. You checked Decision C in PART VIII.

☐ D. Change in PGTC is *entirely* due to a change in household size, rental rate, or utility allowance *(recertifications only)*.

☐ E. The most recently completed PART XIV, "Tenant Certification Worksheet" indicated this tenant is no longer subject to the Tenant Contribution Increase Limits.

☐ F. None of the above apply. IF YOU CHECK THIS BOX, YOU MUST COMPLETE PART XIV, "Tenant Certification Worksheet", enter the answer from Line G-1 of Part XIV on line 26 of Part X.

PART X — DETERMINING NET TENANT CONTRIBUTION (NTC)

26. Gross Tenant Contribution *(See PART IX)* $ [   ]
27. Utility Allowance *(Line 23.b. or Line 24.b.)* $ [   ]
28. Preliminary NTC *(Line 26 minus Line 27)* $ [   ]

Decision: *(check one)*

☐ A. If you checked Decision A in PART VIII (PGTC) enter Line 28 on Line 29 below and compare Line 23.c. and Line 28. If Line 23.c. is smaller, return to PART VIII (PGTC) and check Decision B since this tenant will not receive RA.

☐ B. If you checked Decision B in PART VIII (PGTC), enter the greater of Line 23.a. or Line 28 (but not to exceed Line 24.a.) on Line 29 below.

☐ C. If you checked Decision C in PART VIII (PGTC) enter Line 28 on Line 29 below.

29. Final NTC *(amount Tenant pays Borrower for rent)*
(If Line 29 is negative, Borrower pays difference to Tenant for utilities) $ [   ]

PART XI — PROJECT IDENTIFICATION

30. Project Case Number [   ]

31. Project Number [   ]

PART XII — CERTIFICATION BY BORROWER

I certify that the information on this form has been verified as required by federal law and the tenant household ☐ is eligible to live in the unit, or ☐ has been granted ineligible occupancy by FmHA.

a. Effective Date [M M D D Y Y / 0 1] b. Signature of Borrower or Borrowers Representative c. Date Signed [M M D D Y Y]

PART XIII — CERTIFICATION BY FmHA

Based on information provided by the Borrower, the calculations for this form are correct.

a. Date [M M D D Y Y] b. Signature of FmHA Representative

—2—

Form FmHA 1944-8 (Rev. 5-86)

Figure 11-6 (cont'd). Tenant Certification

PART XIV — TENANT CERTIFICATION WORKSHEET

NOTE: Use only if directed by PART IX. When this worksheet is used, it is subject to the certification statements signed and dated by the borrower (PART XII) and FmHA (PART XIII).

ENTER THE FOLLOWING

From This Form FmHA 1944-8:

From the Most Recently Approved Tenant Certification:

		from Form FmHA 1944-8	from Form FmHA 444-8

A-1 _____ PGTC (Line 25)

B-1 _____ Gross Tenant Contribution   (Line 25)   (Line 9.d. plus Line 10.d.)

A-2 _____ Annual Income (Line 12.f.)

B-2 _____ Annual Income   (Line 12.f.)   (Line 4.a.)

A-3 _____ Adjustments (Line 13.e.)

B-3 _____ Adjustments   (Line 13.e.)   (Line 4.b. plus Line 4.c.)

A-4 _____ Affect of Imputed Income from Assets
[If household has net family assets greater than $5000 and imputed income from Assets (Line 10) is greater than actual income from Assets (Line 11) then enter the difference (Line 10 minus Line 11)]

Test # 1

C-1 _____ PGTC (A-1)

C-2 _____ Portion of PGTC Automatically Allowable (B-1 times 1.10)

C-3 _____ Portion of PGTC Which may be Allowable (C-1 minus C-2)

Decision Test # 1
(check one) ☐ If C-3 is zero or less, enter C-1 on G-1 and omit Test #2 Test #3 and Test #4
☐ If C-3 is greater than zero, go to Test #2

Test # 2

D-1 _____ Change in Annual Income (A-2 minus B-2)

D-2 _____ Affect of Imputed Income from Assets (A-4)

D-3 _____ Net Change in Annual Income (D-1 minus D-2)

Decision Test # 2
(check one) ☐ If D-3 is zero or less, enter C-2 on G-1 and omit Test # 3 and Test # 4
☐ If D-3 is greater than zero, go to Test #3

Test # 3

E-1 _____ Net Change in Annual Income (D-3)

E-2 _____ Change in Adjustments (A-3 minus B-3)

E-3 _____ Total Net Change (E-1 plus E-2)

Decision Test # 3
(check one) ☐ If E-3 is zero or less, enter C-2 on G-1 and omit Test #4
☐ If E-3 is greater than zero, go to Test #4

Test # 4

F-1 _____ Portion of Total Net Change Attributable to Annual Income (E-1 divided by E-3)

F-2 _____ Portion of C-3 Allowable (C-3 times F-1)

F-3 _____ Total PGTC Allowable (C-2 plus F-2)

Decision Test # 4
(check one) ☐ If F-3 is less than A-1, enter F-3 on G-1.

☐ If F-3 is equal to or greater than A-1, enter A-1 on G-1.
(NOTE: When this box is checked, this tenant household is no longer subject to the tenant contribution increase limits.)

Gross Tenant Contribution

G-1 _____ (Enter on Line 26 of Part X)

−3−   Form FmHA 1944-8 (Rev. 5-86)

Figure 11-7. Assistance Payment

The Easy Worksheet for Computing Total Tenant Payment/Tenant Rent (All Programs)

U.S. Department of Housing and Urban Development
Office of Housing
Federal Housing Commissioner

OMB No. 2502-0204 (exp. 3/31/87.)

IMPORTANT: Read Appendix 2 of Handbook 4350.3 before you complete this Form. The Appendix tells you which version of the Worksheet you must use.

Name or Tenant	Name of Project	Unit Number

PART A. COMPUTE THE TOTAL TENANT PAYMENT/TENANT RENT. Complete only one Section. Select the Section that applies to the type of subsidy the Tenant will be receiving.

Sec. 8/RAP Tenants

A-1. _____ Monthly Income (Item 31 ÷ 12).
A-2. _____ Monthly Adjusted Income (Item 43 ÷ 12).
A-3. _____ HCDA Percentage (Item 48).
A-4. _____ Monthly Adjusted Income × HCDA Percentage (A2 × A3).
A-5. _____ 10% of Monthly Income (A1 × .10).
A-6. _____ Welfare Rent (*Applies only to welfare recipients in as-paid States or Counties*).
A-7. _____ **TOTAL TENANT PAYMENT (TTP)** (Enter the **largest** of A4, A5 or A6).

Go to Part B

Rent Supplement Tenants

A-1. ///// Monthly Income.
A-2. _____ Monthly Adjusted Income (Item 43 ÷ 12).
A-3. _____ HCDA Percentage (Item 48).
A-4. _____ Gross Rent (Item 46).
A-5. _____ 30% of Gross Rent (A4 × .30).
A-6. _____ Monthly Adjusted Income × HCDA Percentage. (A2 × A3).
A-7. _____ **TOTAL TENANT PAYMENT (TTP)** (Enter the **larger** of A5 or A6).

NOTE: If this is a *move-in* or an *initial* certification, Tenant is eligible ONLY if Total Tenant Payment (TTP) is less than 90 percent of Gross Rent - i.e., A7 is less than (.90 × A4).

Go to Part B

Section 236 Tenants
Complete only one column under this Part. Select the utility arrangement that applies to this Tenant.

No Utility Allowance

A-1. ///// Monthly Income.
A-2. _____ Monthly Adjusted Income (Item 43 ÷ 12).
A-3. _____ HCDA Percentage (Item 48).
A-4. _____ Monthly Adjusted Income × HDCA Percentage (A2 × A3).
A-5. _____ *Basic Rent (Item 44).
A-6. _____ *Market Rent (From Rent Schedule).
A-7. _____ **TENANT RENT** (Enter the **larger** of A4 or A5 but never more than A6).

Go to Part B

With Utility Allowance

A-1. ///// Monthly Income.
A-2. _____ Monthly Adjusted Income (Item 43 ÷ 12).
A-3. _____ HCDA Percentage (Item 48).
A-4. _____ Monthly Adjusted Income × HCDA Percentage (A2 × A3).
A-5. _____ *Utility Allowance (Item 45).
A-6. _____ A4 minus A5.
A-7. _____ *Basic Rent (Item 44).
A-8. _____ Higher of A6 or A7.
A-9. _____ Minimum Rent (25% of A2).
A-10. _____ *Market Rent (From Rent Schedule).
A-11. _____ **TENANT RENT** (Enter the **larger** of A8 or A9 but never more than A10).

Go to Part B

NOTE: Use the Rents and Utility Allowance that will be in effect on the date this Tenant Rent will become effective.

PART B. TRANSFER THIS WORKSHEET DATA TO THE HUD-50059

HUD-50059 Item No:

- Enter the Answer from Part A in:
  - for Section 236 Tenants — 51
  - for All Other Tenants — 50
- Enter HCDA Percentage from A3 in — 54
- Check "No" in — 55

Prepared By (Name and Date)	Supervisory Review By (Initials and Date)

HUD-50059 e (10-84)
HB 4350.3

Summary

The professional property management field is diversified and varied in classification of properties. Each specialized area has its own unique features and peculiarities, many of which are derived from local customs. The property manager should be confident of expertise and experience in a specialized area, such as mini-storage, before undertaking management.

Industrial buildings are usually classified as single-tenant, multi-tenant, or industrial parks. Industrial tenants are classified into six basic categories:

1. Market-oriented

2. Raw material and resource-oriented

3. Transportation-oriented

4. Labor intensity-oriented

5. Energy-oriented

6. Nondescript-oriented

The government approval process in California for new development usually involves an Environmental Impact Report (EIR) that must consider tenant displacement, historical sites, traffic, air, and water quality, endangered species, etc.

Mobile home park management involves different rules and regulations from apartment management. The notice period to raise rents is 60 days vs. only 30 days for apartments. Copies of the "Mobile Home Residency Law" must be provided to tenants.

Mini-storage is a growing and unique type of management that requires specific expertise and knowledge. The Self-Service Storage Association (SSSA), a trade association, is a source for forms, information, and seminars.

Management of medical buildings is unique in that it has special tenant mix requirements. Maintenance is frequently more intense and specialized, such as disposal of contaminated waste including needles and bandages.

Retirement communities are broken into three basic categories: independent, semi-independent, and supported living.

Federally-subsidized housing programs such as Section 8, where the government pays the difference between 20–30% of the tenant's income and fair market rent, requires special knowledge of HUD rules and regulations. Government forms need to be accurately filled out in order to comply and be paid. Use of special computer programs is very desirable in this area.

In conclusion, in this chapter we covered specialized and unique areas of property management. As pointed out, the property management field is wide and varied and no one book can contain all the answers. Common sense and a willingness to seek out and accept challenges are necessary for successful property management.

NOTES

Chapter 11 Review Questions

1. *Industrial buildings usually have stiffer parking regulations than:*

   a. office buildings.
   b. retail buildings.
   c. medical buildings.
   d. none of the above.

2. *Industrial buildings are usually located:*

   a. near major transportation.
   b. only in rural areas.
   c. only in urban areas.
   d. only in Sunbelt areas.

3. *Management fees for industrial management are usually:*

   a. higher than for residential.
   b. higher than for commercial.
   c. among the lowest.
   d. among the highest.

4. *Which of the following is <u>not</u> a typical industrial lease?*

   a. Gross.
   b. Net.
   c. Percentage.
   d. Sale/leaseback.

5. *R&D buildings are usually:*

   a. skyscrapers.
   b. two to three stories.
   c. a minimum of ten stories.
   d. a minimum of 20 stories.

6. *New mobile homes in service since 1980 are:*

   a. taxed as personal property.
   b. taxed as real property.
   c. not taxed.
   d. double-taxed.

7. *The highest rating for a mobile home park is:*

   a. two stars.
   b. three stars.
   c. five stars.
   d. ten stars.

8. *Mini-storage parks are usually located:*

   a. on prime land.
   b. on cheaper land.
   c. only in rural areas.
   d. near hospitals.

9. *The best location for a medical building is usually near:*

   a. a hospital.
   b. a shopping center.
   c. an office building.
   d. a river.

10. *The most desirable tenants for a medical building are:*

    a. chiropractors.
    b. general practitioners.
    c. veterinarians.
    d. insurance companies.

Chapter 11
Selected Additional References and Reading

American Hotel & Motel Association
  1201 New York Avenue, N.W.
  Washington, D.C. 20005

Bureau of National Affairs, *Guide to Federal Housing Programs*, Washington, D.C.

California Department of Real Estate, *Common Interest Homeowner's Association Management Study*, Sacramento, CA, 1987.

California Department of Real Estate, *A Guide to Mobile-Home Park Purchases by Residents*, Sacramento, CA.

Ellickson, Robert C. and A. Tarlock, *Land-Use Controls*, Little, Brown & Co., Boston, MA, 1984.

The Mini-Storage Messenger (Monthly)
  2531 W. Dunlap Avenue, Suite 201
  Phoenix, AZ 85021

Mobilehome Parks Report (Monthly)
  3807 Pasadena Avenue, Suite 100
  Sacramento, CA 95821

Mobile/Manufacturing Home Merchandise (Monthly)
  203 N. Wabash Avenue, Suite 1819
  Chicago, IL 60611

National Association of Industrial & Office Parks (NAIOP)
  1215 Jefferson Davis Highway, Suite 100
  Arlington, VA 22202

Parker, Rosetta A., CPM, *Housing for the Elderly*, Institute of Real Estate Management, Chicago, IL, 1984.

Self Service Storage (Monthly)
  P.O. Box 110
  Eureka, AR 72632

Society of Industrial and Office Realtors, *A Guide to Industrial Site Selection*, Washington, D.C.

Society of Industrial and Office Realtors, *Industrial Real Estate*, Washington, D.C., 1984.

Society of Industrial and Office Realtors, *Industrial Real Estate Market Survey*, Washington, D.C.

Society of Industrial and Office Realtors, S.I.R. Reports (Bimonthly newsletter), Washington, D.C.

Urban Land Institute, *Hotel/Motel Development*, Washington D.C.

Urban Land Institute, *PUD's in Practice*, Washington, D.C., 1985.

Urban Land Institute, *Shared Parking*, Washington, D.C., 1983.

Urban Land Institute, *Timesharing II*, Washington, D.C., 1982.

Western Mobilehome Association Reporter (WMA) (Monthly)
  1760 Creekside Oaks Drive, Suite 200
  Sacramento, CA 95833

NOTES

Chapter 12

Maintenance

Key Terms

Controllable cost
Service maintenance
Routine maintenance
Preventive maintenance
Security complex
Photoelectric timer
Electrolysis
Recirculation pump
Btu
Circuit breaker
Thermostat
Flow restrictor
Asbestos
Toxic waste
Title 24

Food for Thought

"I'd hate to fly seven miles above the ground in something repaired by the low bidder."

Maintenance

Role of the Property Manager in Maintenance

Maintenance is one of the most important and visible roles of property management. If you ask a tenant if a building is well managed, he or she will reply either, "Yes, they fix things right away" or "No, they always procrastinate and never fix things correctly." The tenant views management and maintenance as the same entity. Since retaining existing tenants is the best method for keeping vacancy low and turnover at a minimum, a good maintenance program is imperative. The property manager, in a quest to increase NOI, must not only increase rents but develop programs and guidelines to reduce costs. Maintenance is a controllable cost, unlike the mortgage payment over which the property manager has no control. Budgeting with a priority plan should be set to handle problems so the property manager controls rather than reacts to maintenance problems (Figure 12-1).

The property manager need not be an expert in maintenance, but should learn the terminology and be unafraid to get dirty when dealing with maintenance personnel and contractors.

Four Types of Maintenance

Service Maintenance

Service maintenance includes maintenance items requested by the tenant or manager. It also includes emergency requests such as stopped-up toilets, leaking faucets, no hot water, broken windows, no heat, etc. Requests should be prioritized with a number marked on the work order as follows:

1. *Emergencies*

2. *Repair within 24 hours*

3. *When time permits*

Figure 12-1. Maintenance Circles

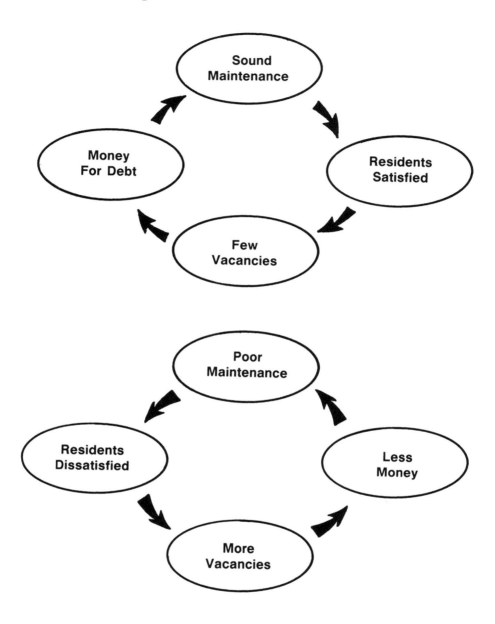

Routine Maintenance

Routine maintenance includes general maintenance to the common areas, landscaping, equipment, and janitorial duties. These items are not tenant-requested, but are necessary to help the building have good "curb appeal" — desirability. In office buildings, the lobby, halls, and restrooms should be maintained on a regular schedule; don't wait for a tenant to complain. See Figure 12-2.

Figure 12-2. Work Order

J. D. MAINTENANCE AND CONSTRUCTION

P.O. BOX 1438
COSTA MESA, CA 92666
(714) 751-2787

WORK ORDER   # 2216

DATE: _____

PHONES

NAME: _____

(H) _____

(B) _____

(MGR.) _____

WORK REQUESTED		MATERIALS		
	QTY.	DESCRIPTION	UNIT COST	

WORKMAN	DATE	IN	OUT	HOURS

Preventive Maintenance

This is a system of performing repair tasks on a regularly scheduled basis to prevent minor problems from leading to major breakdowns or problems. Examples would include replacing air-conditioning filters; lubricating, oiling, and adjusting equipment; exterminating; exterior painting; etc. Many times outside contractors are used for these tasks.

Extraordinary Maintenance

This task involves major rehabilitation, replacement, or refurbishment of units, buildings, or grounds. Examples would include a new facade, roof replacement, replumbing, conversion from master meter to individual meters, etc. The property manager will frequently charge a supervision fee to handle these items.

Licensed vs. Unlicensed Contractors

The basic difference in licensed vs. unlicensed contractors is that licensed contractors have to pass a state exam and meet experience criteria set forth by the Contractor's State License Board (part of the Department of Consumer Affairs). They must also have a bond and are subject to having their license revoked or suspended. An unlicensed contractor doing work (including labor and material) costing $300 or more is committing a misdemeanor. The penalty for a first offense is $1,500, and $4,500 for each additional offense.

Figure 12-3.

---

10 RULES OF SERVICE

1. Do not enter without permission
2. Have a witness, when possible
3. Knock before entering
4. Keep mouth *shut*
5. Authorized work only
6. No false promises
7. Keep mouth *shut*
8. Do not browse
9. Do not touch
10. Be courteous and considerate

Source: E. Robert Miller, CPM

Maintenance Areas

Plumbing

Plumbing is one of the most frequent problem areas. The plumbing system can be divided into three parts: 1) fresh water supply, 2) drainage system, and 3) gas piping.

Areas of Interest to the Property Manager and Onsite Manager

1. Shutoff valve locations in the complex.

2. Electrolysis — corrosion due to dissimilar metal pipes, such as connecting an iron pipe to a copper connector pipe. Steel (gas) pipe laid in close proximity to copper (water) pipe may cause a chemical reaction (electrolysis) to occur between the two dissimilar metals. This results in a pitting action that leads to pinhole leaks in the steel pipe.

3. Insulation of hot water pipes will result in energy savings. A 40°F temperature loss between the hot water heater and a remote outlet can occur without proper insulation.

4. Recirculating pumps also reduce energy costs by constantly keeping hot water in the lines. Pump timers can be used to reduce energy cost during low tenant usage (nighttime).

5. Hot water heaters should be properly serviced to remove heavy mineral deposits which can cause the heater to burst. The temperature should not exceed 120°F, although higher temperatures may be required in special-use buildings (i.e., medical) or for dishwashers (140°F).

6. Repairs — try to replace broken parts with identical parts from the same manufacturer.

7. Parts — faucets and garbage disposals should be purchased in quantity in order to obtain lower prices. One brand for each should be utilized to make replacement or repair easier and less time-consuming.

8. Proper tools — seat-dressing wrench, socket wrench, wax seals (toilet), and pipe wrenches should always be readily available.

9. Always try to standardize the type of repair and replacement parts used.

10. Maintain a working relationship with a qualified plumbing and electrical company to be on call 24 hours a day to handle plumbing and heating emergencies.

Heating System

Like plumbing, lack of heat is a habitability problem, as will be discussed in Chapter 14, and needs immediate attention.

1. The most comfortable temperature range for the human body in summer is 72–79°F, and 68–74°F in winter.

2. Air-flow motion by fans, windows, or vents increases the evaporation rate of heat from the body. This is desirable during the summer months.

3. Drapes (lined) covering windows will prevent heat loss in the winter.

4. Older people usually prefer higher temperatures.

5. A "heat pump" is a system in which the refrigeration system is used to remove heat and discharge it to the outdoors in the summer. In colder weather this process is reversed.

6. Heat exchange is a method of transferring heat from one liquid to another without mixing the liquids; the process is used for hot water systems.

7. British thermal unit (Btu) is the unit of heat required to raise the temperature of one pound of water from 62°F to 63°F.

8. Performance ratio is calculated by converting fuel usage into Btu. These Btu are divided by conditioned square footage of the building — which is then divided by the total heating and cooling days. The lower the performance ratio, the less energy the building consumes per square foot per degree per day. Information on heating- and cooling-degree days can be obtained from the local Weather Bureau.

9. High-pressure gas piping repairs should always be done by a licensed plumber.

Electrical System

1. Wiring systems include the following descriptions and cautions:

   a. 120/240-volt, single-phase, 3-wire system is used for smaller buildings and residential.

   b. 120/208-volt, 3-phase, 4-wire system is usually used in office, apartment, and commercial buildings.

   c. 480/277-volt, 3-phase, 4-wire system is used mainly for large industrial buildings.

2. Electrical repairs should be performed by a licensed electrician for safety and insurance reasons.

3. The property manager should maintain electrical blueprints so the electrician can more readily trace problems.

4. Circuit-breaking vs. fuses—both perform the same function, which is to cut off electricity when the system is overloaded. Appliances should be turned off before replacing fuses or resetting circuit breakers to avoid power surges when the current is restored.

5. Watt (power) — a measurement of electricity is used. Appliances, lights, motors, air-conditioning, etc. should not exceed the capacity of the service panel.

6. Always turn off the power at the circuit breaker before doing any electrical work.

7. In some medical buildings and large office buildings, self-starting diesel generators are installed which automatically activate when the power goes out.

Carpeting

1. Carpeting with patterns and in darker colors hides dirt and wears well. Hi-lo or plush covering is better and more aesthetically pleasing than shag.

2. Padding increases the comfort, quiet, and insulation of residential carpet, but sometimes is not used in commercial areas as it increases wear (increased movement causes more wear on the fibers).

3. Frequent vacuuming will prolong carpet life. A heavy-duty, upright vacuum cleaner is best.

4. Spot and stain removal should be done immediately.
     a. Use a wet cloth to soak up damp spills and transfer the stain from the carpet to the cloth.
     b. Remedies to dissolve stains:
         (1) Water-soluble removers for sugars and starches.
         (2) Dry-cleaning fluids for butter, oils, and fats.
         (3) Detergent solutions:
             (a) Juices — diluted ammonia solution.
             (b) Bleach and urine — diluted vinegar solution.

5. Carpet grade should be FHA-approved to give longer wear — 5 to 8 years in many instances.

Pest Control

Figure 12-4.
Pest Control

1. Regularly scheduled monthly service contracts should be established with a licensed pest control vendor.

2. Cockroaches are best handled by regular spraying or by putting boric acid under sinks and areas they frequent. Caution must be used to keep away from areas accessible to children.

3. Clean premises and good housekeeping are the best deterrent to pest problems.

4. Spraying one unit may cause roaches to flee to neighboring units, so it is desirable to also spray surrounding units.

Roofing

1. Most properly maintained roofs will last 20–30 years.

2. Schedule inspections by a roofing contractor at least once a year, with repair work performed in the dry season for best prices.

3. Don't walk unnecessarily on the roof.

4. When doing repairs, such as major patching, be sure that rotted boards are replaced before putting down new felt and patching. Always have large areas repaired using the same materials and specifications as for the original roof.

Summary

We have covered only the highlights of a few major maintenance areas. An in-depth analysis is contained in Mel Shear's *Handbook of Building Maintenance Management* (Reston Publishing, Reston, VA, 1983).

Maintenance personnel should be carefully screened and selected. Not only should they be competent in their trade, but they should also be honest and trustworthy. A complete reference and credit check should be done on each applicant since they often work alone when a tenant is out and there is a potential for thievery. Ease of entry into an apartment could result in more serious crimes against tenants. Due to potential liability, the prudent property manager should take precautions.

Security and Safety

The property manager is responsible for more than the repair of plumbing and roofs for tenants. To most tenants, security represents the peaceful enjoyment of the unit and a secure complex. It is really a service the tenant has a legal right to expect from the management company or owner. Therefore, the property manager should develop programs and take preventive measures to promote tenant security. However, the manager should never promise more security than is possible to adequately provide.

1. *Hardware* — locks, deadbolts, doors, adequate lighting, fences, gates, etc. If security gates are installed, they should be working at all times to limit liability. A complex should not be advertised as a "security complex." We can't even protect the President of the United States, with all his Secret Service personnel, from being shot. By implying that your building is "secure," you expose yourself to additional liability.

2. *Guards* — to patrol the complex; can be either employees or an outside service.

3. *Tenant participation* — many cities have the COP or Neighborhood Watch program where tenants watch each other's units.

4. *Police* — renting to policemen as tenants at a slightly reduced rate is a good way to ward off problems.

5. *Site improvements* — install lighting in dark areas, high fences, closed-circuit television monitors.

6. *Smoke detectors* — the Orange County Fire Department estimates that an 87% reduction in deaths and serious injury and a 40% reduction in property loss would be achieved through implementation of a comprehensive smoke detection alarm system and maintenance program. Under the amended version of Section 10.307 of the Uniform Fire Code, the burden of responsibility for testing the smoke detector on a regular (annual) basis rests with the owner/manager. It is incumbent upon the owner to notify tenants, provide test forms, and maintain records of compliance for a minimum of three years (see Figure 12-5, Smoke Detector Log).

7. *Telephone jack* — CC 1941.2 says the landlord is responsible for installing at least one jack and maintaining the inside telephone wiring in good working order.

Figure 12-5. Smoke Detector Log

```
                                    SMOKE ALARM
                                INSTALLATION RECORD

                                              INSTALLATION CODE
          PROPERTY:_____   A= New alarm and battery installed
                   _____
                   _____   B= New battery for existing
    UNIT                                                detector
     #     Record date and installation code letter in box farthest left
```


J. D. Property Mgt Form

Lead Paint Standards

Congress passed the Residential Lead Based Paint Hazard Reduction Act of 1992, called Title X for short. This act places a burden on owners of property constructed prior to 1978, the year lead paint was banned, to disclose prior to sale or lease of a residential building.

Energy Management

The largest single expense in office buildings is master-metered utilities, which represents over 32% of operating costs. The cost of master-metered utilities in apartment buildings is over 25% of operating costs. The property manager must therefore institute an energy management program as a means of reducing expenses and increasing net operating income. The cap rate method of valuation assists in increasing property value. The comfort level of the tenant must also be considered as no one likes to take cold showers or wear a coat to bed at night.

Steps in an Energy Management Program

1. Gather background information — past utility bills, prior energy programs.

2. Analyze information — fuel usage per unit or per square foot.

3. Develop alternative measures — hot water heater efficiency, replacement needs, payback period.

Figure 12-6.

Page _____

SMOKE DETECTOR AGREEMENT

THIS AGREEMENT is entered into this _____ day of _____ , 198 ___,

by and between _____ , "Owner" (Landlord),

and _____ ,"Resident" (Tenant).

IN CONSIDERATION OF THEIR MUTUAL PROMISES, OWNER AND RESIDENT AGREE AS FOLLOWS:

1. Resident is renting from Owner the premises located at:

_____ , CA

2. This agreement is an Addendum and part of the Rental Agreement and/or Lease between Owner and Resident.

3. The premises is equipped with a smoke detection device(s).

4. The resident acknowledges the smoke detector(s) was tested and its operation explained by management in the presence of the Resident at time of initial occupancy and the detector(s) in the unit was working properly at that time.

5. Each resident shall perform the manufacturer's recommended test to determine if the smoke detector(s) is (are) operating properly at least once a week.

6. Initial in box ONLY if BATTERY OPERATED: ☐

   By initialing as provided, each Resident understands that said smoke detector(s) and alarm is a battery operated unit and it shall be each Resident's responsibility to:

   a. ensure that the battery is in operating condition at all times;
   b. replace the battery as needed (unless otherwise provided by law); and
   c. if, after replacing the battery, the smoke detector(s) do *not* work, inform the Owner or authorized agent immediately in writing.

7. Resident(s) must inform the owner or authorized agent immediately in writing of any defect, malfunction or failure of any detector(s).

_____   _____
           Owner/Agent   Resident

                                          _____
                                                        Resident

CAA APPROVED FORM
CALIFORNIA APARTMENT ASSOCIATION
FORM 27 0 COPYRIGHT 1984

4. Implement selected measures — purchase equipment and put it into use.

5. Follow up and maintain control — review fuel bills and operating costs periodically.

Specific Measures to Reduce Energy Consumption

1. Caulk outside cracks, joints, holes, vents, pipes, windows, air-conditioners, doors, etc. to prevent drafts which can increase heating and cooling costs by as much as 30%.

2. Install photoelectric timers for inside and outside lighting.

3. Adjust thermostat settings in the common areas to 60–65°F in winter and 78–80°F in summer.

4. Cover room air-conditioners in winter to reduce heat loss.

5. Install hot water recirculating pumps and set hot water at 110°F (when appropriate).

6. Install tamper-proof boxes over thermostats.

7. Sub-meter or separate-meter master-metered buildings if possible. Studies show this reduces energy consumption by 20%. Reminder: Tenants conserve energy when they pay directly.

8. Install flow restrictors on shower heads as this uses 50-75% less water.

9. Repair any plumbing leaks or drips, especially of hot water.

10. Replace incandescent bulbs with low-energy fluorescent bulbs which last ten times longer and use only a third as much energy.

11. Use two dummy bulbs in four-bulb light fixtures, which reduces energy usage by almost 50%.

12. Charge tenants in office and commercial buildings for using air-conditioning after 6:00 p.m. and on Sundays if these are not considered normal operating hours. The lease provision to this effect should be in writing.

Solar Energy

In the past, the property manager recommended purchasing solar to receive large rebates. These rebates are no longer available, but the owner may still get a 20-40% return on investment depending on dollar amount of gas bills, rent structure, and income tax status. A well-designed solar system can reduce gas bills by 50%. In California, the Public Utilities Commission (PUC) allows the gas company

Figure 12-7. Exterior Inspection Report Form

Property_____ Date_____

Address_____ Inspector_____

Item	Condition	Remarks
Roof		
Surface		
Vents		
Flashings		
Gutters		
Other		
Lighting		
Fixtures		
Timers		
Bulbs		
Other		
Surface Walls		
Structure		
Cleanliness		
Paint		
Trim		
Other		
Grounds		
Landscaping		
Cleanliness		
Trash enclosures		
Other		
Signage		
Building sign		
Manager's office		
Vacancy		
Other		
Mailboxes		
Doors		
Locks		
Other		
Decking		
Stairs		
Railing		
Deck		
Other		
Laundry Room		
Cleanliness		
Machines		
Other		
Hallway		
Cleanliness		
Paint		
Carpet		
Other		
Entryways		
Cleanliness		
Paint		
Locks		
Other		

Figure 12-8. Interior Unit Inspection Report Form

Property_____ Date_____

Address_____ Inspector_____

Unit No._____ No. of occupants: Adults_____ Children_____ Other_____

Room	Condition	Remarks
Bedroom(s)		
Carpet		
Windows		
Drapes		
Walls & ceiling		
Doors & locks		
Electrical		
Closets		
Paint		
Other		
Kitchen		
Floor		
Walls & ceiling		
Electrical		
Refrigerator		
Stove		
Sink		
Garbage disposal		
Doors & locks		
Paint		
Other		
Living Room		
Carpet		
Walls & ceiling		
Windows		
Drapes		
Electrical		
Doors & locks		
Paint		
Other		
Bathroom(s)		
Floor		
Walls & ceiling		
Windows		
Shower		
Toilet		
Sink		
Faucets		
Electrical		
Towel racks		
Paint		
Other		

to allocate a discounted baseline rate of $.35 per therm. This allocation does not consider the number of people, bedrooms, bathrooms, or size of the units. Once the building exceeds the baseline allowance, the rate increases to almost $1.00 per therm (Figure 12-9).

It can be seen that large units or those with heated swimming pools have the greatest need to reduce gas expenses. If the building is under rent control, the owner may be able to pass the cost of the solar installation on to the tenants in the form of higher rents and reduce expenses at the same time, which will increase resale value. Solar installations still receive both a 12% federal and state tax credit, plus double-declining depreciation.

Figure 12-9. Gas Bill

Selection of Maintenance Persons

The maintenance person must have not only competence, necessary skills, and preferably his own tools, but must also be trustworthy. A thorough background credit and reference check similar to that for a prospective tenant should be performed. The maintenance person has access to the apartment units and could possibly steal from or rape a tenant. The management company, as well as the owner, may incur liability from the maintenance person's actions. A Pre-Employment Maintenance Person Skills Test should be administered (Figure 12-10) to make sure the person has a basic understanding of maintenance.

Estimating Repair Costs

The property manager often needs estimates of repair costs for budgets, management plans, or specific projects. In some cases, bids by outside contractors are not readily available in a timely manner. Also, having a working knowledge of approximate costs allows the property manager to better interface and negotiate with contractors.

A helpful book is *Means Repair and Remodeling Cost Data for Commercial and Residential.* This book breaks down the unit price by description, crew, equipment cost, daily output, man hours, material, labor, and overhead and profit.

	Crew	Daily Output	Man Hours	Material	Labor	Total	Total O&P
Garbage disposal	L-1	10	1.6	$55.00	$38.00	$93.00	$120.00
Maximum				$190.00			$265.00

In the above illustration, you can see the cost of an inexpensive garbage disposal (such as the Badger I) installed would be approximately $120. The maximum figure is $265 for a more expensive disposal. This book covers items ranging from site preparation to skylights, floor tile, plumbing, electrical, and concrete.

Figure 12-10.

YOU WILL BE GIVEN 15 MINUTES
TO COMPLETE THIS TEST.

Name: _____

Date: _____

PRE-EMPLOYMENT "MAINTENANCE" REPAIRPERSON
SKILLS TEST

CARPENTRY

1.   T   F   Roofing is started at the crown of the roof.

2.   T   F   Sticky locks should be loosened up by spraying WD-40
             in the locking mechanism.

3.   Give two uses for caulking - interior and exterior

     a. _____

     b. _____

4.   What are the four purposes of weatherstripping?

     a. _____   c. _____

     b. _____   d. _____

5.   What are the two common types of material used for patching holes
     in plaster or drywall?

     a. _____   b. _____

6.   List three commonly used materials for floor tiles.

     a. _____   b. _____

          c. _____

7.   What are glazier points and why should they be used when installing
     window glass?

     _____

     _____

8.   T   F   Lock parts from different manufacturers all have their
             own basic designs. They are not interchangeable.

PLUMBING

9.   Whan making any galvanized or black steel pipe repair, one should
     apply _____ to all joints.

Figure 12-10 (cont'd).

10. What are the three important and necessary basic steps in making a sweat joint?

    a. _____

    b. _____

    c. _____

11. Anytime a water closet is pulled, it is always to change the
    _____ gasket.

12. T   F   A gas cock (valve) on a gas hot water heater should always be installed in the gas line before the union.

13. In replacing a nipple for a tub spout, you should use a:

    (check one)   ( ) black steel pipe nipple
                       ( ) galvanized steel pipe nipple

14. A rumbling or knocking noise in a gas hot water heater when the burner is on indicates:

    (check one)   ( ) excessive flame
                       ( ) excessive water pressure
                       ( ) excessive sediment or lime in tank
                       ( ) none of the above

ELECTRICITY

15. The purpose of a circuit breaker is that of a _____ device.

16. Resistance is measured in _____.

17. This device can reduce or increase voltage. It has a primary and secondary coil. It is called a _____.

18. T   F   A high voltage test light is an accurate means of determining voltage.

19. When checking for continuity in an electrical circuit, one should have the circuit: (check one)   ( ) ON   ( ) OFF

20. It is better, when replacing a defective circuit breaker and the proper size is unavailable, to install replacement breaker of:

    (check one)   ( ) larger size
                       ( ) smaller size

Why do you feel you would be a good maintenance repairperson?

_____

_____

_____

Toxic Waste

Superfund Law

Under the Superfund Law passed by Congress in 1980, the Environmental Protection Agency (EPA) has the authority to recover clean-up costs from the present owner or past owners who polluted the property.

Strict liability interpretations include:

1. Present owners are liable even if they did not cause or know of contamination.

2. Deep Pocket Rule means that if one party contributed only 5% of pollution, and if other polluters have no assets, the 5% financially solvent firm could be held responsible for 100% of the clean-up cost.

The property manager should ask owners and tenants to inform him/her of any toxic activities or materials such as heavy metals, cyanides, PCBs, solvents, asbestos, or underground storage tanks, etc. When purchasing property, the buyer should investigate previous usage of the property and have soil tests performed.

California Proposition 65

Under Proposition 65, "businesses are prohibited from exposing the public or employees to chemicals known to cause cancer or birth defects unless they first provide a clear and reasonable warning of the danger" (Figure 12-11). Businesses that violate this law can be fined up to $2,500 per day for each individual exposed. The burden of proof is on the business to prove the chemicals it uses are safe, and the

Figure 12-11. Warning Notice

WARNING
DETECTABLE AMOUNTS OF CHEMICALS KNOWN TO THE STATE OF CALIFORNIA TO CAUSE CANCER, BIRTH DEFECTS, OR OTHER REPRODUCTIVE HARM MAY BE FOUND IN AND AROUND THIS FACILITY.
(CALIFORNIA HEALTH AND SAFETY CODE SECTION 25249.6)

victims need not show they have been injured to receive an award. In addition, a "bounty hunter clause" in this law allows anyone who brings the suit to receive 25% of the fine imposed. The property manager needs to be vigilant, especially when managing industrial property, to be sure tenants *do not* cause toxic waste pollution.

At present, the State of California has classified over 542 chemicals as requiring the warning label. Below is a partial list; the property manager should consult the local health department for an up-to-date and complete list. The first 10 chemicals are cancer-causing.

> 4-Aminodiphenyl — once used in rubber manufacturing
> Analgesic mixtures containing phenactin — used in prescriptions and drugs, including aspirin
> Arsenic (inorganic compounds) used in wood preservatives, etc.
> Asbestos — used in insulation, fireproofing, textiles
> Azathioprine — used to treat diseases such as anemia, liver disease, arthritis, etc.
> Benzene — gasoline additive and solvent used in chemical and drug manufacturing
> Benzidine — used in production of dyes
> Chlornapazine — not used commercially in the United States, but used in foreign countries to treat cancer
> Myleran — used as oral drug for leukemia
> Chemotherapy for lymphomas — used to treat cancer

Refrigerant Management

The Federal Clean Air Act of 1990, Section 608, addresses chlorofluorocarbons (CFCs) and hydrochlorofluorocarbons (HCFCs) which are generally found in air-conditioning systems. The CFCs are R-11, R-12, R-500, R-502; the HCFCs are R-22. Some of the requirements of this law include:

1. Covers systems which require 50 pounds or more of refrigerant.

2. Records of leak repairs must be maintained and the contractor must give written notice of leaks to the owner.

3. Effective November 1, 1994, all technicians must be EPA Section 608 certified and refrigerants will be sold only to certified contractors.

4. It is illegal to knowingly release refrigerants into the atmosphere. Fines of up to $25,000 may be assessed.

The Environmental Protection Agency (EPA) administers the Clean Air Act, but it is supplemental to more stringent local rules such as those of the South Coast Air Quality Management District (SCAQMD).

Asbestos

An issue of increasing concern facing owners and property managers is how to discover and respond to the presence of asbestos in buildings. Asbestos has been routinely used in apartment and office buildings for the last 50 years for a variety of purposes: fireproofing, thermal and acoustical insulation on pipes, ductwork, and boilers. An Environmental Protection Agency (EPA) survey has identified more than 750,000 buildings in the United States that contain asbestos. Over 20% of the office buildings have been found to contain asbestos, which is a carcinogen that has been linked to causing cancer. The cost of asbestos abatement could be as high as $250 billion over the next ten years, according to environmental engineer Peter McDowell.

Federal legislation, the "Federal Asbestos Hazard Abatement Act of 1987," regulates the amount of exposure to workers in office buildings and tenants in rental buildings of ten or more units. In California, under Proposition 65, the "Safe Drinking Water and Toxic Enforcement Act of 1986," liability is imposed for knowing of intentional exposure of individuals to any detectable level of carcinogen without a clear and reasonable warning. On January 1, 1987, a new California State Registration Law for contractors dealing with asbestos removal went into effect that requires training and education before a contractor can perform work. The law "requires registration of any employer whose employees engage in work that will disturb 100 square feet per year of asbestos-containing (more than one-tenth of one percent) material, thereby releasing dangerous fibers into the air."

In California, unregistered licensed contractors may receive hazardous material certification from the Contractor's State License Board. Hall-Kimbrell Environmental Services offers Asbestos Abatement Training Programs to meet OSHA requirements under AHERA (Asbestos Hazard Emergency Response Act) and the AHERA Model Contractor Accreditation Plan (TSCA Section 206.15 USC 2646).

In addressing asbestos problems, the property manager must also consider cost and marketing implications. Removal is usually the most effective method, but also the most costly alternative. Cost ranges from $10 to $30 per square foot. Encapsulation (sealing) the asbestos in a chemical compound and enclosure or containment in an isolated area is less costly, but less permanent. From a marketing perspective, if workers (offices) or tenants (apartments) feel the building is unsafe or hazardous to their health, it may lead to vacancy loss and a poor reputation for the building that could result in lower rental rates.

Title 24

"Title 24" is short for the California Administrative Code, Title 24, Part 2, Chapter 53. It defines energy standards for all new construction in California and describes methods of compliance. The standards were first implemented in 1978 and are continually being revised. Office, retail, and residential uses are included in these standards, which have a goal of reducing energy consumption by 40%. These rules also apply to tenant improvements (TI's) which are divided into two areas:

1. Remodeling of existing conditioned (heated or cooled) space (only what is being changed must conform to Title 24).

2. New conditioned space must meet all of the new standards.

Compliance Approaches

Under Title 24, there are three building components: architectural, mechanical, and electrical. There are two methods of compliance: one, considering each component separately with no interaction to the whole, is called the *package method*; the second, is called the *performance method*, in which the entire building has a standard to meet. In this second method, there can be trade-offs and flexibility, but it is also more complicated.

Injury and Illness Prevention Program

In California, effective July 1, 1991, firms with ten or more employees must have a written Injury and Illness Prevention Program (SB 198). Employing gardeners, handymen, pool cleaners, etc. will subject the property and property management firm to the provisions of SB 198. There are seven areas to be addressed in programs and communicated verbally as well as in written form to employees.

Section I	Philosophy and Policy of Company in Health and Safety
Section II	Compliance with Health and Safety Practices
Section III	Communications of Health and Safety Provisions
Section IV	Procedures of Identifying and Evaluating Hazards
Section V	Accident Investigation
Section VI	Correcting Unsafe Practices or Procedures
Section VII	Training and Instruction

If this program is not in place, it could result in costly CAL-OSHA fines.

Summary

Many tenants view maintenance and management as the same entity. It is therefore important to have a good maintenance program for tenant (customer) satisfaction and reduced turnover to increase income. A second feature of a good maintenance program is to reduce or minimize cost. The above reasons increase the net operating income (NOI) and therefore the value of the property for the owner. The property manager, then, should be familiar with the terminology and maintenance operations, but need not be an expert.

There are four basic types of maintenance:

1. Service — emergencies, repairs.

2. Routine — landscaping, janitorial.

3. Preventive — regular repair tasks; i.e., air conditioning.

4. Extraordinary — rehabilitation, replacement; i.e., roof.

Plumbing is one of the most frequent problem areas in maintenance. Items of concern to the property manager would include location of shutoff valves, electrolysis, insulation of hot water pipes, recirculating pumps, and hot water heaters.

Another major problem area, which is a habitability item, is heating. Temperature settings, air-flow ventilation, heat exchanger, performance ratio, and Btu are some of the items to be considered. Electrical repairs should be done by licensed electricians and blueprints should be readily available on the property.

Carpeting is an area where selection of a good grade and color can add marketing pizzazz as well as reduce replacement costs. Regularly scheduled pest control will prevent serious infestation and tenant unhappiness.

In addition to maintenance, the property manager is responsible for security, which to the tenant means peaceful enjoyment of the unit in a secure complex. Some preventive measures the property manager needs to address include:

Hardware — locks, lighting, gates

Guards — employees or an outside service

Tenant participation — Neighborhood Watch program

Police — reduced rental rate for policemen who live in complex

Smoke detectors — required by law

Chapter 12 Review Questions

1. *Service maintenance would include:*

   a. emergencies.
   b. repairs made within 24 hours.
   c. adding a new roof.
   d. both a and b.
   e. both a and c.

2. *Routine maintenance includes:*

   a. landscaping.
   b. janitorial.
   c. replacing air-conditioners.
   d. both a and b.
   e. none of the above.

3. *An example of preventive maintenance would be:*

   a. repairing a broken water main.
   b. replacing air-conditioning filters.
   c. putting in a new sprinkler system.
   d. replacing burned-out light bulbs.

4. *Extraordinary maintenance involves:*

   a. repairing a leaky faucet.
   b. installing a new hot water heater.
   c. installing a new garbage disposal.
   d. converting the master meter to individual meters.

5. *The onsite manager should:*

   a. know the location of shutoff valves.
   b. be an expert plumber.
   c. be an expert electrician.
   d. be an expert carpenter.

5. *The onsite manager should:*

    a. know the location of the shutoff valves.
    b. be an expert plumber.
    c. be an expert electrician.
    d. be an expert carpenter.

6. *Insulating pipes will result in:*

    a. faster flow of water.
    b. energy savings.
    c. fewer stoppages.
    d. colder water.

7. *Measures to prevent heat loss would include:*

    a. utilizing high thermostat settings.
    b. installing fireplaces.
    c. all of the above.
    d. none of the above.

8. *Electrical work should be done by:*

    a. the onsite manager.
    b. a licensed electrician.
    c. the property manager.
    d. a handyman.

9. *Boric acid helps control:*

    a. cockroaches.
    b. flies.
    c. bugs.
    d. dogs.

10. *Security measures would include:*

    a. locks and gates.
    b. lighting.
    c. security guards.
    d. all of the above.
    e. only a and c.

Chapter 12 Case Study Problem

1. Would you recommend a preventive maintenance program for Civic Center Terrace? If so, why?

2. The present plumbing is copper. What type of plumbing should be used for repairs in order to prevent electrolysis?

3. We need to make some electrical repairs at the complex. What type of maintenance people would be preferable?

4. After a tenant moves out, and before re-renting, should you replace old, worn carpet?

5. Is the cheapest carpet always the best to install?

6. Should the manager purchase highly toxic chemicals and spray the interior of all tenant apartments every three months?

7. Civic Center Terrace has no outside lighting. Should you consider installation? Why or why not?

8. Should maintenance people be selected only for their competence?

9. Since there are deadbolts on all apartment doors, can Civic Center Terrace be advertised as a security complex?

10. List some specific measures to reduce energy consumption.

Chapter 12
Selected Additional References and Reading

Allen, Edward, *The Professional Handbook of Building Construction*, John Wiley & Sons, Somerset, NJ, 1985.

Asbestos Abatement Training Programs
Hall-Kimbrell Environmental Services
4830 W. 15th Street
Lawrence, KS 66044

Building Trade Services, *Tenant Improvement Price Guide*, San Diego, CA, 1987.

California Department of Housing and Community Development, *A New Horizon*, Sacramento, CA, 1985.

Commercial Real Estate Report (Monthly)
Builders Publications of America
6935 Laurel Avenue, Suite 201
Takoma Park, MD 20912

Commercial Renovation (Monthly)
P.O. Box 3192
Oakbrook, IL 60522

Institute of Real Estate Management, *No-Cost Low-Cost Energy Conservation Measures for Multi-Housing*, Chicago, IL, 1981.

International Conference of Building Officials, *Manual of Forms for Building Department Administration*, Whittier, CA, 1985.

Means Co., R.S., *Means Repair and Remodeling Cost Data Commercial and Residential*, Chicago, IL, 1988.

National Association of Homebuilders, *Building Construction Cost Data*, Washington, D.C., 1984.

National Construction Estimator (Annual)
Craftsman Book Company
6058 Corte del Cedro
Carlsbad, CA 92008

Shear, Mel, *Handbook of Building Maintenance*, Reston Publishing, Reston, VA, 1983.

Chapter 13

ADMINISTRATION AND THE MANAGEMENT OFFICE

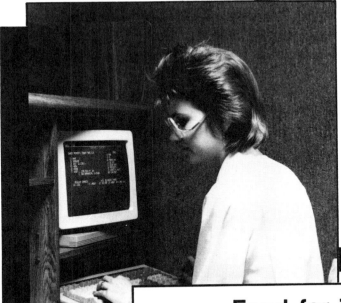

Key Terms

Pro forma budget
Bank reconciliation
Deductible
Endorsements
Modem
Fidelity bond
Worker's
    Compensation
Micro-computer
Check register
Hardware
Software
Co-insurance
FAX
Umbrella policy
Mini-computer

Food for Thought

"Give *someone a fish and they will eat it in a day. Teach someone to fish and they will eat for a lifetime.*"

Administration and the Management Office

Introduction

Real estate management is comprised basically of four major groupings: "Ma and Pa" owners who manage for themselves; institutional investors (pension plans, insurance companies) which self-manage through a professional division within their company; local real estate offices managing to either secure or protect future listings; and professional "fee managers" who, without ownership interest, manage for several clients.

The goals and objectives of the management firm will differ depending on the grouping to which the individual firm conforms. For example, a fee manager will not want to keep a client who pays a low management fee that precludes making a profit. The local real estate office, although it may be running the property poorly due to inexperience, might be willing to suffer a loss in management fees hoping it will make a profit on the sale commission.

Establishing the Management Office

Type of Ownership

Property managers must decide on the legal form of ownership their company will take, such as sole proprietorship, partnership, or corporation. Each has legal and tax ramifications (refer to Chapter 4-3). Consultation with a CPA or attorney is prudent.

Office Location

Office location will depend on the type of clients serviced, goals, and geographic area of the property manager. The property manager should not work out of his/her home, but should have an office to reflect professionalism. Many times the property manager can negotiate with a client to rent space at a reduced rate in a building he/she manages. The owner benefits from the "onsite" proximity. Some offices are located in less prestigious industrial areas. If your clients are professionals, such as doctors or attorneys, a suitable location is a must to portray the proper image. If you are dealing with residential tenants who bring rent to your office, the office should be centrally located, have easy access, be on the ground floor, and have ample parking. Consideration should also be given to expansion — how long is this space going to be large enough to serve your needs? Moving the office frequently is both expensive (moving costs, stationery, etc.) and confusing to clients and tenants.

Office Layout

A nice but small waiting room is necessary, separated by a partition from the work area but with a window so the receptionist can talk to tenants and clients. This gives a feeling of professionalism and keeps tenants and/or visitors from wandering uninvited into the office where files, checks, or money may be accessible. The office should be cheerfully decorated with partitions, and separate offices to reduce noise from copy machines, typewriters, and computer printers (Figure 13-1).

Figure 13-1. Office Layout

Equipment

The property manager provides a service, not a product. There is no inventory or large capital outlay for machinery. Every office, however, usually has typewriters, word processors, calculators, and copy machines. The FAX machine is a contraction of "facsimile" meaning exact copy of an original. These machines are transceivers and can send or receive messages over standard local and long-distance telephone lines. The message is transmitted on a sheet of paper into the FAX machine to be scanned and transmitted by electrical impulses to the receiving FAX machine onto a sheet of paper, much like making a copy on a Xerox machine. The cost is low, at only about $1.00 a page between Los Angeles and New York City, including phone costs and paper. The Group III FAX machine is the most desirable and fastest (12-15 seconds per page) and is compatible with the slower Group II and Group I FAX machines. The applications of the FAX machine are many and varied for the property manager and would include: rent receipts, lease documents, proposals, blueprints, contracts, letters, and reports.

In smaller operations, items such as posting of rents, posting of bills, and checkwriting are usually done by hand. In larger offices, many of these functions are done with the assistance of a computer. Proper equipment increases productivity and reduces costs. Salary usually accounts for 40-50% of property management overhead. Profits can thus be increased significantly by increasing the volume of business and automating at the same time.

Computers

If the management office portfolio exceeds 500 units, a computer is usually necessary in order to automate bookkeeping and generate timely financial reports. There are three categories of computers:

1. *Mainframe* — largest, fastest, and most expensive; usually not necessary for property management.

2. *Mini* — can be networked and has a memory to handle 20,000+ units, but is usually triple the cost of a micro.

3. *Micro* — the least expensive and has the smallest memory (IBM PC is an example). It comes in both hard and floppy-disk drives and can handle several thousand units.

Key computer terms are explained in Figure 13-3.

Figure 13-2. Computer Categories

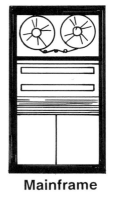
Mainframe

Mini

Micro

Figure 13-3. Key Computer Terms

HARDWARE	The actual physical computer system, including keyboard, printer, and display screen.
SOFTWARE	The programmed instructions used to run the computer; stored on disks or tapes. A. User-friendly: Cursor helps you input data. B. Canned program: Purchase of property management program sold to many other users. Several of these programs can be found in: Real Estate Software, Moore Business Forms, Inc., 1600 S. Highway 100, Minneapolis, MN 55416. C. Custom-designed programs: expensive and written specifically for a firm and its hardware.
CRT	Cathode ray tube, a TV-like display terminal used to show information.
CP/M	Common operating system for microcomputer.
CPU	Central processing unit, the heart of the computer. It controls all operations and does the actual calculating.
DATABASE	Collection of data that can be retrieved by the computer; i.e., security deposit lists.
DISK	Storage device for data.
HARD COPY	The actual paper printout.
LINE PRINTER	High-speed printer as it prints a line at a time rather than one character at a time.
MODEM	A device that allows the computer to send and receive information over telephone lines.
RAM	Random Access Memory, the main type used in small computers; i.e., 128K.
TERMINAL	Typewriter-like keyboard used for input.
WORD PROCESSING	A program used for typing form letters, etc.

Computer Software

Figure 13-4.

The Institute of Real Estate Management (IREM) has completed a list of software vendors who have certified compliance with IREM's Minimum Standards for Property Management Accounting Software. These minimum standards were recommended by an IREM Software Standards Task Force "to assist management firms in defining and locating acceptable software for property management accounting." The task force also provides software suppliers with a better understanding of needs of management firms. In order to receive the Certified Compliance Listing, software vendors must file an affidavit that their products comply in all respects with the minimum IREM Minimum Standards for Property Management Accounting Software. IREM does not, however, evaluate the software to determine if these standards are met. Below is a list of firms which have complied as of a certain date. A more updated and complete list can be obtained by contacting IREM in Chicago.

Alternative Management Systems, Inc.
3100 Wilcrest Drive, Suite 300
Houston, TX 77042
(713) 785-0265

Maxwell Systems, Inc.
CIT
1971 E. Fourth Street, Suite 140
Santa Ana, CA 92705
(714) 285-0501

Yardi Systems
813 Reddick St.
Santa Barbara, CA 93103
(805) 966-3666

Pinetree Software, Inc.
2871 No. 3 Road
Richmond, B.C., Canada V6X 2B8
(604) 270-3311

The Softa Group
450 Skokie Boulevard, Suite 703
Northbrook, IL 60062
(312) 291-4000

The Ten Man Systems, Inc.
1855 Mount Prospect Road
Des Plaines, IL 60018
(312) 699-7500

United Data Systems
501 Greene Street, Suite 220
Augusta, GA 30901
(404) 724-7761

Selection of a Property Management Company

If an outside company is to be used for property management, the question is often asked, "How do we select that company?" The management firm will, after all, be entrusted with several thousand dollars in rent collections each month. It is prudent, therefore, to inquire about the management firm. Some questions which should be asked include:

1. *What is the company's size?*

2. *How long has it been in business?*

3. *Is it bonded?*

4. *Does it have a real estate license (a must in California)?*

5. *Is it primarily in the property management business or in real estate sales?*

6. *Does it have a trust account?*

Just as there are different types of properties, management companies are different for specific types of properties. For example, some management companies specialize in residential units and would be a poor choice to manage a medical building. When selecting a management company, ask for a written proposal which should include its fees, who has responsibility for hiring and training onsite resident managers, payment of bills, leasing proposals, inspection frequency, supervision criteria, a copy of the management agreement, references, and a history of the firm. Visit the management company's office and meet the people who will be in charge of your property. Do its executive managers have a CPM designation? Ask to see a sample of the monthly financial statement you will receive.

In summary, the property manager should bring diversified talents, experience, controls, and computer reporting systems all in one package to help the property perform to its maximum potential. The owner should benefit from the old cliché: "Property management doesn't cost — it pays."

Figure 13-5. Flow Chart

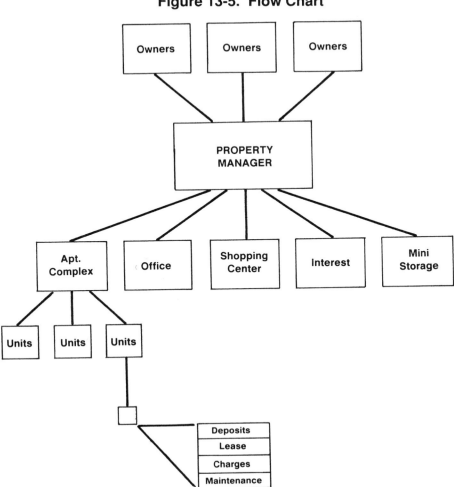

Purchasing a Property Management Company

Purchase a property management company usually involves little in physical assets (computer, furniture, etc.) and is mostly the existing client accounts and goodwill. The present personnel may or may not stay with the new operation after purchase. It is, therefore, difficult to determine the purchase price due to these subjective and nebulous characteristics. One method is a lump-sum payment (3-6 months present management fees) plus incentives at the end of each year, depending on the gross income. If income goes down (as it invariably will due to sales and natural attrition), the seller would receive less. For example, if the gross management fees were $10,000 per month:

Down payment	— 3 mo. ×	$10,000 =	$30,000
End of 1st yr.	— 1 mo. ×	8,000 =	8,000
End of 2nd yr.	— 1 mo. ×	7,000 =	7,000
End of 3rd yr.	— 1 mo. ×	5,000 =	5,000
End of 4th yr.	— 1 mo. ×	4,000 =	4,000
End of 5th yr.	— 1 mo. ×	2,000 =	2,000
		Total price	$56,000

Other methods of determining value include income capitalization, replacement cost, percentage of annual gross management fees, and net earning times a number of years.

Insurance for the Property

The property manager, in addition to increasing the income stream, must also preserve and protect tenants and the property. This involves risk evaluation in dealing with possible liability and loss.

Risk Management

> RETAIN RISK — deductible or self-insurance.
> AVOID RISK — fill in the swimming pool.
> TRANSFER RISK — insurance policy, required by lenders.
> CONTROL RISK — install smoke alarms and safety systems.

The property manager should seek the assistance of a good insurance broker for counsel on insurance needs. Adequate records and files should be kept, as well as a tickler file on expiration dates.

Types of Insurance

1. *All-Peril, All-Risk Policy* — includes fire and extended coverage. Floods, earthquakes, and liability are usually excluded from coverage.

2. *Package Policy* — covers both property and liability.

3. *Rent Loss (Business Interruption)* — pays the owner for loss of rents if a unit is destroyed by fire.

4. *Surety Bond* — an instrument providing for monetary compensation should there be a failure to perform any specific acts within a certain period.

5. *Fidelity Bond* — should cover all employees for losses from dishonest acts in the property manager's office or on property being managed.

6. *Non-Owned Auto* — covers the employer's liability for daily work by employees. It does not cover the employees.

7. *Umbrella Policy* — additional liability coverage to existing underlying policy; relatively inexpensive.

8. *Worker's Compensation* — covers medical and hospital payments for injuries sustained by employees hurt on the job. Rates are set by the state and this policy is not transferable in the event of a sale. Property managers should make sure vendors have certificates of insurance or the property manager may be liable in the event of an accident. The management company may have a master policy or arrange for each property to have a separate policy.

9. *Errors and Omissions* — basically malpractice insurance. It covers legal fees and damages for liability less the deductible. It does not cover dishonest or fraudulent acts and is very expensive and difficult to obtain for the property manager.

10. *Co-insurance* — the owner accepts part of the risk and pays a lower premium. The property is insured for less than its value, usually 80%. The amount of loss collectible is dollar for dollar up to 80% of the value. Since buildings are seldom destroyed, the owner is "betting" his building will survive. For example, if a building worth $1,000,000 is insured for $800,000, and there is fire damage of $600,000, the property owner would receive the full amount ($600,000). If, however, the insurance policy is for only $500,000, the owner would receive only 50% of the loss, or $300,000.

$$\text{Formula} = \frac{\text{Amount of insurance carried}}{\text{Value of building}} \quad \text{or} \quad \frac{\$500,000}{\$1,000,000} = \frac{50\%}{\text{coverage}}$$

It is important, therefore, to make sure the building is properly insured.

Endorsements

1. *Additional Insured* — the management company should be listed as an additional insured on the owner's policy. The cost is usually nominal and it maintains the unity of interests of the owner, management company, and insurance company in the event of a lawsuit.

2. *Host Liquor* — should be carried if liquor is served on the premises.

3. *Premises Medical* — allows for no-fault minimum on minor injuries.

Insurance Suggestions

1. Under new insurance regulations, claims will be covered only if they occur and were filed during the policy period. Notify the insurance company immediately if someone falls down an outside stairway.

2. Include instructions on how to handle losses such as fires or falls in your Standard Operating Procedures manual.

3. The deductible should be at least $500 to eliminate nuisance claims. A higher deductible usually results in lower premiums.

4. Commercial properties should require tenants to carry contents and liability insurance coverage for inside their store.

Files and Recordkeeping

Records and file should be kept in an efficient, organized manner so they can be easily retrieved. The legal retention period for the Department of Real Estate is usually three years on most documents, but you may want to keep some records longer.

1. *Tenant Files* — separate files should be kept for each unit. They are set up when a new account is obtained. Rental and lease agreements, notices, etc. are kept in the files. Retain for three years.

2. *General Correspondence Files* — these can be kept either by date or by subject.

3. *Vendor Files* — where bills, contracts, and bids are kept. Purchase orders (consecutively numbered) should also be retained.

4. *Check Register* — usually kept on computer with each account reconciled monthly. Good accounting procedure dictates that a person other than the one who makes up or signs the checks should do the reconciliation. Also, checks over a certain amount (for example, $1,500) should require two signatures, and a daily balance should be maintained.

5. *Owner Files* — management agreement, monthly statements, correspondence, insurance policies, tax bills, receipts. Most management companies do not keep the owner's bills (receipts), but instead mail them to the owner with the profit and loss statement.

6. *Eviction Files* — usually kept on pending cases.

7. *Wage and Hours Files* — should be kept for three years, including employment applications.

The use of the computer has been previously discussed, but in smaller offices a hand system of posting may be used. A similar system is used in collecting rents. It consists of three parts:

1. *Ledger sheet for the onsite manager.*

2. *Ledger sheet for the management office.*

3. *Individual receipt for the tenant.*

Figure 13-6.

```
                    BOOKKEEPING PROPERTY SET UP

OWNER: _____    DATE TO START:
                                            SUPERVISION:_____

ADDRESS: _____

CITY,ZIP: _____

PHONE: (_____)_____(_____)_____
         HOME                          WORK


PROPERTY ADDRESS: _____   # UNITS: _____

CITY: _____

MANAGER: NAME _____
(if appropriate)
ADDRESS/PHONE: _____


                         INSURANCE CARRIER: _____

MANAGEMENT FEE: $_____   AGENT NAME/PHONE: _____

AREA MGR. FEE:  $_____   _____

RE-RENT FEE:    $_____   POLICY # _____

OTHERS:         $_____   CERTIFICATE ORDERED? _____ BY WHOM?_____


LENDER INFORMATION:

1st: AMOUNT: $_____   DUE: _____   DEL:_____

LENDER ADDRESS: _____

LOAN NUMBER: _____


2nd: AMOUNT: $_____   DUE: _____   DEL:_____

LENDER ADDRESS: _____

LOAN NUMBER: _____


ASSOCIATION DUES:  DUE: _____   AMOUNT $_____

OTHER:             DUE: _____   AMOUNT $_____
```

Copyright 1988, J.D. Publications and Seminars

Figure 13-7.

DATE: _____

NEW PROPERTY INFORMATION

OWNER NAME: _____

ADDRESS/PHONE: _____

PROPERTY ADDRESS: _____

TENANT NAME & PHONE NO.	APT. #	UNIT TYPE	RENT	S.D.	PAID TO DATE	COMMENTS

BE SURE TO GET <u>ALL</u> KEYS - INCLUDING MAILBOX KEYS!

ATTACH RENTAL AGREEMENTS.

DISTRIBUTION: BOOKKEEPING, MAINTENANCE, RENTAL COORD., EXEC. ADMIN.

The old theory (CYA), if followed to the extreme, would result in duplication and a waste of time. Only use forms or keep records that serve a useful purpose or are required by law.

Management Company Income and Expenses

The property manager must not only increase the net operating income (NOI) of the property by good management techniques, but also make a profit for the management company. In many instances the management company bids too low, not knowing its costs, as we discussed in Chapter 4. Many small firms bid too low because the owner, who is also the property manager, does not take a monthly salary. This leads to reduced services, secret profit, or other illegal activities, or the management company going out of business.

The management company should prepare a budget for itself just as it does for the properties it manages. The budget is a road map to help the management company reach its goals. In Figure 13-8 we see that, by categorizing monthly expenses and having an additional column for percentage of total expenses, the management company can review its progress on a monthly basis and make changes and corrections if necessary to stay on its intended course. The net profit as a percentage of expenses will vary, but the 10-20% range seems reasonable.

In order to complete Figure 13-8, a list of employees, salaries, cars, hours worked, and operating expenses is made. Subtracting expenses from revenues gives the monthly profit. By dividing expenses into total units managed, the cost of management per apartment ($15-25) for the management company is obtained. This gives a rule of thumb to use in bidding. All units do not require the same intensity of management, so individual complexes' costs will vary from the average. The Institute of Real Estate Management publishes a yearly research study, *The Real Estate Management Office: Income, Expenses, and Profits*, which gives average costs in the different expense areas. A sample management company profit and loss statement is shown in Figure 13-9.

Consulting Fees

When dealing with the client in the real estate industry, traditionally, the agent gets paid only if the deal is consummated. An example would be if the property manager does a comprehensive inspection and market survey for an owner who is contemplating purchasing an apartment building. The owner promises to give management to the property manager if the building is purchased. If, however, the building is not purchased, the property manager gets zero for services rendered and time spent. It is hard to believe that because the property manager found serious plumbing problems in the proposed building, saving the buyer from financial disaster, the property manager will *not* be paid for expert professional advice. It is nice

Figure 13-8. Management Company Budget

INCOME	1st Mo.	%	6th Mo.	%	12th Mo.	%
Multi-unit fees						
Commercial fees						
Leasing fees						
Miscellaneous						
TOTAL INCOME						
OPERATING EXPENSES						
Advertising/promotion						
Auto expenses						
Computer expenses						
Dues/subscriptions						
Insurance						
Legal/accounting fees						
Licenses						
Miscellaneous						
Office expenses						
Payroll taxes						
Repairs/maintenance						
Referral fees/leasing splits						
Rent						
Salaries						
Executive						
Accounting/clerical						
Property supervisors						
Bonuses						
Telephone						
Taxes						
Utilities						
TOTAL EXPENSES						
NET PROFIT OR LOSS						

NO. OF UNITS MANAGED _____ DIVIDED BY EXPENSES _____ = COST PER UNIT _____

Figure 13-9. Sample Monthly Statement

ABC Property Management Company

Income	$ Amount	%
Multi-unit fees	$25,000	55.00%
Commercial fees	12,000	27.00%
Leasing fees	3,000	7.00%
Broker commissions	5,000	11.00%
Miscellaneous		
Total income	$45,000	100.00%
Operating Expenses		
Advertising and promotion	810	1.80%
Automobile expense	1,710	3.80%
Computer expense	2,250	5.00%
Dues and subscriptions	450	1.00%
Insurance	1,350	3.00%
Legal and accounting	675	1.50%
Licenses	225	.05%
Miscellaneous	900	2.00%
Office expense	2,925	6.50%
Payroll expense	1,350	3.00%
Repairs and maintenance	1,080	2.40%
Referral fees	900	2.00%
Rent	1,800	4.00%
Salaries:		
Executive	5,850	13.00%
Accounting and Clerical	7,650	17.00%
Property supervisors	6,300	14.00%
Bonuses	900	2.00%
Telephone	1,440	3.20%
Travel and entertainment	1,350	3.00%
Utilities	1,170	2.60%
Total operating expenses	41,085	91.30%
Net profit or loss (before taxes)	$ 3,915	8.70%

to be paid for advice, and even nicer to be paid whether or not that advice is followed. Landauer and Associates recently represented NBC, which was considering moving its corporate headquarters. Landauer received a nice fee even though NBC decided to stay at Rockefeller Center.

If the client requests additional services, consultation should be charged on either an hourly or set-fee basis. Such consultation areas include:

1. *Refinancing the property.*

2. *In-depth management plan.*

3. *Appraisals.*

4. *Rehabilitation.*

5. *Zone or use changes.*

6. *Sale or exchange of property.*

7. *Property tax reassessment.*

8. *Special bookkeeping or accounting.*

9. *Leasing.*

Summary

The goals and objectives of a property management company will differ depending on the grouping:

1. Ma and Pa owner

2. Institutional investor (in-house)

3. Local real estate office

4. Professional fee manager

The location of the property manager's office should reflect professionalism, but need not be in an exclusive area or lavishly decorated. The layout and color scheme should be cheerful and have partitions and separate offices to reduce noise and provide privacy. Since the property manager offers a service, not a product, there is no machinery except for computers and office equipment. The three kinds of computers (hardware) are mainframe, mini, and micro (PC). When selecting a computer, the software (program) to be used is most important. The main question to be answered is, "What specific tasks need to be accomplished?"

The selection of a property management company by an owner is based on several criteria, some of which would include: size and length of time in business, bonding, real estate licenses, and professional designations such as Certified Property Manager (CPM). The property manager must also handle the insurance on the property, which involves risk evaluation such as retaining, avoiding, transferring, and controlling risk. There are different types of policies, including: all-peril, all-risk, rent loss, surety bond, fidelity bond, umbrella policy, Worker's Compensation, and co-insurance.

The property management office may purchase errors and omissions insurance for its own protection as well as being covered as additionally insured under the owner's policy for each property. Records and files should be kept for income tax and Department of Real Estate purposes for three to four years.

The management company should, like other well-run professional companies, prepare an annual budget and produce monthly profit and loss statements. The management company should also charge the client for additional services such as: refinancing the property, appraisals, management plans, rehabilitation, zone changes, sale or exchange of the property, special reports, and leasing.

In conclusion, in this chapter we have shown that goals and objectives of management firms differ, as well as how to establish a management office and its layout, design, and equipment.

NOTES

Chapter 13 Review Questions

1. *A type of ownership for a property management office is:*

    a. sole proprietorship.
    b. partnership.
    c. corporation.
    d. all of the above.
    e. none of the above.

2. *Property management offices should:*

    a. *always* be located in a bank building.
    b. *always* be located in a major city.
    c. be cheerfully and tastefully decorated.
    d. be lavishly and expensively decorated.

3. *The goal of the computer in property management is to:*

    a. replace all people.
    b. reduce redundant tasks and improve efficiency.
    c. calculate the management fee faster.
    d. reduce typing costs.

4. *Categories of computers would include:*

    a. mainframe.
    b. mini.
    c. both a and b.
    d. neither a nor b.

5. *Word processing use of the computer is primarily for:*

    a. calculating vacancy reports.
    b. typing letters.
    c. calculating cash flow statements.
    d. calculating delinquency reports.

6. *Disk function is to:*

   a. store data.
   b. display data.
   c. print data.
   d. send information.

7. *Computer hardware would include:*

   a. the keyboard.
   b. the printer.
   c. both a and b.
   d. neither a nor b.

8. *Software is used to:*

   a. repair the computer.
   b. run the computer program.
   c. turn the computer on and off.
   d. reduce emergency requirements of the computer.

9. *The management company specializes in certain properties based on:*

   a. size.
   b. type — medical, apartments, etc.
   c. both a and b.
   d. neither a nor b.

10. *The elements of insurance would be to:*

    a. avoid risk.
    b. transfer risk.
    c. control risk.
    d. all of the above.
    e. none of the above.

Chapter 13 Case Study Problem

1. Should the insurance policy have a rent loss clause?

2. The present maintenance is done by "Ben the Handyman," who works out of his house and isn't licensed or covered under Worker's Compensation. What changes would you make?

3. The liability on the present policy is $200,000. Should this amount be increased?

4. If you, as a management company, were to bid on managing Civic Center Terrace, how much would you bid?

5. If the owners wanted you to do refinancing paperwork on the property, would you charge over and above the management fee?

Chapter 13
Selected Additional References and Reading

Boykin, James H., *Real Estate Counseling*, American Society of Real Estate Counselors, Chicago, IL, 1984.

California Real Estate (Monthly)
California Association of Realtors
525 S. Virgil Avenue
Los Angeles, CA 90020

Downs, James Jr., CPM, *Principles of Real Estate Management*, Institute of Real Estate Management, Chicago, IL, 1980.

Hansen, James M., *Guide to Buying or Selling a Business*, Prentice-Hall, Englewood Cliffs, NJ, 1975.

Mehr, Robert I., *Fundamentals of Insurance*, Richard Irwin, Inc., Homewood, IL, 1983.

The Real Estate Professional (Semi-Monthly)
Wellesley Publications
P.O. Box 6
Winchester, MA 01890

Realtor News (Bimonthly)
National Association of Realtors
430 N. Michigan Avenue
Chicago, IL 60611

Walters, William Jr., CPM, *The Practice of Real Estate Management*, Institute of Real Estate Management, Chicago, IL, 1983.

Chapter 14

CALIFORNIA LANDLORD/TENANT LAW

Key Terms

Constitution
Habitability
Unruh Act
Rumford Act
Retaliation
   Notice to Pay Rent
   Unlawful detainer
   Writ
   Wolfson vs. Marina
     Pt. Ltd.
   Constructive eviction
   Actual eviction
   Repair and Deduct
   AIDS Law
   Waterbed Law
   Arrieta v. Mahon

Food for Thought

"Some people bring happiness wherever they go. Some people only bring happiness whenever they go."
          Oscar Wilde

California
Landlord/Tenant Law

Introduction

This chapter will cover the present landlord/tenant laws in California. The chapter has been divided into sources of law, landlord responsibility, tenant responsibility, landlord protection, and tenant protection.

Sources of Property Management Law

In order to fully understand the nature of landlord/tenant laws, it is important to see how these laws interface with our legal system. Figure 14-1 illustrates the principal sources of law. The significance of these sources is in ranking, starting with the U.S. Constitution, which is the source and comparison for all laws. If any federal, state, or local law or regulation is contrary to the Constitution, as determined by the courts, it is ruled unconstitutional and therefore void.

In order to better understand these sources, rent control will be used as an example. In California, rent control laws are passed by local governments (city or county). These laws can be preempted by state law. Through an Administrative Ruling, the Department of Housing & Urban Development (HUD) can decree that those cities having rent control will have federal housing subsidies cut off unless the rent control laws are repealed. The landlords also can challenge in court the fact that rent control is an uncompensated taking of property which may be unconstitutional.

It can be seen that local, state, and federal laws and regulations are interwoven. The property manager should note, however, the pecking order as federal laws and regulations supersede both state and local laws. Court decisions are ranked last as they interpret the laws and regulations and then will move up the ladder depending on the court and its jurisdiction (i.e., federal court takes precedence over state, which takes precedence over local).

```
┌──────────────────────────────────────────────────────────────┐
│                Figure 14-1. Sources of Law                   │
│                                                              │
│   1) U.S. Constitution (i.e., 14th Amendment)                │
│   2) Treaties (i.e., Treaty of Guadalupe Hidalgo)            │
│   3) Laws of Congress (i.e., 1968 Civil Rights Act)         │
│   4) Federal regulations (i.e., HUD)                        │
│   5) State Constitution (i.e., discrimination)              │
│   6) State laws (i.e., Unruh Act)                           │
│   7) State regulations (i.e., DRE)                          │
│   8) Local ordinances (i.e., rent control)                  │
│   9) Court decisions (i.e., Wolfson v. Marina Pt., Ltd.)    │
└──────────────────────────────────────────────────────────────┘
```

Commercial vs. Residential Laws

In many instances the laws governing commercial and residential management are similar, but not exactly the same. For example, the period for giving the disposition and return of a security deposit is 21 days in residential, but 30 days in commercial. In residential, the maximum deposit collectible is two months rent for an unfurnished apartment and three months for furnished. Last month's rent collected, for the purpose of determining the maximum, is treated as if it were a deposit. There is no maximum in commercial.

The courts will often look differently upon commercial and residential tenants. The commercial tenant is viewed on parity with the landlord, as two Roman gladiators, each with a sword and shield, battling it out in a coliseum. However, the court views residential tenants as unsophisticated underdogs in comparison to landlords, or like the Christians vs. the lions.

Residential vs. Commercial Leases

Leases for real property are traditionally construed as conveyances, as opposed to contracts. The fundamental difference is that conveyances are interpreted by real property law, which provides that the covenants are independently (as opposed to dependently) construed. Commercial leases are generally still interpreted under real property law, with the covenant to pay rent looked upon as independent from the other covenants of the lease. Thus, if a toilet overflows or the roof leaks in a commercial lease, the tenant still has to pay rent. Conversely, in a residential lease, the *Green* case chose to apply the provisions of contract law which provide that the failure by the landlord to comply with the implied covenant of habitability allows a tenant not to pay rent. The *Green* case comes very close to converting residential leases from conveyances to contracts.

Landlord Responsibility

The property manager, acting as agent for the owner, must understand and obey the legal duties of the landlord. Many courts are holding the onsite manager and property manager, as well as the owner, legally responsible.

Habitability

Maintaining habitability is one of the most important responsibilities of the property manager.

Figure 14-2. Habitability

```
         CIVIL CODE 1941.1 PROVISIONS

   1. Waterproofing and weatherproofing
   2. Doors and windows reasonably secure
   3. Hot and cold water (plumbing)
   4. Heating system in good working order
   5. Electrical system in safe working order
   6. Building in good repair (stairs and railings)
   7. Trash and garbage removal
   8. Free from pests
   9. Smoke detectors
```

Government Code Section 17920.3 sets forth conditions constituting a substandard building, such as lack of working toilet facilities or kitchen sink, pest infestation, improper maintenance, etc. The California Supreme Court, starting with *Green v. Superior Court* (1974), said every residential lease has an implied warranty of habitability which the tenant cannot waive. If the premises have breaches of habitability, the tenant may reduce or withhold rent accordingly.

In another related case, *Knight v. Hallsthammar* (1981), the Supreme Court said the owner is responsible for habitability even if the defects were known by the tenant at time of rental. It is therefore necessary for the property manager to respond to maintenance requests and even to make periodic inspections as many tenants fail to report problems that can lead to more serious and costly repairs. For example, a leaky shower on the second floor might cause the bathroom ceiling of the unit below to collapse. Not only will the landlord have a more costly repair, but there is also the potential of liability for injury.

The warranty of habitability is *not* waivable by the tenant, even if the lease or rental agreement excludes habitability provisions (CC 1942.1). Remember, a residential tenant *may not* waive the right to a habitable premise.

A new law (AB 1515 by Assemblyman Mike Roos), passed in an effort to crack down on absentee slumlords who do not make necessary repairs, allows the court to order in-house (subject apartment building) confinement of landlords convicted of building code violations.

Discrimination

In renting or leasing residential or commercial space, the landlord or property manager cannot discriminate against a prospective tenant on the listed bases shown in Figure 14-3. The property manager must be diligent in efforts to have the onsite manager know and observe these laws.

Federal Laws

1. *Civil Rights Act of 1866* — prohibits any type of discrimination based on race.

2. *Fair Housing Act of 1968 (Title VIII of Civil Rights Act of 1968)* — makes it unlawful to discriminate on the basis of race, religion, or color in leasing residential property. It does provide exemptions such as owner occupied fourplexes.

3. *Fair Housing Act Amendment (1972)* — mandates that a real estate agent (property manager) must display the equal opportunity poster (Figure 14-4). Failure to do so is evidence of discrimination.

4. *Jones v. Mayer (1964)* — U.S. Supreme Court decision upheld the Civil Rights Act of 1866 which prohibits racial discrimination.

5. *Fair Housing Amendment Act (1988)* — effective March 12, 1989, on a national basis, prohibits discrimination against families with children and handicapped persons in rental housing.

6. *Americans with Disability Act (1992)* — requires that architectural and communications barriers be removed from public and commercial facilities.

Figure 14-3. Discrimination Chart

	Real Estate Comm. Regs.	Federal Civil Rights Act of 1866	Federal Fair Housing Act of 1968	Federal Fair Housing Act of 1988	Unruh Act	Rumford Act
Race	X	X	X		X	X
Religion	X		X		X	X
Color	X		X		X	X
National Origin	X		X		X	X
Age					X	
Handicap	X			X		
Sex	X		X		X	X
Familial Status				X		

Figure 14-4. HUD Equal Housing Opportunity Poster

EQUAL HOUSING OPPORTUNITY

We Do Business in Accordance With the Federal Fair Housing Law

(Title VIII of the Civil Rights Act of 1968, as Amended by the Housing and Community Development Act of 1974)

IT IS ILLEGAL TO DISCRIMINATE AGAINST ANY PERSON BECAUSE OF RACE, COLOR, RELIGION, SEX, OR NATIONAL ORIGIN

- In the sale or rental of housing or residential lots
- In advertising the sale or rental of housing
- In the financing of housing
- In the provision of real estate brokerage services

Blockbusting is also illegal

An aggrieved person may file a complaint of a housing discrimination act with the:

U.S. DEPARTMENT OF HOUSING AND URBAN DEVELOPMENT

Assistant Regional Administrator for Fair Housing and Equal Opportunity
450 Golden Gate Ave. P.O. Box 36003
San Francisco, CA 94102

HUD-928.1 (7-75) Previous editions are obsolete

☼ U.S. GOVERNMENT PRINTING OFFICE 1982-587-033 359

State Laws

1. *Fair Housing Act (Rumford) (Govt. Code 12955)* — Prohibits discrimination in the sale, rental, leasing, or financing of most types of housing. This act established the Fair Employment Practices Commission which investigates discrimination complaints.

2. *Senior Citizen Housing (CC 51.3)* — Exempts specially designated housing for senior citizens from age discrimination. In other words, children can be prohibited from living in senior citizen developments or associations. The property manager should be familiar with the regulations, including age definition (55-62 years of age, depending on the type of development and its size). Developments exempted range from 150 units minimum size in an urban area to 35 units and must be specially developed or rehabilitated for senior citizens. This code section clarified the *Wolfson v. Marina Pt., Ltd.* case.

3. *Handicapped Rights (CC 54)* — An owner or property manager *is not* required to make special modifications to the leased premises, but *cannot* refuse rental on the basis of handicap. This is a Catch 22 for the property manager — should a walk-up (second-story) apartment be rented to a blind person, thus increasing the risk of an accident? Another example is that a complex may have a "no pets" policy, yet must allow a blind or deaf person to keep a guide or hearing dog.

4. *California Department of Real Estate Commission Regulations (Section 2780 California Administrative Code, Title 10, Chapter 6)* — Prohibits discriminatory conduct by a real estate licensee on the basis of race, religion, color, sex, national origin, handicap, or marital status.

5. *Wolfson v. Marina Pt., Ltd. (1982)* — California Supreme Court ruled a landlord cannot prohibit children from living in rentals.

6. *Village Green v. O'Conner (1983)* — California Supreme Court ruled condominium associations cannot discriminate against children in rental or sale.

7. *Unruh Act (CC 52-53)* — Prohibits discrimination on the basis of race, religion, color, sex, or national origin in business. The operation of an apartment building, shopping center, or property management office is considered a business.

8. *AIDS* — SB 324 amends Section 1710.2 of the Civil Code. The law says there is no cause of action for failure of the seller or landlord or his agent to disclose to the buyer or tenant that an occupant died on the real property, or the manner of the occupant's death, so long as the death was three years prior to occupancy, unless the person died of AIDS. If the person died of AIDS, even within the last three years, you *do not* have to disclose this fact. The bill further states that if an inquiry is made concerning any death, the owner or his agent must answer honestly.

9. *Limits on Occupants per Apartment* — In order to circumvent the law (Unruh Act) that prohibits discrimination against children, some landlords set unreasonable limits on the number of occupants; for example, allowing only three people to occupy a two-bedroom unit. This would probably be interpreted by the California Department of Fair Employment and Housing as discriminatory against children. In order to give guidance to the landlord, this state agency has issued "safe harbor" guidelines. Two persons per bedroom plus one (five occupants for a two-bedroom) for the entire unit is usually deemed acceptable (Figure 14-5). Another limiting factor is the Uniform Housing Code, Section 503(b), which limits the number of occupants per square foot of bedroom space.

10. *Waterbeds (CC 1940.5)* — A landlord may not refuse to rent or continue to rent a unit solely based on tenant possession of a waterbed in any building built after 1972. The tenant must, however, show proof of insurance for at least $100,000 for damages arising from use of a waterbed. The bed must also conform to standards regarding weight per square foot. The landlord also has the right to be present at installation and can make periodic inspections (Figure 14-9).

11. *Pets (SB 1167)* — Extends the right of an elderly person in public housing to keep two or more pets to others such as developmentally disabled who qualify for federal housing assistance (Figure 14-6).

12. *Telephone Jacks (CC 1941.4)* — Makes the landlord responsible for providing tenants with at least one working phone jack. The landlord is also responsible for maintaining inside telephone wiring in good working order.

Tenant Responsibility

1. *Pay rent on time* — Most rental agreements state that rent will be paid on the first of the month. A common-sense approach to rent collection is that if a tenant moves in during the month, rent is prorated during the second month as the property manager should always strive to collect the first month's rent plus a deposit (cashier's check, money order, or cash) before allowing a tenant to move in. Personal checks are not usually desirable for the first month as they may be returned unpaid — a typical ploy of the professional rent-skipper.

2. *Maintain* the rented premises in clean, sanitary, and undamaged condition, excluding normal wear and tear, is a tenant responsibility. These duties are spelled out in CC 1941.2.

3. *Give proper legal notice* in writing (the property manager should not accept verbal notice). For example, moving notice is usually 30 days.

4. *Allow other tenants quiet enjoyment* of their units (i.e., do not play the stereo too loudly).

Figure 14-5. Occupancy Limitation

DEPARTMENT OF FAIR EMPLOYMENT & HOUSING
1201 I STREET, SUITE 211, SACRAMENTO, CA 95814-2919
TDD (916) 323-6000

N O T I C E

As you know, the Department of Fair Employment and Housing (DFEH) is accepting complaints which allege that an occupancy limitation set by a provider constitutes discrimination against families with children. These complaints are accepted under the Department's authority to enforce Civil Code Section 51, the Unruh Civil Rights Act. This is to advise you that DFEH has recently circulated guidelines to our staff for use in accepting and processing these complaints.

Complaints which allege that a provider has an occupancy limitation more restrictive than two persons per bedroom plus one for the entire unit will be accepted and processed in a routine fashion.

Complainants who wish to file, but allege a limitation at least as liberal as two-per-bedroom-plus-one will be advised that it is unlikely their complaint can be sustained solely on an "adverse impact" (numerical) theory. Unless evidence of intent can be established, the case is probably not supportable. A complaint will only be accepted if the complainant still desires to pursue the matter, but the statistical proof questions will be evaluated before an investigative burden is placed on the respondent.

For further information, contact the appropriate Regional Administrator:

       Northern California - George Macias
                    (916) 323-5273

       Southern California - Carol Schiller
                    (213) 620-2630

TALMADGE R. JONES
Director

TRJ:EES:emm

5. *Abide by reasonable rules and regulations* of the landlord (i.e., no skateboard riding on the complex sidewalks, designated parking areas, etc.).

6. *Comply with local laws* such as those on overcrowding as defined in the Uniform Housing Code (UHC 503(b)) which limits the number of people per unit based on bedroom size (70 s.f. for two people and 50 s.f. for each additional person). This usually works out to three persons for a one bedroom unit.

7. *Crimes against property* such as vandalism states that "every person who maliciously (1) defaces with paint or any other liquid, (2) damages, or (3) destroys any real or personal property not his own — is guilty of a misdemeanor" (CC 594(a)).

Landlord Remedies

In residential management, the court system usually favors the tenant, so the property manager must be diligent in documenting a case with facts, pictures, etc., as the burden of proof is usually on the landlord.

1. *Notice to Pay Rent or Quit* — Can be served by anyone over 18 years of age, including the property manager or owner, to the tenant for delinquent rent. The amount can include only actual rent, not damage charges, late payment fees, etc. See Figure 14-7.

2. *Notice to Correct Breach of Covenant or Quit (3-Day)* — Used when the tenant seriously violates the terms of the rental agreement, house rules, or breaks local ordinances. Again, anyone may serve this notice. In residential property this notice should proceed to court only on the advice of an attorney as many judges view the three-day period as insufficient time to require anyone to terminate tenancy except for cases of very serious magnitude.

3. *Notice to Vacate (30-Day)* — This notice, also called 30-Day Notice of Termination of Tenancy, is given to the tenant who is on a month-to-month tenancy when the property manager or landlord wants the tenant to move from the premises. No reason need be given except if required in areas of rent control (check your local ordinances), but the notice cannot be used for retaliatory or discriminatory reasons. Anyone may serve. See Figure 14-8.

4. *Notice of Belief of Abandonment* — Provides the owner with a procedure to recover the premises after the tenant has not paid rent for 14 days and there is reasonable belief the tenant has vacated and will not return. The tenant has to respond within 18 days. Service may be by mail. Refer to CC 1951.2. See Figure 14-10.

5. *Notice of Right to Reclaim Abandoned Personal Property* — Used when the tenant leaves personal property (i.e., furniture, clothing, etc.). The property

Figure 14-6.

PET AGREEMENT

THIS AGREEMENT entered into this _____ day of _____, 198____, by

and between _____, "Owner" (Landlord)

and _____, "Resident" (Tenant)
IN CONSIDERATION OF THEIR MUTUAL PROMISES AGREE AS FOLLOWS:
1. Resident is renting from Owner the premises located at:

_____, CA.

2. The Rental Agreement provides that without Owner's prior written consent, no pets shall be allowed in or about said premises.

3. Resident desires to keep the below described pet hereinafter referred to as "Pet".

4. This Agreement is an Addendum and part of the Rental Agreement and/or Lease between Owner and Resident. In the event of default by Resident of any of the above terms, Resident agrees, within three days after receiving written notice of default from Owner, to cure the default or vacate the premises. Resident agrees Owner may revoke permission to keep said Pet on the premises by giving Resident written thirty (30) day notice.

5. As a special security deposit, Resident agrees to pay Owner the sum of $_____(receipt of which is hereby acknowledged). Owner may use therefrom such amount as is reasonably necessary to take care of any damages or cleaning caused by or in connection with said Pet. At the termination of this agreement, any balance shall be added to the rental agreement security deposit, and disbursed thereafter as required by law. Resident agrees to pay Owner for any excess damages or costs on demand.

6. Resident agrees to comply with:
    a) Health and Safety Code, and
    b) all other applicable governmental laws and regulations.

7. Resident represents the Pet or Pets are quiet and "housebroken" and will not cause any damage or annoy other Residents.

8. Resident agrees that the Pet will not be permitted outside the Resident's unit, unless restrained by a leash. Use of the grounds or premises of Owner for sanitary purposes is prohibited.

9. If the Pet is a cat:
    a) it must be neutered and declawed, and
    b) Resident must provide and maintain an appropriate litter box.

10. If a bird, the bird shall not be let out of the cage.

11. If fish, the water container shall not be over_____lbs. and be placed in a safe location in the unit.

12. No Pet shall be fed on unprotected carpeting within the rental unit. Resident shall prevent any fleas or other infestation of the rental unit or other property of Owner.

13. Resident shall not permit the pet to cause any damage, discomfort, annoyance, nuisance or in any way to inconvenience, or cause complaints, from any other Resident. Any "mess" created by the Pet shall immediately be cleaned up by Resident.

14. Resident shall be liable to Owner for all damages or expenses incurred by or in connection with said Pet, and shall hold Owner harmless for any and all damages or costs in connection with said Pet and shall hold Owner harmless for same.

RESIDENTS:

OWNER: _____
      OWNER/AGENT

_____

_____

Figure 14-7.

NOTICE TO PAY RENT OR QUIT

To _____

      All tenants and subtenants in possession (full name)
      and all others in possession

WITHIN THREE DAYS after the service on you of this notice, you are hereby required to pay to the

undersigned cr _____, his authorized agent, the rent of the premises hereinafter

described, of which you now hold possession amounting to the sum of _____ dollars

($_____) enumerated as follows:

$ _____ Due From _____ 19_____ To _____ 19_____

$ _____ Due From _____ 19_____ To _____ 19_____

$ _____ Due From _____ 19_____ To _____ 19_____

OR QUIT AND DELIVER UP THE POSSESSION OF THE PREMISES.

The premises herein referred to are situated in the city of _____, County

of _____, State of California, designated by the number and street

as _____, apt._____.

YOU ARE FURTHER NOTIFIED THAT, the undersigned does hereby elect to declare the forfeiture of
your lease or rental agreement under which you hold possession of the above-described premises and
lessor will institute legal proceedings to recover rent and possession of said premises which could
result in a judgment against you including costs and necessary disbursements together with treble
damages as allowed by law for such unlawful detention.

Dated this _____ day of _____, 19_____.

_____
          AGENT   LESSOR

To order, contact — California Association of Realtors®
525 South Virgil Avenue, Los Angeles, California 90020

California Apartment Association, revised 4/78.
Reprinted by permission.   CAA-4.0

Figure 14-8.

THIRTY (30) DAY NOTICE
OF TERMINATION OF TENANCY

TO: _____
All residents (tenants and subtenants) in possession (full name) and all others in possession

PLEASE TAKE NOTICE that your tenancy of the below-described premises is terminated, effective at the end of a thirty (30) day period after service on you of this notice.

The purpose of this notice is to terminate your tenancy of the below-described premises.

If you fail to quit and deliver possession, legal proceedings will be instituted against you to obtain possession and such proceedings could result in a judgement against you which could include costs and necessary disbursements.

The premises herein referred to are situated in the city of _____

County of _____ , State of California,

designated by the number and street as _____

Apartment _____

DATE _____   _____
                                                                            Owner/Agent

Figure 14-9.

WATERBED AND/OR LIQUID FILLED FURNITURE AGREEMENT

THIS AGREEMENT entered into this _____ day of _____, 198_____,

by and between _____, "Owner" (Landlord)

and _____, "Resident" (Tenant)

IN CONSIDERATION OF THEIR MUTUAL PROMISES AGREE AS FOLLOWS:

1. Resident is renting from Owner the premises located at:

_____, CA.

2. The Rental Agreement provides that without Owner's prior written consent, no waterbeds or liquid filled furniture shall be allowed in or about said premises.

3. Resident desires to keep the below described waterbed and/or liquid filled furniture hereinafter referred to as "said items":

_____

_____

4. This agreement is an Addendum and part of the Rental Agreement and/or Lease between Owner and Resident. In the event of default by Resident of any of the terms, Resident agrees, within three days after receiving written notice of default from Owner, to cure the default or vacate the premises. Owner may revoke permission to keep said items on the premises by giving Resident written thirty (30) day notice.

5. As additional security, Resident agrees to pay Owner the sum of $_____ (receipt of which is hereby acknowledged). Owner may use therefrom such amount as is reasonably necessary to take care of any damages or cleaning caused by or in connection with said items. At the termination of this agreement, any balance shall be added to the rental agreement security deposit, and disbursed thereafter as required by law. Resident agrees to pay Owner for any excess damages or costs on demand.

6. Resident agrees to furnish Owner a valid certificate of Waterbed Liability Insurance having a minimum policy limit of $100,000.00 for bodily injury and property damage. This certificate of insurance to be furnished to Owner before placing "said items" in the premises and Resident further agrees to furnish another certificate of insurance to Owner upon renewal of policy. Owner to be notified by the insurance company or agent at least ten (10) days prior to any cancellation, lapse or change.

7. Resident agrees to comply with:
   (a)   governing Building Code Requirements;
   (b)   Health and Safety Codes;
   (c)   minimum component standards covering the manufacturing, testing and sale of said items, and
   (d)   all other applicable governmental laws and regulations.

8. As to any waterbed, Resident agrees to use a mattress, a safety liner and a frame. If a heater is provided by Resident and Owner pays for the utilities for said heater, Resident shall pay Owner the sum of $_____ per month on each rent payment date, as a special payment (not to be construed as rent) for the added utility costs.

9. Resident agrees to have qualified personnel install said items according to Manufacturers' specification. Cost of installation is the responsibility of Resident. At time of removal of said items, Resident shall use special care to dispose of water or liquid.

10. Resident shall be liable to Owner for all damages or expenses incurred by or in connection with said items, and shall hold Owner harmless for any and all damages or costs in connection thereto.

11. In an emergency, to prevent injury or damage, Resident agrees to immediately remove said items. If Resident fails to do so, Owner may remove said items.

_____   _____
Owner/Agent   Resident

                                                     _____
                                                     ·Resident

---

UNAUTHORIZED REPRODUCTION OF THIS FORM IS ILLEGAL

manager should make a complete and accurate inventory with an estimate of value. The property manager must store the personal property for 18 days after mailing a notice to the last known address of the tenant. If claimed, by paying reasonable storage costs the tenant can take possession of the goods even if back rent is owed. If unclaimed and under $300 in value, the owner may dispose of the goods in any manner desired. If the value is over $300, a public sale notice must be published in the newspaper and the items auctioned. After deducting reasonable storage and sale costs, the proceeds must be returned to the tenant or turned over to the County to be held for the tenant. If the tenant does not claim the proceeds within five years, they revert to the State. CC 1988 and CC 1989 spell out the exact duties and responsibilities of the landlord. See Figure 14-11.

6. *Comply with local laws* such as those on overcrowding as defined in the Uniform Housing Code (UHC 503(b)) which limits the number of people per unit based on bedroom size (70 s.f. for two people and 50 s.f. for each additional person). This usually works out to three persons for a one-bedroom unit.

7. *Crimes against property* such as vandalism states that "every person who maliciously (1) defaces with paint or any other liquid, (2) damages, or (3) destroys any real or personal property not his own — is guilty of a misdemeanor (CC 594(a)).

8. *Change of Terms Notice* — Must be given before increasing the rent or changing the terms of the agreement (such as allowing pets). The notice time on a month-to-month tenancy is 30 days. See Figure 14-12.

9. *Transfer of Security Deposit* — Upon sale of the property, the rents are usually prorated and security deposits transferred. Notice telling of disposition of deposit must be sent to the tenants within 14 days. This notice should also include the amount of the deposit and the name and address of the new property manager. See Figure 14-13.

10. *Eviction*

a. *Retaliatory Eviction* — The final landlord responsibility to be examined is CC 1942.5 which prohibits retaliation against a tenant who exercises the right to complain about habitability. This complaint can be oral or in writing. The property manager *cannot* evict or increase the rent for 180 days if the reason for that eviction or increase is a result of the tenant exercising the right to complain about habitability. If the tenant is evicted, the landlord or property manager must stand prepared to prove the case is not retaliatory (i.e., proof of nonpayment of rent, severe breach of contract, etc.). This code section also prohibits evicting a tenant for joining a tenant union or exercising certain other legal rights under this law; i.e., suing the landlord.

b. *Constructive Eviction* — Eviction is considered "constructive" if the landlord turns off the utilities, changes locks, removes the tenant's personal property, removes the front door, etc. These actions are prohibited by CC 789.3 and carry penalties of $100 per day for each day in violation.

Figure 14-10.

INSTRUCTIONS
CAA Form 8.0
Notice of Belief of Abandonment (Real Property)

Purpose and Use:

This form provides the Owner with a procedure to recover real property after the resident has not paid rent 14 days after the due date and there is a reasonable belief that the resident may not return. The resident remains liable for rent during the abandonment period or until the property is relet or surrendered by the resident.

Preparation of the Form

1. Insert the names of all residents exactly as they appear on your rental agreement or lease.
2. Completely fill out the address of the abandoned property, your name and address as Owner/agent.
3. Insert the date of mailing.

Copies

Keep one copy and mail one copy to the resident at his last known address and to any other address you might reasonably expect the resident to receive the Notice.

Service

Service may be made by personally serving the notice by anyone over 18 years of age or mailing by first class mail.

Response Period

15 days for personnal service or 18 days for service by mail. Don't count the first day for determining time. The appropriate day that the property is to be considered abandoned must be included in the form.

Resident Responses

The property will not be considered abandoned if:
1. Prior to the date in the Notice the resident responds in writing of his intent not to abandon.
2. The resident pays some portion of the rent due.
3. The resident can show that the owner did not have reasonable belief the property was abandoned.
4. The rent was not due and payable for 14 days.

Resident Fails to Respond

1. If the resident fails to respond in the Notice period then at the completion of the period the owner may enter the premises and take necessary actions to relet the property.
2. If there is personal property then it must be inventoried and stored and an appropriate notice to reclaim property sent. (See FORM instruction for NOTICE OF RIGHT TO RECLAIM ABANDONED PROPERTY).
3. The owner is obliged at the end of the Notice period to take reasonable action in reletting the premises. The former resident remains obligated for any rent due and for any difference between a new resident's rent and the lease rent.
4. The resident may also be liable for costs of repair and fix up where it can be shown that the owner would not have been obligated to incur the expense if the resident had complied with the lease agreement terms.

Pitfalls and Precautionary Notes

1. If the owner relets the property at a lower rate then it is necessary to give the former resident a Notice to that effect if the owner intends to recover from the former tenant the rental difference.
2. Entering into an agreement with the former resident (either oral or written) where the former resident agrees to give up the property is considered surrender and no rent can be collected from the former resident after the date of surrender.
3. Mailing by certified mail return receipt requested is an inexpensive insurance policy.
4. The California Apartment Association does not sanction any CAA form which has been altered or changed in any way.

Figure 14-11.

NOTICE OF RIGHT TO RECLAIM ABANDONED PROPERTY

To:_____ _____ _____

Address:_____

    When you vacated the premises at
the following personal property remained:

    You may claim this property at
Unless you pay the reasonable cost of storage for all the above-described
property, and take possession of the property which you claim, not
later than   this property may be disposed of
pursuant to Civil Code Section 1988.

    If you fail to reclaim the property, it will be sold at a public
sale after notice of the sale has been given by publication. You have
the right to bid on the property at this sale. After the property is
sold and the cost of storage, advertising, and sale is deducted, the
remaining money will be paid over to the county. You may claim the
remaining money at any time within one (1) year after the county
receives the money.

Dated: _____

                     _____

                     _____

Form 10

Figure 14-12.

NOTICE OF CHANGE OF TERMS OF TENANCY

To _____ and to all others

in possession of the premises commonly known as _____

_____   _____ .
Street Address   City

_____ .
State

You are hereby notified, in accordance with Civil Code Section 827, that 30 days after service upon you of this

notice, or _____ , whichever is later, your tenancy of the above designated premises will be changed as
Date

follows:

1. The monthly rent which is payable in advance on or before the _____ day of each month

   will be the sum of $_____ , instead of $_____ , the current monthly rent.

2. OTHER CHANGES:

   Except as herein provided, all other terms of your tenancy shall remain in full force and effect.

DATED: _____

                                    _____
                                              Owner/Agent

To order, contact—California Association of Realtors®
525 S. Virgil Avenue, Los Angeles, California 90020
(Revised 1983)

California Apartment Association   CAA-5.0
Reprinted by permission.

Figure 14-13.

TRANSFER OF SECURITY DEPOSIT

TO: Resident(s) _____

Effective _____ , 198 ____ , we will no longer manage/own the unit in which you reside,

located at _____ , California.

In accordance with the California Tenant/Landlord Civil Code, Section 1950.5, you are being informed that your

security deposit, in the amount of $ _____ , has been:

[_____]   TRANSFERRED TO: _____

_____

_____

[_____]   RETURNED TO YOU. _____
                                        (Date)

YOUR PRESENT RENTAL AGREEMENT/LEASE WILL REMAIN IN EFFECT. FOR MORE INFORMATION ABOUT
YOUR NEW OWNER/AGENT, CONTACT:

_____

_____

_____

On _____ , 198_____, this Notice was:

[_____]   Sent to you by certified mail; or

[_____]   Personally delivered to you;

AND a copy of this Notice was mailed to the new owner/agent.

Dated _____ , 198_____.   _____
                                                        OWNER/AGENT

c. *Actual Eviction (Court-Ordered)* — If the tenant has not paid the rent, the landlord must go to court using an "unlawful detainer action" to remove the tenant and collect unpaid rent. Small Claims Court is inexpensive but time-consuming (75-90 days), so most property managers use Municipal Court. The property manager can go to court to testify, but *cannot* represent the owner in court "in pro per." Therefore, legal counsel should be obtained from an attorney who specializes in evictions. The main goal is to regain possession and rerent the property to a paying tenant as soon as possible. Most times the money judgments obtained are worthless as the tenant is unemployed, on welfare, or leaves the area. Even the self-managing owner who may represent himself "in pro per" will find using an attorney prudent as procedural guidelines must be followed *exactly* or the case will be dismissed and the landlord will have to start again from the beginning with a Notice to Pay Rent or Quit.

Actual forms and a procedural explanation can be found in *California Rental Housing Reference Book*, published by the California Apartment Association, 1107 9th Street, Suite 1010, Sacramento, CA 95814.

Municipal Court, through CC 1179A, gives priority to unlawful detainer cases. This allows for speedy repossession, but strict procedures must be followed before possession and back rent can be obtained. Damage and other abuses by the tenant will not be considered in the unlawful detainer procedure, but must be filed in a separate action.

Certified vs. Registered Mail

Some notices such as a 3-day notice may be sent by regular mail. According to the United States Postal Service, *registered mail* should be used when you are mailing something of monetary value that can be insured, such as money or jewelry. A declared value is made at the time of mailing and, if lost, reimbursement will be made by the Postal Service. *Certified mail* should be used when the item to be mailed has no intrinsic value, such as a letter or notice, and therefore does not require insurance. Certified mail is about 40% cheaper than registered mail. In most instances, a letter sent certified mail, return receipt requested, is adequate to meet notice requirements, even if the lease says registered mail.

Tenant Protection

The tenant has rights that are protected by law from abuses by the landlord. The property manager, by following the Golden Rule of "Do unto others as you would have them do unto you," will avoid many of those hassles and pitfalls. As we discussed in Chapter 4, in addition to avoiding costly legal action for the owner, the property manager is usually paid a percentage of rents collected and will not make a profit if time is consumed in tenant disputes.

Figure 14-14. Stopping Evictions

"We Can Help"

CALIFORNIA PARALEGAL CLINIC

Dear Tenant:

An "EVICTION LAWSUIT" has been filed against you by your landlord. The
purpose of this action is to EVICT you from the premises you now occupy.

You will notice that you have been given five (5) CALENDAR DAYS in which to
file an ANSWER to this SUMMONS. If you fail to answer within this time period,
your landlord will win a Judgment by Default and have the Marshal post a Five
Day Notice to Move (vacate the property) on your residence within a few days.

We can assist you in STOPPING THE EVICTION. Helping tenants faced with an
eviction problem can result in the TENANT retaining possession of the premises
or obtaining the necessary TIME to move in an orderly and dignified fashion.

We can assist you. WE CAN HELP prevent or prolong the abrupt disruption of
your home life.

"YOU MUST ACT QUICKLY"

ACT RIGHT NOW because your time is very short. Call our office for an
appointment, or come in IMMEDIATELY!!!! Bring this letter along with any
other papers you have received.

Sincerely,

CALIFORNIA PARALEGAL CLINIC

O U R   T O T A L   F E E: *$55.00*

Figure 14-15. Eviction Process

Uncontested Unlawful Detainer Steps
1. Service Notice to Pay Rent or Quit (anyone may serve).
2. File Summons and Complaint.
3. Service of Summons and Complaint by disinterested party (best to use marshal or a process server).
4. Tenant, if personally served, has five days to answer, and 15 days if by substitute service.
5. If tenant doesn't respond, file "Request to Enter Default" with clerk. In some jurisdictions you need to go to court for a "prove-up" to get a judgment.
6. After receiving a judgment, file for a "Writ of Possession."
7. File the "Writ of Possession" with the marshal's office for service.
8. Marshal serves "Eviction Notice" and tenant has five days to vacate.
9. Marshal will, after five days, physically evict tenant and turn apartment over to property manager who may immediately change the locks.
10. File declaration to obtain "money judgment" for unpaid rent.

Contested Cases
1. Follow Steps 1–4 above.
2. Tenant files answer to complaint and a "Memorandum to Set Civil Case for Trial" or "Request for Trial" with clerk. A trial date will then be set by the court.
3. When owner wins judgment at trial, he should proceed with Steps 6–10 above.

Proper Service of Notices
1. Attempt must be made for "personal service."
   a. If unable to personally serve, notice may be posted on door with copy mailed first class except for 30-day notices, which should be sent by certified or registered mail.
   b. Summons and Complaint may be filed on the fourth day after personal service of Notice to Pay Rent or Quit, or Breach of Covenant, 31st day for Notice to Vacate.
2. Substituted Service (to occupant other than tenant) or "Post Substituted and Mail."
   a. Pay Rent or Quit or Breach of Covenant must be served three days prior to filing, not counting day of service.
3. Change in Terms or Rent Increase
   a. Served as above or by certified mail.

What is Personal Service?
If you hand the notice to the tenant (or tenants) named on the notice, this is considered personal service. If you hand the notice to anyone else in the unit, who in turn is to give it to the named tenant, this is considered "substituted service." Service must be on an adult, in any case, rather than a child.

1. *Repair and Deduct (CC 1942)* — The tenant may, after a "reasonable" time and after either written or oral notice to the landlord of conditions making the unit uninhabitable, make the repairs himself or have the repairs completed by others. The maximum amount deductible is one month of rent every 180 days.

2. *Non-Waiver of Tenant's Rights (CC 1942.1)* — As discussed earlier in this chapter, the tenant cannot waive rights of habitability.

3. *Entry of Tenant's Unit (CC 1954)* — The tenant must be allowed quiet enjoyment of the dwelling. This code section spells out the four reasons for which a landlord may enter:

   a. Emergency (i.e., water or gas leak).

b. To make necessary or agreed-upon repairs, provide service, show the unit to prospective tenants or buyer, or normal inspection. Twenty-four hours' written notice must be given and entry must be during reasonable hours.

c. Abandoned or surrendered premises.

d. Pursuant to court order.

If the property manager uses tact, reasonableness, and understanding, entry isn't usually a problem. See Figure 14-16.

4. *Forcible Entry (CC 1159)* — Defined as breaking of windows or doors, threats of violence or terror to gain entry. It is strictly illegal.

5. *Soldiers and Sailors Civil Relief Act of 1940* — Protects the rights of persons in the service by providing special methods for serving notices and seizing or holding personal property.

6. *Credit Reporting* — The tenant is protected by the Federal Fair Credit Reporting Act if credit is denied. The reason must be given in writing. When using a credit reporting agency, the property manager should refer tenant requests for information to that agency (i.e., "You were turned down because of information received from Landlord/Tenant Credit.") and not deal in specifics with the tenant.

7. *Seizing Personal Property (CC 1861(a))* — The landlord or property manager may not seize personal property without a court order.

8. *Removal of Vehicles (Vehicle Code Section 22658)* — The property manager must have the property properly posted to conform with local ordinances. A towing service, licensed to operate in the specific local area, must be used to avoid illegal towing and claims by tenants and other persons.

Tenant Abuses

The pendulum has swung in favor of tenant rights with little regard to legally enforcing the tenant to observe the duty not to infringe upon those remaining landlord rights. This legal environment makes it difficult and time-consuming for the property manager when dealing with evictions. For example, Figure 14-14 shows a flyer from a paralegal clinic posted on a tenant's door after an unlawful detainer was served. These clinics search the court records daily and either mail or post a notice on the tenant doors telling them that, for a fee, eviction can be delayed. Another example of the pendulum swing is tenant abuses of the "Arrieta Case" which requires naming all adult habitants on the writ, whether or not their names were on the rental agreement. An Arrieta claim can result in another three- to six-week delay while unnamed inhabitants are enjoined in the suit.

Figure 14-16.

NOTICE TO ENTER DWELLING UNIT
(CC 1954)

Pursuant to California Civil Code Section 1954, Owner does hereby give

notice to:_____, and all

persons in occupancy of the premises located at:

_____, California,

that owner, owner's agent or owner's employees will enter said premises on or about

the _____ day of _____, 19_____, during

normal business hours_____

for the reason set forth in the checked (✓) numbered item below:

_____ 1.   To make necessary or agreed repairs

_____ 2.   Decorations

_____ 3.   Alterations or improvements

_____ 4.   Supply necessary or agreed services

_____ 5.   To exhibit the dwelling unit to prospective or actual purchasers

_____ 6.   To exhibit the dwelling unit to prospective mortagagees

_____ 7.   To exhibit the dwelling unit to prospective tenants

_____ 8.   To exhibit the dwelling unit to workmen or contractors

_____ 9.   Pursuant to Court Order

DATED:_____, 198____.   _____

                                              OWNER/AGENT

_____
UNAUTHORIZED REPRODUCTION OF THIS FORM IS ILLEGAL
_____

Civil procedure should require that tenants disputing eviction be required to post bond or deposit with the court in the rental amount that would be due at the time of trial, at the time they request trial or file for postponement. An evicting owner wins only a hollow victory as most evicted residential tenants are "judgment-proof" (no assets or job), so monies awarded are not collectable. In turn, this leads to higher rent for the rest of the good tenants as owners have to make up their loss. The phrase "CAVEAT FEOFATUS," owner beware, is appropriate.

Landlord/Tenant Court Cases

Throughout this chapter, court cases dealing with areas such as habitability have been cited. Now cases in other areas with which it is important that the property manager be familiar will be covered.

Service and Notice

a. *Arrieta v. Mahon (1982)* — Persons who are in possession at time of the filing of the unlawful detainer, but not specifically listed on the writ, cannot be summarily evicted. This means *all* adults living in the unit — whether or not listed on the rental agreement — must be named in the action.

Effective January 1, 1987, CC 715.010(a) requires the tenant claiming possession to make legal claim and pay a fee. The claim is then heard in court and a decision made as to the validity of the claim of possession. This may take three to four weeks or longer, and leads to further loss of rents.

Arrieta Super Service (SB 2508), effective January 1, 1991, extends the pay or quit 3-day notice period to a 5-day period within which individuals who are not named would have an opportunity to file their claim for possession. This is an option to the current procedure available.

b. *Hernandez v. Stabach (1983)* — Once a landlord allows an apartment to become overcrowded (evidenced, among other things, by accepting rent knowing that the condition exists), the landlord may not thereafter make the tenants reduce the number of people in the apartment unless the landlord has specifically been required by an appropriate governmental agency to reduce overcrowding.

c. *Bekins Moving & Storage Co. v. Prudential Insurance Co. (1985)* — Equitable relief from failure to exercise renewal option was denied where failure was due solely to lessee's negligence.

Liability

a. *Becker v. IRM (1985)* — The landlord is responsible for all defects, including latent ones. This case involved an untempered glass shower door installed by a former owner 16 years prior to the tenant's injury. The landlord makes an "implied" representation that the premises are fit for use.

Figure 14-17. California Court System

```
                    CALIFORNIA COURT SYSTEM


SMALL CLAIMS COURT

1.  Maximum limit is $5,000.

2.  Low cost -- filing fee

3.  No attorney representation.

4.  Limitations on usage.

      a.  Slow and time-consuming, may take 75-90 days.

5.  Appeal -- only defendant can appeal; 20 days to appeal if
    he shows, 35 days if he doesn't appear in court.

6.  Cannot file for eviction in Small Claims Court.


MUNICIPAL COURT

1.  Maximum limit is $1,500 per month rent for commercial
    unlawful detainer, no limit per month for residential,
    $25,000 maximum.

2.  Probably need attorney, but can file "in pro per."  Agent
    cannot act as attorney.

3.  Quickest eviction -- 25-35 days (priority for fast trial,
    CC 1179A).

4.  Limitations on usage:

      a.  Back rent.

      b.  Writ of Possession.


SUPERIOR COURT

1.  Higher attorney costs.

2.  Must be utilized if rent for commercial properties is over
    $1,500 per month or total due is over $25,000.


APPELLATE COURT

1.  An appeals court that hears cases on appeal.


CALIFORNIA SUPREME COURT

1.  Final decision on state laws and the state Constitution.
```

b. *Uccello v. Laudenslayer (1975)* — The landlord is liable for a dangerous condition caused by a tenant if he fails to remedy it (a tenant's dog bit a neighbor).

c. *Rosales v. Stewart (1980)* — A tenant shot and killed a neighbor (not even in the same complex). The court held the landlord liable for failing to remedy a dangerous condition (tenant gun) because the landlord had previous knowledge that the tenant had fired guns on the premises.

d. *Hale v. Morgan (1975)* — Owner in mobile home park shut off utilities and removed ties from mobile home. Court assessed damages at the rate of $100 per day for 173 days, even though the tenant had never paid any rent since possession.

e. *Unpublished Case* — School district was liable for injuries suffered by a Redding, California, youth who was liable for a felony. The youth fell through painted-over skylight while breaking into a building. Won out-of-court settlement for $260,000 plus $1,200 per month for life after being paralyzed. Assemblyman Alister McAlister bill AB 200 barred recovering damages from landlord for injuries received while committing a felony.

f. *Kubichans v. Clinton (1976)* — Anyone who creates a hazardous or dangerous condition on his/her property may be liable for injuries to third parties even after the property has been sold. Case involved a backyard pond in which a child almost drowned. Owner (builder) was found liable for the accident which occurred three years after the property was sold.

g. *Rowland v. Christian (1968)* — Said that the landlord owes a duty of care to persons who enter the property, regardless of their status as invited visitors, business interests, or trespassers.

Discrimination

a. *Hess v. Fair Employment & Housing Commission (1982)* — The landlord or property manager cannot discriminate on the basis of marital status.

b. *Hubert v. Williams (1982)* — The landlord or property manager cannot discriminate against homosexuals.

Rent Control

a. *Fisher v. City of Berkeley (1986)* — U.S. Supreme Court held that regulating rents by the City of Berkeley was not in violation of anti-trust laws.

b. *Carson Mobilehome Park Owners v. Carson (1983)* — California Supreme Court upheld the constitutionality of rent control while refusing to set a firm standard for "fair return."

c. *Pennell v. City of San Jose*

1986 — In Pennell v. the City of San Jose (Rent Control Ordinance), the California Supreme Court declared that an owner may be entitled to less than a "fair return" depending on the income of the tenant.

1988 — Appealed to the federal level, the U.S. Supreme Court, in a 6-2 majority opinion, said:

> "We have long recognized that a legitimate and rational goal of price or rate regulation is the protection of consumer welfare." The ordinance "represents a rational attempt to accommodate the conflicting interests of protecting tenants from burdensome rent increases while at the same time ensuring that landlords are guaranteed a fair return of their investment."

The dissenting opinion by Justice Scalia best describes the landlord's predicament in this case:

> "The San Jose Rent Control Law is no different from a requirement that a grocer charge poor shoppers less than wealthier ones. Rather than putting the social burden on all citizens, the San Jose rent law works to establish a welfare program privately funded by those landlords who happen to have hardship tenants."

This case has been described as a "Robin Hood Law" that steals from the rich (landlords) to pay the poor (tenants).

Summary

It is essential that the property manager be familiar with federal, state, and local regulations and laws in order to properly manage and protect the property from lawsuits. The highest source of law is the constitution, so any local law in conflict with a federal or state law will be void. Local laws such as rent control vary from municipality to municipality and it is imperative to know and follow the regulations, rules, and laws of each municipality. Commercial tenants are viewed as equal to landlords in most courts and are not given the protections (such as rent control) granted to residential tenants.

The owner/manager has a responsibility to maintain a habitable dwelling unit. The definition of habitability includes: weatherproofing, security, plumbing, heating, electrical, repairs, trash, free from pests, and smoke detectors. The courts and legislation have said that the owner/manager cannot discriminate on the basis of race, religion, color, national origin, age, handicap, or sex. These are laws at the federal, state, and local levels as well as the Department of Real Estate Commissioner's regulation (Section 2780).

The tenant has responsibilities, including to: pay rent on time, maintain a clean and sanitary unit, give proper notice, respect the rights of other tenants, abide by reasonable rules and regulations, and comply with laws. Landlord remedies against the tenant include: 3-day and 30-day notices, Notice of Belief of Abandonment, Change of Terms, and eviction. There are two kinds of evictions: actual (court-ordered) and constructive (turning off utilities). Tenant protection includes laws against retaliatory eviction, repairs and deduction for repairs, non-waiver of tenant rights, entry to unit, etc.

Court cases have set precedents over the years which established landlord/tenant laws. Under service and notice, the Arrieta case, involving naming all the tenants living in the unit, whether on the lease or not, is changing eviction procedures in California. When considering liability, *Becker v. IRM* held the landlord responsible for all defects, whether or not he/she knew about the defects. The key discrimination case is *Wolfson v. Marina Pt., Ltd.*, which said the owner/manager could not discriminate against children. When considering rent control, the latest U.S. Supreme Court case, *Pennell v. the City of San Jose*, upheld the right of the city to limit rent increases to poor tenants.

In conclusion, the property manager must be constantly updating and learning about changes and new landlord/tenant laws. A relationship with a good eviction attorney should be established, as a non-paying tenant is worse than a vacancy. The key in landlord/tenant relationships is "treating the other person as you yourself would want to be treated."

Chapter 14 Review Questions

1. *The highest source of law is:*

   a. Congress.
   b. the President.
   c. the Constitution.
   d. local government.

2. *In a conflict of authority between state and federal government, which usually prevails?*

   a. State.
   b. Federal.
   c. Neither.

3. *Green v. Superior Court involves:*

   a. habitability.
   b. discrimination.
   c. liability.
   d. none of the above.

4. *The Unruh Act deals with:*

   a. habitability.
   b. discrimination.
   c. liability.
   d. all of the above.

5. *Rent control usually involves:*

   a. Federal law.
   b. Local law.
   c. State law.

6. *Habitability would include:*

   a. payment of rent on time by the tenant.
   b. always charging market rent.
   c. hot and cold running water in good working condition.
   d. all of the above.
   e. none of the above.

7. *Tenant responsibilities include:*

   a. paying rent on time.
   b. maintaining a clean unit.
   c. giving proper legal notice.
   d. all of the above.
   e. none of the above.

8. *Eviction for non-payment of rent starts with a:*

   a. 30-day notice.
   b. Notice to Pay Rent or Quit.
   c. Summons and Complaint.
   d. writ.

9. *Arrieta v. Mahon involves:*

   a. habitability.
   b. discrimination.
   c. liability.
   d. service and notice.

10. *Which court is usually most prudent to use for apartment tenant evictions?*

   a. Small Claims.
   b. Municipal.
   c. Superior.
   d. Supreme.

Chapter 14 Case Study Problem

1. Civic Center Terrace has some roof leaks that two tenants complained about six months ago. What should be done?

2. In determining the tenant mix for the apartment complex, the owner says he doesn't want to rent one-bedroom units to applicants with children due to the small size of the units. What should you, as the property manager, tell him?

3. A blind applicant wants to rent an apartment on the second floor and asks you (the property manager) to install an elevator. Do you legally have to install an elevator?

4. What rental collection procedures would you implement to reduce delinquencies at Civic Center Terrace?

5. The previous manager started eviction proceedings (gave 30 days' notice) to a tenant she didn't like because he complained about plumbing leaks. What should you do?

6. Would you handle the evictions differently from going to Small Claims Court? Why or why not?

7. Who would you have serve Pay Rent or Quit notices?

8. The previous manager used to change the locks when tenants didn't pay after three months. What would be your policy?

9. The previous manager used her pass key to enter tenant apartments for repairs, to see if they had extra pets, etc. Would you revise that policy?

10. The owner is worried about being sued and wants to include a clause in the rental agreement that prohibits tenants from suing the owner. What should you tell the owner?

Chapter 14
Selected Additional References and Reading

Brown, David and Ralph Warner, *The Landlord's Law Book*, Nolo Press, Berkeley, CA, 1986.

California Apartment Association, *California Rental Housing Reference Book*, Sacramento, CA, 1985.

Casale, William, *Property Management*, California Association of Realtors, Los Angeles, CA, 1983.

First Tuesday (Monthly)
P.O. Box 20068
Riverside, CA 92516

Gordon, Theodore H., *California Real Estate Law*, Prentice-Hall, Inc., Englewood Cliffs, NJ, 1985.

Parkers Uniform Commercial Code for California
Parker and Sons Publications
6500 Flotilla Street
Los Angeles, CA 90022

Real Estate Law Journal (Quarterly)
Warren, Gorham, and Lamont, Inc.
210 South Street
Boston, MA 02111

Real Property Law Reporter (Monthly)
University of California
Department CEB
2300 Shattuck Avenue
Berkeley, CA 94704

Robinson, Leigh, *The Eviction Book For California*, Express, Richmond, VA, 1984.

NOTES

Chapter 15

HUMAN RELATIONS IN PROPERTY MANAGEMENT

Key Terms

Planning
Organization
Staffing
Directing
Controlling
Overtime
Fair Employment
California OSHA
1099 forms
Business plan
Minimum wage
Independent
    contractor
Eviction of manager
Employment
    contract
Withholding
Notices
Task traits

Food for Thought

"Education is a social process . . .
Education is growth . . .
Education is not preparation for life:
Education is life itself."
    John Dewey
    American philosopher/educator

Human Relations in Property Management

Introduction

Previous chapters have examined the mechanics and systems of property management. This chapter will examine how the interaction of these systems is successfully coordinated by the CPM, sometimes referred to as a Certified Property "Magician" rather than Certified Property Manager. As illustrated by one's own body, where the heart, lungs, brain, and kidneys all must work in harmony to enjoy a healthy life, maintenance, rent collection, tenant selection, and accounting must also be in harmony to run a successful building. The property manager, onsite manager, staff, vendors, and tenants must work symbiotically even though their personalities, behavior patterns, approaches, and goals may be dissimilar.

The Management Function

The property manager's function is to deliver a service while dealing with the quality, quantity, cost-effectiveness, and efficiency of the building in the marketplace. The management function is dynamic and constantly changing. In the early 1900s, engineer Fredrich Taylor developed a scientific theory of management and many of his principles are still followed. The basis of property management relies on six steps:

1. *Planning* — develop a management plan to provide goals and objectives.

2. *Organizing* — define jobs; i.e., onsite manager.

3. *Staffing* — hire and train people to fill positions, such as maintenance foreman.

4. *Directing* — lead and motivate the staff, such as by developing goals and rewards for their fulfillment (bonuses, etc.).

5. *Controlling* — measure performance and identify problem areas. Such measurement may be through the monthly profit and loss statements.

6. *Feedback* — test to see if assumptions are valid. Monthly vacancy reports will verify whether the 5% projected vacancy assumption was valid.

Staffing the Management Office

Since the property manager provides a service and not a product, people are the most important asset. Firm sizes range from small (only the property manager and a secretary) to a large office consisting of several layers of personnel (Figure 15-1). The management company should prepare a business plan (budgét — see Chapter 13) to use as a guide as to when to hire additional employees (Figure 13-8).

Figure 15-1. Organizational Chart

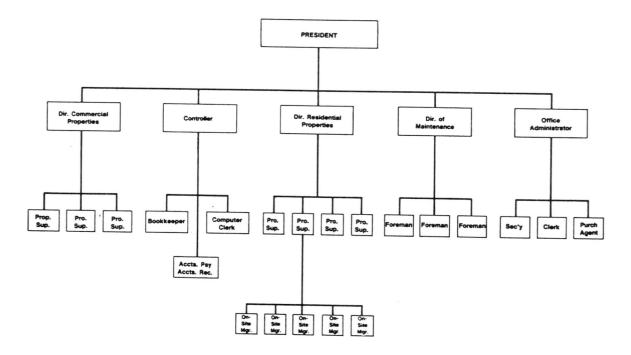

Each employee must be trained in the company's operations and procedures. This task is made easier if there is a company policy and procedures guide for the employee to read, review, and keep for future reference. The future education and professional growth of the employee should also be a company goal (for example, becoming a candidate to achieve the Certified Property Manager designation).

William Walters, Jr., CPM, in *The Practice of Real Estate Management for the Experienced Property Manager* (Chicago: Institute of Real Estate Management, 1979), discusses in depth the staffing of the management office.

Payment of Employees

Persons working permanently on the complex are employees, whether they receive wages or just a rental allowance. As such, state and federal employment laws must be followed.

Minimum Wage Requirements

The current minimum wage rate in California is $4.25 per hour (students should verify this figure due to frequent changes). Onsite managers must be paid at least this amount per hour. The management company can deduct (offset) for SDI (state disability insurance) from the manager's wage the lesser amount of 66-2/3% of ordinary rental value for lodging, but no more than $355 per month.

```
        Example:
            Rental value of $700, 2/3        = $466.20
            Min. rate at $4.25/hr. for
                90 hours                     = $382.50
            Max. deduction (per couple)      = $355.00
            Max. deduction (one person)      = $240.00
            Check to onsite manager          = $142.50
```

As can be seen from the above example, $355 is less than $466.20, which is two thirds of the $700 rental value (Industrial Welfare Commission No. MM-88). The manager, in this case, would receive only an apartment free and $142.50 additional paycheck if it was a single manager ($382.50 minus $240.00 = $142.50). The calculation of manager wages is complex. They must conform to minimum wage laws (both state and federal, whichever is higher). They must also conform to SDI, Worker's Compensation laws, and federal and state tax withholding regulations.

Job Descriptions

In a research project commissioned by the Institute of Real Estate Management (IREM) Foundation, Potential Unlimited, Inc., a firm specializing in employment behavioral analysis and research, concluded that there was no "perfect property manager." No behavior or trait closely correlated with success in the majority of property manager/supervisor positions.

The very nature of property management involves an unusually demanding and conflicting mix of behavioral requirements. One position might require a dynamic "self-starting" salesperson, able to deal with the multiple personalities of tenants, vendors, and owners alike, while another focuses on the pyramid of details and paperwork inherent in lease administration. Thus, when the executive manager looks at a potential job candidate, a definition of the position's priorities through a job description is essential:

1. Who will the applicant be dealing with? Residential tenants? Outside owners? In-house staff only?

2. What will be the primary functions? Leasing? Property supervision? Lease administration? New account solicitation?

3. What technical knowledge is required? Experience with sophisticated building systems? Commercial lease clause familiarity? Accounting?

From an adequately prepared job description, behavioral traits can be matched to job requirements.

Personality Tests

Several personality tests have been developed to help determine behavior traits. Among the best is the Myers-Briggs test of psychological types which breaks personalities down to 16 basic groups. Thus, if the job descriptions calls for the empirical, objective thinking of a senior executive manager responsible for the overall goals and objectives of the management company, results of the Myers-Briggs test would indicate hiring an "ENTJ" (extroverted, intuitive, thinking, judgmental) type. In turn, a job description heavy in the detailed administrative behavior of commercial lease administration might favor an "ISTJ" (introverted, sensing, thinking, judgmental) type.

For a thorough discussion of these behavioral types and their characteristics, read *Please Understand Me* by David Keirsey and Marilyn Bates, which also contains an abbreviated version of the test and answer grid.

An individual considering property management as a career could also take this test to help focus on the area in the industry most appropriate to his personality.

Figure 15-2.

INDUSTRIAL WELFARE COMMISSION ORDER NO. MW-88 REGULATING THE MINIMUM WAGE

Supersedes Title 8
California Administrative Code
Section 11000 and amends
certain minimum wage
Subsections of Sections 11010
through 11150
Effective July 1, 1988

State of California
George Deukmejian, Governor
Ron Rinaldi, Director of Industrial Relations

TAKE NOTICE: The Industrial Welfare Commission (Commission), pursuant to its authority in the California Labor Code, and Article 14, Section 1 of the Constitution of the State of California, has fixed a new minimum wage for all employees in this state, and provided for an alternative wage for certain employees. Also, the Commission has increased the amounts credited against the minimum wage for meals and lodging. The Commission promulgated this order after calling a wage board pursuant to Labor Code Sections 1178.5 (a) and (c) and has proceeded with the authority vested in it by Labor Code Sections 1171 through 1204. This order supersedes Order No. MW-80 and amends certain minimum wage sections of all the Commission's industry and occupation orders as contained in Title 8, Sections 11000 through 11150 of the California Administrative Code. The specific amendments are noted below. The Commission's statement as to the basis upon which this order is predicated includes the above and all that appears on the other side of this sheet.

1. APPLICABILITY

The provisions of this Order shall not apply to employees directly employed by the State or any county, incorporated city or town or other municipal corporation, or to outside salespersons.

The provisions of this Order shall not apply to any individual who is the parent, spouse, child, or legally adopted child of the employer.

Exceptions and modifications provided by statute or in Section 1, Applicability, and other sections of the Industrial Welfare Commission's industry and occupation orders may be used where any such provisions are enforceable and applicable to the employer.

2. MINIMUM WAGES

Every employer shall pay to each employee wages not less than four dollars and twenty-five cents ($4.25) per hour for all hours worked, except:

Tipped employees may be paid not less than $3.50 per hour. A tipped employee is an employee who is engaged in an occupation in which he or she customarily receives gratuities, as that term is defined in Labor Code Section 350 (e), of not less than sixty dollars ($60.00) per month.

3. MEALS AND LODGING

Meals or lodging may not be credited against the minimum wage without a voluntary written agreement between the employer and the employee. When credit for meals or lodging is used to meet part of the employer's minimum wage obligation, the amounts so credited may not be more than the following:

Lodging:

Room occupied alone	$ 20.00 per week
Room shared	$ 16.50 per week
Apartment—two-thirds (2/3) of the ordinary rental value, and in no event more than	$240.00 per month
Where a couple are both employed by the employer, two-thirds (2/3) of the ordinary rental value, and in no event more than	$355.00 per month

Meals:

Breakfast	$ 1.50
Lunch	$ 2.10
Dinner	$ 2.80

4. SEPARABILITY

If the application of any provision of this Order, or any section, subsection, subdivision, sentence, clause, phrase, word or portion of this Order should be held invalid or unconstitutional or unauthorized or prohibited by statute, the remaining provisions thereof shall not be affected thereby, but shall continue to be given full force and effect as if the part so held invalid or unconstitutional had not been included herein.

5. THIS ORDER supersedes Minimum Wage Order No. MW-80, and amends minimum wage Sections 4 (Minimum Wages) and 10 (Meals and Lodging) of the Industrial Welfare Commission's 1980 industry and occupation orders and Order 15-86 contained in the California Administrative Code as follows: It supersedes Title 8, Sec. 11000 (Order MW-80); It also amends subsections 4 (A) and 10 (B) of, and adds subsection 4 (A) (3) to, Title 8, Secs. 11010 (Order 1-80), 11020 (Order 2-80), 11030 (Order 3-80), 11040 (Order 4-80), 11050 (Order 5-80), 11060 (Order 6-80), 11070 (Order 7-80), 11090 (Order 9-80), 11100 (Order 10-80), 11110 (Order 11-80), 11120 (Order 12-80), 11150 (Order 15-86); It also amends subsections 4 (A) and 10 (B) of, and adds subsection 4 (A) (4) to, Title 8, Secs. 11080 (Order 8-80), 11130 (Order 13-80), 11140 (Order 14-80).

Adopted on December 18, 1987 in San Francisco

INDUSTRIAL WELFARE COMMISSION

Lynne Pollock, Chairperson

Muriel Morse   Michael Callahan
David Padilla   James Rude

EMPLOYERS MUST POST WITH THIS HALF OF SHEET SHOWING

QUESTIONS ABOUT ENFORCEMENT of the Industrial Welfare Commission orders and reports of violations should be directed to the Division of Labor Standards Enforcement. Consult the white pages of your telephone directory under CALIFORNIA, State of, Industrial Relations for the address and telephone number of the office nearest you. The Division has offices in the following cities: Bakersfield, El Centro, Eureka, Fresno, Hollywood, Inglewood, Long Beach, Los Angeles, Marysville, Napa, Oakland, Pomona, Redding, Sacramento, Salinas, San Bernardino, San Diego, San Francisco, San Jose, San Mateo, Santa Ana, Santa Barbara, Santa Rosa, Stockton, Van Nuys, Ventura, Whittier. Lloyd W. Aubry, Jr., Chief.

Overtime

Overtime must be paid for any time worked over 40 hours per week. Payment must be at time and a half for the first four hours of overtime each day beyond the initial eight hours, and double time after 12 hours.

Time cards should be kept along with the resident manager agreement since the onsite manager works odd hours (emergency calls). Without time cards, a disgruntled former manager can claim to the Labor Board that he worked 24 hours per day, 7 days per week, for the entire year. As evidenced by the example below, this has disastrous potential.

8 hrs @ 4.25 per hr.	$34.00/day
4 hrs @ 6.38 per hr.	$25.50/day
12 hrs @ 8.50 per hr.	$102.00/day
Total for 24 hours	$161.50/day
30 days	$4,845/month
365 days	$58,947.50/year

Taxability of Manager's Apartment

If lodging (an apartment) is provided on the employer's premises, for the owner's convenience and as a condition of employment, and the rental value is used to meet minimum wage requirements, it is subject to:

* No Federal income tax withholding

* No Social Security (FICA) withholding

* No state income tax withholding

* SDI is withheld on 66-2/3% of rental value, not to exceed maximum deduction

* SUI and ETT are paid by employer on 66-2/3% of rental value, not to exceed maximum deduction

Is the Onsite Manager an Employee or an Independent Contractor?

Under Section 601 of the Unemployment Insurance Code, "employment" is defined as "service performed by an employee or under any contract of hire, written or oral or expressed or implied." Federal guidelines say that if a business grosses over $250,000 per year it is covered under federal law. Most property management companies collect rents in excess of this amount on their combined properties. The onsite manager is then, for all practical purposes, an employee covered by both state and federal law. See Figure 15-3, Assignment of Duties.

Payment When Firing the Onsite Manager

1. *Wages must be paid immediately.*

2. *If the manager quits, he must be paid within 48 hours if he has a contract.*

3. *If the manager quits and doesn't have a contract, he must be paid within 72 hours.*

Eviction of Onsite Manager

Many onsite manager contracts contain a clause that residency is part of the job and the manager must leave within 72 hours upon termination. As yet not fully tested in the courts, this clause, as well as the entire manager employment contract, should be reviewed by legal counsel.

If the manager is a tenant, he may have to be evicted in the normal manner.

Employment Contract

The employment contract with the onsite manager should be in writing and set forth duties, responsibilities, hours, and remuneration (see Figure 15-4).

Payroll

The employer must establish minimum twice-monthly pay periods and give the employee a pay stub with all basic payroll information on it; i.e., number of hours, pay period, taxes, etc.

Records

The company must keep accurate payroll records for three years showing total daily hours. W-2 forms must be given by January 31 to all employees. All documentation relating to hiring, performance, and firing should also be kept for three years.

Withholding from Employees' Pay

1. *Social Security*

2. *Federal and state income tax*

3. *State disability*

Figure 15-3. Assignment of Duties

Exhibit A — Assignment of Duties

Place a ✓ in the box under the title of the one individual who is *primarily* responsible for each duty.

Duty	Manager	Co-Manager	Owner or Agent	Outside Contractor
1. Renting Activities				
Advertising preparation	☐	☐	☐	☐
Inserting ads in newspapers	☐	☐	☐	☐
Sign ordering and placement	☐	☐	☐	☐
Showing vacancies	☐	☐	☐	☐
Completing resident application, rental agreements, and accepting deposits	☐	☐	☐	☐
Keeping vacant units cleaned	☐	☐	☐	☐
Phone answering	☐	☐	☐	☐
2. Rent Collections				
Distributing rental collection cards	☐	☐	☐	☐
Collecting rents when due	☐	☐	☐	☐
Executing receipts for money collected	☐	☐	☐	☐
Serving late rent notices	☐	☐	☐	☐
Collecting late rents and late charges	☐	☐	☐	☐
Serving 3-day notices to move or pay	☐	☐	☐	☐
3. Administration				
Depositing collections in bank	☐	☐	☐	☐
Writing checks for accounts payable	☐	☐	☐	☐
Reconciling bank accounts	☐	☐	☐	☐
Preparing federal and state payroll forms	☐	☐	☐	☐
Preparing employee's bond applications	☐	☐	☐	☐
Keeping reports on rents in competitive units	☐	☐	☐	☐
Compiling rent change notices	☐	☐	☐	☐
Maintaining rent collection records	☐	☐	☐	☐
Preparing late charge or delinquent notices	☐	☐	☐	☐
Preparing 3-day notices to move or pay	☐	☐	☐	☐
Preparing and filing unlawful detainer actions	☐	☐	☐	☐
Enforcement of apartment rules	☐	☐	☐	☐
Filing small claims court actions	☐	☐	☐	☐
4. Record Keeping				
Income receipts	☐	☐	☐	☐
Expenses	☐	☐	☐	☐
Resident name register	☐	☐	☐	☐
Manager's weekly time report	☐	☐	☐	☐
Unit maintenance card	☐	☐	☐	☐
Monthly income statement	☐	☐	☐	☐
Monthly expense statement	☐	☐	☐	☐
Manager's weekly apartment report	☐	☐	☐	☐
Record of location by unit of all furniture and equipment owned by apartment	☐	☐	☐	☐
5. Cleaning Apartments				
Vacuuming carpets	☐	☐	☐	☐
Shampooing carpets	☐	☐	☐	☐
Refrigerator cleaning	☐	☐	☐	☐
Plumbing fixture cleaning	☐	☐	☐	☐
Drape cleaning	☐	☐	☐	☐
Window washing	☐	☐	☐	☐
Screen cleaning	☐	☐	☐	☐
Stove and oven cleaning	☐	☐	☐	☐
Wall washing	☐	☐	☐	☐
Cabinet and closet cleaning	☐	☐	☐	☐
Heater cleaning	☐	☐	☐	☐
Cleaning Apartments (continued)				
Sink, shower, and lavatory cleaning	☐	☐	☐	☐
Floor washing and/or polishing	☐	☐	☐	☐
Ceramic tile grout cleaning	☐	☐	☐	☐
Light fixtures	☐	☐	☐	☐
Tops of doorway and window trim	☐	☐	☐	☐
6. Property Policing				
Facade cleaning	☐	☐	☐	☐
Entry cleaning	☐	☐	☐	☐
Garage oils on floors and pavements	☐	☐	☐	☐
Nite light setting (time clock)	☐	☐	☐	☐
Sign cleaning	☐	☐	☐	☐
Driveway cleaning	☐	☐	☐	☐
Walkway and lawn policing	☐	☐	☐	☐
Garbage area cleanup	☐	☐	☐	☐
7. Maintenance				
Carpet cleaning	☐	☐	☐	☐
Air conditioner cleaning	☐	☐	☐	☐
Recreation, sauna, and bathroom cleaning	☐	☐	☐	☐
Fishpond or fountain cleaning	☐	☐	☐	☐
Laundry room cleaning	☐	☐	☐	☐
Hallway cleaning	☐	☐	☐	☐
Lightbulb replacement	☐	☐	☐	☐
Carport cleaning	☐	☐	☐	☐
Hallway vacuuming	☐	☐	☐	☐
Warm air heat filter cleaning	☐	☐	☐	☐
Warm air heat filter replacement	☐	☐	☐	☐
Water heater draining	☐	☐	☐	☐
Stair and deck cleaning	☐	☐	☐	☐
Stair and deck sealing or painting	☐	☐	☐	☐
Plumbing stoppage	☐	☐	☐	☐
8. Repairs				
Door or window screen repair	☐	☐	☐	☐
Door or window screen replacement	☐	☐	☐	☐
Window pane replacement	☐	☐	☐	☐
Window crank repair	☐	☐	☐	☐
Window crank replacement	☐	☐	☐	☐
Air conditioner repair	☐	☐	☐	☐
Stove burners	☐	☐	☐	☐
Stove and oven handles or knobs	☐	☐	☐	☐
Refrigerators	☐	☐	☐	☐
Dishwasher repair	☐	☐	☐	☐
Door knobs and cabinet catch replacement	☐	☐	☐	☐
Door and cabinet hinge replacement	☐	☐	☐	☐
Carpet repairs	☐	☐	☐	☐
Painting	☐	☐	☐	☐
Plumbing faucet washer replacement	☐	☐	☐	☐
Plumbing replacements	☐	☐	☐	☐
Electric switch replacement	☐	☐	☐	☐
Electric fixture replacement	☐	☐	☐	☐
Stucco patching	☐	☐	☐	☐
Stucco painting	☐	☐	☐	☐
Front door painting	☐	☐	☐	☐
Fence repairs	☐	☐	☐	☐

CAA APPROVED FORM
CALIFORNIA APARTMENT ASSOCIATION
1.4 Revised 7/78 COPYRIGHT 1980

(continued)

Figure 15-4. Resident Manager Agreement

Resident Apartment
Manager-Employer Agreement

This agreement, between _____ , hereinafter referred to as "manager" and
_____ , hereinafter referred to as "employer" for the resident management of
the property known as _____ , located at _____ ,
California, shall be subject to the following conditions:

1. **Compensation:** Either (strike out the subsection which does not apply):
   a. Full compensation shall be $_____ per month, payable semi-monthly by the _____ day and
      _____ day of each month,

   OR

   b. Full compensation shall be $_____ per hour, plus overtime as required by law, for time spent carrying
      out assigned duties. If hours required to carry out assigned duties should exceed _____ hours in any
      workday or ____ ____ hours in any workweek, manager shall notify employer prior to performing such
      services and obtain consent therefore except in an emergency, when manager shall notify employer of
      additional hours worked within 48 hours.

2. **Duties:** Duties assigned to the manager are those shown on Exhibit A, Assignment of Duties, which forms a
   part of this agreement, and which shall be subject to review within 90 days of signing of this agreement and
   annually thereafter.

3. **Apartment:** Since the apartment is provided as a condition of employment and at a reduced rate (see current
   General Information sheet for limitations) the manager will vacate the apartment within 24 hours of termination
   of employment. The rent on the apartment shall be $ _____ per month payable either:

   ☐ (a) By a credit against the agreed compensation

   ☐ (b) By the _____day of each month in cash or check.
   (Initial appropriate box)

   NOTE: Employers subject to Federal laws may use only alternative (b) for exempt employees.

4. **Days Off:** Shall be one day in seven.

5. **Excess Hours:** Manager shall record excess hours worked carrying out assigned duties on Exhibit B, Report of
   Hours Worked, and shall so arrange his time as to carry out assigned duties and to provide the opportunity for
   not less than six hours uninterrupted sleep each 24 hours except for emergencies affecting health or safety.

6. The undersigned have read and understand the CAA Code of Ethics and the CAA Code of Equal Opportunity
   which are set forth on the reverse side of this agreement and are made a part hereof. The parties agree to abide by
   all the provisions thereto.

7. **Termination:** This contract may be terminated by either party (insert termination conditions):

_____

_____

Dated at _____ , California this _____ day of _____ , 19____

Signed _____
                                      Manager

_____
                                      Employer

UNAUTHORIZED REPRODUCTION OF THIS FORM IS ILLEGAL

Employer Contributions

1. *Federal and state unemployment insurance*

2. *Worker's Compensation insurance (7–10% of wages)*

3. *Social Security*

OSHA

California OSHA (Occupational Safety Hazards Acts) covers the safety of employees relative to unsafe work areas and practices.

Fair Employment

Notices of fair employment hours and working conditions must be posted.

1099 Form

Form 1099 on services of $600 or more per year must be sent to nonemployee vendors and filed with the Internal Revenue Service by January 31 each year. The vendor is exempt if a corporation. Non-corporate vendors must supply you with a Social Security or Federal I.D. number. If this number is not given to you, 20% of future payments must be withheld and forwarded to the IRS on a regular basis. Failure to file 1099s can result in penalties to the management company of $50 for failure to send to IRS, $50 for failure to send to vendor, or 10% of the amount of the services rendered, whichever is greater. See Figure 15-5. The management company should request taxpayer identification form (TIN), which is called W-9 (Figure 15-6).

Staff Selection

In order to assist in personnel selection, behavioral assessment reports have been developed. A leader in this field is Phil Herman of Potential Unlimited, Inc. in San Rafael, California. The personal, interpersonal, and work traits of a bookkeeper are different from those of a property manager or leasing agent. For example, under task (work) traits, a prospective property manager who is seldom decisive, orderly, detailed, objective, or persistent would have little likelihood of success. During the employment interview, the candidate's traits should be compared to the task traits of property managers recognized to be competent who scored moderate to often in these categories (Figure 15-9). Using this structured system and open-ended interview questions increases the probability of hiring a successful applicant.

Figure 15-5. 1099 Form

9595 ☐ VOID ☐ CORRECTED For Official Use Only

Type or macnine print PAYER'S name, street address, city, state, and ZIP code	1 Rents $ 2 Royalties $	OMB No. 1545-0115 19 Statement for Recipients of	Miscellaneous Income
PAYER'S Federal identification number / RECIPIENT'S identification number	3 Prizes and awards $	4 Federal income tax withheld $	Copy A For Internal Revenue Service Center
Type or machine print RECIPIENT'S name (first, middle, last)	5 Fishing boat proceeds $	6 Medical and health care payments $	For Paperwork Reduction Act Notice and instructions for completing this form, see Instructions for Forms 1099, 1098, 5498, 1096, and W-2G.
Street address	7 Nonemployee compensation $	8 Substitute payments in lieu of dividends or interest $	
City, state, and ZIP code	9 Payer made direct sales of $5,000 or more of consumer products to a buyer (recipient) for resale . . . . . ▶ ☐		
Account number (optional)	10 The amount in Box 7 is crop insurance proceeds . . ▶ ☐		

Form 1099-MISC 95-2830662 Do NOT Cut or Separate Forms on This Page Department of the Treasury - Internal Revenue Service

Figure 15-6.

Form **W-9**
(Rev. July 1984)
Department of the Treasury
Internal Revenue Service

Payer's Request for Taxpayer Identification Number and Certification

Give This Form to the Payer, Middleman, Broker, or Barter Exchange

Please print or type

Name as shown on account (If joint account, list first and circle the name of the person or entity whose number you enter in Part I below.)

Address

City, State, and ZIP code

List account number(s) here ▶

Part I Taxpayer Identification Number—For All Accounts

Enter your taxpayer identification number in the appropriate box. For most individuals, this is your social security number. If you do not have a number, see *How to Obtain a TIN.*

Note: *If the account is in more than one name, see the chart on page 2 for guidelines on which number to give the payer.*

Social security number

OR

Employer identification number

Part II For Payees Exempt From Backup Withholding (See Instructions)

Certification.—Under penalties of perjury, I certify that:

(1) The number shown on this form is my correct Taxpayer Identification Number (or I am waiting for a number to be issued to me), **and**

(2) I am not subject to backup withholding either because I have not been notified by the Internal Revenue Service (IRS) that I am subject to backup withholding as a result of a failure to report all interest or dividends, or the IRS has notified me that I am no longer subject to backup withholding.

Certification Instructions.—You must cross out item (2) above if you have been notified by IRS that you are subject to backup withholding because of underreporting interest or dividends on your tax return. However, if after being notified by IRS that you were subject to backup withholding you received another notification from IRS that you are no longer subject to backup withholding, do not cross out item (2). (Also see *Certification* under *Specific Instructions.*)

Please Sign Here **Signature ▶** **Date ▶**

Open-ended questions elicit more than a yes or no answer. For example, "Tell me about your family and education." "What are your strengths?" "How do you motivate yourself?" "How do you learn best?" Using a four-page format, Career Potential Analysis (CPA) can prepare written reports on a job applicant for the management company in usually less than ten days.

Selection of a Resident Manager

In many instances a couple is preferred for resident management, which makes the selection process more difficult. One person usually has to be good in maintenance and the other in leasing and bookkeeping. Unless the apartment community is large, over 150 units, it is difficult to pay wages sufficient to attract high-caliber onsite managers. For example, a 20-unit building with a gross collected income of $10,000 per month may pay only 5% or $500, or just give a free apartment. The managers must have another job or other source of income in order to live. This author prefers to find a person good in leasing and dealing with people and have the maintenance done by outside contractors on smaller complexes. In California, if a complex has more than 16 units you need an onsite manager.

In all cases, the prospective manager should be carefully screened. A credit check should be run just as on a regular tenant and references thoroughly checked. A personal interview is also a must; a Resident Manager Pre-Employment Test (Figure 15-7) is desirable. Frequently, the most appropriate place to conduct the interview is at the prospective manager's present home. The manager's housekeeping ability will reflect on the complex.

Motivation

The property supervisor should use methods to reinforce the behavior expected of employees. Dr. Michael Le Boeuf, noted author, in his book *The Greatest Management Principles in the World*, states that "things that get rewarded are things that get done." If you want to reduce vacancy, the manager's compensation should be structured so that fewer vacancies mean more money each month.

In *The One-Minute Manager*, authors Ken Blanchard and Spencer Johnson believe the manager should:

Set one-minute goals
Give one-minute praisings
Give one-minute reprimands
Encourage people
Speak the truth
Laugh
Enjoy work

Figure 15-7. Resident Manager Test

Name: _____
Date: _____

RESIDENT MANAGER PRE-EMPLOYMENT TEST

You will be given thirty minutes to answer these questions. Please circle the best answer for the multiple choice questions.

1. The resident from apartment #107 comes into the office to tell you that a sudden leak of water from apartment #207 has formed a pool of water in her kitchen. You should:

   a. Call the police so you can enter apartment #207. Have a maintenance person or plumber repair the leak with the police there.
   b. Call the resident of apartment #207 and have them come home so you can fix the leak.
   c. Enter apartment #207, have maintenance or plumber fix the leak and leave everything just the way you found it so the resident doesn't know you were there.
   d. Enter apartment #207, have maintenance or plumber fix the leak and leave a notice to let the resident know you were in the apartment and why.

2. A family with two children wants to rent an apartment. There is only a one bedroom available. You may:

   a. Tell them you don't rent to people with children.
   b. Tell them that children of the opposite sex may not share a bedroom.
   c. Tell them the policy of the property will not permit four people to share a one bedroom unit.
   d. None of the above.

3. Pro-rate the following, assuming that the apartment rents for $300 per month, and the resident moves in on the dates shown. Using a 30 day month, calculate the amount of rent that is prorated and due on the first of the following month:

   Move In Date   Pro-rated Amount

   1st of month   _____
   5th of month   _____
   15th of month   _____

4. If a prospective tenant enters the office while you are busy, you should:

   a. Finish what you are working on and greet the person.
   b. Tell the person to sit down and have some coffee.
   c. Stop what you are doing and greet the person immediately.
   d. Ignore the person until they say what they want.

Figure 15-7 (cont'd). Resident Manager Test

5. What can be deducted from a tenant's security deposit after move out?

    a. Any back rent.
    b. Any damage to the apartment beyond normal wear and tear.
    c. A carpet which has become discolored by the sun.
    d. Both a and b

6. The appearance of the rental office is:

    a. A reflection on the property.
    b. A reflection on the manager and employees.
    c. One of the first impressions a potential resident has of the property.
    d. All of the above.

7. When you are showing an apartment, you would:

    a. Take the fastest route to the apartment and the scenic route back.
    b. Take the scenic route to the apartment and the fastest route back.
    c. Take the fastest route to the apartment and back.
    d. Take the scenic route to the apartment and back.

8. In qualifying a prospective resident for an apartment, you ask:

    a. How many people will be living in the apartment.
    b. The move-in date needed.
    c. Where they work.
    d. If they can put down a deposit.
    e. All of the above.

9. A resident named May Smith lives in your building. She has decided to let John Adams move in, and has come to the office to let you know. You would:

    a. Refuse to let them live together.
    b. Take a rental application from John, verify employment and credit, and have a new rental agreement signed by both residents.
    c. Take a rental application from John. You trust May, so there is no reason to check further.
    d. None of the above.

10. May Smith moves out, leaving John Adams in the apartment in question #9, and without giving you notice. She wants her security deposit back.

    a. You advise her to get her share from John and get a statement from her that John now has full right to the security deposit you hold.
    b. Tell her she doesn't get anything back anyway because she didn't give notice.
    c. Ask your property supervisor what to do.

Figure 15-7 (cont'd). Resident Manager Test

11. You have five vacancies. Three of the apartments have been vacant for three weeks. An ad has been running in a newspaper for several weeks and you are displaying signs and banners. Name three things you could also try to increase the traffic and rent those units:

_____

_____

_____

12. You don't like a resident. He acts funny toward you and other residents. You would like to evict him. You may legally do so:

    a. Only if he doesn't pay his rent on time.
    b. By calling the police immediately.
    c. Only if he breaks the terms of his rental agreement.
    d. Either a or c.

13. A tenant meets you in the laundry room and tells you verbally that he will be moving soon. You should:

    a. Prepare a written 30 day notice and take it to him to sign.
    b. Forget about it. If he wants his security deposit back, it's his obligation to comply with the rules.
    c. Call you supervisor and tell her you have a verbal notice.

14. A resident manager may not discriminate against people based on their:

    a. _____
    b. _____
    c. _____
    d. _____
    e. _____
    f. _____

15. A couple who are black want to rent an apartment. You should:

    a. Tell them they really won't be happy living at the property as there are no other black families.
    b. Take their application, show them an apartment just as you would any other prospective resident.
    c. Tell them you have no vacancies and there is a long waiting list.
    d. Add another $300 to the security deposit and charge them more rent.

16. Every morning you should:

    a. Walk the property to be sure everything is clean.
    b. Dust the rent ready apartments or models.
    c. Clean the rental office.
    d. All of the above.

Figure 15-7 (cont'd). Resident Manager Test

17. Complete the following math problems:

$375.00	What is 75%	$374.95	1,879.99
485.00	of 110?	316.39	8,798.13
+ 620.00		333.33	5,455.92
		+ 498.88	+ 8,122.25

18. A resident has moved out on the 15th of the month. You should prepare a Security Deposit Refund Statement form so the main office can process their deposit refund:

    a.   As soon as possible. By law the deposit refund must be give to the resident in 14 days.

    b.   At the end of the month. By law the deposit refund must be given to the resident in 30 days.

    c.   As soon as possible. By law, the deposit refund must be given to the resident immediately at move out.

    d.   At the end of the month if the resident doesn't have a refund. As soon as possible if they have a refund.

19. If the electricity <u>is not</u> working in a tenant's apartment, you should:

    a.   Tell the tenant the maintenance person will be by next week to look at the problem.

    b.   Tell the tenant to buy some candles.

    c.   Consider it an emergency and get it repaired immediately.

20. Please explain briefly why you feel you are qualified for this position, and what knowledge and experience you possess that would make you an asset to this company.

_____

_____

_____

_____

_____

_____

_____

_____

_____

_____

_____

_____

_____

_____

The property supervisor needs to be aware of his/her own behavior and how those actions affect the employees in order to encourage their best performance.

Figure 15-8. Motivation

"WHAT DID THE BOSS HAVE TO SAY?"

Compensation and Rewards

In a recent study conducted by the *Personnel Journal*, job satisfaction is ranked the number one worker concern. In second place was job security, followed by money. Company benefits were in fourth place, followed by challenges and then promotional opportunities.

In today's society, employees are expecting more from their jobs than traditional wages and employee benefits. They are turning to their work as a source of personal fulfillment, social relationships, and community responsibilities.

If the management company has a history of hassling tenants in returning security deposits, and the company develops a poor reputation, employees cannot be proud of the company and are often subjected to verbal and sometimes physical abuse. The key to a successful management company is stability. If a firm is always replacing and retraining its best personnel, it usually indicates a problem with the management company.

15-18

Figure 15-9. Interview Worksheet

EXPLORATORY INTERVIEW WORKSHEET

CANDIDATE _____ DATE _____

POSITION _____ INTERVIEWER _____

RAPPORT/PURPOSE

LIFE EXPERIENCE QUESTIONS
WORK:
EDUCATION:
FAMILY:
INTERESTS:
GOALS

PERSONAL TRAITS	PERSON L M H	JOB L M H
AMBITIOUS		
CONFIDENT		
ENERGETIC		
COMPETITIVE		
FLEXIBLE		
INDEPENDENT		

INTER— PERSONAL TRAITS	PERSON L M H	JOB L M H
EMPATHETIC		
OUTGOING		
TACTFUL		
PERSUASIVE		
ASSERTIVE		
DOMINANT		

WORK TRAITS	PERSON L M H	JOB L M H
DECISIVE		
ORDERLY		
DETAILED		
OBJECTIVE		
PERSISTENT		
ANALYTICAL		
COMPLIANT		

Decision: ☐ Continue ☐ Stop
Company/Job Sell

Selection System Sell

Administer Forms/CPA

Potential
Unlimited
Incorporated

Effective Communication

In order to motivate, the property supervisor must establish effective communication with personnel. Are your plans for managing the apartment building (see Figure 15-8):

1. *Being comprehended?* "Clean the sidewalks every day."

2. *Being accepted?* "No broom, so we couldn't sweep today."

3. *Being understood?* "Clean sidewalks lead to better curb appeal and lower vacancy."

4. *Are you understanding your employees?* "We can't find our broom because we want to buy a motorized sweeper."

Kinds of Communication

1. *Formal* — written notices, letters.

2. *Informal* — custom, the way it has always been done.

3. *Official* — Standard Operating Procedure (SOP).

4. *Grapevine* — how others perceive you and the formal system.

5. *Verbal* — not what we say, but how we say it; i.e., tone of voice.

6. *Nonverbal* — includes body language such as smiling when saying "Thank you."

Abraham Maslow, noted psychologist, developed a hierarchy of needs (Figure 15-10) that managers should be aware of when supervising and motivating employees. When an employee is only making minimum wage, doesn't have a place to live, or enough food to feed his family, trying to motivate through self-actualization such as creativity, curiosity, or independence will probably be futile. This individual still has basic needs (food, shelter, clothing) that must first be met. Exploring how this individual can earn more money would be a successful approach. On the other hand, a Certified Property Manager (CPM) whose salary adequately covers basic needs would be more amenable to creativity and independence as target motivators.

Figure 15-10.

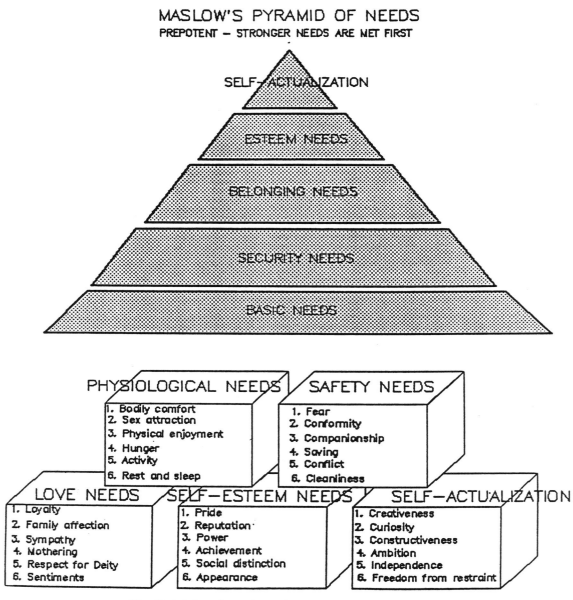

MASLOW'S PYRAMID OF NEEDS
PREPOTENT — STRONGER NEEDS ARE MET FIRST

SELF-ACTUALIZATION

ESTEEM NEEDS

BELONGING NEEDS

SECURITY NEEDS

BASIC NEEDS

PHYSIOLOGICAL NEEDS
1. Bodily comfort
2. Sex attraction
3. Physical enjoyment
4. Hunger
5. Activity
6. Rest and sleep

SAFETY NEEDS
1. Fear
2. Conformity
3. Companionship
4. Saving
5. Conflict
6. Cleanliness

LOVE NEEDS
1. Loyalty
2. Family affection
3. Sympathy
4. Mothering
5. Respect for Deity
6. Sentiments

SELF—ESTEEM NEEDS
1. Pride
2. Reputation
3. Power
4. Achievement
5. Social distinction
6. Appearance

SELF—ACTUALIZATION
1. Creativeness
2. Curiosity
3. Constructiveness
4. Ambition
5. Independence
6. Freedom from restraint

Build Motivation into Management

Summary

The property manager must coordinate operations in various areas such as rent collection, maintenance, tenant selection, and accounting in order for the building to operate harmoniously. Different personalities, behavior patterns, approaches, and goals must be channeled in the right direction. The basis of property management relies on six steps: planning, organization, staffing, directing, controlling, and feedback. When staffing the management office, an organizational chart is usually developed to delineate the chain of command in the organization.

Payment of employees according to local, state, and federal guidelines can be complex and difficult. For example, state and federal minimum wage rates may differ, and credit for the onsite manager is exempt from some withholding taxes. The onsite manager should sign a "Manager's Contract" and be given an assignment of duties and responsibilities. The number of hours worked should equate to at least the minimum wage. The onsite manager is considered an employee, not an independent contractor. Records such as time sheets and wages paid should be kept, as well as a W-2 form issued by January 31 each year. For vendors who are not corporations, a 1099 form must be prepared and sent for any amounts over $600.

In order to help the property manager select personnel, personnel behavior assessment reports are available from outside consulting firms. Incentives should be based on performance, bonus, or reward for the things you want accomplished. To motivate and communicate, the property manager must be aware of the six types of communication: formal, informal, official, grapevine, verbal and nonverbal.

In conclusion, the future of property management looks bright as investors are looking at properties as a business that needs to be run professionally in order to increase cash flow and appreciation. This means that the demand for competent, experienced, knowledgeable, and certified property managers (CPMs) will increase. As the demand for these professionals grows faster than the supply, salaries will escalate and compensation will be greater for those who are the real achievers and producers.

Chapter 15 Review Questions

1. *The management function includes:*

   a. planning.
   b. organizing.
   c. staffing.
   d. all of the above.
   e. none of the above.

2. *Controlling is:*

   a. hiring and training personnel.
   b. developing goals and objectives.
   c. measuring performance and identifying problem areas.
   d. defining jobs.

3. *The property manager provides:*

   a. goods.
   b. products.
   c. a service.
   d. none of the above.

4. *All employees should be paid at least:*

   a. minimum wage.
   b. highest wage.
   c. poverty wage.
   d. comparable wage.

5. *The onsite manager is:*

   a. an independent contractor.
   b. an employee.
   c. a casual laborer.
   d. all of the above.
   e. none of the above.

6. *A fired employee must be paid:*

   a. within 24 hours.
   b. within 48 hours.
   c. within 72 hours.
   d. immediately.

7. *A prudent property manager would have:*

   a. the highest management fees.
   b. a written resident manager agreement.
   c. the lowest-cost employees.
   d. the highest-cost employees.

8. *The property manager should post:*

   a. HUD discrimination posters.
   b. OSHA posters.
   c. Fair Employment posters.
   d. all of the above.
   e. none of the above.

9. *Use of behavior assessment reports considers the:*

   a. sex of the applicant.
   b. personal and work traits of the applicant.
   c. color of the applicant.
   d. all of the above.
   e. none of the above.

10. Laws in property management:

   a. are constantly changing.
   b. change only every ten years.
   c. never change.
   d. are the same nationwide.

Chapter 15 Case Study Problem

1. How much will you pay the new manager at Civic Center Terrace? Does this amount meet minimum wage requirements?

2. Will your new manager be an employee or an independent contractor?

3. How will you fire and evict the old manager?

4. Will the new manager have an employment contract?

5. Should you run extensive credit and background checks on the new manager before hiring?

For students who want to do extra work, here are additional case problems.

6. Prepare a management plan as outlined in Chapter 6. The plan should include rent increases, rehabilitation costs, and increased NOI projections for five years (use your own cost assumptions).

7. What is the new value using the same cap rate of 9 with the increased NOI?

8. Prepare an operating budget (for one month) to show the owner a pro forma projection.

9. Make financing recommendations on obtaining new financing.

10. Write up a proposal to manage Civic Center Terrace.

Chapter 15
Selected Additional References and Reading

Blanchard, Ken and Spencer Johnson, *The One Minute Manager*, Berkeley Books, New York, NY, 1984.

Boykin, James H., *Real Estate Counseling*, American Society of Real Estate Counselors, Chicago, IL, 1984.

Carnegie, Dale, *How to Win Friends and Influence People*, Simon and Schuster, New York, NY, 1977.

Keirsey, David and Marilyn Bates, *Please Understand Me*, Prometheus Nemesis Book Co., Del Mar, CA, 1984.

Nierenberg, Gerald, *The Art of Negotiating*, Simon and Schuster, New York, NY, 1981.

Personal Journal (Monthly)
245 Fisher Avenue, Suite B-2
Costa Mesa, CA 92626

Waitley, Denis, *The Psychology of Winning*, Nightingale-Conant Corp., Chicago, IL, 1979.

Glossary of Real Estate Management Terms

Acceleration Clause: Lease clause that calls for specified rental increases at specific times.

Accredited Management Organization (AMO): Professional designation awarded to qualifying firms by the Institute of Real Estate Management (IREM).

Accredited Resident Manager (ARM): A designation given by IREM to resident managers who have completed certain experience and education requirements.

Actual Eviction: Forcible ouster from rental property of the tenant pursuant to court order (Writ of Execution).

Agency: The relationship between principal and agent by which the agent is employed to act for the principal.

Agent: One who acts and represents another from whom he has derived legal authority.

Air Resources Board (ARB): The state agency that plans and enforces achievements of air quality improvements.

Air Quality Management District (AQMD): A regional agency that plans and enforces achievement of air quality improvements.

Anchor Tenant: The major (key) tenant which will attract other businesses and customers.

Appraisal: An estimate of value as of a certain date.

Assessment (Condo): Monthly fee paid by homeowners to cover operation and maintenance of common areas.

Assignee: One to whom the property shall be transferred.

Assignment: Transfer of existing tenant's rental rights in a property to a third party; i.e., lease assignment.

Assignor: One who assigns or transfers property.

Automatic Extension Clause: A lease covenant providing that a lease can be renewed unless one party gives notice to terminate.

Beneficiary: The lender on the security of a note and deed of trust.

Btu: British thermal unit. The quantity of heat required to raise the temperature of one pound of water one degree Fahrenheit.

Building Code: Regulations adopted by local, county, and state agencies to regulate construction of buildings.

Building Owners and Managers Association (BOMA): An international organization to foster industry standards, educational programs, and publications.

Bylaws: Rules and regulations adopted by associations.

California Association of Realtors (CAR): Association of California realtors to promote professionalism in the real estate industry.

California Environmental Quality Act (CEQA): Law passed in 1970 under which the state and local agencies must analyze the potential environmental impacts of their actions before approving projects.

Capitalization Rate: The rate of return considering interest and risk which an investor desires to achieve; used to determine value based on NOI.

Cash Flow: Net income after expenses and debt financing, but before depreciation.

CBD: Central Business District.

Certified Commercial Investment Member (CCIM): A designation by NAR.

Certified Property Manager (CPM): Professional designation conferred by IREM on property managers who meet stiff educational and experience requirements.

Certified Shopping Center Manager (CSM): Professional designation conferred by the International Council of Shopping Centers after educational requirements are completed.

Community Association Institute (CAI): A professional organization for condominium and cooperative owners and managers.

Condemnation: The taking of a property by government agencies.

Condominium: A system whereby the owner holds title to an individual unit plus an undivided fee-simple interest in the common areas.

Constructive Eviction: Illegal eviction by a landlord through methods making the unit unusable; i.e., changing locks, removing doors, etc.

Covenants, Conditions, and Restrictions (CC&Rs): Usually refers to condominium management and the powers and duties of its governing entity.

Curable Depreciation: Physical deterioration and functional obsolescence which can be repaired or replaced.

Deep Pockets: A term used to refer to a defendant in a lawsuit who had little liability, but more assets than other defendants with more liability in the case.

Deferred Maintenance: Needed but postponed repairs.

Department of Housing and Urban Development (HUD): A government agency which provides financial assistance and construction of housing for low-income tenants.

Depreciation: Loss of value due to physical deterioration, economic or functional obsolescence (also see Tax Depreciation).

Economic Life: Useful period over which the property will yield a return on the investment.

Economic Obsolescence: Loss of value due to factors other than the building; i.e., neighborhood deteriorates.

Economic Rent: The expected or predicted scheduled rent (not actual rent).

Eminent Domain: Right of the government to acquire property for public used by condemnation.

Environmental Impact Report (EIR): The mandated reports prepared by state and local agencies, and CEQA that analyzes environmental matters.

Environmental Protection Agency (EPA): Federal agency responsible for planning and enforcing achievement of air quality improvements within the United States.

Escalation Clause: A lease clause providing for upward or downward adjustment of the rental rate at certain times (usually tied to the Consumer Price Index).

Estate for Years: Leasehold interest that continues for a specific period of time.

Estoppel: A doctrine of law which prevents assertion of rights that are inconsistent with a previous position or representation.

Eviction: Removal of the tenant from the property pursuant to a court judgment.

Eviction Notice: Legal notice given to the tenant when he defaults under the terms of his lease or rental agreement.

Experience Exchange Report: A publication by the Institute of Real Estate Management of operating costs for apartments, office buildings, and condominiums.

Facade: Front of a building.

FDIC: Federal Deposit Insurance Corporation, a government agency that insures bank deposits.

Fee: The payment for services.

Fidelity Bond: Employer's insurance against loss of money or property by an employee.

Fiduciary: Relationship of trust and confidence between the principal and property manager.

Fixed Expense: Property expense that doesn't fluctuate with rental income; i.e., loan payment.

Flat Fee: Management fee expressed as a dollar amount, usually per month.

Foreclosure: When property pledged as security for a debt is sold to pay the debt if payments haven't been made.

Forfeiture: The giving up of rights such as in the forfeiture of lease.

Functional Obsolescence: Loss of property value due to adverse building features; i.e., small elevators, out-of-date electrical wiring, low ceilings.

Graduate Realtor Institute (GRI): Designation by the National Association of Realtors (NAR).

Graduated Lease: Lease that provides for varying rent; i.e., 5% increase every year.

Highest and Best Use: Most productive use a property can be put to in order to produce the highest economic gain.

Holdover Tenant: Tenant who remains after the expiration of his lease.

House Rules: Building rules and regulations under which a tenant will operate, usually in a residential building.

Hundred Percent Location: Best retail location in a geographic area.

HVAC: Heating, ventilation, and air-conditioning equipment.

Hypothecate: To pledge as security an item without giving up possession.

Impounds: An account by lenders to accumulate funds to pay taxes and insurance on properties on which they loaned money.

Income Approach: A process of estimating value by capitalizing the annual net operating income.

Industrial Park: Subdivision to accommodate light manufacturing and distribution uses.

Inflation: When the money supply increases faster than goods and services. Results in raising wages and decreased purchasing power.

Injunction: A writ or court order restraining a party's action.

Institute of Real Estate Management (IREM): Professional organization of property managers which is part of the National Association of Realtors (NAR).

International Council of Shopping Centers (ICSC): Professional organization of shopping center managers and owners which provides information exchange and education for its members.

Key Tenant: Major tenant in an office building or shopping center. Also referred to as the anchor tenant.

Kiosk: Free-standing counter shops located in shopping center malls.

Landlord: Owner of the property.

Lease: A contract given by the landlord to the tenant setting forth conditions, terms, and length of occupancy.

Leasing Agent: The person (agent) who rents the space to another.

Lessee: One who rents property (tenant).

Lessor: The owner or landlord.

Life Support System: Safety and security procedures of a complex.

Limited Partnership: Allows investor to reduce risks, usually by being only "at risk for the amount of investment."

Lis Pendens: Constructive notice of pending lawsuit.

Loss Factor: The ratio of rentable space to usuable space.

Maintenance Contract: Contract which assigns vendors specific duties, usually on a monthly basis; i.e., HVAC contract or landscape.

Leasing Agent: The person (agent) who rents the space to another.

Lessee: One who rents property (tenant).

Lessor: The owner or landlord.

Life Support System: Safety and security procedures of a complex.

Limited Partnership: Allows investor to reduce risks, usually by being only "at risk for the amount of investment."

Lis Pendens: Constructive notice of pending lawsuit.

Loss Factor: The ratio of rentable space to usuable space.

Maintenance Contract: Contract which assigns vendors specific duties, usually on a monthly basis; i.e., HVAC contract or landscape.

Management Agreement: A written contract signed by the owner and agent outlining the duties, obligations, responsibilities, and terms under which a property will be managed.

Management Fee: The cost charged by the management company, usually on a monthly basis, to manage a particular property.

Management Plan: The financial and operational strategy for the management of a property to attain the owner's goals.

Market Analysis: Studies of economic, demographic, sales, and leasing information to evaluate supply and demand and market price and rates for a specific building.

Mechanic's Lien: A lien against the property by a vendor who supplied labor and materials for improvements.

Member of Appraisal Institute (MAI): Designation of a professional appraiser.

Merchants' Association: An organization of merchants of a shopping center to promote joint advertising, promotions, and decorations to enhance their business.

Mini-warehouse: A facility that provides smaller space rentals to individuals and businesses.

Minor: Any person under 18 years of age.

Mixed-Use Project: A planned development that incorporates several uses such as apartments, office, and retail.

Modernization: The updating of existing space or equipment to enhance the value.

Mortgagee: The person who lends the money; i.e., bank or savings and loan.

Mortgagor: The borrower who pledges the property as security.

National Association of Realtors (NAR): Umbrella of all the specialized real estate organizations such as the Institute of Real Estate Management (IREM).

Neighborhood Analysis: Used in management plans to determine the characteristics of the population in a small geographic area.

Neighborhood Center: Smaller retail center (25,000 to 100,000 s.f.) catering to convenience shopping.

Net Lease: A lease in which the tenant usually pays base rent plus extra expenses such as taxes, insurance, and maintenance.

Net Operating Income (NOI): Gross collected income minus operating expenses. Doesn't include debt service or depreciation expense.

Nominal Interest Rate: The interest rate stated in the loan documents.

Non-Competition Clause: Lease clause giving one tenant exclusive right to operate a particular use in a shopping center; i.e., florist shop.

Non-Controllable Expenses: Items the property manager has little or no control over; i.e., taxes, utility rates.

Normal Wear and Tear: Refers to residential units and tenants not being responsible for maintenance due to length of time; i.e., painting of apartments after one year.

Notary Public: Officer who has authority to acknowledge documents and affix a seal.

Notice of Responsibility: Notice to relieve the owner of responsibility of cost of work being done. Must be recorded and posted.

Notice to Quit: Legal notice to tenant to vacate rented space.

Novation: Substitution of a new party or agreement to replace an existing one.

Nuisance Rent Raise: Usually small ($10 or less) increase that the tenant will pay to avoid the cost of moving.

Pass-Through Costs: Certain cost increases (taxes, insurance, etc.) passed from the owner to the tenant.

Percentage Fee: Management cost expressed as a percentage of collected income.

Percentage Lease: Based on percentage of gross sales for retail stores. Usually contains a base or minimum monthly rent.

Physical Life: The length of useful time the building is expected to be functional.

Police Power: Right of government to enact laws for health, safety, and general public welfare.

Power of Attorney: An instrument authorizing a person to act as agent of the principal, granting that authority. Could be general or specific.

Preventive Maintenance: A program of regularly scheduled inspections and maintenance that allows potential problems to be prevented or repaired less expensively than if left to turn into major repairs, i.e., monthly changing of filters.

Principal: The property owner to whom the property manager (agent) is responsible.

Procuring Cause: The cause that results from an agent's employment in the sale or leasing of property, finding a buyer or tenant.

Profit and Loss Statement: Monthly report of the income and expenses sent to the owner.

Property Management: The operation and supervision of a property by an agent to increase the net operating income (NOI) and enhance the value of the property.

Property Supervisor (Manager): Person who usually supervises several onsite (resident) managers.

Proprietary Lease: The right of a shareholder to occupy a specific unit in a building under certain conditions.

Proration: Adjustment of taxes, insurance, interest, etc., on the proportional time in use.

Quiet Enjoyment: Right of the owner or tenant to use the property without interference.

Quitclaim Deed: Relinquishing of a right or claim, if any, one may have had in the property.

Radius Clause: A lease term in which a retailer agrees not to own or operate a similar business within a specific distance of the leased store.

Real Estate Cycle: The pattern of real estate experience over a long period of time in response to the economy and changing conditions.

Real Estate Investment Trust (REIT): A tax entity trust that purchases property and passes at least 90% of its income to its shareholders.

Real Property Administrator (RPA): A property management designation bestowed by BOMA.

Realtor: A real estate broker who is a dues-paying member in good standing in a Board of Realtors associated with NAR.

Recapture Clause: Lease term in percentage leases that allows the owner to terminate the lease if a merchant's sales haven't reached a specified level.

Rescission: Repealing of a contract by mutual consent of the parties to the contract.

Recycling: Changing the use and modernization of a building; i.e., converting an old warehouse into a restaurant.

Referral: Obtaining new business from reference of existing clients or associates.

Regional Center: Large shopping center (500,000 to 900,000 s.f.) that has at least two anchor tenants, merchandises a wide variety of goods and has a large geographic radius of customer attraction.

Reminder Notice: Sent to tenant who is late with rent.

Rent: Periodic payment to the owner or agent by the tenant for space used.

Rent Control: Local government regulations governing the increases in rents and evictions.

Rentable Space: The floor area minus stairs, elevator shafts, ducts, and areas not available to tenant according to BOMA standards.

Rental Schedule: Amount of rent total if all units are rented.

Repair and Deduct: Where the tenant makes necessary repairs for habitability if the landlord doesn't respond within a reasonable time.

Replacement Cost: Cost to replace existing structure with equivalent building, but with modern materials, design, and layout.

Resident Manager (Onsite Manager): Person who is directly responsible for renting, maintenance, and personnel of a building.

Retaliatory Eviction: Illegal action based on reprisal against the tenant by the landlord.

Return on Investment: Owner measure of profitability. Calculated by dividing the cost into the existing or projected profits and then multiplying by 100.

Rules and Regulations: Usually in an apartment building. Set forth guidelines such as pool hours, behavior (no skateboards), etc.

Sale-Leaseback: Owner sells property, but retains occupancy by leasing from the buyer.

Sandwich Lease: A leasehold interest which lies between the primary lease and the operating lease.

Section 8: Housing assistance from HUD through local housing agencies sending payments directly to the owner for part of the qualified tenant rent. The tenant pays the balance to the owner.

Security Deposit: Money held by the owner or agent until tenant moves to cover damage, cleaning, lost keys, and unpaid rent.

Sheriff Deed: Deed given by the court to satisfy a judgment.

Sherman Anti-Trust Act: Federal law that prohibits price-fixing or collusion in fixing of management fees among competitors.

Sign Restriction Clause: Lease clause that regulates tenant signs and displays.

Society of Industrial Realtors (SIR): An organization of industrial realtors.

Special-Purpose Property: Buildings designed for a particular use; i.e., hotels, churches.

Specialty Center: Small retail center (less than 250,000 s.f.) that specializes in unique merchandise. Usually located near resorts or large centers.

Statute of Frauds: Contracts of real property must be in writing if longer than one year in order to be enforceable.

Step-Up Clause: Lease term allowing for rental increases at specified times.

Straight-Line Depreciation: Conservative method of calculating tax depreciation based on equal increments for life of building.

Strip Center: Small convenience center with stores configurated usually in a straight line.

Super-Regional Center: The largest form of shopping center (750,000+ s.f.) and attracting customers from a large radius.

Technical Shortage: A market condition when supply (units)is exceeded by demand (tenants).

Tenancy at Sufferance: When tenant lease has expired and he continues to occupy the premises without the consent of the owner.

Tenancy at Will: Tenant has right of possession for an indefinite period of time or until either party gives termination notice.

Tenancy in Common: Ownership by two or more persons who hold individual interest and without right of survivorship.

Tenant: One who pays the rent. Also called the lessee.

Tenant Improvement Allowance (TI): Allowance for the cost of alterations needed to make the space suitable for the tenant's business.

Tenant Mix: The types of tenants which occupy the building. Thought and careful consideration should be given to compatibility.

Tenants Organization: A tenant union usually formed to control rental increases or to enforce specified actions on the owner.

Time is of the Essence: Contract provision specifying punctual performance.

Trade Fixtures: Personal property affixed to real property that are removable by the owner.

Trading Area: Geographic area in which the customers reside or work.

Trust Account: Separate account maintained by the property manager (broker) for deposit and distribution of owner (client) funds.

Trust Deed: A legal document in which the borrower (trustor) pledges his property as security to pay off the note to the beneficiary (lender).

Trustee: Person or entity holding naked title under a trust deed for the beneficiary.

Trustor: Holds the deed, but owes money to the lender (beneficiary) under a trust deed.

Uniform Residential Landlord/Tenant Act: A model law drafted by the National Conference of Commissioners on Uniform State Laws (1972) to standardize residential landlord/tenant relationships among the different local and state governments.

Unruh Act: California law that prohibits discrimination in the conduct of business, which includes residential apartments and commercial rentals.

Urban Land Institute (ULI): Industry association to provide education and research to its members and the public.

Urban Renewal: A program to rehabilitate and redevelop slum residential properties.

U.S. Housing Act of 1968: Prohibits discrimination based on race, religion, color, creed, national origin, or sex.

Use Clause: Lease provision that states the type of business to be conducted on the leased premises (shopping center).

Usury: Charging interest rates greater than permitted by law.

Utilities: Services provided by public utilities; i.e., gas, water, electricity.

Valuation: The estimated value or worth of a property.

Value: Worth of goods or services in the marketplace.

Variable Expenses: Costs that increase or decrease with occupancy level; i.e., water bill.

Vendee: The purchaser (buyer).

Vendor: The seller.

Void: Unenforceable.

Voidable: Enforceable unless action is taken to void; i.e., contract with person under 18 years old (minor).

Waive: To relinquish or abandon a person's right to enforce.

Waiver: The giving up of specified rights or responsibilities. In California, a residential tenant cannot waive his rights.

Wall Shops: Retail shops to break up long, blank walls in a large shopping center. Usually very narrow in depth.

Yield: Return earned on money or investment.

Zoning: Restriction on type of use or building in certain areas.

NOTES

Appendix B

Index

Index of Figures

Answers to Case Study Problem

Chapter 6

1. Yes. The high employment rate, service-related industry, and growing population indicate an influx of tenants who can pay higher rents for a newly rehabbed complex.

2. Yes. The civic center is an excellent source of employed tenants. There are good public services and nice neighbors, the Catholic Church. The comparable buildings in the area are in good condition.

3. Whiskey Manor excells in location and the fact that it has a play area. However, it lacks the pool, garage, and spa.

4. The curb appeal — like the landscaping — appears to be non-existent. Only at night when the red light shines above Judy Lovelace's apartment does the curb appear to have any appeal.

5. Good management doesn't cost; it pays. Any cost will quickly be recaptured with an applied management plan.

Chapter 7

1. No. In a 20-unit building there will frequently be times of 100% occupancy. A model apartment unnecessarily drains the property cash flow. The manager can make arrangements with the vacating tenant to show his unit, or use the manager's apartment to show.

2. Landscaping is the cheapest and quickest method to improve curb appeal. And how about a new wormwood facade to decry the building's age?

3. A new name means a new identity. The indentification of Whiskey Manor and Big Bertha surely had a reputation. A new name will help prospects forget the nefarious past.

4. Let's identify with the positive aspects of the area. We'll rename the complex "Civic Center Terrace." Now, not only does the property have identification of location, but also a new image. ("Whiskey Manor," indeed!)

5. Yes. Signage is the cheapest form of advertising.

6.

> CIVIC CENTER TERRACE
>
> 1–2 bdrm apts.
>
> $500–$600
>
> Just east of the Civic Center
>
> 12042 Civic Center Plaza
>
> Westminster, CA 92683
>
> (714) 751-2787
>
> "A nice Place to Live"

7. Judy Lovelace will be retired to the Old Bordello Workers' Retirement Home where she'll eventually be laid to rest (FIRE HER!).

8. With as high a vacancy factor as we'll have after evicting the delinquent tenants and undesirables, I'm going to hire a professional apartment manager training company to train my new manager in the art of salesmanship.

9. Easily, with a bit of maintenance and praying, the rents can go up.

10. Read the book! (Comparison grid Chapter 7 and fact sheet in Chapter 5).

11. What security deposit procedure? They are collecting rent. I'd forget last month's rent and charge slightly less than one month's rent as a security deposit. Slightly less so the prospective tenant won't confuse it with rent. From the security deposit I'll be able to deduct damages, lost keys, cleaning, unpaid rent, etc. (see Chapter 7).

12. Written rental agreement, of course, which allows attorney fees to be charged to the tenant if the owner wins in court.

Chapter 12

1. Yes. It prevents minor problems from turning into major ones.

2. Repair with copper pipe.

3. A licensed electrician.

4. Yes, the apartment will show better and can get higher rent.

5. No. Also use a pad.

6. Never do this. Use a licensed pest control vendor.

7. Reduce liability.

8. No, he must also be trustworthy and honest.

9. No, it could lead to a lawsuit.

10. Caulk outside cracks, joints, holes, etc. Install a hot water recirculating pump, separate or submeter, flow restrictors on shower heads, solar heating of hot water, and other improvements.

Chapter 13

1. Yes, would still have to pay mortgage payment.

2. Hire a licensed contractor covered by Worker's Compensation or cover Ben yourself.

3. Increase to at least $1,000,000.

4. Refer to Figure 4-1, Bid Sheet.

5. Yes, either hourly or points on the loan.

Chapter 14

1. Fix immediately as this is a habitability problem.

2. Tell the owner that this would be illegal (Wolfson vs. Marina Pt. Ltd.).

3. No, you can't discriminate, but you don't have to remodel.

4. Presently it is hit and miss. Serve the 3-day Pay or Quit notices by the fifth of the month and then put into legal action. You could also give a $20 rebate off the rent if they pay by the first.

5. Drop eviction as this would be retaliatory eviction, and then fix plumbing problems (CC 1942.5).

6. Yes, forget Small Claims Court and hire an attorney who specializes in evictions (25–35 days usually).

7. The onsite manager.

8. Discontinue. This is illegal (CC 789.3), $100/day penalty.

9. Yes, unlawful entry (CC 1954).

10. Tenant *can't* waive his rights (CC 1942.1).

Chapter 15

1. Must be at least $3.35/hour and offset can't exceed maximum deduction (one person) of $190 or two-thirds of rental value, whichever is less.

2. Employee.

3. Must be paid immediately and given 30-day notice to vacate the apartment.

4. Yes (written).

Answers to Review Questions

Chapter 1	Chapter 2	Chapter 3	Chapter 4	Chapter 5
1. C	1. C	1. A	1. A	1. D
2. C	2. C	2. C	2. D	2. A
3. A	3. A	3. D	3. A	3. D
4. C	4. A	4. B	4. C	4. B
5. D	5. D	5. D	5. B	5. C
6. B	6. D	6. A	6. C	6. B
7. A	7. A	7. B	7. B	7. D
8. B	8. C	8. B	8. A	8. B
9. C	9. A	9. D	9. B	9. C
10. A	10. C	10. C	10. A	10. D

Chapter 6	Chapter 7	Chapter 8	Chapter 9	Chapter 10
1. A	1. C	1. B	1. A	1. B
2. C	2. D	2. C	2. E	2. C
3. A	3. A	3. C	3. A	3. A
4. C	4. B	4. A	4. E	4. C
5. C	5. A	5. A	5. B	5. A
6. B	6. A	6. C	6. C	6. B
7. C	7. E	7. B	7. E	7. D
8. D	8. B	8. D	8. C	8. C
9. D	9. C	9. D	9. E	9. B
10. C	10. D	10. A	10. B	10. B

Chapter 11	Chapter 12	Chapter 13	Chapter 14	Chapter 15
1. D	1. D	1. D	1. C	1. D
2. A	2. D	2. C	2. B	2. C
3. C	3. B	3. B	3. A	3. C
4. C	4. D	4. C	4. B	4. A
5. B	5. A	5. B	5. B	5. B
6. B	6. B	6. A	6. C	6. D
7. C	7. D	7. C	7. D	7. B
8. B	8. B	8. B	8. B	8. D
9. A	9. A	9. C	9. D	9. B
10. B	10. D	10. D	10. B	10. A